$\Big\{$ CONTAINING
the POOR $\Big\}$

SILVIA MARINA ARROM

{ CONTAINING *the* POOR }

The Mexico City Poor House,

1774–1871

DUKE UNIVERSITY PRESS

Durham and London, 2000

*

© 2000 DUKE UNIVERSITY PRESS
All rights reserved
Printed in the United States of
America on acid-free paper ∞
Designed by Amy Ruth Buchanan
Typeset in Janson by Tseng Information Systems, Inc.
Library of Congress Cataloging-in-Publication
Data appear on the last printed page of this book.
The Jane's Chair in Latin American Studies at Brandeis
University generously provided a subvention for this work.
Appendixes with the full text of the Mexico City Poor
House bylaws can be found at the following website,
with URL http://www.brandeis.edu/~arrom/.
The author transcribed this archival material,
which is not otherwise available
outside of Mexico.

To my parents,

SILVIA RAVELO DE ARROM

and

JOSÉ JUAN ARROM,

whose passion for knowledge

and for things Latin American

showed me the way

*

{ CONTENTS }

{ LIST OF ILLUSTRATIONS, TABLES, }
AND FIGURES

{ ACKNOWLEDGMENTS }

I would like to express my gratitude to the generous people and institutions that assisted me during the many years I worked on this book. Financial support came from the Social Science Research Council, the Morse Fellowship of Yale University, a Grant-in-Aid and Summer Faculty Fellowship from Indiana University, a Fellowship for University Teachers from the National Endowment for the Humanities, the Bunting Institute of Radcliffe College, the American Council of Learned Societies, and Jane's Chair in Latin American Studies at Brandeis University.

In Mexico City my research was facilitated by the kind staffs of the Archivo Histórico de la Ciudad de México, the Archivo Histórico de la Secretaría de Salud, the Archivo General de la Nación, the Archivo Notarial, the Archivo de la Parroquia de la Santa Veracruz, the Biblioteca Nacional de México, and the Biblioteca Orozco y Berra of the Departamento de Historia of the Instituto Nacional de Antropología e Historia. In Seville I was aided by the efficient staff of the Archivo General de Indias. At Brandeis I received help from the dedicated staff at the Goldfarb Library, particularly Mark Alpert, and from the Interlibrary Loan Department, which procured a continuous stream of books and articles for this investigation.

As this project developed I presented portions of it as lectures and conference papers. I benefited from the comments of audiences at the IV Congreso de Historia del Derecho Mexicano, the American Historical Association, the Kellogg Institute at the University of Notre Dame, the Universidad Nacional Autónoma de México (UNAM) Conference on the Family and Private Life, the Berkshire Conference on the History of Women, the University of Texas Conference in Memory of Nettie Lee Benson, the IX Conference of Mexican and North American Historians, the Universidad Autónoma Metropolitana (UAM) Conference on Mexico City in the Nineteenth Century, the Boston Area Latin American History Workshop at Harvard University, and History Department seminars at Indiana University, Duke University, Boston University, Mt. Holyoke College, and Brandeis University.

Some of these papers were eventually published as articles. Part of chapter one first appeared as "Vagos y mendigos en la legislación mexicana, 1745–1845," *Memoria del IV Congreso de Historia del Derecho Mexicano* 1, 71–87. A portion of chapter three appeared in "Desintegración familiar y pauperización: los indigentes del Hospicio de Pobres en la ciudad de México, 1795," in *Familia y vida privada en la historia de Iberoamérica*, 119–31. Parts of chapters seven to nine appeared in "¿De la caridad a la beneficencia? Las reformas de la asistencia pública desde la perspectiva del Hospicio de Pobres de la ciudad de México, 1856–1871," in *Ciudad de México: instituciones, actores sociales y conflicto político, 1774–1931*, 21–53.

I am particularly grateful to friends, relatives, and colleagues who helped in numerous ways. John Johnson, Cathy LeGrand, Ann Blum, Susan Porter, John TePaske, Eric Van Young, Silvia Ravelo de Arrom, José Juan Arrom, and an anonymous reader for the Duke University Press read the full manuscript and offered helpful suggestions. Carlos Illades, Dolores Morales, Celia Maldonado, Verónica Zárate Toscano, Erika Pani, William Christian Jr., Christon Archer, Cheryl Martin, Miguel León Portilla, Fritz Schwaller, Armando Alonzo, Marjorie Becker, Randy Hanson, Leslie Berliant, and Marilyn Brooks read portions of the manuscript, answered questions, or helped me locate sources. Valerie Millholland and Rebecca Johns-Danes of the Duke University Press deserve special thanks for seeing the manuscript through to publication. My greatest debt is to my husband, David Oran, for his constant encouragement, and to my children, Christina and Daniel, for their occasional help and frequent distractions which enriched my life during the long years of research and writing.

Note to Reader

1 Monetary values are presented in *pesos*, with the *reales* converted into fractions of pesos.
2 Unless otherwise noted, the sources for tables are in appendix 1.
3 All translations into English are the author's, unless otherwise noted.

{ CONTAINING *the* POOR }

{ INTRODUCTION }

Poverty is one of the striking facts of life in Latin America. Yet few historians have studied the paupers of its cities, perhaps because they consider the homeless, beggars, and unemployed an unchanging feature of the area. In contrast, foreign visitors—myself included—have never taken them for granted. Travelers' accounts over the last two centuries consistently express shock at the destitution of a large part of the populace and wonder at how the wealthy could tolerate such misery. I was therefore intrigued, in sifting through archival materials of the late colonial period, to find that Mexican policymakers of the time did not ignore these problems. On the contrary, in 1774 Mexico City leaders embarked on a bold experiment that the most optimistic believed would eliminate poverty and usher in economic development.

This book focuses on the centerpiece of that experiment. The Mexico City Poor House was founded as part of an effort to sweep beggars and vagrants off the streets of the viceregal capital. The plan was to classify the paupers according to their "worthiness." The undeserving vagrants (the *mendigos fingidos* or "false" and employable beggars) would be put to work in the private sector or sentenced to military service or public works; the deserving beggars (the *verdaderos pobres* or "true" beggars) would be confined in the brand new asylum. There they would be sheltered and simultaneously trained to be good Christians, productive workers, and responsible citizens. They would lose their liberty, too. Whether they entered voluntarily or by force, they were to remain institutionalized until they were claimed by a relative or friend or could support themselves without soliciting alms. The Poor House was therefore designed as a homeless shelter, workhouse, catechism school, reformatory, and—for some—a prison as well.

The 1774 decree that established the Poor House contained two provisions that were new for Mexico. First, it outlawed begging, a significant change in a Catholic society in which beggars had long been considered the beloved of Christ and soliciting alms was a legal and legitimate way to earn a

I STREET SCENE MARRED BY A LÉPERO. By placing the arrest of a delinquent in the foreground, the artist reflects elite fears of the poor intruding in their daily lives. In this case, the idyllic moonlit promenade of elegant city dwellers in front of the Mexico City cathedral is threatened by the lépero in their midst. The desire to gain control of public spaces was one of the motivations for the Poor House experiment.

living. Second, it commanded the roundup and forcible internment of those who violated the ban. The criminalization of begging and the attempt to isolate beggars while they were rehabilitated inaugurated a new type of interference in the daily lives of the urban poor: whereas vagrants had been persecuted for centuries in Mexico, beggars had not. This policy reflected a fundamental shift in attitudes toward the poor, for no one had before considered the indigent so deficient as to need transformation, let alone incarceration.

Although the Poor House quickly became "the foremost of our welfare establishments,"[1] it was unable to achieve its original goal of controlling the poor. For eight decades following the creation of the asylum, Mexico City officials reiterated the decrees against begging and vagrancy—indeed, they expanded the categories of people liable for conviction as vagrants and repeatedly ordered beggars into the asylum. Yet the Poor House project made little headway in suppressing mendicity or transforming the culture of the capital's street people. Eventually Mexican leaders backed down. The 1871 Penal Code relegalized begging, thus terminating the compulsory confinement of those who solicited alms, and reduced the categories of people who could be prosecuted for vagrancy. So ended the century-long experiment, with little to show for its efforts.

This book seeks to discover why this coercive experiment was undertaken, how it worked, and why it ultimately failed. Its fate is difficult to study because the history of public welfare institutions in Mexico has been sorely neglected. With few secondary works to rely on, I have been forced to laboriously piece together the asylum's past from internal accounts, church and government documents, newspapers, and the like. The process has been cumbersome because the surviving records are widely scattered in archives from Mexico City to Spain and, though voluminous, are incomplete. Correspondence with the viceroys has been well preserved, for example, while most daily registers have disappeared, and different kinds of documents are available for different periods, preventing consistent comparisons. At times I fear that I am treading on exceedingly thin ice, for there is still much that I do not know.[2] Particularly frustrating is the scarcity of eyewitness descriptions of day-to-day life in the asylum or of records giving voice to the pauper inmates. Despite the missing pieces of the puzzle, though, enough of a picture has now emerged to challenge many conclusions that have been based on the more easily accessible published sources.

When I began my research, I was imbued with the ideas of the "social control" school, which views the poor as victims of an increasingly powerful state. Historians like Michel Foucault challenged the traditional view of asylums as purely humanitarian institutions, instead arguing that they represented attempts to "discipline" the poor. I was convinced that the Mexico City Poor House was a Latin American example of the state mobilizing its coercive powers against a disorderly populace. My impression was reinforced by the works of Gabriel Haslip-Viera and Moisés González Navarro, the first two contemporary historians to pay brief attention to the asylum,[3] who both assumed that the experiment in practice worked as described in the legislation on beggars and in the bylaws of the institution.[4]

My initial impression vanished, however, as I delved progressively deeper into archival records that no one had systematically explored. As I learned how the Poor House actually functioned, I discovered that the original plan had been modified soon after its inception. Long before 1871 the roundups of beggars had ceased, the asylum had dwindled in size, and the attempt to reform as well as to shelter adult inmates had been discontinued. Indeed, by the middle of the nineteenth century the Poor House had primarily become a boarding school for orphaned children, a clientele not originally targeted by its founders.

The analysis of the Poor House experiment in practice reveals how little control the government exercised over the urban populace. Not only the weak republican administrations but also the supposedly strong colonial state could not impose this policy. Insufficient funding is only one of several reasons for this failure. While the experiment garnered enthusiastic support in some quarters, it never achieved a consensus among Mexico City residents. The elites, its strongest proponents, were more divided—and compassionate—than a study of their legislation would suggest. The Poor House staff and board members responsible for implementing the project were highly ambivalent about combining punishment with protection and had their own notions about which kinds of paupers deserved assistance. The Poor House clients, instead of being helpless victims manipulated from above, were able to shape the kind of institution that emerged by contesting the original plan while applying pressure for the asylum to serve their needs. By the time it was formally abandoned in 1871, the century-long experiment had made few inroads into the traditional "moral economy" of begging, in which the needy had the undisputed right to receive alms and the affluent considered it their duty to dispense them.[5]

This book traces the transformation of the Poor House, and of the Poor House experiment, over that century. This periodization is unusual for studies of Mexico, which normally begin or end with independence in 1821. It creates some problems, such as those of changing nomenclature and boundaries. For example, the colony of New Spain became the nation of Mexico, a unit much reduced in size. The city of Mexico became the Federal District, or D.F. (under federalist regimes), and the Department of Mexico (under centralist ones), both republican units enlarged to include some nearby villages.[6] Since these distinctions are unimportant to this study, I often use the simple but technically incorrect term *Mexico* for the colony as well as the nation, and consistently use the Anglicized name Mexico City to distinguish the capital from the country. Despite such problems, it is worth straddling the colonial and republican periods to follow the logical unit formed by the launching of the experiment in 1774 until its formal demise in 1871. These dates demarcate a period when the policies toward beggars differed, at least on paper, from those of both the preceding and subsequent years.

This periodization has the advantage of revealing long-term trends such as the growing role of the state and of women in social welfare. Although little studied for Latin America, these developments are often incorrectly dated in pioneering studies that focus on a short time period. The rising prominence of women in philanthropy and the staffing of public institutions has been portrayed as a Porfirian innovation, for example, though it dates to at least the Second Empire of Maximilian and Charlotte, with important republican precedents.[7] The shift from traditional Catholic notions of poor relief to modern ideas of secular social welfare has been located in the nineteenth century, beginning with independence and intensifying with the mid-century Liberal Reforma presided over by President Benito Juárez.[8] Perhaps plausible when studies begin in 1821, this interpretation becomes untenable when nineteenth-century liberals are compared to the Bourbon reformers who preceded them.

This book consequently challenges some of the basic mantras of patriotic histories. The nineteenth century has attracted highly polemical treatment. In most accounts, the Bad Guys are the losers of the great Reform War of the 1850s and 1860s: the Church, the Conservatives, and the foreign Emperor Maximilian. The Good Guys are the victorious Liberals, led by the Indian president Juárez. (To be sure, a few conservative historians reverse the parts and execrate the Liberals for opposing the Church.)[9] In reviewing their record in the Poor House, this book finds that Reforma Liberals failed to live up to their glorious image, while Maximilian and Charlotte, whose welfare policies have been neglected even by historians sympathetic to the ill-starred couple, emerge in a favorable light. Another maligned figure, General Antonio López de Santa Anna, also emerges as ripe for reinterpretation. Indeed, this study finds considerably more continuity in Mexican history than is allowed for in the standard historiography. Whether Bourbon, federalist, or centralist, Liberal or Conservative, native or foreign, the regimes that ruled Mexico from 1774 to 1871 shared many assumptions about how the urban poor fit into a broad modernization project. Thus, what might appear as a narrow case study of a single institution provides a window illuminating larger debates about Mexican history.

The Poor House records also provide valuable insights about the paupers of Mexico City. Although their statistics are notoriously unreliable, contemporary observers agreed that the poor were the majority of the capital's population. In 1764 the Spanish monk Francisco de Ajofrín believed that its destitute, "in tattered rags, who stain and disfigure everything," were much more numerous than in European cities. "Of every hundred persons you find on the streets," he wrote, "only one will be dressed and shod."[10] Twenty years later the Bourbon official Hipólito Villarroel put the population of "useless and lazy men and women" at forty thousand, approximately one-third of the capital's inhabitants.[11] A more cautious calculation came from the Prussian scientist Alexander von Humboldt when he noted in 1803 that "the streets of Mexico swarm with from twenty to thirty thousand wretches . . . of whom the greater number pass the night *sub dio*, and stretch themselves out to the sun during the day with nothing but a flannel covering." By his count, these "dregs of the people" represented between 15 and 22 percent of the capital's residents.[12] Similar estimates were made by travelers to independent Mexico, beginning with the U.S. minister Joel Poinsett, who in 1822 found "at least twenty thousand inhabitants of this capital . . . who have no permanent place of abode, and no ostensible means of gaining a livelihood." Poinsett reported that these *léperos* lived in "squalid penury," spending their days begging or stealing and then retiring to sleep "beneath the church porches, in miserable barracks in the suburbs, or under the canopy of heaven."[13] Successive visitors to Mexico City saw little improvement over the next four decades. On the contrary, several authors claimed that the number of *léperos* rose as a result of the political instability and recession that plagued the new republic. By 1855, for example, the French soldier Ernest Vigneaux estimated that they numbered fifty thousand or one-fourth of the capital's population.[14] In addition, the urban poor included laborers, servants, ambulant vendors, and artisans who also filled the city streets—both when working and playing—and who often lived on the brink of destitution.[15]

This sizable group of paupers is difficult to study. Although beggars were apparently everywhere—thronging the streets of the capital, sleeping on benches and in churchyards at night, and soliciting alms at the doors of temples and houses, in plazas, portals, theaters, shops, and restaurants—they left few written traces. Illiterates could not produce documents written in their own hand, and it is impossible to know how much the scribe shaped the rare testimonial. The homeless were not counted by municipal census takers, who went from door to door, often avoiding the slums. Those without substantial property or business had no reason to sign notarial contracts or make wills. And those who were marginalized from the church did not even leave certificates of baptism or marriage. If some indigents appeared in criminal records, they can hardly be considered representative of the capital's paupers as a whole. Likewise, those who appeared in hospital registers were the sick or demented. In contrast, the Poor House—at least, during its first two decades—confined a broad gamut of Mexico City's street people. This inquiry offers a partial glimpse of who they were and how they responded to the Poor House experiment.

This study also helps us understand Mexico City's first "urban crisis." Just as Mexico today boasts one of the largest and most polluted cities in the world, two centuries ago it boasted the largest city in the American hemisphere. By 1803 the capital numbered some 137,000 people, nearly twice its population in 1742.[16] Although the traditional historiography portrays the second half of the eighteenth century as prosperous, more recent historians have noted the impoverishment of the lower classes beneath the dazzling facade of mining wealth.[17] Mexico City's dramatic expansion was caused (then as now) by a rural crisis coupled with rapid population growth. As the Indian villagers finally recovered from the demographic devastation of the conquest, they found that whites had taken over much of their land. Increasingly dependent on cash, the rural population suffered when food prices escalated after 1770. A series of bad harvests and epidemics intensified their misery. Many country people responded by migrating to the capital in search of food, work, medical care, or charity. Unfortunately, they joined a populace already buffeted by inflation, declining real wages, and underemployment. As a result, mendicity became a growing problem.

The response of elite city dwellers to the swelling crowds of beggars ranged from disgust (one colonial bureaucrat proposed building a wall around the capital to keep the migrants out)[18] to initiating the Poor House experiment—the only such experiment, as far as I can determine, in eighteenth-century Latin America.[19] For, if the project owes much to the ideas of the Enlightenment, it was attempted in Mexico City only because it fit local circumstances. And, despite its similarity to contemporary European projects, it was far from a carbon copy of foreign blueprints.

The Social Control School and Its Critics

Ever since 1961, when Michel Foucault's *Madness and Civilization* made the asylum a symbol of the repressive bourgeois state, European and U.S. historians have reexamined the almshouses, orphanages, prisons, mental hospitals, and reformatories that proliferated in the seventeenth to nineteenth centuries during the Great Confinement of the poor.[20] Questioning the benevolence of these institutions, numerous "revisionist" works portrayed them as representing the interests of the elites rather than of the clients supposedly served. For example, David Rothman emphasized the role of social welfare in maintaining civil order. Frances Fox Piven and Richard Cloward explored its role in "regulating the poor" by making relief so degrading that the able-bodied would instead labor under exploitative conditions.[21] Others showed how the asylum movement benefited the philanthropists and the rising professional class, which gained new positions, power, and stature.[22] Angry New Left scholars turned the older sociological theories on their heads. If Emile Durkheim and Norbert Elias had viewed the collective internalization of social restraint as a positive step in the development of civilization (or of capitalism for Max Weber), such "discipline" now represented an insidious kind of mental domination and a violation of individual freedom. If Edward Ross had used the term *social control* to mean the voluntary socialization process essential to achieving social cohesion, it now became an imposition by the ruling class that victimized the poor.[23]

By the 1980s the tide had shifted again. A growing body of "counter-revisionist" studies challenged the social control thesis on many levels, from misusing evidence and establishing incorrect periodizations to being reductionist and conspiratorial, analyzing discourse rather than implementation, overlooking the divisions among the ruling classes, ignoring the genuine humanitarian impulse of social reformers, and failing to recognize the advantages that asylums could offer their inmates.[24] Especially after the publication in 1985 of James Scott's *Weapons of the Weak*,[25] scholars criticized the social control school for denying the agency of the poor. Historians like Ellen Dwyer, Catharina Lis, and Hugo Soly depicted pauper inmates less as passive victims than as active resisters manipulating the asylum system to suit their own ends.[26] At the same time, a related—and equally burgeoning—historiography on philanthropy and welfare grew out of the disenchantment with the modern welfare state. This literature likewise moved from emphasizing the motives of the benefactors to focusing on the experiences and perspectives of the recipients.[27]

The Latin American historiography has remained aloof from these trends. For Mexico there are a few studies of the numerous hospitals for diseased paupers founded since the sixteenth-century conquest.[28] The historian Josefina Muriel investigated convents, then hospitals, and finally the *recogimientos de mujeres*, the quasi-conventual houses of refuge for women that flourished in the sixteenth and seventeenth centuries.[29] Yet the favorite asylums of the Enlightenment that confined the physically healthy poor are only now beginning to receive the attention they deserve.[30] The study of charity and welfare has likewise been largely neglected until recently.[31]

Consequently, the nineteenth-century literature remains the most useful, despite its unmitigated glorification of the welfare establishments and the philanthropists who founded them. Most Mexican works consist of brief surveys of many institutions, with relatively little detail about any one. These books began to appear in the 1860s, when a series of short-lived reorganizations of the welfare system focused attention on institutions of public assistance.[32] Subsequent surveys were included as part of the city guides and histories that became popular at the time when urban planners were redesigning the face of the Mexican metropolis.[33] In fact, the destruction of the original Poor House building in 1905 as part of the "beautification" of the downtown capital elicited the first history of the asylum, written by its secretary, Martiniano T. Alfaro.[34]

In contrast, there has been growing interest in the daily lives of the urban poor in Mexico, although this literature still lags behind the studies of peasants.[35] Elite policies toward the poor have also attracted increasing attention. The pioneer in this field is the Jesuit historian Norman F. Martin, who analyzed colonial policy toward paupers, mostly before the Poor House experiment was initiated.[36] Recent works by Michael Scardaville, Juan Pedro Viqueira Albán, Pamela Voekel, William French, and others have moved beyond the legislation to show a repeated pattern of popular resistance to government or elite projects promoting various kinds of urban reform.[37]

The most complete study of Mexican welfare is Moisés González Navarro's *Poverty in Mexico*.[38] In the midst of the terrible economic crisis of the 1980s, which tragically worsened the lot of the poor, this eminent Mexican historian published his mammoth work to stir the conscience of the Mexican rich to support government measures to aid the destitute. His survey of elite policies toward indigents since the conquest builds a case for the superiority of public assistance. González Navarro argues that private and church philanthropy were never effective because they were disorganized, piecemeal, and treated the symptoms rather than the causes of poverty. Yet he does not examine how these policies were applied in practice, what impact they had on the poor, or how the client population responded to them.

This is the major weakness of works in this field outside of Latin America as well. As Peter Tyor and Jamil Zainaldin lamented in 1979, the field of social welfare history "may be considered a variety of intellectual history" that relies upon the analysis of policy statements and rarely explores the hidden "internal" history of welfare institutions.[39] Unfortunately, the situation has changed little since they wrote these words, as few historians have taken up their call to study individual institutions from the inside over their life course.[40]

This study therefore fills a considerable gap in the historiography. It amply demonstrates the dangers, to borrow Peter Mandler's felicitous phrase, of reading "prescriptions . . . as descriptions."[41] There was a huge gulf between how the Poor House experiment was supposed to work, as analyzed in the first two chapters of this book, and how it actually worked, as documented in the seven chapters that follow. The explanations for this gulf contribute to the reassessment of social control theories. The appraisal of the Mexican Poor House project is particularly relevant today as poverty increases in the developed as well as the underdeveloped world. It raises many questions we still grapple with and reflects familiar ambiguities such as whether government or private solutions are more effective, whether the poor are worthy or unworthy, whether they should be confined or allowed to remain at liberty, and whether money spent on shelters and orphanages is an effective response to poverty, unemployment, broken families, and homelessness. Likewise, the lessons from the Poor House experiment continue to be useful. Then as now effective solutions are exceedingly expensive, and stopgap measures inevitably fall short. The poor will always be with us as long as relief programs fail to address the structural problems of land tenure, jobs, and education. Plans designed without the input of the people affected—including the staff of welfare institutions—are doomed to failure. If the record of the Mexico City Poor House is any guide, institutionalization should be a last resort, for it was far from an ideal solution under any of the regimes that ruled Mexico from 1774 to 1871.

{ I }

THE PROBLEM OF BEGGARS AND

VAGRANTS, 1774–1871

On the fifth of March, 1774, Viceroy Antonio María de Bucareli announced a radically new policy toward the beggars of Mexico City:

> I have resolved . . . that the opening of the Poor House shall be on the nineteenth of this month, to which end I order that all beggars of both sexes present themselves to said hospice, where they shall be treated with charity and allowed to leave . . . if their fortunes vary, be it through inheritance, donation, or a means of earning a living, taking advantage of the training they shall receive, so that they cease to be beggars. . . . I assign the term of eight days, counted from the publication of this decree, for them to present themselves voluntarily, letting it be known that they shall not importune the faithful by asking for alms, and that henceforth all who are found begging in the streets, plazas, houses, and churches shall be picked up by the watchmen stationed in the different neighborhoods of the city and by the sentinels who shall be commissioned for the task. And to ensure that this news reaches everyone, and none can claim ignorance, I mandate that this resolution be published as a decree in the accustomed manner.[1]

So began the Poor House experiment, which consisted of prohibiting begging and forcibly confining—and attempting to transform—the paupers caught soliciting alms. Consciously designed to impose social control, the landmark decree bore few signs of benevolent intent. Beyond commanding that they be "treated with charity" in the new asylum, it ignored the needs of the verdaderos pobres, the "many persons of both sexes who are totally prevented from seeking sustenance with their labor, either by advanced age or

✠

EL BAILIO FREI DON ANTONIO MARIA BUCARELI Y

Vrfua Heneftrofa, Lafo de la Vega, Villacis y Còrdova, Caballero Gran Cruz y Comendador de la Bòbeda de Toro en el Orden de S. Juan, Teniente General de los Reales Exèrcitos de S. M., Virrey, Governador y Capitan General del Reyno de Nueva Efpaña, Prefidente de fu Real Audiencia, Superintendente General de Real Hacienda y Ramo del Tabaco, Juez Confervador de efte, Prefidente de fu Junta, y Subdelegado General de la Renta de Correos, en el mifmo Reyno.

POR QUANTO EL Sr. Dr. D. FERNANDO ORTIS CORTES, DIGNIdad de Chantre que fue de efta Santa Iglefia, condoliendofe de que muchas Perfonas de ambos fexos, fe hallan totalmente impofibilitadas de bufcar el fuftento con fu trabajo, ò por fer de edad abanzada, ò por haver padecido graves enfermedades, que les han inutilizado, y fe veen precifadas à mendigàr, en las Iglefias, en las Cafas, y en las calles, expueftas à muchos peligros de alma, y cuerpo, porque en las enfermedades carecen de focorros efpirituales, y temporales, por fer tanto fu defamparo que no fuelen tener, ni aun quien les llame al Confiffor; por lo que haviendofe tenido las licencias necefsarias, fabricò à fus expenfas una Cafa Hofpicio, en que fe recogieffen todos los Mendigos, con el piadofo objeto de que los verdaderos Pobres, fean afsiftidos con todo lo correfponde ente à una vida Chriftiana, precaviendo el que fe defrauden las Limofnas de los Fieles, por los vagos, mal entretenidos, y holgazanes, que abufan de la Charidad que encuentran, en Pueblo tan piadofo, como el de México, quando con fu trabajo debieran contrebuir à la indigencia del ò cefitado. Y haviendofe dado cuenta a S. M. fe dignò fu Real Clemencia, por Cedula dada en Madrid, 9. de Julio de 1765. aprobàr el proyecto manifeftando, haver fido de fu Real agrado la aplicacion del Fundador, à una obra tan grande, piadofa, y fanta, infpirada por la providencia Divina; rogandoles, y encàgandole, que continuaffe efte loable afsumpto, hafta verle enteramente puefto en pràctica. Para cuyo efecto, fe firviò S. M. de mandar, fe formaffen Ordenanzas, y fe le informaffe fobre varios puntos. Por lo que tuve à bien crear una Junta, que las formaffe, y entendieffe en lo conducente à dicho Hofpicio: la que me confultò, feria conveniente al fervicio de Dios, y del Rey, y à la utilidad del Público, con quanto antes fe pufieffe en ufo la Cafa; y en inteligencia de lo que pidió el Sr. Fifcal, y del Dictamen que me diò el Real Acuerdo, à donde remitì el Expediente por voto confultivo, y baxo de los mas efcrupulofos exàmenes. Hè refuelto, por providencia provifional, è interinaria, por depender fu continuacion de la Aprobacion de S.M. à quien darè cuenta de todo que la Apertura del Hofpicio fea el 19 del corriente, para lo que ordeno, que todos los Mendigos de ambos fexos fe prefenten en dicho Hofpicio, en el que feràn tratados con Caridad; y podràn falir, pues à ninguno fe le conducirà por fuerza, fiempre que variada fu fortuna, ya fea por herencia, Legado, ò proporciones de mantenerfe, ufando de los Oficios en que fe les inftituià, dejen de fer Mendigos: y por que la entrada ha de fer voluntaria, les afigno el termino de ocho dias, que fe contaràn, defde la publicacion de efte Vando para que fe prefenten voluntariamente, debiendo tener entendido, que pafado el dicho termino, no deben importunar à los Fieles pidiendo limofnas; por que à todo el que fe fepa, que fe hace en las Calles, Plazas, Cafas, è Iglefias ferà recogido por los Zeladores que eftaràn repartidos, por los diferentes Barrios de efta Ciudad, y por los otèros, à quienes tuviere por conveniente dàr Comifsion para ello. Y para que llegue à noticia de todos, y por ninguno fe alegue ignorancia, mando fe publique efta Refolucion por Vando en el modo, y forma que fe acoftumbra. México 5. de Marzo de mil fetecientos fetenta y quatro.

El Bo. Fr. D. Antonio Bucareli y Urfúa.

Por mandado de fu Exâ.

V Exà. por providencia Provifional, è interinaria, refuelve que la Apertura del Hofpicio de Pobres, fea el 19. del corriente y ordena que todos los Mendigos de ambos fexos fe prefenten en èl, dentro de ocho dias, que feràn tratados con Caridad, y en la forma que fe exprefa: con Apercebimiento que pafado dicho termino, no deben importunar à los Fieles, pidiendo Limofna, porque à todo el, que fe fepa, que lo hace, ferà recogido por los Zeladores que eftaràn repartidos por los diferentes Barrios de efta Ciudad.

2 DECREE FOUNDING OF THE POOR HOUSE. With this decree Viceroy Antonio María de Bucareli proclaimed the Poor House experiment on March 5, 1774. In announcing the aperture of the new asylum he simultaneously outlawed mendicity and warned the capital's beggars that they would henceforth be confined in the Poor House or forced to work. The landmark decree initiated the repression of Mexico City's beggars as part of a broader effort to discipline the urban poor.

by having suffered a serious illness that left them incapacitated." Instead, it focused on the twin goals of redirecting the able-bodied into the work force and deterring future mendicity.

The preamble to the viceroy's decree shows that his attack on the "moral economy" of begging was primarily aimed at combating vagrancy. Like many of his contemporaries, Bucareli was obsessed with the "professional beggar." In his 1816 *Periquillo sarniento*, the "Mexican Thinker" José Joaquín Fernández de Lizardi immortalized those rogues who "pretend[ed] to be blind, crippled, legless, lame, leprous, [and] unfortunate." "All ragged, dirty, be-patched and bedeviled-looking," they "importuned the whole world" with their "sorrowful supplications." Yet upon returning home they experienced a miraculous transformation. Some "straightened up; some stood their crutches in a corner and walked well enough on their own two feet; others stripped off the patches they wore and were clean-skinned and healthy; some took off great thick grey beards and grey wigs and were young men again; others stretched and unbent themselves on entering; everyone left his infirmities at the doorway" and gleefully proceeded to count up the day's take.[2] The viceroy had concluded that such pretenders could never be eliminated while indigents freely roamed about receiving alms. As long as they could mingle with "true" beggars, the "vagrants, troublemakers, and bums" would continue shunning work and "abusing the charity they encounter in such a pious city as Mexico." All beggars therefore had to be removed from public spaces, the "false" ones immediately put to work for the government or private employers and the "true" ones institutionalized. Meanwhile, alms-givers were encouraged to contribute directly to the Poor House, where their donations would reach only those who merited assistance.

It was not solely the difficulty of separating the deserving from the undeserving paupers that led the viceroy to restrict the liberty of all beggars. His decree portrayed "true" beggars as troublesome individuals in their own right, who could no longer be left to their own devices or to the care of private and ecclesiastical charity. They needed to be sequestered because they bothered the faithful with their solicitations and because their idleness set a bad example for the working poor. Those who could be rehabilitated were to be trained and returned to society; the others were to be aided but also deprived of freedom and kept from public view. In the foundational decree, the humanitarian concern for relieving suffering thus took a backseat to utilitarian goals.

Because policies toward beggars and vagrants were inextricably linked, the opening of the Poor House launched an intense campaign against both—at least on paper. The legislation of the next eight decades reveals remarkable continuity between the aims and methods of the colonial and republican regimes. Both shared the optimistic view that mendicity could be eradicated. Both also shared considerable hostility to the urban poor, as shown in the increasing conflation between the "unworthy" vagrants and the "worthy" beggars of yore. In keeping with a broad reformist agenda, both attempted to impose many kinds of "discipline" on the paupers of Mexico City, including religious discipline as well as the labor discipline analyzed by Frances Fox Piven and Richard Cloward, the civic discipline emphasized by David Rothman, the time discipline discussed by E. P. Thompson, the mental discipline highlighted by Michel Foucault, and the refinement of manners chronicled by Norbert Elias as a hallmark of the development of Western civilization.

Background to the Poor House Experiment

The creation of the Mexico City Poor House coincided with the Bourbon kings' ambitious program to modernize Spain and its empire. Particularly during the reign of Charles III (1759–88), the Spanish state carried out sweeping reforms that included strengthening the provision of welfare services. María Jiménez Salas, the pioneering historian of welfare in Spain, divided such institutions into three types: those that aided the poor, those that repressed them, and those that attempted to prevent poverty.[3] Yet the favorite institutions of the Enlightenment fulfilled the three functions simultaneously. The Bourbon goal of creating a productive and well-ordered society required that philanthropy be combined with the disciplining of the poor.

In Mexico City four new welfare establishments appeared during the late eighteenth century, two of which were part of a new strategy for dealing with destitution. The two ecclesiastical foundations, the Foundling Home (Casa de Cuna) of 1767 and the General Hospital of San Andrés of 1779, represented traditional types of assistance. An orphanage had existed in the sixteenth-century capital, although it had long ago disappeared.[4] The hospital, opened in the midst of a devastating smallpox epidemic, joined eleven other hospitals and three asylums for the mentally ill in Mexico City, most of these dating from the sixteenth century.[5] The two secular institutions departed from this tradition. Instead of sheltering only limited groups of dependent paupers in need of immediate care (babies, the sick, and the mentally ill), the Poor House targeted adults who, when begging was legal, had been able to fend for themselves. The asylum was designed to isolate and reclaim social marginals rather than merely assist them. The Pawn Shop (Monte de Piedad), founded in 1775, was designed to prevent the indigence of the working poor by offering low-cost (and in some periods free) credit.[6] In addition, the crown established pension funds (*montepíos*) from the 1760s on to provide for the survivors of civil servants, thereby preventing the impoverishment of their widows and orphaned children.[7] In 1769 it founded a huge Royal Cigar Factory to generate employment for thousands of unoccupied men and women.[8] Taken together, these initiatives embodied the utopian ideal of eliminating poverty itself.

The Poor House was also part of an attempt to upgrade the labor force and "civilize" the lower classes. The crown's agenda was extremely complicated. Some new measures were aimed at maintaining civil order and fostering economic development. The promotion of free elementary instruction, to be provided by parishes, convents, municipalities, and asylums, reflected the enlightened view that education was the most effective way to achieve "progress."[9] Beyond basic literacy, schools and asylums were to inculcate new values. The work ethic and a sense of civic responsibility were of paramount importance. So were industrial time and work discipline, which were to replace the casual, episodic, and flexible work habits of artisans who set their own schedules and regularly took off "St. Monday" in addition to the innumerable religious holidays.[10] Other measures were aimed at effecting a broad cultural transformation that was not strictly utilitarian. In keeping with the development of a more refined sensibility, municipal authorities took steps to ban public nakedness; to reduce concubinage, public drinking, and gambling; to tame the boisterous celebrations of religious holidays such as Holy Week and Corpus Christi; and to curb such distasteful behavior as urinating on the walls of buildings. The *buena policía de los pobres* thus encompassed not only the narrow policing of the poor but also attempts to impose new moral codes and manners.[11] These were accompanied by efforts to sanitize and beautify the capital city by cleaning the filth that was everywhere — as well as by removing the poor from the streets where they congregated to socialize, work, eat, very often sleep, and, of course, beg.[12]

The repressive organs of the state were simultaneously overhauled to facilitate the implementation of these reforms. In Mexico City, the police force and the system of criminal courts were expanded in 1782 as part of the division of the capital into eight administrative districts (*cuarteles mayores*). Each had its own district court, and each was further subdivided to create thirty-two smaller units (*cuarteles menores*) with their own neighborhood sentinels. In 1790 a ninth court was established and the police force was further expanded with a force of *guardafaroles* to guard new gaslights and patrol the streets at night.[13] These officials were charged not only with arresting criminals but also with bringing beggars to the Poor House. They were further instructed to monitor the people in their districts by drawing up censuses to locate undesirables and by "watching the inclinations, lifestyle, and customs" of those under their charge.[14]

These initiatives resembled those of Bourbon Spain, where beggars and vagrants were likewise a favorite target. The Spanish ministers Bernardo Ward, the Count of Campomanes, and Gaspar Melchor de Jovellanos encouraged the policing, internment, and reform of paupers as part of their strategy to modernize Spain. They viewed idle vagrants who undermined Spanish wealth and industry as a potential resource that, if properly tapped, could provide labor to increase production and soldiers to defend the empire. They also believed that many social problems (from the migration that fueled unprecedented urban growth to increased social unrest, crime, and immorality) could be controlled by eradicating this "scourge." Religious reformers hoped, in addition, to reclaim a marginal group that was largely lost to the Church and thus to the primary institution of moral education.[15]

The Spanish campaign against vagrants went into full swing after the 1766 riot of the Esquilache (in which vagrants allegedly swelled the menacing crowd that invaded the royal palace in Madrid to protest an unpopular decree) and continued strong in the next few decades as Spain's foreign wars created a steady demand for soldiers.[16] It was accompanied by a spurt of asylum building throughout the Iberian Peninsula.[17] And it culminated, in 1777, in a royal decree prohibiting begging and ordering the confinement of the beggars of Madrid.[18]

Although these developments were not without precedent in Spain, they took on a new character and intensity during the era of the Bourbon reforms. Campaigns against vagrants had existed sporadically for centuries. The diverse asylums founded since the sixteenth century had included an occasional hospice for paupers, though hospitals for the sick were far more common. Following the publication of Juan Luis Vives's influential *Del socorro de los pobres* in 1526, some Spanish cities had experimented with restricting mendicity by licensing "legitimate" beggars and arresting all others as vagrants, and by limiting beggars to their native towns. These restrictions had since lapsed, however.[19] In the late eighteenth century, when reformers focused on the "infestation" of "false" beggars as a cause of Spanish decline, the persecution of vagrants mounted, the number of asylums for paupers increased, and these became more coercive as entry ceased to be entirely voluntary.

In Mexico these trends marked a dramatic departure from previous policies. Although campaigns against vagrants had been tried in the past, especially in the sixteenth century,[20] the colony had never before restricted the right to beg. Likewise, there had never been an asylum for beggars in Mexico City. Some of the recogimientos de mujeres came close because they sheltered healthy adults: spinsters, widows, and abandoned wives who wished to live apart from the world in a religious atmosphere. Unlike the Poor House, however, these houses of refuge were designed to serve clients from all social classes and entrance was voluntary—except in those established as reformatories for prostitutes. Besides, these institutions had declined considerably by the late colonial period, with some becoming female prisons, schools, or hospitals and others closing entirely.[21] Policies of supervised enclosure had likewise been applied during the sixteenth century to Indians in mission towns,[22] but never before to the urban poor. Indeed, unlike earlier welfare projects that targeted particular racial groups (such as the Royal Indian Hospital and the special legal assistance offered Indians who as a group were considered the *pobres miserables* of the colony),[23] the Poor House experiment was meant to control a multiracial populace. Reflecting the decline of caste society,[24] late-eighteenth-century reformers rarely mentioned race in their discourse about the unruly street people of Mexico City.

Although the Mexican Poor House experiment was launched at the same time as similar projects in Spain, it was not motivated simply by a desire to imitate the metropolis. It was initiated by Mexican leaders because it addressed local needs created by the "urban crisis" gripping Mexico City. The massive migration of people from rural areas had caused it to grow from approximately 98,000 inhabitants in 1742 to 137,000 in 1803. This population made the turn of the century capital nearly the size of Madrid and the fifth largest city in the Western World. The surge in migration was particularly acute in the 1770s and 1780s, when a series of bad harvests and epidemics forced the sick and hungry to flee the countryside in search of assistance, and again after 1810, when the independence wars sent refugees to seek safety in the city. Following a wartime peak of some 169,000 in 1811, Mexico City's population briefly dropped but then resumed its earlier growth to reach 200,000 by 1870.[25] Unfortunately, the colonial migrants joined city dwellers who were increasingly impoverished because of a dramatic rise in the prices of basic staples: corn prices, for example, doubled in the decade of the 1770s alone, while earnings remained flat.[26] In the republican years, migrants joined residents buffeted by the deep recession that followed independence.

Until this point Mexico City had been able to maintain a "charitable equilibrium" in which the capital city provided for its own destitute as well as for those from the surrounding region.[27] By the late eighteenth century, however, the proliferation of paupers overwhelmed the existing system of poor relief. The public granary, ecclesiastical soup kitchens, hospitals, lay confraternities, and individual almsgivers could not keep up with the growing demand. It is likely that the guilds, already in decline, no longer provided sufficient assistance for the large artisan population.[28] Neither could the outdated law enforcement institutions keep up with the task of controlling the crime, alcoholism, promiscuity, and other social problems that contemporaries believed had escalated as the size of the marginal population swelled.[29] The fear of milling crowds of potentially unruly paupers even led the Bourbon official Hipólito Villarroel in 1785 to propose expelling all vagrants from Mexico City and building a wall around it to keep new migrants out.[30] Instead, authorities adopted the two-pronged approach of increasing social services and employment opportunities, on the one hand, while reorganizing the system of law enforcement and unleashing the campaign against the capital's beggars and vagrants on the other.

If these policies looked like those on the peninsula it was because Mexican officials faced the same problems of precipitous urbanization and widespread unemployment—coupled, paradoxically, with a scarcity of soldiers and disciplined workers—that motivated their counterparts in Spain. Indeed, in some ways Mexico City was on the cutting edge of Spanish social policy. Most of the metropolitan decrees against vagrants were reissued for the colony soon after their proclamation in the mother country. The initiative to establish the Mexico City Poor House dated from 1760, only one decade after the publication of Bernardo Ward's *Obra pía* and prior to most Spanish proposals for confining paupers in asylums.[31] And, although a few eighteenth-century poorhouses on the peninsula antedated the one in the viceroyalty, the ban on begging was decreed three years earlier in Mexico City than in Madrid.

Rather than viewing the Mexican Poor House project as an example of cultural dependency, it should be seen as part of an experiment conducted simultaneously on both sides of the Atlantic—and one to which the colony contributed substantially. Not only did its viceroy pioneer the ban on begging, but the archbishop of Mexico provided one of the earliest and most cogent justifications by a Spanish cleric for the forced institutionalization of beggars. Attempting to obtain royal approval for the Mexico City Poor House in 1770, Archbishop Francisco de Lorenzana sent the king a twenty-nine-page *Memorial que presentan a todas las comunidades, y gremios los pobres mendigos de México por mano de su Arzobispo*, beautifully printed and bound in embossed leather with gold leaf. When he returned to Spain as the cardinal of Toledo, Lorenzana would become a major proponent of repressing mendicity and confining Spanish paupers.[32] As the *Memorial* demonstrates, he developed his ideas while serving in New Spain from 1766 to 1771.

Lorenzana's *Memorial* shows how the Poor House project responded to the specific problems of the Mexican viceroyalty. Such an asylum was necessary, he argued, to control the hordes of "half-naked idlers . . . who beg from

door to door in Mexico City, Puebla, and other cities of America." He attributed this "plague" to urban migration, which he explained in terms of moral
decline. Recently, he claimed, "laziness" had even spread to the native population: "The Indians, who previously never solicited alms, are now coming
in troops to the cities to live at their liberty. The King loses tributaries, . . .
the lands lie uncultivated, haciendas are abandoned for lack of workers, sugar
mills are brought to a halt, priests lose their parishioners, mayors lose track
of their subjects, and many [Indians] even stay on in Mexico City as deputies
to litigate constantly against everyone." Such freedom was intolerable, he insisted, because people "are not born for themselves alone but for the greater
good of the nation." His solution, restricted for the time to the colony's
major metropolis, was "to confine the indigent, that is, maintain the disabled,
make the lazy ones work, train them in useful arts, and . . . teach them Christian doctrine."

The archbishop's treatise demonstrates that, contrary to what William
Callahan argued for Spain, clerical support for confinement derived as much
from secular as from religious concerns.[33] In a long list of the ills of vagrancy,
Lorenzana only briefly mentioned the vagabonds' isolation from the Church.
He vividly condemned them as a "sink of corruption, . . . sponge absorbing
poison, pump sucking up grime, . . . [and a] cancerous sore consuming the
body politic." He maintained that they "insidiously undermine the strength
of the Sovereign, . . . which consists in the wealth and industry of his Vassals."
They caused sin, vice, and crime. Their "tongues inflame citizens to sedition
and riots, disseminate gossip, . . . upset families, and render people indifferent
to obeying their superiors." Their wandering and filthy habits spread epidemics. Their drunken milling about in crowds caused "the murders and frequent injuries which are a daily occurrence in Mexico City." Their nakedness
caused "horror in the men, disgust and shame in the women." They usurped
the alms that rightfully belonged to the truly needy. And, finally, they were
"Catholics without religion, Christians only in name, . . . nuisances to all,
useful to none, and harmful even to themselves."

Most of Lorenzana's attention focused on the economic damage caused
by vagrancy. A recurrent theme of the *Memorial* was that America was poor,
despite its vast natural resources, because of its many idle inhabitants. The
archbishop believed that the extraordinary fertility of the soil and the benign
climate made it so easy to survive that people did not exert themselves—not
even to "cover their flesh" with "decency," despite the low cost of clothing
"a man or woman of the people." The "wealth of nations,"[34] wrote Lorenzana, "does not depend on one or more powerful persons, but on the trade,
activity, continuous movement, and manufactures of all its people. . . . Hol-

land and Flanders, where the land does not easily produce fruit, are none-theless wealthy because they do not allow a single inhabitant to remain idle and without a licit means of earning a living." In contrast, "in this America, where the fruits of the land are so copious, there is more poverty because each individual is free to spend the entire day sitting on his hands."

Underneath this climatic determinism lay a cultural interpretation of Mexico's ills. Lorenzana may be considered an early proponent of the "cul-ture of poverty" thesis (although the term itself would not be coined for another two centuries) because he blamed the poverty of Mexican paupers on their laziness and lack of ambition. Like many modern analysts who locate the source of poverty in the values and attitudes of the poor themselves,[35] Lorenzana's prescription was to transform the moral character of the lower classes by "rooting out the rotten part of their customs, waking them from their lethargy, and teaching them their obligations." Like his modern coun-terparts, he overlooked the structural obstacles faced by the poor (e.g., a study conducted for Mexico City in 1790 discovered that the cost of buying clothing was in fact out of reach for a large segment of the urban poor).[36] Above all, the archbishop wanted to instill the work ethic so that "the humans of this kingdom" would not be inferior to the "admirable" and "industri-ous" ants.

Thus, Lorenzana's proposal mixed utilitarian with humanitarian con-cerns. He was apparently sincere in his belief that the institutionalization of deserving beggars would improve their living conditions. He described how the Poor House would benefit its inmates by providing nutritious meals, proper clothing, shelter from inclement weather, rooms free from dampness, and doctors and medicines as needed. Their spiritual health would improve because they could regularly "attend Mass, frequent the Sacraments, and live as Christians." They would "be entertained in ways that will not mortify them . . . and will achieve a happy old age." Finally, those temporarily disabled by sickness would be cured so that they could resume their normal activities.

At the same time, Lorenzana intended to "regulate" the poor by encourag-ing the able-bodied to enter the labor market. Anticipating that his proposal would not be welcomed by Mexican paupers, he counted on the threat of con-finement to have a deterrent effect: "All will do their utmost to cover their flesh, so they will not be judged lazy and taken to the Poor House, and con-sequently more decency, less dishonesty, more modesty in the women and honor in the men, will be achieved." Others "will cease feigning sickness and will no longer open sores on themselves with herbs and poultices" to elicit pity. All will be stimulated to exertion, and "in this manner so much land will not lie idle in America, artisans will work harder, servants will be more obedient, and people, houses, and possessions will be secure from theft . . . because all will know that they can expect internment, either in an asylum to receive charity or in a jail to receive punishment."

As the *Memorial* makes striking clear, the Mexico City Poor House was central to a much larger project to discipline the poor. Lorenzana saw the institutionalization and reform of beggars not only as a way to save souls and aid the elderly, infirm, and disabled but also as a way to combat idleness, increase production, and control the migration, crime, epidemics, and social dissolution undermining the viceroyalty. For him the Poor House experiment was the panacea that would produce peace, prosperity, and progress. The archbishop's treatise further demonstrates that, although promulgated by the viceroy as a representative of the royal state, the project had strong ecclesiastical support.

Beggars and Vagrants before the Law, 1774–1870

The Poor House experiment unleashed a flood of legislation mandating the persecution of beggars and vagrants in the Mexican capital. Orders to arrest vagrants were reiterated at least thirty-five times between 1774 and 1870.[37] The confinement of beggars was decreed at least fifteen times, usually within ordinances aimed at vagrants, in 1774, 1782, 1783, 1786, 1794, 1797, 1800, 1806, 1809, 1830, 1843, 1845, 1850, 1851, and 1863.[38] Henceforth, only designated persons licensed by ecclesiastical authorities to raise funds for the Church would be free to solicit alms.[39] After the 1774 decree targeted beggars and vagrants together, the distinctions between the two became increasingly blurred. Moreover, in the three-quarters of a century after the Poor House experiment began, ever larger numbers of Mexico City paupers became subject to the repressive crusade against vagrancy.

In theory, there was a clear separation between beggars and vagrants. The *verdaderos pobres*, or "legitimate" beggars incapable of working because of age or an infirmity, were the deserving or worthy poor. The vagrants (*mendigos fingidos* or *voluntarios*) who were capable of working but did not, were the unworthy poor. Their treatment was supposed to diverge, with the "true" beggars receiving "love and charity" in the Poor House and the "abominable" vagrants forced to work in the private sector or sentenced to government service, which included service in the army and the marines and, after 1806, colonization of the Californias and other northern border areas.[40]

In practice, the two groups began to overlap from the moment the 1774 decree made begging a criminal act for which a person could be arrested. This ordinance insisted that the new policies were for the beggars' own good since

PL. 16

COSTUMES MEXICAINS.
Manière de porter des mendiants pour exciter la pitié.

3 A "TRUE" BEGGAR. The verdaderos pobres were the elderly and incapacitated who could not support themselves with their own labor. The Italian lithographer, Claudio Linati, was struck by the manner in which this crippled beggar was carried about to excite the pity of almsgivers. That an able-bodied man devoted himself to this task suggests that the elderly beggar earned enough for both of them, a testament to the generosity of Mexico City almsgivers.

they would be removed from the dangers of the streets and sheltered. Subsequent decrees clarified that, unlike the treatment of vagrants, the seclusion of beggars was "not a penalty or punishment."[41] Yet it clearly was. After 1774 beggars had no more choice about being in the Poor House than vagrants had about being conscripted. They either entered voluntarily or, if caught begging, were forcibly interned. Moreover, the beggar who resisted confinement immediately became a delinquent, with his punishment proportional to the "scandal and commotion" he caused.[42] In some ways the beggar's penalty was harsher than the vagrant's because it was open-ended. Although the sentences mandated for vagrants were of limited duration (e.g., service in the armed services was set at eight years in 1779 and at two in 1820 and 1828, rising to four for repeat offenders),[43] beggars could leave the Poor House only when they demonstrated that they could survive without soliciting alms.

The internal regime of the Poor House further confounded the two groups. As chapter two shows, the inmates were supposed to work in the asylum's workshops, making clothes and bed linens for their own use as well as for sale to raise funds for the institution. Even the infirm were to work according to their abilities, if not in the workshops then in cleaning, doing laun-

COSTUMES MEXICAINS.
(Lepero) Vagabond

4 A LÉPERO OR VAGABOND. By the middle of the nineteenth century the derogatory term *lépero* was used to describe the sturdy beggar, or vagrant. Usually men, the léperos were decried as recalcitrant characters who refused steady work and lived by their wits on the margins of the law. The writer Guillermo Prieto depicted them as picaresque types, devoted to love, drink, and fighting. Travelers to Mexico City feared these rogues, who picked their pockets with ease.

dry, and performing other household tasks. Forced labor, the centuries-old penalty for vagrants, was therefore prescribed for beggars from the inception of the Poor House experiment.

Finally, beggars had come to be regarded as people in need of moral rehabilitation, just as vagrants had been for centuries. Today we would distinguish between two types of vagrant in the eighteenth-century legislation: the person who did not work though capable of doing so (the unemployed) and the lazy, vice-ridden bum who abandoned his family, hung around bars, gambled, stole, and led his peers astray (the deviant or delinquent). But legislators of the time did not make these distinctions. They combined the unemployed and the deviant in single phrases: *vagos y viciosos* (vice-ridden vagrants) or *vagos, ociosos, y malentretenidos* (vagrants, idlers, and troublemakers). Vagrants were viewed not as victims of unemployment but as pernicious people who suffered from a moral defect that caused them to choose their lot voluntarily; otherwise, they would have been productively employed. After 1774 the "true" beggars, though still considered worthy of public assistance, were also judged morally defective. This is why Mexican policymakers tried to change them, as if the causes of mendicity were in their "idleness, lack of discipline, and poor upbringing," as the 1777 bylaws of the Poor House put it, and not in the structures of society that denied them education and employment. The Poor House therefore sought to teach them not only vocational skills but also such habits as industriousness, punctuality, temperance, the fear of God, and obedience to authority.[44]

Within the next few years the distinction between the two groups of paupers was further eroded by decrees that permitted the confinement of vagrants who were ineligible for military service in the asylums designed for beggars. If Spanish legislation had once provided methods for dealing with vagrants of all ages and sexes, that was no longer the case by the eighteenth century, when antivagrancy laws dictated military conscription. Female vagrants, who in the fourteenth century could be sentenced to personal service, were omitted from the antivagrancy laws of the sixteenth to mid-eighteenth centuries. Penalties that once were applied to vagrants ineligible for the military, such as service in textile mills or public works, had likewise disappeared.[45] Yet the armed services only accepted men between the ages of 16 and 18 and 36 and 40 (depending on the year), subject to additional requirements of minimum stature (five feet for the army, none for the marines), physical and mental health, and in some periods single marital status.[46] In New Spain Indians were also barred from the armed services.[47] Consequently, the Bourbon state found that many vagrants were beyond its reach, an unacceptable situation if the new experiment in social control was to succeed.

Beginning in 1775 the Spanish crown began dictating alternative methods for dealing with ineligible men, underage youths, and women. In addition to reinstating the option of forcing them to work in textile mills, bakeries, *tocinerías* (where pork was cured and sold), haciendas, or public works projects,[48] they were occasionally confined in asylums. A royal order of May 7, 1775, confined in "*hospicios y casas de misericordia*" male vagrants who were "inept for arms" because they were too young, too old, too short, or "not robust enough."[49] An order of July 12, 1781, mandated that "vagrants of both sexes" who were "inept for military service" must be forced to work. It left the procedures for disciplining adults rather vague, for its main concern was with the children of beggars, who were growing up without an occupation. These youths, both girls and boys, were to be apprenticed to a reputable master or placed in an asylum to learn a trade.[50] The new form of treating mendicity thus allowed the state to intervene directly in the lives of paupers of all ages and sexes—and even to confine children who were in danger of becoming future vagrants even if they had not yet begged or otherwise misbehaved.

Similar edicts were issued specifically for New Spain beginning in 1786, the terrible Year of Hunger when, following two years of unseasonably wet and cold weather that damaged crops and caused widespread famine and illness, a flood of starving migrants arrived in the viceregal capital begging for assistance.[51] By March of 1786, the authorities took steps so that the "multitude of poor people of both sexes" who lived by begging, "many of them half-naked and burdened with children," would not get used to "the detestable and prejudicial vice of idleness." On April 10, Viceroy Bernardo de Gálvez decreed that healthy men and boys age ten and older should be put to work building roads, while women and girls should be sent home; a woman caught begging again, however, was to be placed in the Poor House "for as long as seems convenient."[52] Male vagrants who were ineligible for military service were confined to the Poor House by Mexican decrees of 1792, 1828, 1834, 1845, 1850, 1853, and 1857.[53] The asylum was to convert these able-bodied idlers into productive members of society—or at the very least, as an 1820 decree explained, allow them to "work without getting into trouble or being a burden to the state."[54]

A royal decree of January 11, 1784, recognized that for all practical purposes the punishment of vagrants who did not qualify for military service might be indistinguishable from that of beggars. Confirming that vagrants and beggars were often mixed together within asylums, it stipulated that delinquents should be isolated from the other inmates in separate rooms or sections (an isolation that was, however, difficult to enforce). In addition, the 1784 decree specified that when vagrants were placed in asylums their terms of confinement became open-ended, like those of the beggars.[55]

The differences between beggars and vagrants diminished even further as the legal definition of vagrancy expanded over the next three-quarters of a century. The proliferation of people subject to persecution can be seen by comparing an 1845 law of the Mexican congress, which listed twenty-one types of vagrant, to a royal edict of 1745.[56] The 1745 decree, with sixteen types of vagrant, had already enlarged the traditional narrow definition of vagrants—as unemployed troublemakers, including "false" beggars—to include some underemployed and socially undesirable persons.[57] The 1845 decree continued that trend by adding several new kinds of vagrants. Even though the nineteenth-century catalogue of vices was simplified, omitting some of the details and explanations of the earlier decree, only one type of vagrant was dropped: the person who illegally bears arms, being of such an age that the normal penalties for this infraction could not be applied. In addition, the 1845 decree incorporated five categories that had appeared in scattered legislation over the previous century and added two entirely new ones.

In the century between 1745 and 1845 the vagrant had come to include the underemployed as well as the unemployed. Although the 1745 decree was already moving in this direction, it left considerable room for discretion on the part of the authorities when it designated as a vagrant the person who had a trade only if he "did not exercise it for most of the year, without just motive for failing to do so." A decree of 1778 was also sympathetic to the unemployed in stating that "those laborers who are occasionally idle because they have nothing in which to work shall not be considered vagrants."[58] In contrast, the 1845 decree designated as a vagrant not only the underemployed "without just cause" but also the day laborer who worked less than half the week, "spending the other days without an honest occupation." Leaving little margin for those suffering from difficult economic times, this definition incorrectly assumed that employment opportunities were plentiful for those who wanted them. Despite the severe economic depression afflicting independent Mexico, the authors of an 1834 decree similarly insisted that reformed vagrants would easily find work because "the arts, commerce, and industry reclaim the arms to whom they offer useful and honest occupations, to interest them in public prosperity and separate them from a career in crime."[59] In their desire to enforce work and maintain law and order, these legislators apparently felt no ambivalence about condemning the unemployed to punishment as vagrants.

Another new category of vagrant that appeared in the nineteenth century is the man or woman who did not work hard enough, namely, people who sold *billetes y papeles*—broadsides, political propaganda, and lottery tickets. This was easy work best left to invalids according to the 1845 decree. The sale of *papeles impresos*, "printed papers," was first prohibited in 1810 as a measure to combat the insurgent movement.[60] After independence, in the midst of continued political turbulence, republican leaders three times repeated this ban "to prevent the alteration of public tranquility."[61] Although one goal of this legislation was to prevent opposition to the government, this was not the reason given by a decree of October 3, 1834. In designating as vagrants those who sold papeles impresos without official permission, the decree cited "the demoralization caused by the ease of earning money selling printed papers in the portals, streets, and other public places, which causes a multitude of men and women, particularly youths, to abandon the jobs in which they once worked and could have earned an honorable subsistence, because it is more comfortable to roam the streets and make a living by surrendering themselves to degrading vices." Clearly, hanging around street corners selling broadsides and talking to passersby was not "honest" employment for those suited for harder work. This new category of vagrant shows the authorities' desire to improve the work habits of the lower classes.

CONTAINING THE POOR

In addition to the underemployed or marginally employed, the 1845 decree defined as a vagrant the libertine even if he had a job. Again, this development expanded on a trend inaugurated when the 1745 decree augmented the traditional narrow definition of vagrants with youths who defied their parents or local authorities, men perpetually "distracted by concubinage," and those "who without visible motive abuse their wives with public scandal." The 1845 decree added people who whiled away the time playing cards or gambling or who sold indecent pictures, made obscene comments or gestures in public, or otherwise "promoted immorality"—even if they had "honest" jobs. There was some precedent for including people of means among the vagrants subject to persecution: a 1781 decree had ordered that noble libertines, who had legitimate sources of income, be rounded up as vagrants.[62] Since noble titles were abolished after independence, noble vagrants were not specifically referred to in the 1845 decree. Yet profligates with means were comprehended in the articles on socially undesirable behavior (arts. 2, 5, 6, 9, 13, 17), which applied to those with jobs and income. Thus, by 1845 vagrants were no longer just unemployed rowdies—or even just poor people, as they had been in 1745—but occasionally included those with some education and wealth whose behavior was considered unsavory if not strictly criminal.

The 1845 decree also defined as vagrancy some jobs once considered to be valid employment. Classifying certain ambulant vendors as vagrants, the 1745 decree echoed the traditional persecution of gypsies in Spain—and reflected the double meaning of the Spanish word *vago*, which can best be translated as "vagabond" since it means "wanderer" as well as "loafer." The 1845 decree added several stationary occupations. Foremost were musicians in popular bars (*vinaterías, bodegones*, and *pulquerías*), which offered bawdy entertainment that offended the sensibilities of elite policymakers. These bars were considered part of the magnet that diverted industrious workers into a life of drink, idleness, and vice.[63] A 1789 decree, condemning those who subsisted on odd jobs and spent most of their time hanging out in "cafés, saloons, pool halls, taverns, and other such diversions," explained that these entertainments were permitted, "but only for the relief of those who work."[64] In other words, recreation was to be a supplement to a life of work, not the most important part. This legislation reflects the rejection of the aristocratic and plebeian culture that valued leisure, as well as the desire to instill the ethic of hard work. At the same time, it shows the desire to moralize the culture of the poor already evident in the persecution of those who indulged in "licentious" activities.

Another formerly legal occupation newly designated as vagrancy was that of *tinterillos* or *huisacheros*, unlicensed attorneys who made their living by representing others in court. An 1842 decree of the Ministry of Justice and Ecclesiastical Affairs, which introduced this new category of vagrant, explained that tinterillos—along with *curanderos* (healers), who were considered vagrants in 1842 but not in 1845—were offensive because they practiced a profession without a license: "The occupation that for a licensed practitioner is honorable is for the person without a title but an illegal entertainment."[65] This preoccupation with restricting the exercise of medicine and law reflects the institutionalization of the medical and legal professions during this period. The Mexican government had additional reasons, however, for "clearing the courts and neighborhoods of this kind of vagrant."[66] Framing its argument in terms of public protection, the 1842 law explained that just as curanderos threatened public health tinterillos threatened "the peace of families and the proper administration of justice." What made them dangerous was that "without obtaining title or legal authorization they encourage, agitate, and promote other people's lawsuits by hanging around the courts of justice to offer their services . . . and often involving them without necessity." It was thus to reduce the number of lawsuits—especially those brought by poor people, who presumably used the services of the untitled attorneys— that tinterillos were classified as vagrants. Again, the desire to suppress the offensive activities of the poor was behind the inclusion of this group. The primacy of the social control impulse may explain why unlicensed healers, who posed no threat to public order, were omitted from the 1845 catalog of vagrants.

Finally, by 1845 certain "true" beggars were included for the first time among the social undesirables classified as vagrants. These were not just the "voluntary" beggars considered vagrants by the 1745 decree, which had included able-bodied adults, crippled soldiers who received pensions, and youths who spent their time begging even though they were capable of learning and practicing a useful trade. The 1845 decree added true beggars positioned outside of churches and those who carried around *alcancías* (collection boxes), virgins, or rosaries without the permission of the ecclesiastical judge and district governor.[67] The two new categories probably encompassed the majority of beggars, for whom churches were a favorite station and appeals to religious piety were standard. An 1834 decree had already targeted blind paupers who harangued the public with their loud recitations about religion.[68] By 1845, however, these beggars were no longer just a nuisance to be confined in the Poor House, as was the case in 1774 and even 1834; they were now condemned as the far more despicable vagrants. Beggars and vagrants had thus become intertwined, at least in the minds of Mexican legislators.

The two groups remained confused in the antivagrancy laws of the next decade. Comprehensive presidential decrees of 1853 and 1857 trimmed the list of people who qualified as vagrants. They dropped disabled soldiers who received pensions, probably because the government could no longer afford to pay them. They dropped people who sold newspapers, broadsides, and obscene pictures, although people who scandalized the public with obscenities could instead be arrested as criminals.[69] They also dropped some of those who committed "moral offenses," namely, the son who did not respect his parents or the husband who abused his wife (although, again, the latter could be punished as a criminal).[70] Yet they kept the morally offensive musicians in bars as well as (in 1853 only) the tinterillos who promoted popular litigiousness. They also retained the unlicensed beggars who used religious images in soliciting alms.[71] Republican leaders thus not only continued but in some ways intensified the colonial campaign against the street people of Mexico City—at least in their legislation.

Besides expanding the types of beggars liable for conviction as vagrants, the Mexican statutes introduced new weapons to the arsenal available to fight these undesirables. First, the municipal police and court systems were enlarged or reorganized several times during the republican years. For example, a new police force of 250 celadores públicos was established in 1826.[72] In 1833 the city council hatched a plan, specifically aimed at controlling vagrancy, to increase the number of alcaldes auxiliares maintaining vigilance over their neighborhoods. It bore fruit in 1834, when one police official was appointed to surveil each city block.[73] A civic militia was created in 1834.[74] In 1837 the court system was restructured.[75] In 1848, in the wake of the Mexican-American War, a system of guardias de policía was created.[76] In 1850 followed the creation of a new corps of guardas diurnos charged with myriad duties to maintain public order because "unfortunately in this city nearly all the previous police dispositions have fallen into disuse or are viewed with public scorn."[77] Then in 1853 the government undertook a major expansion of the judicial system explicitly aimed at repressing vagrants and criminals, repeatedly referred to in the linked phrase vagos y malhechores. The 1853 decree created an additional layer of judges, the jueces menores, charged with "dedicating themselves in particular to prosecuting vagrants and malefactors."[78]

The campaign against vagrancy assumed such a high priority that a new judicial institution was created to facilitate their conviction. A presidential decree of March 3, 1828, created a national system of Vagrants Tribunals, which lasted until April 23, 1846, and was again revived on January 5, 1857. This system consisted of a special court in each major city. In 1828–46 the tribunals were composed of members of the city council on a rotating basis and were required to meet twice a week and process accused vagrants within three days. In 1857 the tribunal in the Federal District was composed of its governor, one city councilman, and several *jueces menores*. In both 1828 and 1857 some attempts were made to protect the rights of the accused, for example, by requiring evidence that they were vagrants, allowing them to produce witnesses on their behalf, and giving them the right to appeal. Yet the main purpose was to obtain speedy sentences. Even with an appeal, the process was complete in eight days. Furthermore, the right to appeal was watered down since the accused had only twenty-four hours in which to file a petition in 1828 and one week in 1857. In both years the tribunal that originally convicted a vagrant was the same one that heard his appeal.[79] Thus the desire to capture vagrants led the state to restrict the civil rights of the men[80] brought before the Vagrants Tribunals.

On March 7, 1828—only four days after the creation of the Vagrants Tribunal—the governor of the Federal District decreed three further measures to clear the capital's streets of beggars and vagrants.[81] First, he imposed a fine of 25 pesos on those who gave alms to beggars in public places as well as a fine of 10 to 100 pesos on those who sheltered vagrants. This measure marked a radical change in approach because all those who collaborated with the offensive paupers could be punished in addition to the paupers themselves. Fines of 100 (or even 25) pesos were exceedingly steep for the time. The ban on almsgiving was particularly audacious. Although there was ample precedent in Spanish law for punishing those who sheltered criminals, only one narrow—and recent—precedent existed for limiting the right to give alms: a decree of 1800, reiterated in 1825, that prohibited godparents from distributing the *volo* (the coins thrown to beggars who congregated in the churchyard where a baptism was taking place).[82] The 1828 decree therefore represented the first blanket prohibition on almsgiving in Mexican history. The attempt to dry up the supply of alms so as to reduce the demand in effect deprived the well-to-do of their freedom to give alms, a right that had been recognized for centuries.

A second measure of the 1828 decree attempted to avert future mendicancy by sentencing beggars' children under 16 years of age to placement as apprentices or servants so as to learn a useful trade. Although a similar law had been issued in 1781, a third measure designed to make it effective went far beyond the colonial admonitions that parents comply with the state's plans for their children:[83] the republican decree denied a priori any petitions that parents might file for the release of their children on the grounds that they had waived their parental rights by "abandoning [their children] to idleness and consequently vice."[84] Again, the desire to regulate the capital's street people had led the state to intervene in new areas of peoples' lives, in this case by circumscribing the rights of pauper parents over their children, who in effect became wards of the state.

On August 8, 1834, the Secretary of Relaciones dictated a series of additional measures to contain the "abundance of vagrants infesting the capital."[85] First, it explained that the colonial decrees of 1745, 1775, and 1788 were still binding in republican Mexico, a necessary clarification because of the absence of a new penal code. Second, in order to locate vagrants, it ordered a municipal census that would register people's occupations and note the houses of prostitution, gambling, and "scandal" where vagrants congregated. Third, in order to eliminate the favorite alibis used by vagrants, it required salesmen and servants to prove their occupations. In an unprecedented intrusion into the lives of working people (and one that would be partially reiterated in 1862 and 1879) it required salesmen to show their books or merchandise and servants to carry a *boleta*, or identity card, that listed their employers, salaries, and job descriptions.[86] Since servants were the largest single group of workers in the Mexican capital,[87] a significant portion of the lower classes stood to be affected by the government's new right to stop them at will. Thus, in order to improve its ability to ferret out vagrants the state had increased its powers of surveillance over the urban poor.

The 1834 decree further intervened in the lives of paupers by mandating, first, that "unoccupied children" between the ages of 7 and 15 must attend school, and, second, that prisoners could not be released until they had learned a trade. The indefinite expansion of the term of prisoners' incarceration was clearly aimed at preventing vagrancy or, as the decree put it, "making useful to the state those members who can always be counted on to disturb it." So was the first republican law making schooling obligatory, for school was mandated only for children at risk of becoming vagrants. Although this requirement was extended to all children in 1842 (and regularly reiterated, though not enforced, throughout the nineteenth century), it is worth noting that obligatory primary education was initially explicitly linked to the disciplining of the poor.[88]

These measures strengthened the project in social control initiated in 1774. In the three-quarters of a century since the Poor House experiment was launched, the state had expanded the reach of its authority over the poor. It had issued edicts that steadily infringed on individual liberties and gave it new powers over parents, children, almsgivers, servants, salesmen, popular musicians, unlicensed attorneys, bawdy revelers, and even workers who did not apply themselves with sufficient diligence. By the time the new vagrancy code was promulgated in 1845, the "true" beggars were barely distinguishable from the much-maligned vagrants in the legislators' rhetoric.

5 THE RAGGED POOR, Labeled Desnudos in the Late Eighteenth Century. This Mexico City scene shows the streets crowded with half-naked paupers who mingled with well-dressed ladies in lace mantillas. The torn and scanty attire of the majority of the populace made it difficult to distinguish the "mendacious" vagrants from the "true" beggars and working poor. That is why Bourbon officials attempting to deter vagrancy decided to outlaw mendicity and institutionalize all beggars who could not immediately be put to work.

Changing Attitudes toward the Urban Poor

These attempts to control the street people of Mexico City reveal an increasingly hostile attitude toward the urban poor. From its inception the Poor House experiment embodied the decline of the traditional Catholic view of poverty. The pre-Tridentine Church idealized paupers as the representatives of Christ on earth. It taught that their presence benefited the rich, who gained salvation by sharing their property with the less fortunate. The rich therefore had a sacred duty to give alms, just as beggars had a sacred right to request them. The Seven Acts of Mercy (feeding the hungry, housing the wayfarer, dressing the naked, giving drink to the thirsty, visiting the sick, dowering orphans, and burying the dead) delineated a broad range of claims that the poor could make on the rich.[89] Indeed, Spanish religious manuals taught that the person who refused to give alms to the needy "sinned against the providence, mercy and justice of God."[90] This is what made the attack on the "moral economy" of begging such a fundamental change in a Catholic society. To be sure, reformers insisted that providing for beggars in an asylum was a more efficient way to exercise Christian charity since alms channeled to a central institution would not be wasted on vagrants.[91] Yet the desire to remove beggars from public spaces and transform them rejects the traditional notion of the virtuous poor, "who represent the Lord and who were made poor in this world for our benefit."[92] By the late eighteenth century paupers had come to be viewed as an obstacle—and occasionally even a threat—to public tranquility and economic development.

The elite contempt for the urban poor is likewise demonstrated in the late-eighteenth-century campaign against *desnudos* (literally, naked ones) that accompanied the campaign against beggars and vagrants in Mexico City. The desnudos were indigents who instead of "covering their flesh with decency" wrapped themselves with blankets, shawls, and other coarse cloths, "which they call *chispas* or *sarapes*."[93] A series of decrees banned from public places "all classes of people in *mantas* and blankets, beggars, the barefoot, naked, and indecent."[94] The most severe edict, of May 22, 1799, prohibited their presence "in [religious] processions, . . . in the streets where these pass, . . . in public promenades, [and] in solemn functions celebrated in the cathedral churches." It further stipulated that, "nakedness being a vehement index of idleness or immoral customs," the ragged poor should be arrested and imprisoned.[95] The 1799 decree recognized that "a large part" of the populace—and according to a decree of April 18, 1801, "the majority of the plebes"[96]—went about in this "indecent and shameful nakedness . . . with no clothes other than a disgusting blanket or filthy rag that does not even cover them entirely."[97] Although public outrage forced the crown to rescind the most severe strictures of the 1799 decree,[98] the wording is significant because it shows that the colonial authorities had come to consider a large part of the population as indecent and disgusting.

The disdain for the poor is articulated in elite discourse throughout the Bourbon period. For example, in 1771 Viceroy Marqués de Croix advised his successor that "There are many *castas* mixed up among the populace, which causes it to be naturally vicious."[99] If, following the racist notions of the time, he only condemned the mixed-race castes, other writers made no such distinctions. In 1785 Villarroel lamented "the deplorable state of this unhappy city . . . uninhabitable for cultured peoples" because of its "dirty vulgar poor" and "lazy, daring, insolent, shameless, and untamed multitude."[100] In 1788 the anonymous author of a treatise on the policing of Mexico City affirmed that the "vile plebeians" had been ruined "since birth" by parents who, instead of offering them an education, "gave them only their depraved customs, which they inherit by example and tradition."[101] Increasingly, during the eighteenth century, the neutral *el pueblo* was replaced by such derogatory terms as *el populacho, el pueblo vil, el vulgo, la ínfima plebe, la gente vulgar,* and *la gente ruin y ordinaria,* which stood in marked contrast to *la gente culta* and *decente.* Moreover, the traditional Spanish term for beggar, *pordiosero* (recalling the beggar's plea of "for God's sake"), was increasingly replaced with *mendigo,* a linguistic shift that obliterated any reminder of the religious duty to give alms.[102]

These negative attitudes did not disappear after independence, despite the republican embrace of democracy. The idea of popular sovereignty certainly created contradictions for those who proposed social control measures.[103] And some writers defended the urban poor, as did Florencio del Castillo, who in 1856 insisted that the generally upright and docile pueblo had been unfairly maligned.[104] Yet others never harbored any illusions about the lower classes. The patriotic author of an 1821 proposal to improve the capital city at least laid the blame for the "ignorance and boorishness of the populace" on three hundred years of an "oppressive colonial regime." [105] For others, an initial flirtation with admiration for the "sovereign people" was quickly soured by the destructive Parián riot of December 4, 1828, the worst rioting the capital had witnessed in over a century. Even the Yorkino leader Lorenzo Zavala, whose party the plundering masses supported, backed off from "exaggerated democracy" and admitted that the "popular triumph" was a "catastrophe" because the lower classes were not yet sufficiently "civilized" to take on a responsible civic role.[106]

The continuing scorn for the urban poor can be seen in the words used to describe them. The term *desnudos* fell out of use in republican Mexico, and even *mendigos* became infrequent—and usually linked with an adjective such as *viciosos.* For example, the city council in 1827 condemned the "swarms of vicious beggars that infest the streets." [107] An 1850 decree, instead of distinguishing between the "true" and "false" beggars, simply mandated that they all be rounded up as unsightly repositories of "the most degrading vices of the human species." [108] Increasingly, republican commentators replaced the older terms with the phrase *gente perdida* [109] (lost people) or more often with the derogatory *léperos.* This term, which literally means "lepers," was used in Mexico to denote the ragged poor that nineteenth-century elites wrote about with horror.[110] As far as I can tell, *lépero,* which lumped beggars and vagrants together as rogues, emerged as a synonym for *paupers* only after Humboldt popularized it by referring to the Mexican plebes as *lazaroni* in his widely read *Political Essay on the Kingdom of New Spain.*[111] Already used by Fernández de Lizardi in his 1816 description of professional beggars, the term came into widespread use after independence.[112] The distinction between the older *desnudos* and the more modern *léperos* or *gentes perdidas* is meaningful, for if "naked ones" connotes a certain innocence the republican terms do not. "Lost people" recalls the colonial euphemism for prostitutes: *mujeres perdidas*.[113] "Lepers" were even worse: an outright threat to public health (though few contemporaries made the connection) as well as to property and moral sensitivities.[114] The change in terminology parallels the conflation of beggars with vagrants in the legislation, which progressively robbed the beggars of the "worthiness" they had once enjoyed.

The derogatory republican view of paupers is also expressed in voting laws that denied vagrants—and perhaps also beggars—the rights of citizenship, a tacit admission that they were inferior to other men in the nation and therefore not entitled to representation. This exclusion from suffrage was one of the few restrictions consistently repeated (along with the disqualification of women, minors, and convicted criminals) in national and state constitutions and in local voting regulations from the 1814 Constitution of Apatzingan to the Liberal Constitution of 1857. It even applied in the 1824 Constitution, which granted men suffrage regardless of literacy and wealth—a right that was quickly curtailed in the wake of the Parián riot.[115] Furthermore, the customary phrase denying suffrage to "those without a job, trade, or honest means of subsistence" could be interpreted as excluding beggars as well as vagrants because the solicitation of alms, since 1774 an illegal activity, was hardly "an honest means of subsistence." Thus, male beggars and vagrants became second-class members of the body politic.

To some extent, these changing attitudes converged with utilitarian needs. In particular, the campaign against vagrants during the independence period, and its renewal between 1828 and 1846, reflects the government's desire to enlarge the army. The Spanish state conscripted many vagrants after 1797.[116] Beginning in the late 1820s, when measures such as the abolition of slavery were enacted to discourage the immigration of U.S. citizens to Texas, Mexican authorities redoubled their attempts to recruit soldiers and reorganize the troops in preparation for a military confrontation on the U.S.-Mexican border.[117] Nationwide efforts to facilitate the conviction of vagrants were central to this process.

Since they were largely aimed at recruiting soldiers, the harshest republican measures came from the national rather than municipal authorities and applied nationally rather than only to Mexico City—which had not been the case with many of the earlier measures. Thus, it was Congress that created the Vagrants Tribunals in 1828. In 1834, as tension grew on the border with the United States, it was the Minister of Relaciones who decreed the unprecedented measures to restrict the freedom of servants and salesmen. In 1845 it was Congress that expanded the pool of potential vagrants (and soldiers) by adding new categories of people who could be convicted as vagrants. In 1846, on the eve of the Mexican-American War, it was the president who abolished the Vagrants Tribunals because "the critical circumstances in which the country finds itself require the immediate filling of military quotas, while the tribunals established to sentence vagrants, due to their peculiar organization, function with a slowness prejudicial in this case." [118] The new system was much less cumbersome: vagrants were simply sentenced by local judges, mayors, or other officials without the pretense of a formal trial.[119]

Just as it is no coincidence that the most extensive legislative assault on vagrants came in 1845 when manpower was desperately needed, it is likewise no coincidence that their persecution decreased briefly when the war with the United States was over. Immediately after the Mexican-American War, the government seems to have reversed its policy of recruiting vagrants for the armed services. Since Mexican leaders blamed the disastrous defeat in part on the demoralization of the troops, a decree of November 4, 1848, stated that only those "with an honest means of subsistence" who "have not been sentenced to a defamatory penalty" could be conscripted. An 1852 commentary on Mexican law, the *Nuevo Febrero*, explained that these phrases disqualified vagrants from serving in the armed forces.[120] Yet this ban, if it ever existed, did not last long in the contentious climate of peasant uprisings and strife between Liberals and Conservatives. A presidential decree of August 20, 1853, though slightly narrowing the definition of vagrancy, reiterated most of the 1845 dispositions, including the penalty of serving in the armed forces for healthy draft-age men.[121] Then, on January 5, 1857, in the midst of the War of Reform, President Ignacio Comonfort revived the Vagrants Tribunals to facilitate impressment.[122]

Still, the need for soldiers does not entirely explain the persecution of ever-growing categories of the urban poor. The expansion of the scope of vagrancy began in the mid–eighteenth century, long before recruiting soldiers became imperative. Decrees against vagrants targeted foreigners as well as women, youths, and ineligible men who could not be conscripted.[123] They continued to include social undesirables even during the short period when vagrants may have been disqualified from the armed services. For example, a decree of 1849 repeated the injunction against tinterillos, and an 1850 decree classified as vagrants the youths who sang lewd songs during the Jornadas de la Virgen as well as those who used obscene ditties to hawk their wares. Instead of being sentenced to the armed forces, their penalty was to serve in the Poor House for one year, working as servants for those "who live there for honest reasons." [124] In fact, it was only in the 1790s and 1840s that the legislation cited the urgent need for soldiers as a reason to arrest vagrants.[125]

Instead, the reasons legislators gave for pursuing vagrants consistently echoed those so elaborately presented by Archbishop Lorenzana in 1770. The claim that they posed both a moral and physical danger to other citizens was made across the entire century of the Poor House experiment. A 1767 decree explained that, "vagrants only serve to introduce vices, pervert good habits, and commit crimes."[126] An 1806 decree added that they were "vicious and indolent people who, disguised with the cape of misery, live in the depths of abandonment and pervert with their bad example many individuals who without them would be useful to the state."[127] That was why, in 1834, the government would not allow vagrants "to continue to mingle in society with the artisans, merchants, and others who sustain it with their work and industry."[128] Again, in 1850, they were blamed for damaging "the good morals of youth, so that in time crime will be rampant and society its victim."[129] In addition, vagrants were consistently condemned for stealing alms from generous citizens and thereby depriving the worthy poor of their well-deserved aid.

The claim that vagrants directly endangered the economy was also made throughout the entire century, although republican leaders grappling with the recession that followed independence put less emphasis on the economic costs than did their colonial predecessors. For example, a decree of July 1810 (two months before the outbreak of the independence war) denounced the "transcendental damage to mining, agriculture, and the arts and crafts" caused by vagrants, who lived in "indolence" instead of applying themselves to work.[130] At times the economic damage was linked to migration, especially during 1786, the Year of Hunger, which saw the promulgation of three antivagrancy decrees—the most I have found in a single year. Because the viceroy blamed the "loss of many *milpas*" on the exodus of the agricultural labor force, he ordered men of all castes "who wander shiftless and idle" to return to their villages and haciendas to work the fields.[131] Even after the crisis had passed, the authorities tried to limit the migration of Indians to the capital. A decree of 1799, which restricted to two the number of men from each Indian village who could go to the city to pursue suits representing their community, explained that the exodus from the rural areas "deprived agriculture of many workers, accustomed the inhabitants of villages to the idleness and vice of large cities, . . . and increased the consumption of food in the capital."[132]

The decrees against beggars followed a slightly different logic. They were related to the utilitarian attack on vagrancy since the only way to locate "false" beggars was to round them all up without distinction. But the campaign against beggars was far more than that. From the beginning of the Poor House experiment, enlightened legislators cited the nuisance caused not just by vagrants but also by the worthy beggars themselves. For example, a 1783 decree on the "proper policing of the poor" aimed not only "to improve their customs by applying them to work" but also "to liberate the community from the importunities of beggars." [133] A decree of June 1806 explained that it was necessary to "eliminate the burgeoning number of beggars that afflict and mortify the citizens of this populous city with their incessant petitions and supplications." [134] An 1830 decree explained that respectable citizens had to be freed from "the constant clamor of beggars who hound them everywhere." [135] An 1850 decree likewise deplored the "beggars who swarm on the streets . . . disturbing the people from whom they solicit alms not only with impertinent and tenacious declamations but also with their filthy demeanor." [136] In other words, the elimination of beggars was a way to make Mexico City a more peaceful and pleasant place to live—for those who were lucky enough to avoid destitution.

The desire to remove indigents from public view—if not by arresting them as desnudos then by rounding them up as beggars or classifying them as vagrants subject to criminal prosecution—reflects a new tendency in relations between the rich and the poor. The dramatic urbanization of Mexico City helped convert paupers into undesirables. Many migrants were detached from the traditional web of clientage and patronage relations. Moreover, as "outsiders" they had an ambiguous claim on the capital's resources. As the population of the capital city burgeoned, it became more difficult for its elites to consider the destitute a legitimate part of the community. Hence the proposals to keep out new migrants (by a licensing system, if not a wall),[137] and to purge the existing beggars from the streets of Mexico City.

This disdain for the poor also reflects the secularization of the era and the rise of the bourgeois age in which materialism reigned supreme. The increasing valorization of wealth as the definition of worth undermined the religious idealization of poverty. Instead of being viewed as a virtue, poverty came to be seen as evidence of individual failure. The glorification of production as the primary measure of well-being led to the desire to instill the work ethic and root out all remnants of an older culture of aristocratic—and plebeian—leisure.[138] This shift in attitudes was even shared by pious clerics like Archbishop Lorenzana, who had come to see the beloved of Christ as offensive people who deserved pseudopenal correction.

The broad attack on popular customs—whether aimed at suppressing the use of obscene language in public, outlawing certain music in popular taverns, banning public nakedness, limiting lower-class drinking and gambling, or banishing boisterous religious celebrations from the center of Mexico

City—reflects the growing gap between elite and popular culture. According to Juan Pedro Viqueira Albán, the increasingly Frenchified and "refined" elites simply found the traditional conduct of the populace distasteful.[139] Whether they termed it "repulsive" or "ridiculous" (as did one republican decree),[140] the capital's elites wanted to change many aspects of plebeian culture. As Villarroel put it, the city's "barbarous" populace "filled the God-fearing and judicious classes with horror" and made the capital "uninhabitable for cultured people."[141]

Thus, the projects to reform plebeians had a psychological dimension that went beyond the utilitarian goals of raising production, maintaining social order, improving sanitation, and preventing crime. As Pamela Voekel noted, attempts to root out the "moral turpitude" of the masses and impose their own "good taste" provided the elites with a sense of identity that legitimated their superiority at a time when older justifications based on race or metropolitan birth were crumbling.[142] During republican years, when Mexican elites began to conceive of their country as underdeveloped, the reformation of the populacho also became a way for them to alleviate their sense of inferiority. The writer and statesman Manuel Payno exemplified the sensitivity of educated Mexicans to foreign opinion when he wrote in 1845, "Mexico will never deserve to be labeled a civilized country until the foreigners who visit and observe us see that the populace is productively employed, the roads are secure, and the people neatly clothed and without those disgusting vices that so degrade them today."[143] If the proper policing of the poor did not "elevate the Republic to the level of the civilized nations of the world,"[144] as the governor of the Federal District, José María Bocanegra, dreamed in 1841, then removing ragged paupers from public view would at least eliminate a daily reminder of Mexico's underdevelopment. Thus, the poor unwittingly continued to serve the rich, if no longer by guaranteeing their salvation then by becoming the objects of reform from which social reformers could distinguish themselves and by providing them with a project that gave them an alternate source of status and justified their continued rule.

The Legal Death of the Poor House Experiment, 1871

The campaign against the beggars of Mexico City formally ended when the 1871 Penal Code legalized mendicity and reduced the categories of people considered vagrants. Article 858 explained that "until there are enough asylums and workhouses for beggars," those who were incapable of working and lacked a means of subsistence could beg with the license of local authorities.

Article 854 returned to the centuries-old narrow definition of vagrancy by eliminating references to immoral and undesirable conduct and only designating as vagrants those who, "lacking property or income, do not exercise an honest trade, craft, or profession for a livelihood without having a valid impediment." [145]

The formal demise of the highly interventionist project did not end the hostile legislation targeting paupers, however. Other articles in the Penal Code severely restricted the rights of beggars. Article 857 stipulated that those who "habitually begged" without a license were subject to arrest for one to three months and to surveillance for a year—unless they could post the prohibitively high bond of 25 to 100 pesos. Articles 860 and 861 added that beggars who used threats or insults in requesting alms, as well as those begging in groups of three or more, would be imprisoned for up to six months, even if they had the required license. Article 862 made beggars generally suspect by specifying that if they (or vagrants) were found in suspicious circumstances, such as wearing a disguise or carrying weapons or picklocks, they would be presumed guilty of theft and subject to a three years' imprisonment without further trial. Likewise, although the Penal Code reduced the categories of people liable for conviction as vagrants, it did not end the harassment of those who qualified. Article 855 made vagrants subject to arrest unless they could post a bond of 50 to 500 pesos or show that they lived by "honest work." These penalties applied in full only to those over 18, but even those between the ages of 14 and 18 were to be punished with reduced penalties (arts. 225–28). Moreover, parents who led their children into a life of vagrancy or mendicity were also subject to arrest (art. 620). The continued association of begging with delinquency in the Penal Code shows that the end of the Poor House experiment did not signal a return to the traditional Catholic view of the virtuous poor, at least among Mexican legislators.

How, then, can we explain the legal death of the Poor House experiment? Certainly, it had not achieved its goals. If nineteenth-century observers are to be believed, little had changed since the project was initiated in 1774. Foreign travelers continued to note the crowds of beggars, usually depicted as wild-eyed léperos whose favorite pastimes were drinking and stealing and who resorted to deceit by feigning disabilities to elicit alms. [146] The remarks of Colonel Albert Evans, who visited the Mexican capital in 1869–70—just as the new Penal Code was being framed—are reminiscent of colonial descriptions: "Beggars lounge around everywhere, and accost you upon every street and on every block. You can only escape their importunities while in your own house or hotel, by giving the strictest orders to your servants to exclude them. Many of these beggars are really needy, sick, maimed and help-less; but many others are graceless impostors." Evans hinted at the reason for the policy shift in the 1871 Penal Code when he explained: "There is no pub-lic provision for the helpless and deserving poor, and every year the beggars increase in numbers. The increase of late years has been very great." [147]

Thus, purely practical considerations led to the partial return to the pre-1774 policy of allowing "true" beggars to solicit alms. Article 858 of the Penal Code recognized the failure of previous policies when it stated that beg-ging would have to be relegalized "until there are enough asylums and work-houses for beggars." This article implied that the shift might only be tempo-rary, until the government could afford to maintain the indigent in asylums. Mexico City authorities had not lost their desire to isolate beggars: their con-finement had been decreed as late as 1863, and would be revived in an 1879 order to intern those who begged without a license.[148] It was similarly the failure to convict the new types of vagrant that led to the return to the nar-rower prosecution of unemployed rowdies.[149] Despite the rise of positivism, which assumed that economic growth would eliminate many social problems without the need for heavy-handed state intervention, the repression of pau-pers was not abandoned. If attempts to transform the character and lifestyle of the lower classes centered on public education, the drive to control the urban poor also persisted in the regulation of prostitution, the impressment of drunks to serve as contract workers in the Valle Nacional, and the institu-tionalization of certain indigents in mental hospitals, for the "insane" often included the simpletons, alcoholics, and epileptics who wandered the streets and might formerly have been confined to the Poor House.[150]

Yet, even while the Poor House experiment was in force, the law over-states the extent to which paupers were persecuted in the Mexican capital. As the following chapters demonstrate, the hostile decrees were not effec-tively implemented over the century from 1774 to 1871 and the asylum itself was less repressive than it was designed to be. The picture we get from the legislation — of constant campaigns against Mexico City beggars as well as vagrants, the criminalization of ever-expanding categories of behavior, and the increasing encroachment of the state on the lives of the urban poor — is highly misleading. Much of the repetition of decrees to round up street people was necessary because the orders were not being enforced, a fact often recognized in the preamble to the subsequent decree. Much of the expansion of the definition of vagrancy likewise represents an attempt on the part of national leaders to pressure local authorities to act by expanding their pool of potential vagrants and taking away their excuses for convicting so few. The contrast between the policy prescriptions analyzed in this chapter and the Poor House experiment in practice highlights the danger of relying on laws as a source for social history. By richly documenting the goals and attitudes of elite reformers, the legislation on beggars and vagrants is an excellent source for intellectual history. Is is far less useful, however, for illuminating the experiences of the urban poor.

{ 2 }

THE FOUNDATION OF THE POOR HOUSE

The Mexico City Poor House was conceived, according to legend, when Don Fernando Ortiz Cortés, the choirmaster of the Mexico City cathedral,[1] took a walk near the slums at the edge of the city one balmy day in May 1760. Hearing a baby's mournful cry, he followed the sound to a squalid hovel. There he came upon a heart-wrenching sight. A woman lay on the dirt floor, dead from hunger, he later learned. At her breast a starving infant searched in vain for nourishment and warmth. So deeply moved was the charitable priest that from that day forward he dedicated himself to establishing a Poor House on that very spot to prevent the repetition of this pitiful scene.

This story, which first appeared in mid-nineteenth-century accounts, cannot be definitively confirmed.[2] Similar stories are told to explain the establishment of other welfare institutions in eighteenth-century Mexico.[3] The plot invariably involves a wealthy gentleman who comes upon a shocking scene, which changes his life and inspires his philanthropy. These tales of personal transformation praise the humane and selfless generosity of the founders. As Martiniano Alfaro, the early-twentieth-century secretary of the Poor House, stated in his brief history of the asylum, "These facts, . . . though unverifiable, will at least serve to teach the inmates about the noble sentiments that motivated their benefactors."[4]

The foundational story did not exaggerate the founder's devotion to this good cause. Ortiz Cortés dedicated his last years, as well as his entire fortune, to establishing the Poor House. He bought a lot facing the southeastern corner of the Alameda Park (then on the outskirts of Mexico City) from the Convent of the Concepción. With viceregal permission,[5] he designed a large, solid building and set the groundbreaking for December 12, 1763, the day of

6 POOR HOUSE FOUNDER FERNANDO
ORTIZ CORTÉS. The choirmaster of the
Mexico City cathedral dedicated the last
years of his life, as well as his entire
fortune, to establishing the Poor House
to aid the paupers of Mexico City. He
designed the asylum to serve not only as a
homeless shelter but as a school for
religious indoctrination and vocational
training, a workhouse, a reformatory, and
a prison. The good prelate's philanthropy
thus combined benevolence with the
desire to discipline the poor.

the Virgin of Guadalupe, to whom he dedicated the institution. On April 2, 1764, he submitted bylaws for the governance of the asylum for approval to King Charles III along with a request for royal protection of the institution. Ortiz Cortés was still waiting for a response when he died three years later.[6]

With equal devotion the executor of his estate, the eminent ecclesiastic Dr. Don Andrés Ambrosio Llanos y Valdés, took over the project. Even while serving as doctoral canon of the Mexico City cathedral and consultor to the Inquisition, he oversaw the completion of the asylum's construction. After the founder's estate was depleted he drew on his personal funds. It is said that he paid the builders so generously to expedite the work during 1768, the year the building was finished, that other construction in the capital was nearly paralyzed.[7] Llanos y Valdés then guided the asylum through complicated negotiations with the crown. Finally, when the Poor House opened on March 19, 1774, the loyal executor became its first director, serving without salary for nearly eighteen years and contributing much of the first year's expenses out of his own pocket.[8] Fourteen years of diligent effort had been required to fulfill the original dream.

Yet the foundational story contrasts with the kind of institution the two prelates set up. If aiding the downtrodden had been their only goal, the Poor House would have taken a very different shape. It could have been a no-strings-attached shelter where the indigent came and went voluntarily and organized their time as they desired. It was not, however, because it embodied two additional goals that do not appear in the inspirational tale: punishing and rehabilitating paupers. From its inception, the Poor House was designed to serve not only as a homeless shelter but also as a school for religious indoctrination and vocational training, a workhouse, a reformatory, and a prison. Even the kindly Don Fernando Ortiz Cortés saw it as part of a larger project to deter vagrancy and change the culture of the urban poor. His humanitarianism was thus combined with a desire to discipline the street people of Mexico City.

In many ways, the Poor House reflected the shift from traditional notions of Catholic charity to modern concepts of poor relief. The channeling of alms to a central asylum was part of a plan to rationalize the distribution of assistance. It aimed to replace indiscriminate charity, carried out primarily to save the giver's soul, with philanthropy that distinguished between the worthy and unworthy poor, as an individual almsgiver could not. The granting of aid was part of a utilitarian project to benefit society rather than the pious individual. The recipients could no longer be left as they were. They needed to be institutionalized and transformed, by force if they did not consent to the prescribed confinement—and not just for their own good but to shape them to serve a larger national project. This emphasis on changing the character of the pauper inmates shows that poverty was no longer considered inevitable or even desirable as a stimulus to good works. It had instead become a problem to be eliminated.[9] Moreover, the Poor House was a modern welfare establishment because it was not directly run by the Church or staffed by a religious order. Since the state was not yet strong enough to take it over entirely, however, it was managed and financed by the partnership of Church, state, and private philanthropy so characteristic of the Bourbon period.

The Battle for Control of the Poor House

The Bourbon era is often portrayed as one in which the government consistently increased its power at the expense of the Church.[10] Although there is much truth to this view, the process of expanding state jurisdiction over public welfare was not as smooth as this statement implies. Certainly, the government staked out a new area of authority when it began to regulate begging and almsgiving. The jurisdictional struggle that delayed the opening of the Poor House clearly shows the Church and the state battling for control of the asylum, with the Church ultimately losing the directorship of the governing board. Yet the state did not entirely displace the Church or private philanthropists. When the Poor House finally opened under royal patronage it was as an independent civil institution under the supervision of a board composed by representatives from the Church, the royal and municipal governments, and private corporations. It was jointly financed by all of these groups. Indeed, the founding of the asylum reflects cooperation—as well as conflict—among the Church, state, and private sectors. Far from representing a new kind of compromise, this arrangement was a continuation of the pattern that had characterized the welfare system since the sixteenth century in a colony where the Church had never totally dominated the institutions of poor relief, where individual institutions often received mixed funding, and where the crown had always insisted on exercising its patronage.[11]

Several histories of the Poor House copy each other in incorrectly stating that Ortiz Cortés received royal permission to proceed with his foundation on July 9, 1765.[12] The prelate's petition to King Charles III on April 2, 1764, actually opened a decade-long jurisdictional battle that held up the inauguration of the asylum for six years after the building was completed. Although the king granted general royal protection to the project in 1765, he withheld his formal license and approval of the bylaws until after the original proposal had been significantly revised. The crown's first response to Ortiz Cortés's petition came in a rescript of October 14, 1764, directed to Viceroy Marqués de Cruillas.[13] The king expressed his dismay that the Poor House targeted only "poor beggars vagabonds and idlers instead of including foundlings and orphans, the two groups most needy" of assistance and royal attention. He asked the viceroy to visit the building site with Ortiz Cortés to see if it was possible to revise the Poor House plan to include foundlings and orphans, to investigate whether the proposed funding arrangements were sufficient, and to rewrite the "irregular" statutes submitted by the cleric six months earlier so that they followed "to the extent they are adaptable to this country" the bylaws of the Poor House in Oviedo. Finally, the king ordered the viceroy to consult with the archbishop, the ecclesiastical chapter, the *fiscal de lo civil* of the Audiencia, the city attorney, and the Real Acuerdo and to send him a detailed report with his recommendations. Since Viceroy Cruillas never sent this report, the royal order of July 9, 1765, reiterated the 1764 instructions and clarified that the king wanted the project suspended until his requirements were met.[14] This request for information, no more successful than the first, was followed by directives to the next two viceroys (to Viceroy Croix on April 2, 1769 and to Viceroy Bucareli on April 24, 1772) reiterating the king's desire for a detailed report before they proceeded any farther.[15]

Although each of these directives urged the viceroy to consult with ecclesiastical officials to "avoid subsequent controversies and disturbances," these were already brewing. Recommendations from the *fiscal* of the Council of the Indies, which accompanied the royal order of July 9, 1765, explained the matter in detail.[16] In addition to wanting the institution to shelter orphans and foundlings, the king was dissatisfied with the complex funding arrangements proposed by Ortiz Cortés, which included the imposition of new taxes on the public.[17] More importantly, the king did not want to approve an institution controlled by clerics, for Ortiz Cortés had proposed that the *junta*, or governing board, consist of the archbishop and five Church officials. There the matter stalled, even after the building was completed in December of 1768. Despite Llanos y Valdés's efforts to enlist the aid of the archbishop and the viceroy, the royal licenses were not forthcoming.

On August 12, 1769, Archbishop Lorenzana stepped in with his characteristic vigor, petitioning the king for approval of the Poor House.[18] Lorenzana explained that Mexico City already had a functioning orphanage, which he had himself established two years earlier. It made no sense to combine the institutions, he argued, because they should be governed differently and because two separate buildings already existed. The Foundling Home was centrally located, as it must be for people to take their infants "and not throw them into the ditches out of convenience." The Poor House was on the outskirts of the city in an area "free from infection and providing the large space required, clean air, and an abundance of water" (see fig. 1). Although he did not mention it, its peripheral location also kept the inmates out of sight, for the asylum faced only the Acordada Prison on one side and the Convent of San Diego on the other. Beyond that were "*egidos* and arches" where the inmates could take Sunday walks without disturbing the residents of the capital.[19] As to financing, the archbishop proposed that the Poor House open solely on the basis of ecclesiastical and private contributions to avoid burdening the city with new taxes. He had already obtained a pledge of 12,000 pesos from Llanos y Valdés to defray the first year's expenses.[20] The archbishop believed that the charitable funds and meals regularly distributed to beggars by the various religious communities, as well as the alms he gave out every week "at my door" (later converted to a firm pledge of 3,000 pesos a year)[21] would provide the asylum with a sufficient income. Lorenzana demanded, however, that, since it had been founded by a cleric and was primarily funded by the Church, the Poor House should be under ecclesiastical control.

Two months later the archbishop sent the king a new set of bylaws that improved on Ortiz Cortés's idiosyncratic proposal in many areas.[22] Yet these statutes were never approved because of the archbishop's continued insistence on ecclesiastical jurisdiction. Although his proposed eight-member governing board attempted to placate the king by reducing the number of

FIGURE 1 Poor House location, 1774, with dark area marking interior patio.

clerics to two (plus five officials of the secular government and the prior of the Merchants' Guild),[23] it was headed by the archbishop of Mexico and omitted the viceroy altogether. Lorenzana's eloquent *Memorial*, which followed the next year, did not persuade the sovereign to change his mind.

Lorenzana's proposals only served to provoke the government's ire. On July 18, 1771, the fiscal of the Council of the Indies, citing the "irregularity and strangeness" of the viceroy's being "deprived of control over an institution founded under the protection of his sovereign," decided that it would be premature to authorize the Poor House to open.[24] A subsequent royal directive to the new viceroy, Antonio María de Bucareli, on April 24, 1772, reprimanded him for not submitting the requested information and reminded him that it was improper for the archbishop to submit the report on the Poor House rather than the viceroy, as requested.[25]

Finally, Viceroy Bucareli acted to break the impasse. On November 30, 1772, he named a board of directors, this time headed by the viceroy. The junta had full authority to govern the Poor House: it oversaw every aspect of the asylum's operation from setting policy to checking its books, hiring and firing employees, and inspecting it regularly. It was composed of six members in addition to the viceroy: two representatives from the ecclesiastical chapter, two from the city council, the city attorney, and the prior of the Merchants' Guild. The Church and the municipality were thus in theory equally represented, although the city attorney in fact tipped the balance in favor of the municipality. The private sector may have been underrepresented with only one member from the Merchant's Guild, yet it was nonetheless an official partner in the governance of the asylum.[26] And the board was firmly under the control of the viceroy as the representative of the crown. Indeed, if the viceroy could not attend a board meeting the dean of the Audiencia (the judicial body directly beholden to the crown) was supposed to preside instead.

Viceroy Bucareli informed the king of this progress on December 27, 1773. Then, too impatient to await royal approval, he took a bold step: apparently confident that he was in good standing with his sovereign, Bucareli presented the king with a fait accompli. The Poor House board voted to open the asylum and announced its decision on January 12, 1774, in a fundraising letter circulated to the principal citizens and corporations of the capital. With the junta's "authorization" the viceroy decreed the aperture "provisionally and tentatively" while awaiting the king's license and the arrangement of permanent funding. Ever counting time with religious markers, the opening was set for an auspicious date, the saint's day of "our Glorious Patriarch Saint Joseph."[27] The gamble paid off: the Poor House opened its doors to the public on March 19, 1774, and royal acceptance followed.

The king's reaction to the viceroy's initiative highlights the danger of concluding that "the state" was in control of the Poor House. Far from being a hegemonic Leviathan, the Bourbon state was a complex entity ridden with internal conflicts. Royal endorsement of the Poor House aperture was grudging—and only partial. King Charles III sent his response more than two years later in a decree of August 14, 1776.[28] After expressing his pleasure that the poor and orphans were being cared for, the king chastised the viceroy for having proceeded without royal permission instead of merely submitting the oft-requested information. The 1776 rescript gave royal authorization to the Poor House board but not to the bylaws. The king continued to insist on seeing a report along with a revised set of statutes, which Viceroy Bucareli finally submitted in July 1777. In 1781, in conceding lottery funds to the Poor House, the royal ministers meeting in a *real acuerdo* recommended that the bylaws be accepted with minor modifications. Yet the king granted his approval only in 1785, after Archbishop Núñez de Haro y Peralta resubmitted the identical bylaws with an addendum incorporating the ministers' suggestions.[29] The prolonged struggle to obtain royal approval for the Poor House statutes suggests that there was less than perfect harmony between the king and his viceregal representatives.

Although the royal deputy "won" the battle with the Church for ultimate supremacy on the Poor House board, his authority over the asylum was shared with representatives from the Church as well as from the municipal and private sectors. In fact, since the Poor House director for its first seventeen years was the powerful ecclesiastic Antonio Llanos y Valdés, the Church in practice had considerable influence over the institution. Its heterogeneous nature is reflected in the names by which the Poor House was known during its early years. Its official name, the *Real Casa de Hospicio de Pobres Mendigos*, emphasized the preeminent royal jurisdiction. Yet the public (and in internal documentation even its staff) more often referred to it simply as the *Hospicio de Pobres*, the *Casa de Misericordia*, the *Casa de Caridad*, the *Casa de Nuestra Señora de Guadalupe*, or the *Santo Hospicio*, names which recognized the asylum's important ties to the Church as well as the religious and charitable component of its mission.

The Financial Partnership of Church, State, and Private Philanthropy

A complete and accurate picture of the Poor House finances is difficult to come by since it must be pieced together from many different, and sometimes contradictory, sources. Moreover, it is at times unclear whether a given source of revenue should be classified as of ecclesiastical, private, or govern-

CONTAINING THE POOR

ment origin. For starters, it is difficult to separate "state" from "ecclesiastical" when all establishments required royal permission and when, through the *patronato real*, religious institutions were under the ultimate authority of the crown. Funds I have classified as state were often based on the taxation of private individuals or corporations or, as with the Temporalidades de los ex-Jesuitas, on assets confiscated from the Jesuits when they were expelled from the colony in 1767. *Limosnas* could include donations from all three groups; indeed, a comprehensive 1804 report that summarized Poor House funding from 1774 to 1803 listed as the second-largest category "ecclesiastical and secular alms" lumped together (see table 1). Clouding these distinctions further, some major benefactors represented more than one sector. For example, Archbishop Alonso Núñez de Haro y Peralta (whose contributions I have designated ecclesiastical), served as viceroy for three months in 1787 and thereafter "retained the treatment and honors due a viceroy until his death."[30] Ortiz Cortés presents a more complicated knot to disentangle. Although he was a priest, his financial contributions to the Poor House should be considered private rather than ecclesiastical because they came from his personal estate rather than Church funds. Yet, given his prominent position in the Church (as one of the top five dignitaries of the cathedral chapter), it would be difficult to designate his initiative in founding the asylum with the same label.

Despite these problems, the picture that emerges of Poor House financing during its first quarter century is unambiguous. From the start, Ortiz Cortés conceived of an independent institution supported by mixed sources of funding. His vision prevailed in general terms, if not in precise details: the Church, state, and private philanthropists cooperated to support the asylum straight through to the independence years. Although by then the state had won a dominant position in controlling the Poor House, it made no similar effort to dominate its funding.

The bulk of the initial building costs came from private sources. Ortiz Cortés spent lavishly on the physical plant, somewhere between 100,000 and 120,700 pesos, depending on the source consulted.[31] His executor, Llanos y Valdés, collected additional "alms" of approximately 28,000 pesos to complete the construction and furnish the asylum.[32] Although ecclesiastical and corporate bodies, as well as private individuals, may have contributed to the supplemental fund, the Church and the state took no official role in paying for the initial foundation of the asylum. It was only after the Poor House opened that they stepped in to help defray its operating expenses.

In his 1764 petition to the crown, Ortiz Cortés proposed several ways of assuring a regular income for the asylum. The first was the alms he was cer-

TABLE 1   Sources of Poor House Funding, 1774–1803

Sources	Pesos	Percentage of Total Funding
Private		
From Ortiz Cortés (excludes cost of building)	6,759.8	
Income from various legacies	126,131.6	
Income from rental of two houses bought with 20,000 donation from Diego Alvarez	21,097.0	
Donations from Don Juan de Sierra, 1774–87	13,500.0	
Don Andrés Llanos y Valdés during nearly 18 years as director	10,720.4	
The current director, Don Simón de la Torre	3,631.2	
Captain Zúñiga's estate over past two years	5,320.2	
Yermo (supplies of lamb)	8,340.0	
Loans to Don Castañiza and others	1,818.4	
SUBTOTAL	197,318.6	17
Ecclesiastical		
Archbishop Núñez de Haro from 1774 to June 1800	59,408.0	
Current Archbishop Lizana, nine months	846.0	
Ecclesiastical Dean and Cabildo, since 1774	15,000.0	
Convent of Santo Domingo, since 1774	10,152.0	
SUBTOTAL	85,406.0	7
State		
Tablas de carnicería	91,547.1	
Royal lottery since December 18, 1781	325,513.5	
Junta de Temporalidades, 1794	4,658.8	
City council from July 1774 to August 1787	14,858.0	
SUBTOTAL	436,577.4	38
Mixed (private/ecclesiastical)		
Special alms collected in 1786	30,299.5	
Other ecclesiastical and secular alms since 1774	224,309.5	
SUBTOTAL	254,609.0	22
Mixed (state/private)		
Raised by Viceroy Bucareli for addition, 1774–76	59,580.9	5

TABLE I *Continued*

Sources	Pesos	Percentage of Total Funding
Inmate Earnings		
Sale of surplus cloth made by inmates	78,181.5	
Earnings from accompanying funerals since 1776	35,455.2	
Pensions paid by relatives since 1791	7,852.8	
SUBTOTAL	121,489.5	11
TOTAL	1,154,981.4	100

Source: 1804 report.
Note: Funding excludes 7,310.5 pesos "owed the Poor House" from 1774–91 and 1796, presumably unpaid interest or rental income on its investments.

tain would be forthcoming from the generous citizens of the capital, among whom he included ecclesiastical, municipal, and corporate bodies. His petition explained that members of these groups imitated the archbishop, who "with a liberal hand in the streets, and at his own palace, daily distributes a considerable sum to impoverished beggars." Ortiz Cortés hoped that the archbishop and viceroy as well as the ecclesiastical chapter, guilds, city council, nobility, and businessmen would give their accustomed daily alms directly to the Poor House, thereby "liberating themselves from importunate solicitations."[33]

Ortiz Cortés also envisioned substantial state support in the form of tax exemptions and concessions. Thus, he requested that the king grant the Poor House exemptions from paying taxes on its food and supplies. In addition, he asked the king to concede to the Poor House the half-real tax paid on each wagon load of flour that entered the capital and the real levied on each pig slaughtered in Mexico City butcheries. The prelate claimed that since these taxes were already being levied, they would not impose a new burden on the capital's citizens. They would not harm the bakers and butchers who currently received them because they were merely being wasted on "selfish litigation." In proposing these subsidies Ortiz Cortés followed timeworn patterns in which tax concessions or exemptions, rather than direct royal grants, were used to support public institutions.[34]

Finally, Ortiz Cortés hoped that the Poor House would become partially self-sustaining. He envisioned the asylum as a productive enterprise where inmates would weave wool and cotton cloth, sew their clothes, make their shoes, and produce their own food whenever possible. He believed that a considerable sum could be raised by selling the surplus wool and cotton cloth that would remain after the inmates' needs had been met.

When the Poor House opened a decade later it was on the basis of private pledges of support and with no arrangements in place for permanent funding. Viceroy Bucareli later explained that when he decided to go ahead with the aperture he only had the 12,000 pesos promised by Llanos y Valdés for the first year's expenses,[35] 19,000 pesos raised by the Poor House board from the capital's citizens, and the certainty that official support would soon follow.[36]

The Poor House quickly obtained ecclesiastical funding, as shown in table 1. The cathedral chapter pledged 50 pesos per month, a sum it paid steadily from the day the Poor House opened until at least December 31, 1803, the date of the last statistics covered by the 1804 report.[37] The Convent of Santo Domingo contributed some 30 pesos per month "without fail" over the same period. Archbishop Núñez de Haro provided 200 pesos a month until his death in 1800, a generous sum (if somewhat less than the 250 originally pledged by Lorenzana).[38] After a brief interruption Archbishop Francisco Javier Lizana y Beaumont also took on this commitment, though with the smaller monthly contribution of 100 pesos per month.[39] Taken together, the average annual revenue from Church sources until 1800, not including the unquantifiable ecclesiastical component of the "alms" listed in the 1804 report, was 3,360 pesos. Although a modest 7 percent of all Poor House revenues from 1774 to 1803, this income was made available immediately after the asylum opened and was paid regularly—though not increased—over the next quarter century.

Given that the Poor House aperture had proceeded without the necessary royal permits, it is hardly surprising that the anticipated government funding took longer to fall into place. In 1777 the viceroy lamented that he was still waiting for the crown to grant the requested tax exemptions.[40] Indeed, although in 1774 the first administrator of the Poor House petitioned the city council for tax relief on the institution's flour purchases, his successor was still petitioning for that relief twenty years later.[41] The city did grant the Poor House a free supply of water for both drinking and household use (*mercedes de agua delgada y gorda*) from the time the asylum opened.[42] Gradually, other state contributions grew until by the end of its first decade state support had eclipsed that provided by the Church.

During its first year Viceroy Bucareli played an important role in protecting the Poor House. Only three months after it opened, when the original building proved too small to meet the demand, he spearheaded a drive to enlarge it. First Bucareli donated two houses and a lot adjacent to the asylum,

CONTAINING THE POOR

which he bought for 8,000 pesos from the Convent of Concepción. Then he raised 59,580.9 pesos in limosnas to build the addition, which was inaugurated on November 14, 1776, during the celebration of "the days of the Monarch Charles III."[43] The source of funding for this addition defies categorization, since the "alms" probably came from many different groups and individuals, and it is unclear whether the viceroy's 8,000 peso contribution was from his personal or viceregal funds or whether he used money collected from the public to pay for the building lot as well.[44] As the fiercely patriotic (and thus anti-Spanish) Juan Abadiano pointed out a century later, the initiative should not be attributed exclusively to the viceroy because the request for the expansion came from Llanos y Valdés and the Poor House board. Moreover, the construction required city council approval to take over three neighboring homes (including an *adobe de Indios*) and to close an alley between the original building and the addition; the city granted its permission and "donated" the alley on September 28, 1774.[45] It is nonetheless evident that the viceroy had supplanted the archbishop as the main patron of the Poor House.

Thanks to the viceroy, the Poor House soon became the beneficiary of substantial revenues available because of the expulsion of the Jesuit order. On August 16, 1774, Bucareli assigned the asylum the *tablas de carnicería* of San Pedro y San Pablo, taxes on the butchering of cattle that had previously supported that Jesuit college. In 1775 he added the proceeds of the tabla of Querétaro, and by 1777 he had assigned to the Poor House the tablas of Puebla, Zacatecas, and San Luis Potosí as well.[46] In some years these taxes produced a large income for the Poor House—a total of 4,751 pesos in 1777 alone. Yet this revenue was variable and eventually diminished when the Poor House lost the benefit of the tablas of Zacatecas, Puebla, and San Luis Potosí.[47] Early on, the Junta de Temporalidades de los ex-Jesuitas also assigned the Poor House properties worth 23,985.6 pesos, which produced an income of 1,999.3 pesos in 1777.[48] Although the performance of these properties is difficult to follow, they were apparently producing some 3,725 pesos annually by 1785.[49] Thus, during its first three decades the Poor House had derived approximately 8 percent of its revenues from the tablas de carnicería and perhaps another 8 percent from the confiscated Jesuit properties.[50]

The asylum's reliance on state funding increased with the concession of proceeds from the Royal Lottery, which was approved in a royal decree of November 26, 1782. The crown initially applied 2 percent of the lottery earnings to the Poor House and created two additional annual lotteries in its favor. At some point a separate Lotería del Hospicio de Pobres was established (for which the Poor House paid the costs of printing tickets) and its share was regularized at 1,000 pesos a month.[51] In addition, the asylum was occasion-

7 TICKET FROM THE ROYAL LOTTERY. The lottery provided the Poor House with steady revenues of approximately 12,000 pesos per year from 1782 to 1817. The asylum began as an independent institution jointly funded by the Catholic Church, the state, and private philanthropists. By the end of the eighteenth century, however, the role of the state had grown so much that it eclipsed the support of ecclesiastical and private donors.

ally awarded grants, such as *billetes caducos* (unclaimed lottery prizes) worth 51,608.5 pesos in 1788. According to the 1804 report, the lottery income began to arrive on December 18, 1781, and soon became the largest single source of Poor House funding (table 1). By December 31, 1803, it had provided 28 percent of the asylum's total revenues (not including capital costs) since it opened in 1774.[52]

While royal and viceregal support grew, municipal support declined. The city council early on began contributing 100 pesos per month. According to the 1804 report, the municipal subsidy began in July 1774 and lasted until 1787.[53] I have been unable to discover why the city discontinued its support of the asylum after thirteen years.[54] The discrepancy between royal and municipal trends serves as a reminder that the state sector was far from monolithic. Since Mexico City was the seat of a viceregal regime as well as a major metropolis with its own municipal government, the Poor House interacted with more than one "state" entity. The small and relatively short-lived municipal subsidy for the asylum ran counter to the royal and viceregal trend.

Private support likewise appears to have decreased over time. In a 1781 petition to the Poor House board warning of the asylum's impending bankruptcy, Llanos y Valdés indicated that in the first few years the bulk of the operating expenses had come from private contributions.[55] The 1804 summary report lists two early donors by name: the merchant Don Juan Sierra, who contributed 13,500 pesos from 1774 to 1787; and Don Diego Alvarez, the priest and university professor whose 20,000 peso donation the Poor House had invested in two houses bought in 1780 to produce rental income (see table 1).[56] The substantial income of 126,131.3 pesos received by the Poor House over thirty years from "various legacies" suggests that other individuals left bequests to the asylum, although the bulk of these probably consisted of the confiscated Jesuit properties. A large number of charitable individuals must have "assigned" regular alms to the Poor House as well, judging from the large size of the alms categories in the 1804 report as well as from the notation next to the special contributions of 30,299 pesos raised in 1786 "in addition to those assigned" because of the widespread "hunger" that battered the Valley of Mexico that year.[57] Moreover, the Poor House continued to benefit from the indirect support provided by Llanos y Valdés, who served without charge as director until he became the bishop of Linares in 1791,[58] and who paid the doctor's retainer out of his own pocket, thereby sparing the asylum considerable expense over eighteen years.[59] Although it is impossible to quantify the total "private" support for the Poor House, given the difficulty of separating the private portion from both the various legacies and mixed alms categories, it is evident that many citizens of Mexico City greeted the opening of the asylum with enthusiasm.

By 1781, however, Llanos y Valdés was bewailing a decline in the ardor of private philanthropists. He explained that the principal source of revenue, which consisted of voluntary contributions, had diminished "due to the death or impoverishment of the original donors."[60] The result was a grave deficit facing the institution, which moved the state to step in to rescue the asylum with funds from the Royal Lottery, the first use of lottery funds for public welfare since it was established in 1771. His complaint was echoed two decades later by the Poor House administrator, Juan Antonio de Araujo, who faced yet another fiscal crisis. In his cover letter to the 1804 report, Araujo lamented that "the monthly alms which used to total more than 1,600 pesos have lately diminished to less than 206 pesos, 7 reales."[61] Two years later an article in the *Gazeta de México* likewise noted the lack of support from a public "whose charity cooled" when it saw that the Poor House was unable to clear the city streets of beggars and who "withdrew the alms" that formerly had been the mainstay of the asylum.[62] Thus, the decline in private giving, usually portrayed by late-nineteenth-century writers as a result of the independence wars or the mid-nineteenth-century Reforma,[63] was already being felt by the Poor House within a few years of its aperture.

The private contribution to the Poor House nonetheless remains immense if capital costs (not included in the 1804 report) are taken into account. A few individuals with special connections to the Poor House, usually board members, though occasionally the director, administrator, or chaplain, continued to make the asylum the object of their personal patronage. Noteworthy was Captain Francisco Zúñiga, a board member who stepped in to bail out the Poor House with some 27,000 pesos[64] at the end of the eighteenth century and who generously endowed a new wing designed as a boarding school for orphans (see chapter four). Yet regular alms from the general public apparently shriveled. The founders' dream that the "indiscriminate charity" distributed daily by the capital's residents would be channeled to a centralized asylum therefore failed to materialize.

The hope that the Poor House could become largely self-sustaining also remained unfulfilled. Table 1 shows that sales of surplus cloth made by the inmates only provided 6 percent of the institution's income between 1774 and 1803.[65] Another source of inmate earnings came from accompanying burials, a service the Poor House began offering in 1776 by "renting out" inmate mourners to march in the funeral processions of city residents who wished to be laid to rest with splendor. The 1777 bylaws set the rate at 4 reales per inmate, and by 1781 it had been increased to one peso for each rented mourner.[66] This service produced a small but regular income worth some 3 percent of total revenues by December 31, 1803. In 1791 the Poor House also began taking in paying "pensioners," whose relatives paid a small fee for them to be cared for in the asylum. Despite these attempts to increase its earnings, the Poor House was only able to produce some 10 percent of its revenues during its first thirty years.

In sum, the Poor House's own earnings took a backseat to contributions from the Church, the state, and private philanthropists. During the three decades after it was established, ecclesiastical support remained steady but modest, while broad private support declined. State support grew, at least that reflected in royal if not municipal funding. Still, the institution depended on contributions from all these sectors. The collaboration of Church, state, and private donors in funding the Poor House is symbolized in the oil paintings that hung in the asylum during the nineteenth century. The five colonial benefactors rewarded with prominently displayed portraits represented the three types of support: the presbyter Ortiz Cortés, Poor House founder; Viceroy Bucareli, who was instrumental in arranging its aperture; Archbishop Núñez de Haro y Peralta, who provided consistent support over its first twenty-six years; Captain Zúñiga, who bequeathed vast sums to the Poor House in the late eighteenth century; and Don Ciriaco González Carbajal, the royal official and board member (as *oidor decano* of the Audiencia) who convinced Zúñiga to donate the bulk of his estate to the asylum. In addition, Ortiz Cortés and Zúñiga were singled out to have their statues placed in the main stairway, a reminder that, although the state took on an increasingly prominent role, clerics and private philanthropists were still critical partners in supporting the asylum.[67]

All parties seemed content with the collaborative funding arrangement. Despite its regalism, the perpetually penurious crown was not prepared to support the institution singlehandedly. Indeed, it only granted the lottery concession under pressure, when the asylum's impending bankruptcy threatened its closure. Even then, a royal minister protested that "it had never been the king's intention" for the Royal Treasury to fund the Poor House. His report of August 17, 1781, cited the doctrine of "some writers who affirm that the primary responsibility for providing poor relief is the King's, as Father of the Poor, orphans, and foundlings"—but only to refute it. On the contrary, he insisted, the royal decrees showed that the crown always counted on "this rich and flourishing City" to maintain its beggars on its own.[68] Yet the municipality did not want this responsibility either. The city council had discontinued its direct funding after the first decade (although it renewed it again at some point after the 1804 report was filed).[69] A notation in city council records shows how ideology and practicality commingled in its decision not to renew its old monthly commitment. In denying an 1802 petition from the Poor House administrator for financial aid, an alderman explained that the city could not afford to help because everything had become exceedingly expensive, and, besides, "the maintenance of the poor should devolve on the rich, who have plenty of wealth."[70] The expansion of the Bourbon state should not therefore be overstated. Although it fought to wrest control of the Poor House board from the Church and it came to furnish a substantial share of the asylum's revenues, the government was reluctant to further enlarge its role in providing for public welfare.

The Prelate's Plan: From Traditional Charity to Modern Poor Relief

Consensus rather than conflict among Church and state is evident in the three sets of Poor House bylaws sent to the king for approval in 1764, 1769, and 1777 (see appendix 2). These blueprints show remarkable agreement about the institution's goals as well as its day-to-day regimen, even though the first two were submitted by priests and the third by a viceroy. All three embody the shift from traditional Catholic notions of charity to modern conceptions of poor relief. Indeed, the statutes written by the prelate Ortiz

Cortés and by Archbishop Lorenzana demonstrate that the shift was spearheaded by enlightened clergymen themselves, rather than being a subject of contention between clergy and crown.[71]

It may not be surprising to discover "modern" ideas in Archbishop Lorenzana's bylaws of 1769, given his 1770 *Memorial*, which was analyzed in chapter 1. It is perhaps more unexpected to find them in the document written by Ortiz Cortés in 1764, two years before Lorenzana was posted to Mexico City as archbishop of Mexico. It is easy to see why the king was displeased with the prelate's "irregular" draft. Although detailed in such areas as religious observances, it was overly general in others (e.g., omitting the inmates' daily schedules). Moreover, the document was disorganized and included such digressions as Ortiz Cortés's belief that the medicines prescribed for the inmates should not be too expensive, "for they should be cured as are the poor, and not with the apparatus of the rich and powerful, since I am not persuaded that they will thus regain their health any sooner." Yet a close analysis of this first set of bylaws, and of the rambling petition that accompanied it, suggests that the Poor House experiment launched by the Spanish viceroy Bucareli in 1774 — the quintessential enlightened plan to discipline the poor in the service of a larger national project — originated a decade earlier in the proposals put forth by the Mexican cleric.[72] In fact, Bucareli's decree announcing the aperture of the Poor House took most of its opening paragraph directly from the petition that Ortiz Cortés had submitted to King Charles III on April 2, 1764.[73]

In his petition Ortiz Cortés emphasized how the Poor House would help the city's beggars. "It is useless to enumerate the many advantages of this system," he wrote. The inmates will receive shelter, food, clothing, and medicines. Instead of "wandering dispersed in the streets," they will be brought together "to live a sociable life, spared from idleness, made to work in what they can, instructed in Christian doctrine and the mysteries necessary for their salvation, taking the sacraments, hearing Mass, and praying the rosary every night." Yet his goals clearly went beyond tending to the physical and spiritual needs of Mexico City paupers.

Ortiz Cortés's Poor House also aimed to reform the poor and clear bothersome beggars from the streets of the Mexican capital. From the first sentence his petition mixed concern for the "unhappy" paupers forced to beg because of their advanced age or infirmities with the desire to alleviate the "great prejudice they cause the residents of this city." He mentioned the harm caused by beggars, "whose annoying clamor disturbs the sick; who block the entrances to churches and distract the attention of the faithful," before he described the suffering of the piteous "people of both sexes" who "endure great difficulties, exposed to the inclemencies of the weather, and suffering heat, cold, wind, and rain" because they had no other means of earning a living. Immediately after this brief expression of compassion, he launched into a long diatribe that condemned even those unfortunates who had legitimate cause for soliciting alms: "I have noticed that this caste of people never gets close to the confessional, and even less the communion rail, to frequent the sacrament of Penance and the sacrosanct of the Eucharist; they are so intently concerned with collecting alms that they totally ignore their souls, and so absorbed by this difficult life that the women give no other career to their children than begging, without placing them in honest and virtuous houses to serve, which engenders such a pernicious habit that it cannot be outgrown, so [their children] put all their study into going about in rags, and purposefully looking downtrodden, to move pious hearts to give them succor." Thus, Ortiz Cortés showed a profound ambivalence toward Mexico City's "true" beggars, whom he simultaneously portrayed not only as deserving recipients of charity but also as faulty Christians and irresponsible parents.

The prelate's plan relied upon coercion. A decade before begging was outlawed in Mexico City, Ortiz Cortés proposed forcibly confining beggars in the Poor House. In fact, it was he who, in his letter to the king, requested that the government issue the appropriate decree authorizing their detention. Not expecting the state to shoulder the entire burden of policing the streets, he proposed that the asylum hire a sentinel (and pay his annual salary of 50 pesos) for the sole purpose of patrolling the capital and the surrounding archbishopric to pick up paupers caught soliciting alms—including those "who do not wish to go willingly and voluntarily." Those who qualified for assistance would then be indefinitely sequestered. Other than being permitted supervised outings on Sundays and holidays, they could leave only if someone hired them or promised to maintain them.

In another manifestation of "modern" rather than "traditional" poor relief, the Poor House was to discriminate between the worthy and unworthy poor in offering assistance. Only the "true" beggars were eligible for institutional aid. Although Ortiz Cortés did not specify what would happen to the vagrants, his petition repeated several times that the "lazy, as well as the false and fraudulent" would be "separated" from the asylum. In fact, he argued that one of the main benefits the Poor House could provide the "pious" inhabitants of Mexico City was to guarantee that their alms would not be wasted on "vagabonds and lazy bums who pretend to be unfit for work, thereby defrauding the truly needy of their well-deserved charity, while [using these handouts] to support the vices of womanizing, gambling, and drinking." Ortiz Cortés believed that the capital's citizens would gladly redirect to the asylum their accustomed daily alms, which currently supported "infinite numbers of destitute beggars" without "obtaining in many the desired effects of charity." Thus, the prelate wanted to replace indiscriminate almsgiving on the city streets with a system that would rationalize the distribution of charity through a central institution.

Even then, the worthy recipients of aid could not be left as they were. Although Ortiz Cortés only vaguely sketched out his plan, he wanted to rehabilitate the inmates through a strict regimen that included close surveillance, constant work, and heavy doses of religion. The deserving paupers were to live with order and decorum under the watchful eyes of a live-in chaplain, lay administrator, and two wardens: the *mayordomo* for the men, and the *rectora* for the women. The men and women were to be segregated, except for married couples, who would be housed in a separate section with their children. The inmates would be kept busy and would contribute to the sustenance of the asylum by working according to their abilities in its workshops, kitchens, and laundry and in the performance of various cleaning chores. Master artisans would be hired to provide vocational training, especially so the inmates' children could return to society as productive citizens who would not beg in the future. Misbehavior (including laziness) would be punished, with penalties ranging from "reforming rations" to placement in the stocks.

If this Poor House in some ways resembled the carceral regimes that were the product of the Great Confinement of the eighteenth century, it was less repressive and dehumanizing than the "total institutions" described by Foucault. Although Ortiz Cortés wanted the asylum to control many aspects of the inmates' daily lives, his plan allowed married couples and their children to live together, an environment that would be more familial than penal. Rather than attempting to "normalize" the inmates into a homogeneous mold, it catered to the varied customs of the different ethnic groups that would inhabit the asylum. The Spanish inmates were to have chocolate for breakfast, a cup of broth and lamb for lunch, and beans with lamb and bread for supper. The Indians, mestizos, and mulattos would be "happier," according to Ortiz Cortés, with a cup of *atole* for breakfast, and beef and tortillas with their other two meals, all of them "well seasoned and made with care." Inmates would wear shoes and sleep on mattresses only if this was their usual practice. Each inmate who desired it would also be given two packs of cigarettes each Thursday. Anticipating the king's disapproval, he explained that "this vice . . . is in New Spain baptized with the name of medicine and is so widespread that there are few people who do not use them, and if they were deprived of smoking they would be disconsolate, and perhaps harmed, since they have been accustomed to it since their youth." Thus, although the inmates were to be disciplined, the prelate appears to have been sincere in his desire to make them comfortable.

The racial integration of his proposed Poor House distinguished Ortiz Cortés's asylum from earlier colonial establishments, which targeted a single racial group, as well as from contemporary asylums in the United States.[74] His preface to the bylaws explained that they could not look like those of the recently founded poorhouse in the Spanish city of Oviedo "because the countries are different, the temperaments diverse, and the individuals so varied, since in Oviedo all are Spanish [i.e., white], while in Mexico it is necessary to mix Indians, mulattos, Spaniards, and mestizos." The prelate was not philosophically opposed to racial discrimination: in a follow-up letter attempting to overcome royal objections, he explained that his Poor House could take in orphans and foundlings if the crown insisted but in that case it should only admit infants of Spanish descent to avoid the institution's becoming swamped by so many children that there would be no room for beggars.[75] Instead, it was the asylum's goal of combating the idleness and immorality of the popular classes that required it to take in all the capital's "legitimate" beggars without distinction.

The building Ortiz Cortés designed for the Poor House reflects his complicated agenda.[76] It aimed to provide cheerful and wholesome quarters in a spacious two-story structure that took up a full city block. Its many rooms were arranged around airy patios flanked by arched corridors. In addition to the requisite dormitories and offices, there were several *salas de labores*, or workshops. One was for the women to sew quilts, knit socks and stockings, and weave "all types of shawls." Another was for the men to weave coarse cotton and woolen cloth, baize, and blankets.[77] A room with an oven was for baking bread. Another outfitted with *metates* (stones for grinding corn) was for making tortillas and atole, which, Ortiz Cortés explained to the king, were the staple foods of "the natives of this kingdom." Other rooms were set up for producing cigarettes and hats, for making shoes "for those persons accustomed to wearing them," and for sewing and mending the inmates' clothes. There were two washrooms, "one for the men and one for the women, so that they can always be clean and neat," and also two refectories and two infirmaries, one for each sex. The chapel's single nave was likewise divided so that the male and female inmates could hear Mass without mingling. A cramped room under the stairs was designed as a dungeon where recalcitrant inmates could be locked up as punishment.[78] And a locked entrance gate and grated windows enforced the inmates' enclosure.

The architecture was solid and simple—so massive and stark, in fact, that later generations would consider the building an eyesore,[79] though Ortiz

8 EXTERIOR OF THE POOR HOUSE BUILDING. This huge edifice occupied an entire city block. By the middle of the nineteenth century its austere architecture, considered beautiful when it was first built, had come to be viewed as an eyesore. It was destroyed in 1905 as part of an effort to beautify the center of Mexico City. The Hospicio de Pobres, by then an orphanage, was moved to a new site on the outskirts of the capital.

9 POOR HOUSE CHAPEL with a View of the Main Altar. This elegant neoclassical design was by the renowned architect and sculptor Manuel Tolsá. The only ornate section in an otherwise stark building, the chapel was the centerpiece of the asylum. It symbolized the importance of religious ritual and instruction to the rehabilitation of the disorderly poor.

Cortés boasted of its "great size and beauty, which compares favorably with others of this city."[80] Only two areas punctuated its overall plainness, a sign that they held special significance for the founder. One was the elegant neoclassic chapel designed by the renowned architect and sculptor Manuel Tolsá and decorated with ornate statues and an oil painting above the four pillars that flanked the altar. Clearly the centerpiece of the asylum, the chapel highlighted the importance Ortiz Cortés assigned to religion in moralizing the pauper inmates. The other was the frontispiece above the main entrance door. As he explained in his 1764 petition, it represented St. Peter on the right, St. Paul on the left, the Virgin of Guadalupe, "universal patroness of this kingdom," on the top, and the royal coat of arms in the center, in recognition of His Majesty's expected protection of the asylum. The juxtaposition of religious and secular emblems symbolizes the joint role Ortiz Cortés expected church and state to play in protecting and funding the independent asylum—even though he tilted more toward the ecclesiastical side by proposing a board of directors exclusively composed of clerics.

The Revised Bylaws of 1769 and 1777

It is remarkable how little the subsequent bylaws departed from Ortiz Cortés's plan. Archbishop Lorenzana completely rewrote the original document. In response to royal criticism, his 1769 statutes omitted the prelate's charming digressions and became systematic and detailed. They covered everything from how often and where the board of directors should meet to how the books should be kept, what time the outside doors should open and close, and who should have keys. They spelled out how the inmates were to be treated from the time they were picked up, "with the greatest gentleness" and "without causing disturbances," until they were dismissed or died. They provided a carefully laid out schedule that specified what they should do throughout each day, how they should be motivated and punished, what they should eat, and what they should wear right down to their undergarments. They introduced a revenue-producing enterprise, renting out mourners to accompany funerals, of which Ortiz Cortés surely would have approved. Consequently, the original 21 articles grew to 77. Yet, beyond reducing the number of clerics on the governing board, the archiepiscopal statutes mostly fleshed out the sketchy proposals Ortiz Cortés had made in 1764.[81] Similarly, the bylaws submitted by Viceroy Bucareli in 1777 (and resubmitted by Archbishop Núñez de Haro in 1785 with an addendum incorporating the four minor modifications recommended by the Council of Ministers in 1781)[82] made few substantive changes besides putting the viceroy in charge of the board of directors. With 112 articles, the 1777 statutes were considerably longer than Lorenzana's. Yet the new articles mostly clarified or added to the details of the archbishop's version. For example, they specified that male and female vagrants had thirty days to find a job or be sent to the viceroy for placement. They explained that the asylum should not admit mentally ill or sick paupers, who could be sent to the capital's hospitals or mental institutions, and that the only children to be admitted (aside from the disabled) were the offspring of Poor House inmates, who were to be housed and trained until they reached the age of fourteen. On matters of principle, however, there was total unanimity between the archbishop and viceroy. Indeed, the viceroy (or perhaps the board, whose members signed the 1777 document) copied many phrases and even paragraphs verbatim from the 1769 statutes. For example, the list of various kinds of discipline the asylum sought to impose by teaching "Christian doctrine, the rule of good manners, moderation in all things, and, finally, the holy fear of God, respect for the sacred, and obedience to the sovereign and other superiors" was mostly borrowed from the archbishop. For both, religion and work were the twin pillars upon which the reform of the inmates rested.

The viceregal and archiepiscopal statutes outlined a daily regime that combined many hours of work with regular religious observances. In the viceroy's 1777 version, the inmates rose by 5:30 A.M. in the summer and 6:30 in the winter, when it was too cold to rise earlier.[83] They then went to Mass, had breakfast, and worked for a few hours in the asylum's workshops or at household chores. At 11:30 they stopped for lunch and rested until 2:00 P.M. In the afternoon they again worked, until 5 in the winter and 6 in the summer, and then went to evening Mass, had supper at 8, and retired early. In winter the inmates spent a total of seven hours working, in summer eight and a half hours. This schedule varied only on Sundays and holidays, when the inmates either suspended work or worked less, spending more time in religious instruction and "honest" recreation. The work requirements were even heavier in the archbishop's 1769 version, in which inmates rose half an hour earlier and spent eight and a half hours working in the winter and ten in the summer, with an hour less for lunch and lights out promptly at 9 P.M. This strict timetable was crucial to rehabilitating the pauper inmates.

The inmates' constant labor fulfilled several purposes. One was to teach them good work habits and vocational skills so that they could hold jobs outside the asylum, especially in the textile industry or service sector. Another was to earn income for the asylum by producing cloth that could be sold for a profit. A third goal was to save the asylum money by using inmate workers whenever possible. The 1777 statutes provided a detailed list of inmate positions. Selected inmates with particularly good character and the "fear of God" could assist the wardens in supervising the dormitories and preserving "silence, circumspection, and good order" at Mass and meals. Those with specialized knowledge could teach other inmates Christian doctrine, how to work cotton and wool, mend clothes, or clean the asylum. A literate inmate could teach reading and writing to the "quick and talented" children (girls as well as boys) until they were old enough to become apprentices in the asylum's workshops. A few "immaculate" women could serve as cooks, an inmate *proveedor* (purveyor) could dispense food and tableware from the locked storeroom, and a *repostera* could portion out the meals. The inmate-employees were not without cost: the statutes specified that those who filled these positions or whose labor produced a profit for the asylum should be paid a small gratuity "so that they will work with greater punctuality and effort." The final reason for making the inmates work was merely to keep them occupied, for work was considered a kind of therapy that could improve the undesirable customs of the poor.[84] On this point the bylaws were quite explicit, charging the administrator with finding tasks that even the disabled and frail elderly could perform—if only to comb the children's hair or comfort the sick in the infirmary—so that they would not become used to indolence. The constant regimen of labor also kept the inmates out of trouble and instilled obedience, an essential element of the discipline the Poor House sought to impose.

Religious ritual and instruction played an equally important role in the moral reformation of the pauper inmates, and they were just as valued in the viceregal as in the archiepiscopal statutes. In addition to twice-daily Masses, the inmates were to pray for the health and happiness of the king, the viceroy, the archbishop, the board members, the founder of the asylum, and its other benefactors both dead and alive. After daily Mass and on holidays the chaplains were to review some aspect of Christian doctrine. Those found to be deficient in their comprehension of the doctrine would be assigned to a more knowledgeable inmate for tutoring. The inmates were to confess and take Communion once a month, the men on the first Sunday of the month, the women on the second. They were to observe the precept of annual Communion, the men on Holy Monday, the women on Holy Tuesday. Special Masses were to be said on the saint's day of the founder (May 30, San Fernando) and of the religious patrons of the institution (December 12 for the Virgin of Guadalupe and March 19 for San José). On Good Friday and other fast days beans, fish, or eggs were to replace meat in the inmates' menus, and special feasts with "extra lamb and rice pudding" were to mark the celebration of the three *Pascuas* (Christmas, Easter, and Pentecost), Corpus Christi, the feast day of Saint John the Baptist, the Assumption, and the days of the asylum's patrons, Guadalupe and José.

Physical and moral cleanliness also contributed to reforming the inmates. The bylaws specified that they were to change their clothes once a week and their bedsheets once a month. Entertainment on holidays was to be equally pure, with cards, gambling, and liquor strictly prohibited—except the alcohol prescribed by a doctor for individual ills, as *pulque* was believed to have medicinal properties. Only "licit" and "honest" diversions were permitted, with fights and arguments to be avoided. And the men were to be kept strictly separated from the women while working, eating, sleeping, and attending Mass, except for the married couples who shared separate living quarters with their children until these turned five and entered the common dormitories.

The concern with the inmates' morals was just as strong in the viceregal as archiepiscopal bylaws. Indeed, the viceregal version added detailed instructions on guarding against improper sexual contact. For example, the inmate assistants who supervised the dormitories at night were to make sure that (except for the married couples) "no pauper sleep accompanied . . . even those of the same sex." The 1777 statutes devoted five entire articles to dealing with couples in order to facilitate the reunion of husbands and wives while preventing the visits of lovers who, given "human malice," might falsely claim to be wed. The man and woman were to be kept apart until they could prove they had been married. If they were engaged in "illicit correspondence" but wished to legitimize their offspring "and avoid the perdition of their souls," they could be married in the Poor House, with the chaplain waiving the customary fees if necessary.

Both the viceregal and archiepiscopal statutes assigned a pivotal role to the chaplain in the daily workings of the asylum, with the viceregal version increasing the number of chaplains from one to two. In addition to performing the many religious rituals, the chaplains were to sit with the inmates at lunch and supper (one in the men's refectory, another in the women's) and help supervise the inmates, resolve disputes, and determine punishments for those who violated the rules, were "rebellious, disturbed the peace and harmony that should reign, or set a bad example in word or deed"—or even those who failed to care for their clothing properly. The chaplains were also to check the administrator's books on a daily basis. Thus, although the two chaplains were outnumbered by the lay employees (the doctor, barber/surgeon, secretary, and scribe who lived outside the asylum, and the administrator, mayordomo, and rectora who lived on the premises),[85] they were instrumental in guiding the inmates and supervising the asylum. Moreover, even the viceregal version gave ecclesiastical officials considerable authority. Not only did two representatives of the Church serve on the Poor House board, but the archbishop (along with the viceroy, the Poor House administrator, and its board members) were permitted to authorize the entrance of paupers into the asylum.

The viceregal and archiepiscopal statutes came closer to Foucault's "normalizing" institutions than those proposed by Ortiz Cortés. Each set of bylaws progressively erased the ethnic differences that he had been careful to accommodate. The 1769 bylaws omitted direct references to special foods and bedding for paupers of different racial backgrounds, although they still permitted Indian inmates to wear their traditional clothes. By 1777 each pauper was supposed to dress in identical uniforms made of coarse cloth and sporting the emblem of the Poor House: a medallion of the Virgin of Guadalupe and Saint Joseph. It is unclear whether this innovation simply catered to the king's instructions to conform with peninsular practice or whether it reflected the decline of the caste system in the late eighteenth century,[86] already evident in the racial integration that distinguished the asylum from early colonial institutions. In either case, the introduction of a visible mark of indigence had the effect of setting the inmates apart from other city residents. The 1777 bylaws explicitly recognized that wearing a uniform would humiliate the inmates because it "manifests that they are maintained at the expense of charity." The uniform can therefore be interpreted as part of the punitive regime imposed on Mexico City beggars.

The Poor House outlined in the three sets of bylaws had much in common with the "total institutions" portrayed by the social control school. The disciplining of the poor required their enclosure and constant surveillance. It imposed on them the strict time distribution that had long characterized monastic communities. It attempted to control all aspects of individual behavior, including the pauper's "aptitude to work, his everyday conduct, his moral attitude, his state of mind." It subjected them to "a whole micropenality of time (latenesses, absences, interruptions of tasks), of activity (inattention, negligence, lack of zeal), of behaviour (impoliteness, disobedience), of speech (idle chatter, insolence), of the body ('incorrect' attitudes, irregular gestures, lack of cleanliness), of sexuality (impurity, indecency)."[87] By 1777 it sought to homogenize the inmates in their clothing and diet as well.

Yet in some ways the Poor House was not designed to be as repressive as Foucault's carceral institutions. Although daily life was strictly regulated, down to the hours of sleep and the amount of food allowed the inmates, the atmosphere may have been more that of a rigid boarding school than a prison. The founders did not intend the Poor House to provide the foul quarters and starvation diet Piven and Cloward describe as a deterrent for moochers. On the contrary, the spacious new building was designed to be comfortable and healthy. The prescribed diet was much better than the minimum required to sustain health. Indeed, with sixteen ounces of meat each day and special delicacies on feast days, it was far superior to the diet paupers could expect on the streets. And the provision for married couples to live with their families would distinguish their environment from the oppressive prison cell.

In addition, the Poor House inmates were not as isolated as those of "total institutions." Relatives were allowed to visit, although we do not know with what frequency or under what conditions. Occasional outings were also possible, not only in supervised Sunday walks but also on an individual basis with the permission of the director (the inmates wishing to obtain such permission had to show sufficient cause, especially the women, who were considered to be more vulnerable to moral and physical peril while out on their own). The 1777 bylaws also allowed any "honest" citizen who wished to "spend the rest of his or her days in this house receiving spiritual and temporal assistance" to do so by contributing the cost of room and board. These paying pensioners presumably would not enter the asylum to be rehabilitated or punished and would be free to leave whenever they wished because they had the funds to guarantee that they would not become beggars. Thus, even in conception, the walls between the Poor House and the city had some porosity.[88]

Indeed, the funeral-accompanying business, introduced in the 1769 bylaws and considerably elaborated on in 1777, gave the Poor House inmates a visible and legitimate role in the life of the community. The viceregal statutes described how selected inmates, dressed in dark clothing and holding lighted candles, were to march in procession behind one of the chaplains while "praying with great devotion and composure for the soul of the dead." This service was available for a price to people "of any rank" who requested such assistance; the only exception was that twelve inmates should attend the funerals of Poor House employees and board members free of charge. The function of serving as paid mourners prevented the asylum's inmates from being locked away and forgotten.

The paupers' agency was not completely obliterated during their confinement, either. Expanding on an idea already present in Ortiz Cortés's bylaws, the 1777 statutes stipulated that the inmates should have recourse to outside authorities if they were displeased with their treatment. The *juez protector*, or judge protector of the asylum (the oidor of the royal Audiencia), was to visit the Poor House at least four times a year and hold a hearing in the main upstairs room where inmates could present their complaints and requests. The judge was to "hear them benignly" and grant them confidentiality if they wanted to keep their discussions secret. Moreover, the use of paid inmate-workers in positions of responsibility, as well as their right to keep a por-

N. S. DE LA CARIDAD.

DEVS CHARITAS EST

Dando Limosna para el sustento delos pobres Inocentes, se gana 40. dias de Indulgencia, enlas Esca'erill de Mexico.
Sylverio, Sc. ā, 1755.

10 TRADITIONAL CHARITY. This illustration of Mexico City beggars before the image of Our Lady of Charity dates from 1755. The
caption, "Giving alms for the sustenance of the innocent poor earns
40 days of indulgence," embodies one of the tenets of traditional
Catholic charity, which was practiced for the spiritual benefit of the
giver as well as the material assistance of the recipient. Enlightened
reformers sought to replace these attitudes, which encouraged indiscriminate almsgiving and professional begging, with modern, utilitarian forms of poor relief that would deter idleness and enforce the
work ethic.

tion of the profits they produced, would distinguish these privileged paupers from the others. It would also give certain inmates a measure of control over their daily lives—though never as much as before the Poor House experiment went into effect, when they could roam the capital's streets doing as they pleased. The reliance on selected inmates to fill supervisory positions would also undermine the strict regulation of daily activities.

Still, if the Poor House envisioned in the bylaws was not as rigid or normalizing as the classic Foucauldian asylum, it was not a purely benevolent institution, either. With the possible exception of the pensioners, its inmates were to be deprived of their liberty. Life in the asylum involved considerable regimentation and loss of privacy. Efforts to mold the inmates' characters were pervasive, and punishment was part of the prescribed daily regime. Reform rather than retribution may have been the paramount goal, but the asylum nonetheless aimed to impose social control.

Conclusion

Studies of public welfare in Europe have found that enormous changes occurred in the concept of poor relief in past centuries. Earlier generations of historians attributed these changes to Protestantism, which replaced the traditional Catholic notion of charity as an act of religious piety with a new form of discriminating relief directed by secular authorities and conceived of as part of a utilitarian project to benefit society.[89] More recent works have questioned the dichotomy between Protestantism and Catholicism by showing that Catholic countries shared in this transformation from the sixteenth century onward.[90] For Spain, although Maureen Flynn and William Callahan found strong popular resistance to the new reforms, the strengthening of secular and utilitarian notions of social welfare has been amply documented, particularly for the late eighteenth century.[91]

Yet studies of Latin America, still dominated by a strong tradition of patriotic historiography, generally assume that enlightened ideas about poverty and poor relief only appeared after independence. For example, Teresita Martínez-Vergne's study of Puerto Rico and Shannon McGhee Hernández's study of Guatemala both date such changes to the nineteenth century, although the former attributes them to liberalism and the latter to conservatism.[92] Most studies of Mexico correlate the "modern" attitudes with nineteenth-century liberalism. Some note that the secularization of welfare institutions was a two-step process that began with independence in 1821 and ended with the Reform Laws of 1856–59. But the shift in ideology from traditional religious notions of charity to modern ideas of secular social welfare—what González Navarro labels the modern bourgeois conscience—is usually linked to the triumph of the Liberal Reform in the middle of the century.[93] The continuities between colonial and republican policies have been obscured by the tendency of Mexican historians to begin or end their studies in 1821, for students of the national period failed to follow through on the hints in brief seminal studies of the colonial period that the Bourbon period witnessed important innovations in social welfare policies.[94]

In contrast, this study of the Poor House suggests that a true watershed occurred in the late eighteenth century. The desire to substitute traditional indiscriminate almsgiving (*la caridad mal reglada*) with "well-regulated charity" that disciplined the poor is embodied in the first paragraph of the 1769 bylaws proposed by Archbishop Lorenzana:

> The saintly and exalted object . . . of repressing feigned mendicity, preventing idleness that, dressed in the clothing of true poverty, defrauds and usurps the assistance that is its due; of disciplining and instructing the worthy poor in politics and morals; of forcing the healthy to work and even making the invalids laborious; of imposing the order of well-regulated charity on the distribution and consumption of alms which with devotion the residents of this city and archbishopric lavishly hand out without determining whether the need is real or simulated, and only attending to the corporal maintenance of those who receive them; and, finally, of preventing the nakedness widely visible on the streets, with the prejudice it causes the public, and the spoiling of so many people who in these parts make mendicity their profession while abandoning agriculture, the mechanical arts, manufactures, and such, instead relying for their sustenance and the support of their vices and debauchery on the funds of poorly administered charity, moved Dr. Don Fernando Ortiz Cortés . . . to build this Poor House at his own expense, to confine the poor.

Such "modern" ideas about poverty and poor relief were also emphasized by the Poor House board when it announced the project in its fundraising letter of January 12, 1774. Echoing Ortiz Cortés's 1764 petition to the crown, the junta's letter assured the public that supporting the Poor House was the best way "to exercise charity without the danger that their alms will support drunken binges and other vices, or sustain vagrants, troublemakers, and idlers who defraud the alms of the deserving poor, . . . and equally defraud society of the work and services to which they should be dedicating their strength, . . . and who acquire much more with their simulated infirmities and indigence than they would earn if they applied themselves to honest work, being one of the causes of the scarcity of servants." It appealed to utilitarian rather than religious sentiments when it argued that, by contributing directly to the Poor House instead of handing out alms indiscriminately, Mexico City residents would be freed of the "bothersome clamor that currently inconveniences them in church, in their houses, and on the streets."[95] The city council explicitly linked the Poor House project with national progress. In approving its monthly support of the asylum in 1777, it explained that "One of the most important features of a well-ordered republic is the banishment of beggars from the streets." The Poor House experiment was consequently worth supporting so that Mexico could rank among "the most civilized nations" in the world.[96]

At the same time, the humanitarian desire to relieve suffering coexisted with the desire to impose social control. Indeed, the older view of the sacred poor occasionally surfaced alongside the disdain exhibited by Lorenzana. The tone of the viceregal bylaws was considerably softer than that of the archbishop's earlier document. The 1777 statutes harkened back to traditional religious notions of charity from their opening sentence, which described the inspiration for the Poor House as "desiring to better serve God Our Father and seeking the greatest spiritual benefit of all souls." They exhorted Poor House employees to take particular care of the inmates who needed temporary care in the infirmary, for they were "the poor of Jesus Christ." They labeled the seclusion of paupers "a work of piety." The funeral-accompanying service in particular shows that contemporaries still believed the poor could contribute to the salvation of the rich. Yet that did not prevent the Poor House bylaws from prescribing the confinement and correction of the pauper inmates.

All the elements of modern public welfare were not yet fully developed in Bourbon Mexico. The secularizing tendency was already strong, as witnessed in the crown's insistence that the viceroy, not the archbishop, preside over the Poor House board (not to mention in the expulsion of the Jesuit order and the confiscation of its property in 1767). Once it was established, the state took a dominant role in funding and protecting the institution. Yet the initiative for founding the Poor House came from a priest. If the asylum was from the start an independent institution staffed primarily by lay people, its director during the first seventeen years was a cleric and its chaplains played an important guiding role. Moreover, the state was reluctant to take it over entirely, instead welcoming ecclesiastical as well as private funding and representation on the governing board. At the same time, the Bourbon state permitted the Foundling Home and the General Hospital of San Andrés to open as entirely ecclesiastical foundations. Although the crown encouraged the creation of a "national" network of poorhouses,[97] it did not attempt to centralize the various hospitals and asylums under one office or agency. Thus Reforma liberals would certainly take the process of secularization and centralization farther than did the Bourbon regime.

The Poor House experiment nonetheless supports Raymond Carr's conclusion, for Spain, that "There is no practical reform of the nineteenth century, no reforming attitude of mind, that cannot be traced back to one of the servants of Charles III."[98] This statement is accurate only if the king's "servants" include ecclesiastical officials, however, for in Mexico clerics spearheaded the reform of traditional Catholic customs. In light of the central role played by priests in disseminating the new attitudes toward poverty and poor relief, it is more accurate to label them enlightened rather than secular or bourgeois.[99] On the treatment of paupers, the Bourbon crown and clergy were more often in consensus than conflict, acting in concert with private philanthropists to promote this experiment to shelter and discipline the poor.

{ 3 }

THE EXPERIMENT IN PRACTICE,

1774–1805

Within five days of its inauguration, Viceroy Bucareli proclaimed the Poor House a success. It opened on March 19, 1774, with 250 "paupers of all ages and sexes who came forward of their own volition." By March 24, even before the eight-day grace period for beggars expired, there were 292 inmates, "none of them brought by force." The capital, reported the viceroy to the king, would soon be free of beggars and the "many vagrants who though able to work steal the alms of the legitimate poor" would be left without recourse.[1]

The number of inmates continued to grow after the ban on begging went into effect on March 27, with beggars thereafter forcibly confined in the asylum. Within three months the Poor House was so crowded that the director, Dr. Don Andrés Llanos y Valdés, petitioned the city council for permission to expand the building. "So many paupers have entered," he wrote on July 9, "so many more than we expected . . . that they are suffering many discomforts, which increase as the number grows each day."[2] By August 16 the institution housed five hundred inmates, twice what it had opened with six months earlier.[3] Given the unexpected demand for its services, the viceroy, city council, and Poor House board quickly moved to add a new wing.[4] After it opened in November 1776, the Poor House could take in even more paupers. Over the next two decades it housed approximately six to nine hundred inmates at a time.

In 1781 Llanos y Valdés boasted that the Poor House experiment had worked as planned. It had reduced begging, not only by legitimate paupers but also by the "many idlers and vagabonds who currently abstain for fear of being taken to the *Hospicio*."[5] In 1784 a committee of distinguished citizens, reporting to the viceroy on the state of Mexico City, affirmed that the Poor

House had contributed to a notable improvement in social order and a decline in "the nakedness of the plebes," for "those who knew Mexico [twenty years] before recognize that each day there is less laxity of behavior among all classes of people."[6]

There may have been some truth to these claims, at least for the first few years after the Poor House opened. Yet close inspection of its internal records suggests that from the start the capital's citizens began using the institution in ways its founders had not intended. Its deterrent effect on begging gradually diminished, as did attempts to discipline the adult inmates. By the turn of the century its function was more custodial than rehabilitative. In addition to containing disorderly street people, the asylum increasingly devoted its resources to sheltering the groups served in the past by traditional charity: respectable persons fallen on hard times, vulnerable maidens, and abandoned children. Although beggars continued to be sporadically confined, humanitarianism was gradually gaining the upper hand over the imposition of social control.

The Flourishing Early Years

The Poor House was at its apogee in 1777 when the priest Juan de Viera, who directed the Colegio de San Ildefonso, visited the asylum.[7] Sparing no superlatives, he declared it "so magnificent that it looks more like a Palace of Princes than a House for the Poor." Seven "vast" patios with beautiful fountains provided "superabundant" water. The corridors had elegant iron railings. The dormitories were "so spacious" that they housed 650 paupers with "utmost comfort." The inmates slept in wrought iron beds with "blankets, pillows, and a mattress appropriate to each individual's station." Their clothes were plain but "honest and very decent." Their food was plentiful, with the asylum consuming fourteen *arrobas* of lamb, an entire bull, and twelve hundred loaves of bread every day. "They are given all that is necessary and their children are raised with the saintly fear of God because they have schools and teachers for those of both sexes. Each one works in whatever he can and knows, and those who cannot are attended in all their needs." Viera added, approvingly, that the inmates never went out except with special permission of the superior, as he called the administrator. Several inmates were also sent out each day to collect alms, which were "so copious" that at the end of the year there was still money left over. Finally, the institution had its own sentinels who brought beggars to the asylum, where they were "cloistered," even against their will.

Aside from this eyewitness description, only spotty documentation sur-

11 INTERIOR OF THE POOR HOUSE BUILDING. The late-eighteenth-century visitor Juan de Viera considered it "so magnificent that it looks more like a palace of princes than a house for the poor." These early-twentieth-century photographs show the patio of what was by then the Children's Department flanked by arched corridors (*top*), the statue of one of the founders in the central patio (*middle right*), the massive and plain exterior (*middle left*); and the boys' dormitory, with beds lined up in two straight rows (*bottom*).

vives on the Poor House during the first two decades of its existence. Financial records and correspondence with the viceroy suggest that the time of plenty portrayed by Viera did not last long. By 1781 the asylum was facing its first financial crisis. For several years the Poor House had been operating in the red, with Llanos y Valdés lending it the money necessary to meet its obligations. In March of 1781 he submitted his resignation. Claiming to have spent 28,806.8 pesos from his own pocket, he informed the board that it could either find a new director or close the Poor House altogether. The government moved with unusual celerity to save the asylum. After considering various options (including an additional tax on pulque, which was rejected) Viceroy Martín de Mayorga proposed subsidizing the Poor House with revenues from the Royal Lottery. Moved by the argument that if the asylum closed "eight hundred paupers will spill onto the streets, where they will offend the public by stealing and engaging in other crimes and sins," the crown approved.[8] The crisis was resolved, at least for the moment, and Llanos y Valdés returned to the directorship.

Despite the crown's concession of regular lottery funds, the shortage of revenue became a constant refrain. The Poor House board again claimed insolvency in a 1785 petition to the king.[9] Their request for an increase in the lottery income was rejected, although the crown granted the institution an occasional subsidy such as the windfall of 51,608.5 pesos in unclaimed lottery tickets awarded on September 20, 1788. The situation worsened with the departure of Llanos y Valdés, who was appointed bishop of Linares in 1791. The director's deep pockets had continued to shield the asylum from budget deficits, for example, by paying the doctor's retainer out of his personal funds. The Poor House never again found such a strong—or wealthy—leader. Thus, beginning in 1791 it was forced to seek pension-paying inmates.[10] By 1794 Viceroy Revillagigedo, in his *Instrucción reservada*, informed his successor that the asylum's strained finances were threatening its capacity to function adequately.[11]

Still, the Poor House was not yet forced to retrench. The summary totals available for the first two decades show that during this period it housed more inmates than ever again. It responded effectively to the demands placed upon it during 1786, the terrible Year of Hunger when famine and disease ravaged the Valley of Mexico and sent thousands of destitute country people to seek aid in the viceregal capital. Alarmed by the flood of "nearly naked" migrants of both sexes, who, "reduced to mendicancy by the grain shortages . . . solicit alms in the streets, plazas, temples, and everywhere,"[12] Viceroy Bernardo de Gálvez collected donations from the capital's citizens, confraternities, and corporations; reestablished public granaries to feed the starving; set up public works projects to occupy the sturdy men and boys over the age of ten; and ordered the Poor House to take in the "miserable" paupers who needed succor, especially the women who were not eligible for public works assignments.[13] Charitable citizens rose to the occasion, with one Col. Mariano Bruno de Azeta feeding one hundred people daily from his own kitchen on the street of Las Ratas.[14] For its part, the Poor House raised special contributions totaling some 30,300 pesos, and temporarily expanded to accommodate fourteen-hundred needy paupers.[15]

After the famine and epidemics subsided, the institution reverted to a more manageable size. The printed totals for the 1790 census list 910 inmates. The next available statistics, for the year from December 31, 1793, to December 31, 1794, list 777 and 743 inmates on those two dates. By April of 1795 the inmate population had increased to 820. The Poor House therefore maintained a large number of paupers throughout its first two decades. This evidence suggests that its funding was more solid during the late eighteenth century than at any time until the 1860s, when the number of inmates returned to these early levels.

Table 2 shows that the asylum housed mostly adults, just as its founders had intended. From the first week it opened until 1794 between 81 and 89 percent of the inmates were fifteen or older, the age at which colonial documents classified people as adults. Between 56 and 63 percent of these were men.[16] Some 267 surviving entrance slips for 1774–76 suggest that the few children who entered the asylum accompanied their parents, especially their mothers, and occasionally other relatives such as godparents or grandparents. Only 8 percent of the children in 1774–75 and 10 percent in 1776 came on their own, and (since the entrance slips do not list their ages) they may have been adolescents rather than young children.[17] Thus, the original division between the Poor House and the Foundling Home was largely respected. The Casa de Cuna took in orphans and cared for them until they turned fourteen.[18] The Poor House concentrated on adults, with male inmates having a slight edge.

From the start the Poor House was racially integrated, again fulfilling the intentions of its founders. Although there is no systematic information on the racial makeup of the inmate population during the first two decades, occasional references to race as well as the racial identifications given for 104 paupers confirmed on August 2, 1779, show that the inmates represented every racial group in Mexico City. Some paupers were listed as español, or Spanish, a term that can be loosely translated as "white" since it included both Spaniards and their American-born descendants. Some were Indians. Others were members of the mixed-race castes, including, according to the confir-

TABLE 2   Poor House Inmates, 1774–1803

Year	Total	Women (as % adults)	Children (as % total)
1774 (March)	292	38	11
1774 (August)	500	—	—
1777	650	—	—
1780	644	44	16
1781	780	—	—
1782	568[a]	37	15
1790	910	—	19
1793	777	—	19
1794	743	—	18
1795	820	46	21
1801	464	49	23
1802	609	51	27
1803	555	57	20

[a] This total is too low because the 1782 count, taken for ecclesiastical purposes, omits an unspecified number of gentile Indians.

mation list, many mestizos, a few mulattos, *castizos*, *lobos*, and *moriscos*. One was a Negro.[19]

Many of these inmates were the beggars whom the Poor House experiment was meant to control. As planned, the opening of the asylum initiated the persecution of people caught soliciting alms in the Mexican capital. In fact, the early period—at least until the crusading Llanos y Valdés departed in 1791—was the only time when the institution regularly attempted to confine beggars. Although it never entirely eliminated them from the streets of Mexico City, the Poor House came closer to fulfilling its original goals during the first two decades than at any time in the future.

The Campaign against Mendicity

The energetic early campaign against mendicity is illustrated by two very rich, though only partially preserved, sources. Loose entrance and exit slips from 1774–78, in which the Poor House director gave the live-in administrator Don Joseph de Elizalde y León permission to admit or release the named inmate, illustrate how often and why paupers entered and left the asylum.[20] Eight petitions to Viceroy Gálvez in 1785 requesting the release of forcibly confined inmates describe the conditions under which beggars were detained and contain occasional traces of the paupers' voices as well as of Llanos y Valdés's opinions of them.[21]

Regular roundups of beggars began as soon as the newly decreed ban on begging went into effect. Several requests for the release of an inmate, included among the surviving exit slips for 1774, allege that a mistake was made in picking up a certain person. For example, Don Francisco de Espinosa, writing on behalf of "a poor, half-witted pauper picked up on Sunday because he was seen asking for a real from a lady at the cathedral," explained that "he is not like the rest who are in the Hospicio since he has a brother who supports him." The chaplain Joseph Abarca asked that Miguel Xuarez be released because "although a poor invalid, he can work and does not solicit alms; he supports himself by manufacturing combs." Likewise Doña Juana Paula de Zavaleta y Peña alleged that her maid's husband, Cayetano Galicia, though "poor and half-blind, does not bother people by begging because he eats at my house. . . . He was apprehended not begging but going to take Communion."

Petitions to the viceroy throughout the 1780s indicate that the forcible confinement of beggars continued into the asylum's second decade.[22] The very existence of these documents shows that inmates had access to the viceroy, as president of the Poor House board, to appeal the decisions of its director. The fact that half the petitioners in 1785 did not know how to sign their names did not present a barrier. Yet only a minority achieved their goal: three paupers who were in the asylum for the first time and found a *fiador* (guarantor) to vouch for them were released; the other five were not released because Llanos y Valdés determined that they were habitual beggars who would not be able to earn their living "honestly."

These documents indicate how much some inmates hated the Poor House. Several vigorously resisted their apprehension. Two of their relatives labeled it a "prison." The 65-year-old Domingo Castro, sequestered against his will for six months, pleaded to be freed from "the captivity in which I have been placed without cause," for he (like the other petitioners) denied having begged. The octogenarian Mariano Montiverio, confined along with his wife for five years "only because I was found at the side of the royal palace wearing a torn cape and trying to sell an armoire," protested the "difficulties we suffer in this House and especially our loss of liberty." Their petitions were denied because the director insisted that the two men had been caught soliciting alms and that they were too elderly and infirm to exercise their respective professions of gold-wire drawer and blacksmith.

These records suggest that Llanos y Valdés was conducting a vigorous personal campaign against mendicity. Three petitions contain vivid images of how he patrolled the streets, picking up beggars and taking them directly to the asylum in his coach. For example, Castro described how the Poor House director found him on Tacuba Street (near the central plaza) as he left the Hospital of San Juan de Dios and "made me enter his coach and brought me to this House of the Poor." Llanos y Valdés added that "I took him with great difficulty, because of the resistance he put up." Castro argued that his detention was unjust because he had a trade and his unmarried daughters relied on him for support. Although the viceroy approved his petition, Llanos y Valdés refused to release Castro on the grounds that this was his second confinement in the Poor House, that he had violated the promise he made five years earlier to refrain from begging, that an illness (unnamed) prevented him from practicing his trade, that other inmates confirmed that his only profession for forty years had been to beg at the doors of churches, and that he had lied when he claimed that his daughters needed him because he had none. Thus, because of his fierce determination to discipline beggars, Llanos y Valdés was not above overruling the viceroy's orders.

The one-handed María Petra suffered a similar harsh confinement. After an earlier release from the Poor House she made the mistake of "requesting half a real" from Llanos y Valdés himself as he traveled in his coach, apparently because she was nearly blind and failed to recognize him. Seized on the spot and returned to the asylum, she was still there three years later with little hope of release. When her husband, Juan de Lizalde, visited—two and a half years later—he was apprehended as well. Llanos y Valdés explained that he had earlier "found him begging but did not take him because he resisted, as they tend to do; so I gave an order that if he went to see his wife, he should be detained, as was done." The director had concluded that Lizalde, too, was an incorrigible beggar. Although the mestiza Juana de Dios, who claimed to be their daughter-in-law, petitioned for their release, it was denied on the grounds that since both Lizalde and his wife "are over eighty years, they are incapable of earning their bread." Llanos y Valdés added that he doubted the petitioner was a relative, for the couple had repeatedly failed to identify family members who might be able to support them.

In memos responding to the viceroy's queries, Llanos y Valdés revealed his exasperation with habitual beggars. Recommending the denial of Juana de Dios's petition, he referred to "the custom these people have of lying." He refused to consider several petitions from the soldier sons of Bonifacia Moreno, held in the Poor House for ten months, because he felt that even with her sons supporting her she, like all those "accustomed to begging, cannot usually refrain even if they have what they need." During seven months he likewise denied petitions from the daughter of an elderly Indian, María de

Olbera, on the grounds that "my experience shows that, even if they have no need, they beg due to their habit and vice." The viceroy ordered both these paupers freed when suitable guarantors were found.

The unsuccessful petitioner Castro accused Llanos y Valdés of denying him due process, "for he makes a farce of everything, believing himself to be absolute, since he has no one who can give him orders." Admitting that he had refused to comply with the viceroy's directive to release Castro to an unknown guarantor, the director explained that he did so to avoid a future lawsuit, for when Castro was again caught begging (as he surely would be) the director would have to take the fiador to court to collect the bond, "present proofs, and waste on lawsuits (which tend to last a long time) the time I need to attend to the asylum." The director's own memos thus contain evidence that he treated recidivists with high-handed toughness occasionally bordering on arbitrariness, further proof that clerics enthusiastically led the drive to eliminate begging rather than merely following the dictates of state authorities.

The petitions from 1785 demonstrate that civil and ecclesiastical authorities joined the Poor House director in confining paupers. The regent of the Audiencia, a member of the Poor House board, sent Bonifacia Moreno to the asylum when he found her begging. Priests occasionally sent beggars who were bothering their parishioners. For example, the priest of San Felipe Neri sent the elderly Doña Manuela de Sotomayor to the asylum because "she solicited alms, not only in the streets, but also in the churches from people who were attending Mass or praying." (A niece's petition on her behalf was denied because Llanos y Valdés convinced the viceroy that the niece could not earn enough by sewing to support her aunt.) The 1776 exit slips likewise contain a notation that the sacristan of the cathedral placed 90-year-old Alfonsa de San Joseph in the Poor House *por limosnera*.

While the campaign against mendicity was in full force, the Poor House appears to have confined a sizable portion of Mexico City's beggars, if only temporarily. The six to eight hundred inmates in the asylum at any one time cannot have been all the beggars in the huge Mexican capital, where by all accounts thousands rather than hundreds relied on charity for their sustenance. Yet the totals are not an accurate indicator of the institution's impact on Mexico City's street people because high turnover rates meant that many more paupers passed through its doors than were listed on any single day.

The exit slips for 1774 and 1776–78 show that a steady stream of inmates were released, many of them soon after they were detained. Some were let out on their own after promising not to beg again. Most were released to a

Mes, y Abril 3, de 1774 añ.

Digo yo D.n José Antonio Mínguez Mo Examinado en las Artes de prime ras letras, que me hago cargo de la manutenci on de José Medina, y soy responzable en qualesquiera tiempo, que sepa, q. mendiga bolverlo á esta Casa, y Ospicio de Pobres de donde lo saco en cuya obligacion doy este firmado de mi puño en dho dia mez, y Año

José Antonio Mínguez

12 STATEMENT OF FIANZA. With this document the primary school teacher Don José Antonio Mínguez claimed a Poor House inmate, José Medina, on April 3, 1774. Mínguez pledged to maintain the pauper and return him to the asylum if he should ever beg again. Similar statements were signed by respectable citizens when retrieving their relatives, friends, employees, or clients. In theory, institutionalized paupers could only leave if they were so claimed, if they were placed in a job, or if they could show that they had the means to support themselves without reverting to mendicity.

guarantor, who signed a formulaic declaration promising to support (or provide employment for) the named pauper and to return him or her to the Poor House if he or she reverted to begging.[23] Some of the exit slips referred to "the customary bond" (*fianza*) of 50 pesos promised as a guarantee of this obligation. Given Llanos y Valdés' complaint about having to take fiadores to court, this sum was apparently only paid in the event that the contract was broken and the released inmate returned to the Poor House. A few exit slips also mentioned that the inmates' clothing had either been paid for or returned to the asylum.

The exit slips confirm that the traditional web of kinship and clientage still protected many beggars. Even though most of these declarations were signed by people who did not state their relationship to the inmate being released, many claimants identified themselves as relatives, patrons, or employers. The first surviving petition came from the vicar of the parish of San Miguel, who on March 21, 1774, claimed Mathías Final because "he was raised in my house, and for that reason I have often helped him and his family." The second came from the daughter and granddaughter of the elderly Francisco Sumaya, who insisted that "we fear the loss of liberty will cost him his life." The men were released on March 23 and 24, the fourth and fifth day after the Poor House opened. The relatives were usually spouses, parents, or children who claimed their loved ones and, like the illiterate wife of Don Juan Joseph Castaño (one of the very few claimants who could not sign his or her name), promised "that he will not go about bothering the public with solicitations." An occasional employer stepped forward to claim an employee who had strayed, as did Sor Anna, a nun of an unspecified convent, who petitioned on behalf of the water carrier Felis Morales "because we need him to go to the plaza and bring us syrup." One shoemaker claimed his apprentice's parents and brother, who were to be supported with the boy's wages.

Although most of the exit slips have been lost, they are numbered (unlike the entrance slips) so that we can calculate release rates. In the first nine months after the Poor House opened some 900 paupers entered, with one-third of them released within the same period.[24] In 1778, when approximately 620 paupers left the Poor House[25] — as many as were recorded as being there on any given day — at least 1,240 paupers were confined altogether.[26] The 1794 summary statistics specify that 1,537 paupers entered the asylum that year, with 45 percent of them released and another 7 percent dying before the year was out (table 3). It is therefore likely that many of the capital's habitual beggars passed through the institution at one time or another during the first two decades of its existence. This lends support to Llanos y Valdés's claim that the Poor House reduced begging in the capital, for much of its impact

TABLE 3 Inmate Totals and Turnover, 1793–94

	Adults	Children	All
December 31, 1793	628	149	777
Entered in 1794	629	131	760
Left in 1794	561	125	686 (45%)
Died in 1794	89	19	108 (7%)
December 31, 1794	607	136	743

was as a deterrent, with the fear of being detained acting to curb potential mendicity.

Pressures to Serve as a Reformatory

Not all of these inmates were beggars, however. The original plan began to be modified from the first week the Poor House opened by citizens who turned to it for help in disciplining unruly youths and, somewhat later, by viceregal authorities who used it as a prison for indigenous war captives who did not fit into the existing penal system. By accommodating their demands, the Poor House diluted its focus on the street people it had been designed to restrain.

Under pressure from the capital's residents, the asylum began to serve as a reformatory for juveniles placed by patrons and masters who could not control their clients or apprentices. Among the entrance slips we find that five days after it opened a gentleman (whose signature is illegible) wrote Llanos y Valdés that he was sending "an orphaned Indian girl I took into my home since childhood with the intent of raising her in a Christian manner; but now that she is grown she has turned out bad and routinely flees my house, and I have not been able to reform her despite repeated punishments." He asked that the young woman be "perpetually shut up in the Casa de Misericordia and put to work . . . in order to avoid her perdition." She was apparently accepted even though the Poor House was not originally meant to house wayward women, who were supposed to be placed in a recogimiento instead. On September 16, 1776, the master silversmith José Salvatierra brought his apprentice Agustín Cabrera and asked that he be given "the punishment deserved for carelessness." Similarly, the 1785 petitions reveal that the priest of Santa Catarina Mártir sent the young Juana Rodríguez to the Poor House "for nothing worse," according to her mother, "than having gone to a baptism and leaving drunk." The mother's petition for her daughter's release was denied when the priest testified that the girl was a perpetual drunkard. Since none of these youths had solicited alms, they were not the target population for which the Poor House had been intended.

Neither were the *mecas*, the Indian prisoners of war who appeared for the first time in a 1782 Communion list and reappeared in every inmate count of the next three decades. *Mecas*, a term probably derived from *chichimecas*, were "barbarous" Indians from northern Mexico. The historian Silvio Zavala has documented how, from the 1780s until at least 1810, captives taken in the brutal wars against the Apaches and other rebellious northern tribes were brought south in chain gangs to Mexico City and beyond—eventually to Veracruz and even Havana. The prisoners of war proved so "fierce" and adept at escaping that the government continually shifted its policies on how to handle them. At various times they were forced to labor in public works, given to "citizens of good reputation who will teach them Christian doctrine and use them without treating them cruelly," allowed to stay in Mexico City, not allowed to stay in Mexico City, placed in prison, sent to the fortress of San Juan de Ulúa, or transported to Cuba, from where it was believed they would be unable to escape and return home to continue the war against the white colonizers.[27]

Many mecas also ended up in the Poor House. Since its building provided security, some may only have been temporarily deposited there while awaiting deportation further south, especially after the royal deportation order of 1799. Yet before that others stayed for an extended period of time. Indeed, a 1788 decree directed that meca youths be transferred from the Acordada Prison in Mexico City to the Poor House "to learn the Christian doctrine and a useful trade."[28] The adult meca women were supposed to be placed in a recogimiento with their infants and young children; the adult men were to stay in prison until another destination could be found for them. Perhaps because most of Mexico City's retirement homes had closed by that date,[29] meca women and children went to the Poor House along with the male youths. As early as 1782 some mecas had been in the asylum long enough to learn Spanish and become Catholics. The Communion list counted ten baptized mecas, all under the category of women rather than girls and using the designation Meca instead of a last name. It also referred to an unspecified number of other mecas and one Otomita who were not counted because, as gentiles, they were unable to participate in the "annual obligation of our Saintly Mother Church.[30]

Although they were a minority of the Poor House inmates, the very presence of these groups modified the asylum's stated mission. By admitting and Hispanizing the mecas, as well as by accepting and punishing the juvenile delinquents, the Poor House strayed from the original project of combating mendicity, even while it maintained its disciplinary function.

The Willing Clients

The repressive thrust began to weaken, however, as the city's poor incorporated the Poor House into their strategies for daily survival. The asylum filled a real need for many paupers, who became its willing clients. In addition to the elderly and disabled for whom it had been designed, homeless families used it as a temporary shelter, especially single mothers having difficulty supporting themselves and their children on their own. The unemployed sought admittance so they could work on the asylum's looms or in its kitchens and save the small wages paid to working inmates. Struggling families placed dependent members in the Poor House to relieve themselves of the burden of supporting them. Indeed, some paupers wanted to enter so badly that they lied in order to gain admittance. One unnamed man, for example, believing that his chances would improve if he were handicapped, asked to be admitted "out of charity" because he was "mute and cannot speak." The director noted that "it is false that he is mute, but take him anyway." The youth Mariano Joseph de Estrada, believing that orphanhood would improve his chances, "said he had no mother." In fact, he may have been trying to escape her, for the director determined that his mother, Doña Nicolasa de Castro Biexo, was still alive.[31]

The demand for shelter was greater than the Poor House could accommodate. Scattered notations on the entrance slips show that the director regularly turned some applicants away. He tried to exclude demented or diseased paupers who could be sent to the capital's mental asylums and charity hospitals. For example, María Antonia Andrade was rejected because she was demented; in contrast, María Josepha de Villanueva was accepted—but only after a doctor examined a sore near her nose and determined that, far from being a sign of leprosy, it was only mud. He rejected others if they had relatives who could support them. For example, on November 18, 1776, he admonished a woman identified as "la Olguín," who presented herself at the Poor House door with her children, to rejoin her husband, "for we cannot divorce you" (an indication that she may have been trying to escape an unhappy marriage, though on this subject the records remain mute). On July 20, 1774, he likewise turned away Don Martín Josef de Aguilar, "*pobre de solemnidad* and unable to earn a subsistence due to his ailments," because he had a family that could take him in.

The entrance slips for 1774 and 1776 indicate that many homeless families sought refuge in the Poor House, although we cannot determine their exact proportion because these records survive for only one-sixth of the inmates admitted.[32] In 1774, 30 percent of the listed adults (and in 1776 26 percent) entered in family groups—and these records miss some related inmates since paupers like "María del Carmen, who is a daughter of a woman who is there," or "María Antonia, who is the godchild of la Mercado," joined relatives who had entered previously. Of the 141 adults who were admitted in 1776, for example, there were 7 married couples (4 with children), 2 sisters, and 2 men with their children. Another 19 were mothers with children, and in two cases with their own mothers as well. The entrance slips do not record the marital status of these women, many of whom were probably widowed or legally married but separated. We only know that the 18 "single" mothers who entered in 1774 had an average of 2.1 children apiece. These included "María Bernarda with her *hijito*," "Mariana Enríquez with her 2 *chicos*," "Michaela Campos with her 4 children," and "la Valbas with her mother and 2 daughters." The pattern is similar in 1776, when 19 "single" mothers brought an average of 2.5 children each.

A second group of inmates whose presence further distorted the original Poor House experiment was that of the "distinguished" paupers who appear sporadically in the surviving documentation. Of the adult inmates listed in the entrance slips for 1774, 18 percent (and in 1776 10 percent) used the honorific title *don* or *doña* usually associated with high status in colonial society. Of the 104 inmates receiving confirmation in 1779, 28 percent were listed as don or doña—especially jarring since most of them were children. Only 14 percent were identified as illegitimate, a low proportion for a time when approximately one-third of all births in Mexico City were out of wedlock.[33] Fully 61 percent were listed as español, another 27 percent were members of the mixed-race castes, and only 6 percent were Indian. These proportions may not be representative of the inmate population as a whole, for only 1 of every 6 inmates required confirmation. The available records nonetheless suggest that people who declared themselves to be Spanish and legitimate, and who rated an honorific title, were well represented in the institution.

Although there were certainly white beggars in Mexico City, many of the white inmates were not among them. Like Don Martín Josef de Aguilar, whose petition was rejected, some of the white inmates were the "solemn poor" (*pobres de solemnidad*), also known as the "shamefaced poor" (*pobres vergonzantes*), who were too proud to beg. Members of respectable families fallen on hard times, such paupers had in Spain for centuries been eligible for public assistance in the form of free legal aid and exemption from certain taxes.[34] When the Mexico City Poor House was established, they evidently considered themselves entitled to receive free room and board as well—though on their own terms.

Once in the Poor House the "distinguished" paupers apparently refused to be homogenized, as were the inmates in Foucauldian institutions. The entrance slips for 1774 and 1776 note that Llanos y Valdés ordered one Doña Josepha Mesa placed in a second-story room "with la Domínguez," a room that was undoubtedly drier and more private than a downstairs dormitory. Doña Francisca Rita de Arteaga was placed in "one of the new rooms above" (a reference to the new wing added to the original building in 1776). Similarly, Don Agustín Saravia was assigned a special room. Like the two women, he brought his own "bed and box" so that he could sleep on a comfortable mattress and use some personal possessions. The presence of distinguished inmates who lived apart from the rest is corroborated by the 1795 Communion count, which has a separate listing for vergonzantes, all of them dons and doñas of Spanish descent. The placement of this category at the end of the census suggests that the chaplain moved on to a separate section of the asylum when he offered communion to the "solemn poor." An 1808 count, which lists pobres de solemnidad separately, clarifies that they lived upstairs in different quarters from "los de abajo."[35]

Yet these "respectable" paupers were not those for whom the Poor House had been established. None of the numerous edicts decreeing the Poor House experiment or the long justifications requesting funds from the crown or citizenry had mentioned vergonzantes or pobres de solemnidad as the target clientele. In fact, a royal order issued for Spain on February 14, 1778, explaining how to enforce the new ban on soliciting alms, specified that, while beggars should be confined in asylums, vergonzantes should be cared for in their own houses.[36] Although the Poor House bylaws of 1777 contained provisions for pension-paying paupers to be admitted, none of the "distinguished" petitioners from the first decade offered to pay their way; indeed, the 1804 report dates the first pension payment to 1791.[37] Finally, when Viceroy Bucareli recommended expansion of the Poor House six months after it opened, it was not to create private quarters for a privileged group of paupers. Bucareli had requested that a portion of the new upstairs addition be reserved for women needing a place to give birth and recuperate;[38] otherwise, it was meant to house the overflow crowd of beggars removed from the city streets. Thus, traditional notions of who constituted the worthy poor, apparently shared by both the asylum's staff and the "solemn poor," reasserted themselves to modify the original Poor House plan.

Soon after the asylum opened, relatives of its staff also began to demand special consideration. Thus, on November 7, 1777, Don Martín Josef Verdugo, a cousin of the administrator, requested the admission of his 14-year-old godchild, "the son of our deceased uncle Dr. Don José Verdugo." The godfather claimed that the youth could not work because of a chronic illness and that his mother, "a poor widowed woman, alone," could "barely support him and even less control him to prevent his perdition." The boy's attempt to become a tailor's apprentice had failed because the master refused to pay for the apprentice's food. His godfather therefore petitioned that the youth be placed in the Poor House to learn a trade, "perhaps weaving or writing, or even that of tailor, so that in time he will be able to support his aforementioned mother." A similar petition came on August 30, 1778, from Francisco Mariano Roxas y Vergara on behalf of his niece, Gertruditas, the daughter of the former rectora Manuelita Cortés.[39] In providing shelter to these "respectable" paupers, the Poor House began to reproduce the relations of patronage and clientelism that permeated Mexican society.

The Quality of Discipline

Given the diversity of its inmates—and the dearth of eyewitness accounts of the asylum's internal regime—it is difficult to judge how effectively the Poor House disciplined its residents during the first two decades. In all likelihood, it was simultaneously coercive and benevolent, though perhaps for different sets of paupers. The forcibly confined were punished merely by their detention. Several references in the exit records to *las voluntarias* and *las forzadas* (as well as separate statistics on forced and voluntary entrants in 1803) suggest that the staff did not collapse these distinctions after the paupers entered the asylum and may have treated each group differently.

For those who voluntarily sought refuge, the Poor House functioned more as a humanitarian shelter than as a vehicle of punishment. Although these paupers had to submit to institutionalization to receive assistance, the Poor House regime was not onerous enough to serve as a deterrent—perhaps because conditions outside the asylum for many of Mexico City's poor were so bad that life inside it offered an improvement. To be sure, most would have suffered a loss of privacy. If it adhered to the ordered daily regime prescribed by the bylaws, the inmates would have been regulated by the strict schedules which imposed time discipline and obedience. Yet there is considerable evidence that these routines were not always followed.

Certainly, they did not apply to the "solemn poor" living in private quarters, who were not subject to communal life.[40] Their distinctive treatment went beyond the different food, clothing, and bedding that Ortíz Cortés had prescribed for inmates of different racial backgrounds. In addition to having

separate upstairs rooms, the 1795 Communion count noted that one vergonzante couple had a mulatta slave serving them in their private quarters and
a vergonzante lady had two servant girls helping raise her three young children.[41] Documents from 1824 and 1833 specified the separate rations given to
one favored lady and the "double rations" given another, evidence that they
did not take their meals with the other inmates.[42] The Poor House thus reproduced within it the hierarchies of colonial society. It also reproduced the
social geography of Mexico City, where people of some social standing lived
higher (literally) in multistoried buildings and left the lower floor to their
social inferiors.

The asylum did not apparently try to moralize the solemn poor. One unusual letter sent by a Poor House resident to a Church court judge indicates
that some vergonzantes maintained their sense of superior class standing despite being reduced to living in the asylum. In 1774 "a poor but honorable
Spanish woman" in the Poor House attempted to prevent her daughter's marriage to an artisan, whom she labeled a chino or lobo, by which she meant a
person of mixed Indian and black descent. The mother protested that, since
the groom "was not her daughter's equal, being of low rank," her family lin-
eage would be "stained by such a match."[43] That this lady did not consider
her dignity lost by institutionalization demonstrates that wealth was not the
primary determinant of worth or self-worth in late colonial society. It also
shows that, unlike the Foucauldian institution, the Mexico City Poor House
did not stigmatize its inmates or at least that some did not feel the stigma.

It is unclear how well the Poor House reformed the "common" paupers,
either. For the many inmates who entered with relatives, life in the asylum
was less disciplinary than familial. Just as the bylaws prescribed, couples who
could prove they were legally married (as did several who inserted marriage
certificates into the entrance records) lived together in their own section.
Thus, the 1795 Communion count had a separate category for *matrimonios*
placed after the listings for men, women, boys, and girls. Married couples
probably lived with their children night and day, at least until these turned
five (when the 1777 bylaws required children to join the older inmates of the
same gender in their respective dormitories). Most of the "single" mothers,
listed under the *mujeres* category in 1795 with their children immediately following, lived in the communal dormitories with the other women, where they
would have accompanied their offspring at all times. It is difficult to believe
that the families with small children could have followed an orderly regime.

In fact, the scarcity of work meant that for most inmates only mealtimes,
Mass, and bedtimes were regulated. Early on, Viceroy Bucareli complained
that the asylum's work regime was inadequate. In the 1777 bylaws he pro-

posed that, since the Poor House manufactures and chores were insufficient to occupy its numerous inmates, it should solicit jobs from the outside such as sewing uniforms for the army.[44] In a 1785 exposé of the problems that blighted the Mexican capital, the Bourbon official Hipólito Villarroel condemned the Poor House for failing to rehabilitate its inmates. Accusing the institution of wasting resources to maintain its inmates "in luxury," he particularly decried the presence of "idle, vagrant women," who, instead of being forced to work, merely "fatten in the Hospicio."[45] The problem had not been solved by 1794, when Viceroy Revillagigedo explained that the asylum failed to provide adequate vocational training because it could not afford to install enough workshops and hire master artisans.[46]

Although a few adult inmates worked within the asylum, only the youths (perhaps including a few aged fifteen or older whom the censuses would classify as adults) received vocational training. Financial records for April 1778, for example, show that 43 pesos were distributed that month to "the poor of both sexes" as payment for their services.[47] The 1804 report lists forty-eight positions that had been filled by inmates over the past three decades, twenty-three of them by women and twenty-five by men (table 4). Some helped the asylum run smoothly, as did two *porteros* (gatekeepers), the nurses in the male and female infirmaries, a barber, nine office helpers, four ward supervisors, two carpenters, two masons, and numerous bread bakers, cooks, and laundresses. One man trained youths in the workshops, and two women taught the children Christian doctrine. The adult inmates gained few new skills from these positions, since they would already have entered the asylum with the required knowledge. In contrast, some of the girls did learn to spin and sew or to keep house and cook. Some boys learned to make shoes, cigarettes, and mattresses for their fellow inmates or to weave the textiles that were sold for a profit. Others attended funerals and kept one real of the peso they earned, although it is unclear what marketable skill they obtained in the process.

It is difficult to consider the Poor House regime exploitative when the inmates were paid for their labor. Indeed, the opportunity for paid work made the asylum attractive to some of the capital's paupers, like the man who asked to be admitted in 1774, saying that "he is a cook and wishes to enter the Poor House to work like the other inmates." The gratuities they received may have been comparable to wages earned on the outside. One inmate who served as a *portero* received 96 pesos, the same salary the 1777 bylaws had set for a noninmate employee.[48] When the Royal Council amended the Poor House bylaws in 1785, it stipulated that any boys who voluntarily chose to stay on past age fourteen to work the looms should be paid a fair wage.[49] This statement suggests that, whether because market rates were actually paid or be-

TABLE 4   Inmate Positions and Wages, 1803 (annual salaries for each worker in pesos)

Males		Females	
1 portero (street)	96	1 president	96
1 portero (patio)	72	1 portera	72
1 pantryman	96	4 atoleras	72
1 nurse	96	3 laundresses	48
1 cook	96	2 catechism instructors	48
1 master artisan	96	2 patio supervisors	48
1 barber	96	2 refectoleras	48
2 celadores	96	1 nurse	72
1 refectolero	72	3 nurse's assistant	36
9 office assistants	48	1 cook	72
		3 cook's assistants	36
2 carpenters	4 reales/day		
2 masons	4 reales/day		
2 peons	3 reales/day		

cause there was a dearth of work in Mexico City, some inmates preferred to remain in the Poor House saving up their earnings—or using them to purchase the small luxuries that softened the severity of institutional life—rather than rushing to leave at the first opportunity.

The placement of some of these workers as apprentices or servants shows that the Poor House was able to move some of the city's unemployed paupers into the labor force—especially the youths who had been taught Christian doctrine, good working habits, and vocational skills. The exit slips for 1774 and 1776–78 indicate that many people who signed for released inmates wanted to hire them.[50] Francisco Hernández, a master silversmith, was typical of those who requested a male assistant. On May 5, 1774, he took Miguel María de Vega, a Spanish youth, to teach him the art of working silver. Hernández agreed either to return him in two months or, "if the boy shows promise," to keep him as an apprentice. Several other silversmiths, shoemakers, and owners of wine shops sought help, as did a barber and the owners of a candle-making shop and a confectionary. Girls were frequently sought as maids or, less often, as *chichiguas* (wet nurses). Many of the capital's wealthy residents (including the Countess of Tepa) came to the Poor House with requests. For example, one lady stated that she needed a chichigua and hoped that a woman whose baby had died would be available "if her milk has not dried up." Llanos y Valdés many times ordered the administrator to find "a loyal girl to serve as chambermaid in a house I trust, where she will be treated very well."

The Poor House had only limited success in training and placing its juvenile delinquents, however. Marginal notations on the exit slips for maids, for example, suggest that the administration attempted to select girls for their virtue and docility. Llanos y Valdés often specified that the girl "should be Spanish," or "one of the voluntarias," or "none of the forzadas." This selectivity may explain why Villarroel found "vagrant" women vegetating in the asylum rather than being placed in outside jobs. In fact, when the young workers failed to satisfy their employers, or when their help was no longer needed, the paupers were returned to the asylum, as was occasionally recorded on the entrance slips.[51]

The Poor House had even less success in rehabilitating its adult inmates. The Confirmation and Communion lists show that the asylum took seriously its duty to bring the undoctrinated masses into the Church. Some, like the 66-year-old mestizo Benito Lázaro de la Fuente, who was confirmed in 1779, had lived in Mexico City all his life without receiving proper religious instruction. In contrast, only a small proportion of the adults were put to work within the asylum—some 8 percent in 1794, for example, if all forty-eight positions for inmate workers were filled by adults. Instead of being trained for new jobs that could prevent their future indigence, the few working adults filled positions for which they were already qualified. Moreover, their gratuities perpetuated the deficiencies of the labor market that had reduced so many to pauperization in the first place. In particular, the payments demonstrate the prevailing wage discrimination against women (table 4). On average, the women received 54.3 pesos per year, compared to 70.8 pesos for the men.[52] Male and female inmates received unequal compensation for comparable work. The female nurse, *portera*, and head cook earned only three-fourths of what was paid to men in those positions, while the female *refectolera* received two-thirds and the female *celadoras* received only half of what was paid to their male counterparts. By reproducing the inequalities in the capital's labor market, the Poor House did little to solve the problem of inadequate wages that plagued female workers in Mexico City. In all fairness, though, the asylum did little to combat the future destitution of the adult males, either. And, with the possible exception of the boys placed as artisans, the inmates' work regime did not open up opportunities for upward mobility—which, in any case, had never been the founders' intention.

In short, even during its prosperous early years the asylum was better at simply sheltering rather than reforming the adult paupers who were the great majority of its inmates. The lack of vocational training may have been partly caused by insufficient funding, as Revillagigedo claimed in 1794, for it cost money to hire master artisans and buy tools and raw materials for the workshops. Yet two more fundamental reasons for the lax discipline are hinted at in 1785 by Villarroel, whose short but vivid critique of the Poor House suggests that he may have visited the asylum.

First, Villarroel blamed the inexperienced director, "a good ecclesiastic, adorned with a Christian heart, zealous, and well intentioned," who ruled the Poor House on his own without a junta or bylaws to help guide him. Villarroel was only half wrong about the absence of bylaws. Although three sets had been submitted to the crown (a fact of which he may have been unaware), they had not yet been approved when he wrote his treatise. Moreover, the casual visitor apparently saw no evidence of the strict regimen prescribed by these statutes. Villarroel was wrong about the absence of a board of directors, for a notation on the margin of a 1785 petition attests to its continued existence.[53] Since Llanos y Valdés did not always follow the viceroy's orders, however, it is probable that he did not follow the board's advice, either. Villarroel was right that Llanos y Valdés was a powerful director, as well as dedicated cleric, who during his nearly eighteen-year tenure put his personal imprint on the asylum. Although he singlehandedly rounded up beggars from the streets of the capital, he was evidently more concerned with providing religious instruction than labor discipline. Indeed, Viera's use of conventual terms in his 1777 portrait of the Poor House, with paupers "cloistered" and governed by a "superior," shows that to some contemporary eyes the Poor House under Llanos y Valdés resembled a monastic rather than a carceral regime. Although Viera acknowledged that some inmates were forcibly confined, like Villarroel he considered them luxuriously housed rather than degraded. Thus, the staff, from the director on down, may have lacked the desire to impose a harsh transformative regime on the inmates.

Second, Villarroel accused the institution of wasting its resources maintaining "in luxury" inmates who should not have been admitted in the first place. He could have mentioned the pobres vergonzantes as a group whose presence modified the original Poor House plan. Instead, he focused on the "idle, vagrant women . . . more apt for procreation or domestic service than to fatten in the Hospicio," who spent their days "cursing their involuntary confinement" while they "consumed the endowment and alms" collected to help the truly needy. Such a regime merely served to "punish poverty," according to Villarroel, while providing "little utility to the state or to the contributors, who do not achieve the true goal of their donations." There may have been some basis for Villarroel's charge that able-bodied women took up resources that could have been spent on the elderly, disabled, and infirm. Although the majority of inmates during this period were men,[54] there were certainly inmates like the incorrigible Indian servant brought by her master or the girl held in the asylum for two years because she left a baptism drunk. In addition, Villarroel may have included the many single mothers in his description. Since the normal penalties for vagrancy applied only to men, the authorities had a difficult time figuring out what to do with disorderly women or mothers who were unemployed though healthy. Reflecting the ambivalence toward female vagrants, Archbishop Lorenzana's 1769 bylaws had proposed setting aside a separate section of the Poor House for "lazy, dissolute, or vagabond women" who needed punishment and rehabilitation. His plan had been rejected by the time the asylum opened. In a 1774 fundraising letter the Poor House board assured potential donors that their contributions would not be used to support the able-bodied,[55] and the 1777 bylaws explicitly excluded female as well as male vagrants. In practice, however, such women found their way to the Poor House. Applying a gendered definition of vagrancy, the staff may even have viewed them less as rogues than as vulnerable and pitiable paupers who were worthy of institutional aid.

Thus, although the Poor House attempted to implement the original experiment to control the poor, it began to be undermined when, as early as its first week, the asylum took on new groups and functions. Its myriad roles were reflected in the widely varying length of the inmates' stays. These can be glimpsed by comparing the ecclesiastical counts of 1779 and 1782.[56] While many of the adults confirmed in 1779 were still in the Poor House to receive Communion in 1782, most of the children had left. To be sure, the Confirmation list is a skewed sample of the Poor House residents because 71 percent of those confirmed were children under 15 and another 21 percent were youths between the ages of 15 and 24. Yet five of the seven older inmates remained to be counted again three years later. Other documents confirm that most children and youths (unless they were disabled) stayed only a short time because they were claimed by relatives, placed as servants or apprentices, or trained to earn a living on their own. The elderly who lacked relatives or patrons—as well as recidivists caught begging after being released from the Poor House with a warning—might remain there for the rest of their lives. Young, healthy adults might stay long enough to recover from a crisis or gain the confidence and skills to start anew—although a few, like María Trinidad Gallardo and her children, might be released only to relapse into destitution and have to return a second time, as noted on an entrance slip for October 10, 1776.[57] Recalcitrant youths might stay on indefinitely because of employers' preferences for the well-behaved *voluntarios* rather than the *forzados*.

CONTAINING THE POOR

The Poor House had therefore become a large, multipurpose institution, punitive for some and beneficent for others. In addition to the beggars for whom it was designed it took in homeless families, the temporarily unemployed, pobres vergonzantes, and, by 1791, pension-paying paupers seeking refuge. At the request of respectable citizens and authorities, it also accepted unruly youths and indigenous prisoners of war. Its clientele had expanded to include not only the diverse pauper inmates themselves but also those who turned to the institution to control juveniles and mecas as well as the employers who used it as a placement agency. In responding to these multiple pressures, however, the asylum compromised its original goals.

The Paupers of the Poor House, 1795

As it entered its third decade, one of the Poor House chaplains produced a remarkable document: a detailed count of the inmates taken on the occasion of the annual Communion on April 12, 1795.[58] The only complete surviving enumeration of the inmate population during the eighteenth century, it lists the name, race, age, marital status, and place of origin of every inmate except eighty-two gentile mecas who could not confess and take Communion (but who are nonetheless counted, unlike in earlier ecclesiastical lists). It even includes babies and children too young to have been confirmed.[59] This census provides the best portrait of the paupers of the Poor House since it opened. It shows how thin the asylum had spread itself by taking on roles that had never been envisioned by its original founders, as well as by taking in paupers from outside the geographical boundaries of the archbishopric of Mexico.

By 1795 the number of incarcerated mecas had risen to eighty-nine, or 11 percent of the Poor House inmates. Seven of these had been converted to Catholicism (four boys aged 10 to 14 and three women aged 24 and 25). The others were only listed as twenty-three male and forty-eight female mecas who were not given names because, since they were not baptized, they lacked a Christian name to list.[60] In addition, the 1795 census listed two female mecas, aged 11 and 30, working as servants for Poor House staff members who had apartments in the building. These "rehabilitated" mecas were no longer counted as inmates but as members of the employees' households. They had become part of the patronage networks that could develop between inmates and staff and temper the repressive thrust of the asylum.

Another group of people incarcerated in the Poor House were forty deserters from the army. They were mostly Spanish, single, and between the ages of 16 and 37. The only officer, Sgt. Don José Núñez, was a 54-year-old widower—the sole don and widower in the group. They came from all over Mexico, with one, José Robles, hailing from Cádiz, Spain. The document gives no information on where they served, why they deserted, or how they arrived in the asylum.[61] Since these soldiers appeared in only one document, they may have been in the Poor House under security awaiting a chain gang to Veracruz or some other location.[62] Apparently held apart from the rest of the inmates, the *soldados desertores* were listed as a separate category after the men and boys. If they were only recent arrivals, that might help explain the jump in the Poor House population from 743 on December 31, 1794, to 820 only three months later. That they were there at all, however, shows how overextended the asylum had become. Moreover, the deserters were unequivocally vagrants: men who were capable of working and whose presence violated the bylaws. Obviously, they could not be given the preferred penalty for vagrancy, which was to be sent into the armed forces from which they had already deserted. Still, their presence (along with the meca prisoners) provides additional proof that the Poor House was accepting "unworthy" paupers whom its founders had wished to exclude.

When the two groups forcibly brought from afar are excluded (since mecas and soldados desertores never begged on Mexico City streets), the 1795 Communion count provides a rare glimpse of who was reduced to destitution in the Mexican capital, and why. Besides the 129 Indian captives and soldiers, there were 691 inmates who represented a broad gamut of Mexico City's paupers. In the twenty years since the founding of the Poor House, this inmate population had changed little in terms of the two variables consistently documented in the earlier counts. Most were still adults, although the proportion of children under 15 (labeled *muchachos* and *muchachas* or in some documents *niños* and *niñas*) had slowly crept up from some 15 to 24 percent. Notwithstanding Villarroel's misogynist portrait of vulgar women "fattening" in the Poor House, a slight majority of the adults (55 percent) were still male. In addition, the 1795 enumeration systematically confirms some intriguing characteristics only hinted at in the earlier impressionistic data, for in several respects the inmates failed to fit prevailing stereotypes of Mexico City's homeless and destitute population.

Table 5.A shows that, even though Indians constituted the lowest class in Mexico City, the majority of inmates in 1795 (52 percent) were of Spanish descent. Only 25 percent were classified as Indian, and another 24 percent came from the variety of caste groups (mostly mestizos, with a few mulattos and *castizos* and one each *pardo* and *negro*). This racial breakdown is remarkably similar to that of the city as a whole in 1790, when 49 percent of the capital's population was enumerated as Spanish, 27 percent caste, and 24 percent Indian. If anything, white paupers were slightly overrepresented in the

TABLE 5   Inmate Characteristics by Sex, 1795

	MALE		FEMALE		ALL		Mexico City (%)
	Number	%	Number	%	Number	%	
A. Race							*1790*
Spanish	192	51	165	52	357	52	49
Caste	94	25	69	22	163	24	27
Indian	89	24	82	26	171	25	24
ALL	375	100	316	100	691	101	100
B. Title							
Don/doña	21	6	45	14	66	10	
Untitled	354	94	271	86	625	90	
ALL	375	100	316	100	691	100	
C. Place of Origin							*1811*
Foreigners	5	1	3	1	8	1	2
Mexican migrants	101	32	83	27	204	30	38
Born in Mexico City	249	66	230	73	479	69	60
ALL	375	99	316	101	691	100	100
D. Marital Status (age 15 and over)							
Single	130	45	96	41	226	43	37
Married	70	24	57	24	127	24	44
Widowed	91	31	83	35	174	33	19
ALL	291	100	236	100	527	100	100
E. Age groups (age 15 and over)							
15–29	47	16	98	42	145	28	43
30–44	63	22	74	31	137	26	33
45–59	97	33	48	20	145	28	16
60 plus	84	29	16	7	100	19	8
ALL	291	100	236	100	527	101	100
F. Mean age (age 15 and over)							
	47.3		34.8		41.7		

Sources: The statistics for the entire city in 1790 come from Humboldt (1966), 1:293. The 1811 statistics come from my sample of the 1811 census, described in Arrom (1985), 271–76.

Note: Totals for 1795 exclude forty soldados desertores and eighty-nine indios mecas (Chichimeca prisoners of war) who never begged on the streets of Mexico City.

asylum. The numerous indigents of Spanish descent demonstrate either that the inmates were not always from the bottom rungs of society or that our view of the lower classes is too simplistic. The correlation between race and class was so weak by the late colonial period that whites were found in every level of society.[63]

Table 5.B shows that even dons and doñas were not immune from destitution, since 10 percent of the Poor House inmates were "respectable" enough to use the honorific title. As might be expected from their higher social status, however, the dons and doñas were exclusively of Spanish descent. Yet most white inmates did not rate an honorific title, and only 18 percent of those listed as Spanish merited this distinction. Only half the dons and doñas were in turn distinguished enough to live apart as pobres vergonzantes, who comprised 5 percent of the inmates in 1795. That the census maintained these differentiations without conflating all whites into one group shows how important these distinctions were to the inmates, the Poor House staff, and the chaplain who took down the information.

The Poor House inmates were also remarkably similar to the capital's population in terms of their place of origin. Although it is reasonable to expect that migrants would be disproportionately represented because of their difficulties in adjusting to city life, table 5.C shows that nearly two-thirds of the pauper inmates were natives of Mexico City. The proportion of migrant inmates was apparently no higher than that of migrants in the city at large. By 1811 (the date of a municipal census that provides information on place of origin, although the independence war had by then increased the influx of migrants), 38 percent of the city's population listed a place of birth outside the capital compared with only 31 percent of the pauper inmates in 1795.[64] Thus, migrants were no more likely to end up in the Poor House than were the city born.

The patterns of migration for those inmates born outside of the capital likewise resembled those of Mexico City's population as a whole.[65] Migrant inmates came from a wide area of Mexico and even from abroad. The foreign migrants—all men—came from Spain (5), Florida (1), the Philippines (1), and France (1). The 199 national migrants whose place of origin could be located (five places, like San Juan or San Juanico, could have been almost anywhere)[66] came from seventeen of Mexico's present-day states.[67] Only the far north, the far south, and the west coast were not represented (unless we include the mecas who were forcibly relocated from the northern states and the deserters who came from all over the realm). As with migrants to the city in general, the majority of inmates came from the cities and small villages close to the capital. One-third came from the present-day state of Mexico alone and half from such villages as Coyoacán, San Angel, and Tacubaya, which are today part of the Federal District. Another 17 percent came from the state of Puebla, and 16 percent from Hidalgo. The city of Puebla, beset with a declining textile industry, accounted for the single largest contingent of migrant inmates, with 21 paupers having been born there.

If gender, ethnic background, and place of origin did not predispose a particular group of people to end up as paupers (or shield them, for that matter), demographic variables did, although they often affected men and women differently. The most obvious reason for pauperization—at least for men—was advanced age. The age breakdown of the inmates in 1795 (excluding the robust soldiers and mecas) was unlike the capital's as a whole. The Poor House sheltered fewer young people, with only 28 percent of the inmates between 15 and 29 years of age, versus 43 percent in the capital (table 5.E). The discrepancy was especially striking among those over 60: the inmates were more than twice as likely to be extremely elderly as the city residents were, since only 8 percent of the capital's population but fully 19 percent of the Poor House inmates had reached that ripe old age. On closer inspection, however, the differences were entirely due to the prevalence of elderly men in the asylum, for 29 percent of the men were over 60 compared with only 7 percent of the women. The average male inmate (based on those 15 or older) was 47.3 years old, or 12.5 years older than the average woman. In fact, the age distribution of the female inmates was similar to that of city residents at large. For men, aging evidently brought the loss of the ability to earn a living as well as the death of family members who could support them. In contrast, women's greater dependence at all ages made them vulnerable to pauperization even when young.

Another feature associated with pauperization, for both men and women, was being single or widowed. Table 5.D shows that the Poor House inmates were married in smaller proportions than city residents (only 24 percent of the adult inmates compared with 44 percent of the city residents).[68] The preponderance in the asylum of single and widowed paupers (43 and 33 percent of adult inmates) makes sense because married people had spouses, in-laws, and often children on whom to rely. Not unexpectedly, most of the married inmates were separated or abandoned (78 percent). Married men without spouses were as prevalent as their female counterparts (19 percent of the male inmates and 18 percent of the female). Thus, family disintegration or loss was an important factor in reducing people to pauperization. Solitary individuals—whether single, widowed, or separated from their spouses—were disproportionately represented in the asylum. Indeed, the absence of family was one of the criteria used to determine the eligibility of certain paupers for institutionalization. As shown by the cases of paupers turned away from the asylum in 1774 and 1776, whenever possible the Poor House staff tried to convince relatives to care for their own.[69]

Yet, if family provided an important resource, it did not always prevent the pauperization of its members. At least sixty-eight family groups resided together in the asylum. These identified family units should be taken as a minimum because, except in the matrimonios and vergonzantes sections, relationships usually have to be inferred from the order of the census listings and from last names.[70] The identified family groups consisted of 14 married couples (5 with children), 48 mothers with at least 70 children, 2 elderly men and 2 elderly women with what appear to be their grandchildren, and 2 sets of siblings. In addition, later documents suggest that two consecutively listed single vergonzante ladies were related in some way, perhaps as aunt and niece.[71] The members of these families represented one of every six adult inmates—a minority, to be sure, yet a significant enough segment of the inmate population to affect the quality of its day-to-day life. Among the adult women the proportion was higher, as one of every five was a mother raising children on her own. For these women, family was a two-edged sword. If lack of family explained the pauperization of some, especially elderly male inmates, for widows and women abandoned by the fathers of their offspring—or fleeing abusive relationships—the very existence of maternal responsibilities contributed to their indigence. Moreover, as shown by the presence of the married couples, even intact families sometimes had to resort to institutionalization.

Most of the "single" mothers had once been married: 54 percent were listed as widows, 33 percent as married (though evidently separated from their husbands), and only 13 percent admitted to being single, or *sin estado*, as that marginal status was termed at the time. Although some single mothers may have claimed the more respectable status of widow, the extremely high proportion of legal marriage among these women nonetheless belies the elite view of rampant "immorality" among the lower classes. So does the rarity of teenaged motherhood. When the age of the oldest child is subtracted from the mother's age, only 12 percent of the mothers appear to have been under twenty when their first children were born. The youngest mother was the married castiza Gertrudis Sambrano, enumerated along with her 20-year-old husband and infant in the section for married couples. Among the "single" mothers, the youngest woman had had her first child when she was seventeen.

The peculiarly female burden of motherhood partly explains the striking gender difference in the age structure of the inmate population. Another reason why the female inmates tended to be younger than the male is that women's opportunities for earning a living were far more restricted than men's. The scarcity of work for women, as well as their comparatively lower earnings, contributed to the difficulty of supporting themselves.[72] Even if Mexican legislators sometimes classified unemployed women as vagrants who were ineligible for institutional aid, the Poor House staff that implemented their policies applied a gendered definition of vagrancy. They evidently found it difficult to turn many young women away, for nearly half the women (42 percent) were between 15 and 29 years of age. Thus, the distinctions between the worthy and the unworthy poor appear to have been more difficult to draw than the Poor House founders had envisioned. In practice, able-bodied women and even "immoral" mothers who had borne children out of wedlock were offered shelter.

Since the lack of alternatives was particularly acute for women of respectable backgrounds, there were many more doñas than dons in the Poor House, with 14 percent of the female inmates using the honorific title compared with only 6 percent of the male (table 5.B). Because educated men had more job opportunities and earning power than their sisters, "genteel" women were more likely to end up impoverished. In a society in which the work force was highly segregated by class and there were very few "honest" jobs for women, some of these women may have considered living in an asylum to be less demeaning than taking jobs usually reserved for their social inferiors. Their brothers experienced a comparable inability to support themselves only with advanced age.

The heightened dependence of genteel women can also be seen in their preponderance among the vergonzantes, for 86 percent of the twenty-one adult vergonzantes were female — more than double the proportion of women among the other inmates. Three of them were wives accompanying their husbands, in two cases with children as well. Three were "single" mothers, two of them listed as married and one as widowed. The other ten distinguished ladies declared themselves to be sin estado. Most of these solitary damsels were surprisingly young. Although two were in their fifties and one was 66 years old, the others were in their twenties or thirties; their average age was only 38. As with the three single mothers, it was the lack of a breadwinner to depend on, rather than old age, that had reduced them to penury. In an earlier era these ladies might have entered one of the capital's seven recogimientos, but since the last retirement home for "virtuous" women had closed in 1794 (the others having become female prisons or schools), the Poor House apparently picked up some of their clientele.[73]

The contrast with the portrait of male vergonzantes is striking, for there were no solitary vergonzante men. The only three adult males were husbands who for some reason could not support their families. The three vergonzante couples were considerably younger than the eleven couples living in the matrimonios section of the asylum. Whereas all but two of the eleven plebeian couples were headed by elderly men, the oldest vergonzante man was only 52 years old, with a 45-year-old wife and 13-year-old daughter. Another, 25-year-old Don Agustín Troncoso, must have suffered from some disability that prevented him from supporting his large family, for he was accompanied by his 24-year-old wife, four young children, and two unmarried sisters. Likewise, some adversity must have befallen the childless 38-year-old Don Manuel Aristorena. Evidently having had some wealth in the past, he and his 31-year-old wife brought a mulatta slave to serve them in the asylum. Unfortunately, the 1795 census provides no hint as to why these relatively young, distinguished couples were living in the Poor House (albeit in private, upstairs apartments) rather than on their own. We do not even know if they were among the pension-paying inmates who began to enter the asylum after 1791.

It is likewise difficult to explain the presence of so many young men in the "common" dormitories of the Poor House. If the majority of male inmates were old enough to suffer some infirmity (55 percent of the men were at least 50 years old), many were in the prime of their lives. Even excluding the robust soldiers and mecas, 28 percent of the male inmates were between the ages of 15 and 39. Thus, a surprising number of draft-age men were institutionalized rather than punished as vagrants or conscripted into military service. It is highly unlikely that all the young men were disabled. The 1795 enumeration only identifies two male inmates as demented and two as *inertos* (possibly paralyzed or dull), but there must have been more, given occasional references in other documents to "half-wits" and epileptics. Still, if data from 1803 are any indication of earlier trends, nearly three-quarters of the inmates were in fact healthy. Men were more likely to be disabled than women, for approximately half the adult men in 1803 were listed as disabled or infirm compared with only one-third of the women.[74] Nonetheless, the other half of the men were institutionalized without a handicap or chronic illness. Some of these healthy young men must have been placed in the Poor House to be reformed or trained. Others must have sought shelter while they faced a temporary setback, evidence that the asylum's staff was more sympathetic to the plight of the unemployed than the legislators who classified them as vagrants. Thus, even though the male inmates as a group were older and more disabled than the women, they too were a heterogeneous group.

The inmates' resemblance to the capital's residents, except for the misfortune of not having a source of income, supports Frederick Shaw's contention, for a later period, that very little differentiated the "honest laboring poor" from the léperos.[75] His study of the Vagrants Tribunal from 1828 to 1852 suggests that a crisis such as the loss of a job, a death in the family, or an illness or disability—to which we might add aging, for men, or losing a breadwinner for women—could easily cause the destitution of the artisan, laborer, shopkeeper, peddler, or servant who already lived close to the margin of subsistence. Such a fate could also befall the *gente de bien*, especially the women who had so few options for supporting themselves without an inheritance or relatives. Since the poor comprised approximately three-fourths of the capital's population,[76] it is little wonder that the paupers who ended up in the Poor House shared so many characteristics with the city's population as a whole. The 1795 census captures a portrait of one of the last moments, however, when the asylum was able to serve such a varied clientele.

Mounting Problems during the Third Decade

Its third decade was a difficult one for the Poor House. Every viceroy from the Count of Revillagigedo, Juan Vicente de Güemes (in 1794), to Miguel de la Grúa Talamanca y Branciforte (in 1797), Miguel José de Azanza (in 1800), and Félix Berenguer de Marquina (in 1803) reported on its plight in his *Instructions* to his successor, and all concurred that its principal problem was insufficient revenues. As Marquina explained, it was no longer possible to "banish from the churches, streets, and public places the swollen number of beggars of both sexes, some true and some false, which necessity obliges us to overlook and tolerate, without trying to confine them and give them work in the Poor House, whose income and funds are not enough to maintain them."[77] When the Prussian scientist Alexander von Humboldt visited the asylum in 1803, he found an "establishment in which both order and cleanliness may be seen, but little industry."[78] The institution housed fewer inmates than at any time in the past, and the Poor House experiment was in jeopardy.

The magnitude of the asylum's fiscal crisis is illustrated in the 1804 report submitted by its administrator, Juan Antonio de Araujo. Despite its inconsistencies and information that occasionally contradicts other sources, the report shows that the Poor House's expenses of 35,027 pesos for 1803 exceeded its income by 4,508 pesos (see table 6). On top of that it was saddled with 13,782 pesos in old debts, mostly to its director and food suppliers.[79] Moreover, it was barely controlling expenditures. It spent approximately the same on 555 inmates as had been spent on 780 in 1780. Although we do not have a detailed budget breakdown for 1780, it is likely that much of this growth was due to inflation in food prices during the last quarter of the eighteenth cen-

13 FIRST PAGE OF A DETAILED REPORT ON THE STATE OF THE POOR HOUSE. This document was submitted by the asylum's administrator, Juan Antonio de Araujo, in 1804. It contains comprehensive statistics on the institution from the time it opened on March 19, 1774, to December 31, 1803. Unfortunately, comparable data are rarely available for other years. Information on the Poor House is particularly spotty during the times of its worst crises, especially those that accompanied independence, the Mexican-American War, and the Reforma.

TABLE 6   Annual Income and Expenses, 1803 (in pesos)

Source	Pesos	Percentage
A. Expenses[a]		
Food	17,590.7	50
Medicine	1,221.6	3
Salaries	3,667.2	11
Inmate wages	869.8	2
Divine cult	335.4	1
Office	98.2	
Materials	6,855.5	20
Clothing	285.9	1
Tools	1,082.2	3
Building	3,020.2	9
TOTAL	35,026.7	100
B. Income		
Royal lottery	12,000	40
Tablas de carnicería	2,500	8
Interest income[b]	2,817.2	9
Rental, two houses	926.7	3
Funeral attendance	2,100.7	7
Sale of cloth	951	3
Zúñiga's estate	1,300	4
Zúñiga for infirmary	3,020.3	10
Regular pledges	3,317.9	11
Pensions	934.9	3
Alms	500	2
TOTAL	30,368.7	100

[a] Omits 13,782.2 pesos in debt repayment.

[b] Interest on 56,343.6 of assets. Another 11,535.3 pesos in interest payments on other assets had been suspended.

tury.[80] By 1803 the asylum was spending some 32 pesos a year on food for each inmate, an expense that represented half its budget. Another problem was that some costs were inelastic: no matter how few inmates it housed, the asylum had to repair the aging building and pay the salaries of its six live-in employees (the administrator and his assistant, two chaplains, the mayordomo, and the rectora) as well as the retainers of a doctor, surgeon/pharmacist,

TABLE 7   Poor House Employees and Salaries, 1769–1803 (annual salaries in pesos)

	1769 (Prescribed)	1777 (Prescribed)	1795 (Type)	1803 (Paid)
Administrator	1,000[a]	1,000[a]	live-in	1,000
First chaplain	500[a]		live-in	500
Second chaplain	none		live-in	400
Assistant administrator	none	none	live-in	556
Mayordomo	—	300	live-in	300
Rectora		120[a]	live-in	160[b]
Master Artisan			live-in	—
Master Artisan			live-in	—
Master Artisan			live-in	—
Surgeon/pharmacist			live-in	300
Doctor			—	180
Bleeder			—	96
Secretary		200	—	200
Scribe		300	—	50
Accountant			—	50
TOTAL				3,792

Sources: Bylaws, 1769 and 1777; 1795 Confirmation list; 1804 report, f. 11.
[a] In addition to their salaries, the bylaws specified that these employees were to receive free lodging in the Poor House building plus rations of unspecified value.
[b] The rectora is the only employee noted in the 1804 report as receiving rations.

bleeder, secretary, scribe, and accountant (table 7). If these wages had not risen since they were first set nearly thirty years earlier, neither had they declined in response to the shrinking inmate population.[81]

Araujo tried to put the best possible spin on the budget figures. He emphasized how much the Poor House had saved over the years by producing some of its own food and clothing. He pointed out that it had economized by replacing with knowledgeable inmates the portero (gatekeeper), the purveyor, three *mozos* (assistants), the master weaver, and the "master of all trades" it had "once" hired. Indeed, three *maestros* (master artisans) listed as live-in employees in the 1795 Communion count had disappeared by 1803, further proof that vocational training had declined.[82] Still, the gratuities took up a large portion of the budget: the 869 pesos paid to inmate workers in 1803 was considerably more than the approximately 516 pesos they received in 1778. Moreover, the savings on master artisans is misleading since it reflected the elimination of potentially profitable workshops whose lost earnings put the Poor House even deeper in the hole. Although 20 percent of the budget was still spent on materials for the looms and 2 percent on tools, by 1803 the sale of cotton, wool, and other textiles manufactured by its inmates brought in only 951 pesos (table 6), much less than the several thousand pesos contributed in earlier years.[83]

Another factor, which Araujo failed to mention, was that institutionalizing paupers had proved to be phenomenally expensive. In 1780 alone the Poor House spent 36,079 pesos,[84] an annual average of 46 per inmate. This sum was considerably more than many hardworking residents of Mexico City earned in a good year. For example, a worker who toiled at piecework rates six days a week in the huge Royal Cigar Factory was lucky to earn 35 pesos— and would still be thankful to have steady employment.[85] By 1803 the annual cost per inmate had increased to 63 pesos,[86] putting it even further out of line with working-class wages, which appear to have remained flat.[87] Thus, the efficiencies which the Poor House founders hoped to achieve by placing paupers in a central asylum had failed to materialize. The extremely high cost of confinement made it an inadequate response to widespread poverty.

Yet the budget deficits were not its only problem. The Poor House had become dangerously overextended by taking in too many "unworthy" paupers. Police logs analyzed by Michael Scardaville show that by its third decade the Poor House routinely took in petty criminals picked up for minor infractions such as intoxication and curfew violations. Equally divided among men and women, the court-confined inmates were mostly elderly white or mestizo paupers who did not have steady jobs. Only 4 percent of those arrested for vagrancy ended up in the Poor House because the courts placed most vagrants as apprentices to learn a trade or sentenced them work in bakeries or textile mills.[88] In the single year of 1798 those sent to the asylum constituted less than 1 percent of the 4,352 people arrested by the municipal police. The 30 petty criminals sent to the Poor House that year were also a small proportion of its inmates, perhaps 3 to 4 percent. Yet they were enough, when combined with the mecas, deserters, and juvenile delinquents, to threaten to change the character of the asylum. Indeed, by 1798 Viceroy Branciforte felt it necessary to ban the practice of using the Poor House as a prison. On February 6 he decreed that the asylum "is not a house of correction and punishment, but rather one of charity, whose scarce funds barely cover the institute's goal, which is to shelter the truly needy and disabled."[89] With this admonishment the viceroy hoped to refocus the Poor House on its original target group of "true" beggars.

The asylum also experienced difficulties with its governing board. In 1794

Revillagigedo described a functioning junta, albeit with a slightly different composition from the one appointed in 1772.[90] The only problem Revillagigedo noted was that the corregidor should be a member. Soon thereafter the board of directors collapsed, perhaps because the original six-member board had ballooned to forty-eight, evidently too many to function efficiently.[91] A completely new board was created on January 20, 1800. An article in the *Gazeta de México* curtly reported that the junta was "reborn from the ashes in which various incidents buried it, which are not of this time and place" to recount. It added that the viceroy had "reassumed" the presidency of the board, an indication that earlier he had lost it.[92]

There were also problems with the Poor House administration. Viceroy Marquina's *Instrucción* of January 1, 1803, hinted at a confrontation with the asylum's administrator and even recommended that the next viceroy try to replace "a particular penniless administrator who seeks the job to support himself and his family" with some "distinguished, powerful, and pious" gentleman of independent means who would serve without salary.[93] In addition, there must have been a conflict with Don Simón María de la Torre, who had served as director since 1798. Torre presented his resignation to the junta in April of 1803, citing some "measure" he had proposed that had not been accepted. The resignation evidently did not go through, since he was still at his post in 1806.[94] Unfortunately, the surviving documentation of the period offers little explanation of these troubles.

The Poor House made it through this decade as well as it did largely because of generous contributions from Capt. Francisco de Zúñiga, a wealthy member of the Poor House board. Captain Zúñiga provides a rare example of rags to riches upward mobility. The story of his life, as recounted by the late-nineteenth-century historian Manuel Rivera Cambas, reads like fiction. Yet key parts are confirmed by the captain's last will and testament. Zúñiga was born to a humble Indian couple in Tula—so humble that in his will he declared himself not only a *natural del Pueblo de Tula* but also an *hijo natural* whose parents were never married by the Church. Indeed the notary, who had automatically penned the standard phrase "legitimate son of legitimate matrimony" in the opening line of Zúñiga's will, crossed it out to insert the declaration of illegitimacy, so unusual among his propertied clientele. On his travels as a muleteer Zúñiga discovered a mine, the Real de Catorce, which brought him fabulous wealth. Eventually he was appointed a captain in the prestigious Dragones de San Carlos regiment as well as a member of the Poor House board, apparently representing the Merchants' Guild. The captain's fortune and position did not buy him happiness, according to Rivera Cambas, for Zúñiga's proposal of marriage to a noble damsel was rejected despite his riches. Supposedly seeking solace in philanthropy, he devoted his entire fortune to charitable works favoring "the divine cult," the imprisoned, and the poor. Had he married and had children, he would presumably have left his entire estate to his family instead.[95]

The Poor House was the prime beneficiary of Zúñiga's largesse. Before his death on November 30, 1797, the captain donated some 27,000 pesos to help pay immediate operating expenses, much of it apparently used to repair the crumbling building, which was now a quarter century old.[96] Zúñiga also bequeathed the asylum vast sums of money. Yet some calamity, which Viceroy Marquina referred to but did not describe in his 1803 *Instrucción*, prevented the institution from "enjoying the favorable results that Zúñiga had intended." For one thing, much of his donation was earmarked for his favorite project, the creation of a Patriotic School in the asylum, which would serve as a boarding school for orphaned children. Construction of the new wing began in 1799 and had consumed at least 420,000 pesos by the time the school opened in 1806.[97] Zúñiga had not forgotten the rest of the asylum, to which he left a third of the products of his mines, valued at 250,000 pesos at the time of his death. The Poor House never saw a penny of this income, however, apparently because the mines ceased producing.[98] For a while it even looked as if it would fail to obtain the 250,000 endowment that Zúñiga had left for the Patriotic School. Just why remains a mystery. Marquina obliquely mentioned "resistance and quarrels" which he had done his best to smooth over.[99] A few months later Humboldt noted that "a rich merchant lately bequeathed to it by his testament six millions of francs, which the royal treasury laid hold of, on the promise of paying five percent for it."[100] Eventually the Poor House secured the regular payment of the interest from this endowment. Meanwhile the institution was forced to contract in an atmosphere poisoned with recriminations and discord.

Two reports submitted by the embattled administrator Araujo in 1803 and 1804 show that the number of inmates had dropped precipitously, from 820 in 1795 to 464 on the last day of 1801, 609 a year later, and 555 a year after that. Although the population of Poor House residents fluctuated considerably from year to year (a reminder of the risks of drawing conclusions from the data for any one day), the downward trend is clear. The asylum still managed to provide adequate care for the remaining paupers, as is suggested in the mortality rates available for 1802 and 1803, when only 4 to 6 percent died despite the many elderly paupers who came to be comforted in their last years (table 8).[101] By the opening of the nineteenth century, however, the Poor House was a pale shadow of its former self.

As the Poor House took in fewer paupers, its repressive function weak-

TABLE 8   Inmate Totals and Turnover, 1801–3

	Men	Boys	Women	Girls	All
December 31, 1801	180	78	175	31	464
Entered in 1802	225	90	282	90	688
Left in 1802	151	74	195	50	470 (41%)
Died in 1802	34[a]	—	39[a]	—	73 (6%)
December 31, 1802	220	94	224	71	609
Entered in 1803	282	84	287	54	707
Left in 1803	280	103	239	82	704 (53%)
Died in 1803	31	4	18	4	57 (4%)
December 31, 1803	191	71	254	39	555

[a] The report does not specify whether those who died in 1802 were adults or children, only whether they were male or female. I have arbitrarily listed them as adults.

ened. It probably stopped taking in petty criminals sentenced by municipal courts after Viceroy Branciforte banned that practice in 1798. No deserters ever again appeared in the asylum's records, and by the time of the next inmate enumeration in 1808 the number of mecas had declined from eighty-nine to fifty-one. At the same time the Poor House reduced its emphasis on disciplining beggars, although it did not totally abandon the policy of forcible confinement. The 1803 statistics, which for the first time document how many inmates were forzados and how many voluntarios, show that a substantial 40 percent had been forcibly interned (table 9.A).[102] The men were most likely to have been coerced, with 44 percent of the male inmates classified as "forced" compared with only 35 percent of the women. Yet, when we focus on the other side of the coin—the proportion of "voluntaries"—it is evident that the majority of inmates, even among the men, had sought refuge on their own. Moreover, given the dramatic reduction of the inmate population, the Poor House cannot have been aggressively rounding up beggars, a fact confirmed by Marquina's comments as well as by the many contemporary observers (including Humboldt and Araujo himself) who noted that the capital was once again beset by mendicity.

The beleaguered Poor House contained slightly more women and children than in the past. Although the summary statistics for 1801–3 are not directly comparable to those of 1795 (e.g., omitting information on race), they show that in most respects the inmates were similar to those of the late eighteenth century. As before, the asylum housed inmates of all ages, with

TABLE 9   Portrait of Poor House Inmates, December 31, 1803

	MALE		FEMALE		ALL	
	Number	%	Number	%	Number	%
A. Entrance Status						
Forced	116	44	104	35	220	40
Voluntary	146	56	189	65	335	60
B. Age Groups						
1–7	15	6	25	9	40	7
8–20	81	31	83	28	164	29
21–40	55	21	98	33	153	28
41–60	78	30	65	22	143	26
61–90	33	13	22	8	55	10
C. Health						
Healthy	176	67	224	76	400	72
Impaired	86	33	69	24	155	28
Blind	25		23		48	
Epileptic	17		24		41	
Crippled	16		6		22	
Paralyzed	17		7		24	
Chronically ill	11		9		20	
ALL	262	100	293	100	555	100

the men tending to be more elderly than the women (table 9.B). It sheltered healthy as well as disabled paupers, with the majority of the handicapped being blind or epileptic, and smaller numbers suffering from paralysis, crippling or chronic illnesses (table 9.C). It experienced a similar high turnover rate, with approximately twice the number of inmates passing through in one year as were there on any given day (table 8). Most of the inmates were still adults. However, women and children together represented between 61 and 66 percent of the inmates in 1801–3, compared with 57 percent in 1795. The growing proportion of children continued a gradual trend already evident in the 1780s and 1790s, as those under fifteen rose from 11 percent of the first week's inmates to 16 percent in 1780 and 21 percent in 1795. In 1801–3 they fluctuated between 20 and 27 percent of the asylum's residents. By 1802–3, women were in the majority, representing between 51 and 57 percent of the adults. The Poor House clientele was therefore becoming increasingly dependent.

It would be a mistake to conclude from these changes that the asylum was simply refocusing on its initial priorities. Although it shed some extraneous functions, such as housing petty criminals and deserters, it also reduced its impact on the capital's street people—the principal group for which it had been established. Moreover, it seems to have maintained its commitment to the vergonzantes. Indeed, Francisco Sedaño, whose diary described the Poor House in 1806, asserted that the asylum was designed to shelter beggars and vergonzantes; he was apparently oblivious to the fact that the latter were not among the original target clientele.[103] As the Poor House took in pension-paying inmates after 1791, it also increased its focus on caring for a slightly "higher" class of pauper whose relatives could afford to pay their keep. In 1803 the Poor House received a substantial 935 pesos from its pensioners; at the monthly rate of 4 to 5 pesos noted in the daily register for 1807–8,[104] this sum would have provided for some twenty pensioned inmates. Thus, the Poor House was increasingly catering to inmates who were not the poorest of the poor.

The growth in the proportion of children shows that the asylum was acquiring a new function. The Poor House came under pressure to take in orphans after a royal directive, issued for Spain and its dominions on New Year's Eve 1797, ordered children over the age of six to leave all orphanages and, if no one wanted them, to be transferred to poorhouses to learn a trade.[105] Yet the presence of children had begun to rise long before King Charles IV issued his edict. Rather than simply responding to the order, it is more likely that the Poor House staff shared the king's heightened concern for children, the most helpless kind of pauper—and one that was easier to mold than the adults who had proven so difficult to transform. Zúñiga's project of adding a boarding school for orphans also preceded the royal edict, which was issued after the benefactor's death. Perhaps the increasing emphasis on children also reflects the demands of Mexico City's paupers, for some homeless youths may have welcomed shelter and tolerated confinement in ways that adult street people did not.

Conclusion

If the Poor House experiment was reasonably successful during its first few years, it never worked exactly as planned. From the start the "kindler, gentler" goals of traditional charity competed with the asylum's disciplinary function, as the Poor House took in unexpected groups of paupers in addition to the elderly and disabled beggars it was designed to serve. Pressure from the "solemn poor," who had never begged on the city streets, as well as from young, unemployed men and women and homeless families, began to modify the original plan. So did pressures from well-to-do citizens and authorities who asked the asylum to take in juvenile delinquents, petty criminals, prisoners of war, and, at least on one occasion, military deserters. Although the Poor House attempted to accommodate the multiple demands placed on it, it proved much better at providing lodging than at reforming its inmates. Thus, a fundamental goal of the original project remained unfulfilled.

During its first two decades the Poor House was nonetheless large enough to confine many of the city's bothersome beggars alongside the other groups. Thus, in 1781 the director could claim that the asylum had reduced mendicity in the Mexican capital. Although it began suffering from budgetary shortfalls, the Poor House functioned without severe restrictions until its third decade. Then, as its financial situation deteriorated, the asylum retrenched, not only by taking in fewer paupers but also by reducing the diversity of people and purposes it served. In the process its priorities shifted even further, from controlling the poor to assisting the capital's most vulnerable women and children as well as genteel paupers fallen on hard times.

In his 1804 report its administrator boasted that the Poor House had served 24,819 paupers during its first twenty-nine years. He likewise boasted that it had fulfilled its religious goals by teaching its inmates Christian doctrine: "Every year since March 19, 1774, in which this saintly house opened, we have not lacked for paupers of 2, of 6, 8, 18, and even 60 years who had never confessed in their lives; we consequently had to give them an instructor who could teach them the basics of Christian doctrine so that the Fathers could confess them." Yet he did not boast about retraining them to become productive citizens, for in that arena the asylum's successes were limited to adolescents rather than adults. Nor did he boast of its impact on reducing mendicity, where the Poor House had evidently failed.

Like all good bureaucrats requesting money, Araujo attributed the immediate crisis entirely to a decline in operating funds. Yet his cover letter to the 1804 report also hints at additional reasons for the decline in the asylum's effectiveness: "In the thirty years and one month that I have managed this saintly house," — presumably as assistant administrator at first, when he began serving under Elizalde at age 25 [106] — "I have seen paupers who daily amassed in the churches and streets 12 reales, 2 pesos 3 reales, and even four pesos by pretending to be crippled or blind and who, upon entering this house, could suddenly see, stand up, and put aside their crutches. . . . Of these, Excellent Sir, few are brought to this House because they have money with which to free themselves in the prison and with their payments have bought off the sentinels so that, although they see them begging, they do not arrest them, and the only ones who are brought are those who do not pay them off." Indeed, he added, even when "legitimate beggars" are picked up "and deposited in prison, they are never transferred to the Poor House . . . because the subordinates hide them and give them liberty."[107]

This statement suggests that the Poor House experiment was foundering not only because of financial problems but also because it was contested by many of the capital's residents. According to Araujo's account, beggars were resisting internment and policemen and prison wardens were refusing to cooperate (or at least they were willing to collude with the beggars by accepting their bribes). The decline of private contributions also suggests that the capital's wealthy had lost their enthusiasm for the Poor House project. Instead of channeling donations to the central institution, they continued to dispense alms directly to those who solicited them. Indeed, by 1800 the Mexico City authorities had become so frustrated with the number of beggars spawned by the almsgivers that they began to restrict the right to give alms in the decree forbidding godparents from distributing the volo at baptisms.[108] Yet mendicity remained as good a business as ever. Thirty years after the Poor House experiment was launched, it had failed to make significant inroads into the "moral economy" of begging.

In many ways the Poor House functioned less like an oppressive "total" institution than like a traditional asylum devoting a large portion of its resources to sheltering the groups served in the past by charity: "shamefaced" persons, vulnerable women, and children.[109] It did not consistently enforce the strict regimen described in its bylaws. Neither did it filter out all the "unworthy" poor. The Poor House staff was evidently more compassionate than the legislators, who would have denied assistance to the healthy unemployed, including "single" mothers. The older idea embodied in the recogimientos—that unattached women needed to live in a cloistered environment—survived in the Poor House even as the retirement homes themselves disappeared. So did the centuries-old view that the vergonzantes deserved special assistance. Especially after the departure of Llanos y Valdés, who had conducted an energetic personal campaign against begging, the asylum's staff responded more to humanitarian aims based on timeworn assumptions than to the modern goal of disciplining the poor. Thus, they permitted the Poor House experiment to be shaped by the demands of its willing clients as well as by their own notions of who constituted the worthy poor.

In the face of such multiple impediments to imposing the original plan, the reforming zeal of many enlightened officials increasingly gave way to sober realism. Viceroy Marquina, for one, no longer shared his predecessors' optimism that beggars could be banished from the streets or that future poverty could be eradicated. By 1801 he had concluded that there would never be a Poor House wealthy enough to confine "all of the eligible poor." [110] Yet his pessimism was not universal. Over the next five years the asylum was reorganized under a new set of statutes designed to help it attain its goals of deterring vagrancy and rehabilitating paupers. It would never again be the institution, however, that was envisioned by its founders in 1774.

{ 4 }

REFORM OF THE POOR HOUSE,

1806–1811

The Poor House was reformed with great fanfare in 1806. In his diary chronicling unusual events in the late colonial capital, Francisco Sedaño noted the inauguration of its Patriotic School for orphans on July 1. He described a splendid ceremony presided over by the viceroy, Don José de Iturrigaray, and the vicereine, Doña María Inés de Jáuregui y Aróstegui. A "sparkling" audience was in attendance. The Escuela Patriótica opened with the benediction of its chapel and a solemn Mass, after which were introduced to their halls the boys and girls who would there be raised and educated under the direction of a Junta de Caridad composed of the principal gentlemen of Mexico."[1] The *Gazeta de México* deemed the event worthy of a special supplement, published the next day.[2] After sketching the history of the asylum, it offered a lengthy account of the inauguration that reproduced the flowery speeches given by the viceroy; the Poor House board's vice president, Don Ciriaco González Carbajal; and its secretary, Don Juan Francisco de Azcárate. It also publicized a contest in which the board offered two prizes of 200 pesos each for the best essays eulogizing Don Fernando Ortiz Cortés, its founder, and Captain Don Francisco de Zúñiga, the philanthropist who had funded the Patriotic School addition and endowed it in perpetuity.

The importance of the event in the life of the capital is reflected both in the groups that participated in the ceremony and in its high public profile.[3] A 7 A.M. Mass, blessing the "magnificent" new chapel, was sung by Dr. Don Francisco Beye Cisneros, abbot of the Colegiata de Guadalupe and one of the four executors of Zúñiga's estate. At 9 A.M. the viceroy left the Royal Palace with his retinue, accompanied by the city council in full regalia. The procession marched ten blocks to the Poor House, where it was met by the members of its board and a company of grenadiers that rendered the accustomed honors. Afterward followed speeches, a Mass of thanksgiving, and the opening of the school, attended by representatives of the city's churches, tribunals, schools, and other corporations, its "distinguished citizens," and its "principal ladies." Then fifty boys and thirty girls were taken to their new quarters by the fifty gentlemen and thirty ladies who, led by the viceregal couple, had volunteered to become their godparents. Thus dawned a "brilliant era" for the Poor House thirty-two years after its foundation.

The ceremony symbolized the revitalization of the ailing asylum. The Patriotic School was part of a larger effort to reform the Poor House. It was simultaneously placed under a revised set of bylaws, the "Prospecto de la nueva forma de gobierno político y económico del Hospicio de Pobres de esta Capital," reorganized into four departments, and entrusted to the new board of directors—all with the approval of Charles IV, generous "Father of the Poor."[4] With its physical plant nearly doubled by the Patriotic School wing, the renovated Poor House was designed to serve sixteen hundred paupers at a time. Enjoying two new endowments from Zúñiga's estate, the asylum was also fortified by a fundraising drive to assure its ability to deliver the enhanced services.

The reform resurrected the goal of clearing beggars and vagrants from the streets of the capital city. A viceregal decree of June 25, 1806, reiterated the ban on begging and again mandated the confinement of those caught soliciting alms (after the "imposters," or vagrants, were weeded out and separately punished).[5] The forcible internment of beggars became effective on July 1, thus coinciding with the inaugural ceremonies and the publication of the new bylaws. The revival—and improvement—of the original Poor House experiment led Azcárate to declare July 1 a "glorious day that will never be erased from Mexican memory." It would assure "the felicity of the public" by exterminating the plague of mendicity while "educating the populace" and promoting "industrial arts and manufactures." Echoing his claims, the *Gazeta* predicted the end of destitution and "the shameful nakedness [of the poor], the blackest blot on this handsome metropolis."[6]

This day did indeed signal a turning point in the asylum's history, though not the one envisioned in the inaugural speeches. Its reorganization into four departments was designed to separate the inmates by age and needs so that the Poor House could deliver more specialized, and thereby more effective, services. It enlarged the institution's mission as well. If the Department of Worthy Paupers resembled the original asylum, the three other departments represented new functions: the Patriotic School was a boarding school for orphaned children; the Department of Correction was a reformatory for delinquent youths of both sexes; and the Department of Secret Births was a maternity ward where respectable women who had strayed could give birth clandestinely. Yet this ambitious agenda was more than the Poor House could fulfill. Although given equal space in the 1806 bylaws, the four departments were never equal partners. The Department of Correction folded soon after it opened, and the Department of Secret Births remained small, while the school flourished from the start. By expanding what had been an ancillary function of the eighteenth-century asylum, the Patriotic School initiated its transformation from an institution that primarily served adults to one that eventually served only children. Along the way, the disciplining of the capital's paupers was abandoned. In retrospect, July 1, 1806, was a turning point but one that marked an important step toward undermining rather than strengthening the original Poor House experiment.

Origins of the Poor House Reform

Some of the new initiatives mirrored trends in contemporary Europe. The school closely followed the model of the identically named Patriotic Schools that proliferated in Spain during the 1780s. These schools reflected the enlightened view that pauper children needed primary education instead of just apprenticeship. In Mexico City, the new philosophy was reflected in a 1786 directive (issued in the midst of the Year of Hunger, when thousands of children roamed about, begging in the streets) that required convents and parishes to provide free education in "pious schools."[7] A second innovation, the division of the Poor House into separate departments for different kinds of inmates who were isolated from each other, was part of a larger tendency toward specialization in the delivery of welfare services.

To some extent, then, the 1806 reforms represented attempts by a new generation of reformers to update Ortiz Cortés's original project. To some extent, they also ratified modifications that had already taken place when the eighteenth-century Poor House took in children, juvenile delinquents, and genteel ladies in violation of its original bylaws. Moreover, they illustrate the degree to which the Church had dropped out of the partnership with the state and private sector that supported the Poor House. In contrast with their prominent role in founding the asylum three decades earlier, ecclesiastical officials were notably absent from the reform effort, although they did bless it.

The creation of a Patriotic School had been in the works for at least a decade. It was the favored project of the Poor House board member and benefactor Zúñiga, who spent a fortune to construct and endow a large school

14 PATRIOTIC SCHOOL
FOUNDER FRANCISCO DE
ZÚÑIGA. This oil painting was
hung in the Poor House to
commemorate the donor who
generously endowed a boarding
school for orphans in the
asylum. The Patriotic School
quickly became the core of the
institution. Zúñiga's life is a rare
rags to riches story, as the
humble Indian muleteer
discovered a mine that gave him
great wealth and earned him a
position on the Poor House
board. Zúñiga did not live to see
the opening of the Patriotic
School on July 1, 1806.

attached to the Poor House building. Yet the new boarding school was not just one man's project. The *Gazeta* credits González Carbajal, oidor decano of the Audiencia, with first proposing the separation of children from adults and persuading Zúñiga to fund this worthy endeavor. Don Simón de la Torre, director of the Poor House and the administrative executor of Zúñiga's estate, pushed the project through after the philanthropist's death in 1797.[8] Azcárate, city attorney and honorary *regidor* of the city council, obtained royal authorization for the school. The three men served on the drafting committee, which wrote the bylaws for the reformed asylum, and then continued as active members of the newly constituted Poor House board.[9] Evidently, these distinguished gentlemen were highly committed to establishing the Patriotic School.

We know very little about the impetus for the other reforms beyond the skeletal history provided in the *Gazeta* article. It seems that when Azcárate began applying for royal approval of the Patriotic School, he was told that the king wanted the Mexico City Poor House to follow the model of the Casa de Misericordia of Cádiz, which was divided into four departments and governed by a small (and thus presumably efficient) board of directors.[10] Azcárate proceeded to reorganize the institution along these lines. A new board, the Junta de Caridad, was appointed on January 20, 1800, to replace the old Junta Real. After receiving royal approval on March 20, 1801, it oversaw the revision of the bylaws. It did not become officially responsible for the Poor House until July 1806, however, when the old board was formally disbanded.

Although royal approval of the Poor House reform is said to have been granted because the bylaws copied the statutes of the Cádiz poorhouse,[11] the Mexican board in fact exercised considerable discretion in adopting the Spanish model. The board followed the lead of Cádiz by adding a Department of Correction, though without any enthusiasm. It substituted a Department of Secret Births—an entirely Mexican innovation—for the Cádiz Department for Foundlings. It apparently made this substitution at the last minute, arguing that Mexico City already had a separate Foundling Home.[12] Even the composition of the governing board, which supposedly followed the Cádiz formula to the letter, was different. Section 5 of the "Prospecto" emphasized that, "like the one that governs the Casa de Misericordia de Cádiz," the Junta de Caridad would be composed of a vice president, two city councilmen, one member of the ecclesiastical chapter, the most senior priest from the cathedral, the city attorney, and twenty *vocales*. These protestations were deceiving, for the new junta also included the members of the old governing board, along with "other distinguished individuals worthy of serving." The bylaws explained that, since vacancies would not be filled, the board would eventually be reduced to the prescribed twenty-six members.[13] In 1806, however, it numbered forty-eight gentlemen serving life terms, who divided among themselves the responsibility for supervising the asylum and its employees (see appendix 4).[14] Individual members were assigned to serve as secretary, treasurer, and accountant; to oversee each of the four departments, the physical plant, and the provision of food and clothing; and to solicit contributions. Indeed, fundraising was such an important part of their duties that twenty-five members shared this task, taking turns to cover each week of the year as well as to approach the major corporations in the capital city. Moreover, the viceroy served as the president of the board, a feature that further distinguished it from the one in Cádiz. The reformed Mexico City Poor House was consequently far from a carbon copy of the one in the Spanish port.

The New Poor House in Theory

The division of the Poor House into four departments represented an effort to separate its multiple functions, with the Department of Worthy Paupers becoming more purely a homeless shelter, the Patriotic School concentrating on preventing future poverty, the Department of Correction focusing on disciplining the recalcitrant, and the Department of Secret Births specializing in obstetrical services. Yet the reform also brought an expansion in the asylum's mission and clientele. Although the Poor House was originally authorized to take in the children of inmates while they were institutionalized, the 1777 bylaws explicitly stated that "it is not the principal role of this House to take in orphans." Likewise, the schooling of children was only a minor part of the eighteenth-century Poor House. Its bylaws provided for rudimentary instruction in reading and writing offered by a knowledgeable inmate rather than a professional teacher, but only for the most "alert and intelligent children" and only until they were old enough to serve as apprentices in the institution's workshops.[15] Moreover, although pregnant paupers had previously come to the asylum to give birth, the maternity ward reached a new group since it was designed exclusively for women of Spanish descent who were not necessarily indigent.

THE DEPARTMENT OF WORTHY PAUPERS The goals of the Department of Worthy Paupers had changed little since it was first envisioned—as the entire Poor House—nearly half a century earlier; that is why the "Prospecto" also referred to this department simply as the Hospicio. Since school-age children and youths were supposed to be placed in the two new departments, the reform restored the original focus on adults, which had become diluted in the late eighteenth century as the proportion of children in the asylum grew.

The "Prospecto" explained that "because all individuals in society cannot be well off" the department for the verdaderos pobres would take in those "deserving of public compassion." These were the elderly, chronically ill, and disabled who could not earn a living. Vagrants were to be excluded, as before, and forced to work for the good of society in the army, public works, arsenals, or northern colonies. Explicitly prohibiting any authority from using the Poor House for punishment (except for the juvenile delinquents in the correctional department), the bylaws mandated that any such inmate must be transferred elsewhere.

As before, the asylum was to assist "legitimate" beggars in all their spiritual and temporal needs as well as instruct them in the "mysteries of religion" and put them to work producing textiles, shoes, hats, boots, and other apparel. The workshops were justified—and required for all those of both sexes who were capable of working—not to "establish a profitable commercial house" but to "banish idleness" and "promote popular education." The manufactures would also assist the "truly needy," because the products would clothe the inmates and the excess would be sold to support the institution. Care was to be taken, however, not to compete with the industries of the mother country; thus, inmates were supposed to produce only the coarse textiles "necessary for daily consumption," such as shawls and blankets, rather than fine luxury goods. This caveat implicitly recognized that the restrictions of the colonial system prevented the Poor House from training inmates in the most profitable lines of manufacturing. The emphasis on work consequently seems designed more to instill the work ethic and keep the needy out of trouble than to lift them out of poverty.

The "Prospecto" glossed over the daily routines that had been so carefully detailed in earlier regulations, probably because few changes were introduced in 1806. As before, the inmates were to live in an orderly manner and be punished if they broke the rules. Those whose "conduct merited distinction" could go out on Sundays and holidays, although they would lose that privilege if they returned late or drunk or were caught begging. The married inmates and their young children would be placed in separate rooms where each family could live in privacy with the required decorum and comfort. In a departure from the 1777 bylaws, their children were to be transferred to the Patriotic School when they reached the proper age. The only other innovation was that inmates were to be clothed in "honest dress" free of any emblem or sign "that would make it odious," a signal that the reformed Poor House wanted to avoid stigmatizing its inmates.

THE PATRIOTIC SCHOOL The Patriotic School was primarily designed for orphans, although its regulations also permitted it to admit the children of Poor House inmates as well as pensioners whose parents paid 15 pesos a month for their maintenance. It was to provide a full primary school curriculum in addition to the vocational training that had originally been considered sufficient. Although the "Prospecto" does not specify the age range of the students, the school was apparently intended to take students from the age of six, when the Foundling Home was required to transfer children to the Poor House, until they were ready to support themselves.[16]

Provisions allowing students to be "adopted" (from a Spanish term somewhat broader than our *adoption*)[17] reflect the asylum's new function as an orphanage for older children, for no such provisions existed in earlier bylaws. The restrictions placed on these adoptions also illustrate the board members' ambivalence about this process. The "Prospecto" allowed adoption only under special conditions. Adoptive parents would be subject to a strict investigation of character. Only "honest and virtuous" citizens would be allowed to adopt children so that their education would not be "wasted." When

CONTAINING THE POOR

girls were adopted, special care was to be taken to ensure that "the cloak of charity" not be used to corrupt young girls, "especially the good-looking ones." Moreover, adoptive parents would have to repay the Poor House for its expenses on behalf of the child. The authors of the "Prospecto" evidently preferred to keep children in the asylum until their education was complete, for the goals of the Patriotic School were much broader than raising orphans.

The Patriotic School strove to rescue its students from the "culture of poverty" so that they could become useful members of society. Various statements in the "Prospecto" show that the school was designed to improve the moral character of the working classes as well as to upgrade the work force. The students were to be shielded from vulgar language and behavior, and they were to maintain the utmost cleanliness, decorum, and order. Their teachers were to be the best available, free of the "defects of conduct that make artisans despicable." Their vocational training should follow "the most perfect models brought from Europe to inspire in them good taste" and thereby raise the quality of popular industry. Such an education would produce the "honest citizen" who would know "the path that would make him a happy and worthy son of the nation [*patria*]" and could be "useful to his peers, never corrupting them with bad examples and retrograde behavior." As the *Gazeta de México* put it, the Patriotic School would "liberate" its students from "the rocky shoals upon which they have been thrown by their poor upbringing, which threatens to prejudice society and damage their souls eternally." [18]

These aims would be achieved through a "Christian and civil education" that combined religious, academic, and vocational instruction. It was also a highly gendered education. For boys it would consist of learning Christian doctrine, reading, writing, arithmetic, drawing, and a useful trade in the school's workshops. For girls it would consist of religious instruction, reading (but apparently not writing or arithmetic), sewing, embroidery, "and everything else required for the sex." Girls would likewise be given "an honest trade with which to help themselves." The different goals for male and female students were reflected not only in the distinct curriculum prescribed for each but also in their destiny after graduation. The girls were to be married to "honest artisans"; the boys were to establish themselves in a trade. Thus, even though the girls were supposed to be given marketable skills, it was marriage and not a career that defined their identity. In contrast, boys were identified with their work, although they would presumably marry as well. Thus, the bylaws allowed boys to keep a portion of the profits from their manufactures so that they could set themselves up as master artisans upon their graduation. Girls, on the other hand, would be helped by soliciting dowries for them "from the many charitable funds set up for orphans to marry."

THE DEPARTMENT OF CORRECTION The Department of Correction was designed as a reformatory for juvenile delinquents of both sexes. Its goal of "correcting the vices and customs that disrupt the peace of families, distract from work, set a bad example, and cause scandal" was not totally new, for the original Poor House was also supposed to achieve the moral regeneration of its inmates. The language used to describe unruly youths was, however, virtually indistinguishable from that denoting vagrants, a group that had in theory been excluded from the asylum. The reformed Poor House committed itself to taking in such youths up to the age of 25 who were placed by judges, parents, or guardians. Orphans were to be taken free; the others would pay a pension of 15 pesos per month. Indeed, according to the "Prospecto," the orphans should be given preference, in keeping with Zúñiga's wishes.

These *corrigendos* were to be treated very differently from the students of the same age. They were to be confined for a fixed term, depending on their transgressions. They were to wear a uniform distinguishing them from the other inmates, with whom they were to have no contact. Their rations were to be less than those of the other paupers, and their bread was to be "of the common and ordinary variety." The "disobedient and haughty" were to be disciplined with "rigor." Finally, the youths would be denied the visits from parents, relatives, and friends that were allowed for the other inmates. The delinquents would not be released to go home even if they became ill; instead, they were to serve out their sentences and be cured within the asylum "with as much charity as possible." These youths were therefore incarcerated and subject to a humiliating regime unlike that experienced in the rest of the reformed asylum.

The rehabilitation of juvenile delinquents was to be effected through religion and work as well as punishment. When they arrived they were to be examined in their knowledge of Christian doctrine, and could only be released when they had learned it. They were to say a rosary morning and night and hear twice weekly sermons exhorting them to change their ways. The women and men were to be kept entirely separate and constantly busy. The females were to wash the laundry for all the Poor House inmates and then spin and sew "so as not to spend one instant idle." The males were also to work continuously, at unspecified tasks, for their "punishment and correction." Literacy was not considered an important part of their rehabilitation. The "Prospecto" thus made a sharp distinction between the undeserving youths in the correctional facility and the deserving students in the Patriotic School.

THE DEPARTMENT OF SECRET BIRTHS The Department of Secret Births, the main innovation of the Mexican junta, expanded on a goal envisioned by Viceroy Bucareli in 1776 when he added space for a maternity ward on the second floor. By 1806, however, the idea had been considerably modified. The department was not to aid just any woman in giving birth. It would admit only the Spanish woman—of any marital status—who could not give birth at home without risking her person and reputation, and her family's honor. The department reinforced the tendency of the colonial Poor House to favor an increasingly "respectable" clientele. Apparently believing that only white families had sufficient honor to be stained by out of wedlock births, the authors of the "Prospecto" discriminated against the majority of pauper women for whom the asylum had originally been intended. The Poor House therefore accorded "wayward" Spanish women the privilege of asylum denied to others, who, at least in theory, were to be excluded from the institution as vagrants.

For the favored Spanish group, the department was to serve the important pronatalist function of preventing the abortions and infanticides to which women resorted out of "fear, shame, and desperation." It would also protect the woman's life by providing a doctor and midwife to assist her[19] rather than letting her attempt to deliver "in a solitary place far from human aid." Once the baby was born the mother could choose to keep it or send it to the Foundling Home. The woman's stay was to be totally secret, her name registered in a box with a double lock that would be opened only if she died and it became necessary to retrieve the information. Otherwise, her presence was to be revealed to no one—not even to her parents or husband. Because of the need for secrecy, the board member supervising this department was required to be a priest.

The New Poor House in Action

Four detailed sources available for the first five years after the 1806 restructuring show how the reformed Poor House worked in practice.[20] A daily register book lists the 487 paupers who entered the Departments of Worthy Paupers and Correction during the seven months from August 3, 1807, to March 9, 1808, and the 348 who exited during the ten months between August 3, 1807, and June 4, 1808. The only complete surviving register for any period, it often notes why inmates came and went. The municipal census of 1811 provides the most comprehensive enumeration in the institution's history, for it contains full demographic data on all Poor House inmates and live-in employees. An ecclesiastical count of 1808 furnishes information on the live-in employees and some inmates who took Communion, although it omits the students in the Patriotic School as well as the "gentile" mecas.[21] These statistical records are supplemented by a thick file of correspondence with the secretary of the Poor House board between 1804 and 1812.

These documents demonstrate that the reformed Poor House did not live up to its lofty goals. Table 10 shows that although it was initially reinvigorated, it fell far short of serving sixteen hundred paupers, as Azcárate had hoped. At first, the inmate population did grow. Even without counting the students in the Patriotic School, the 1808 Communion list includes 24 percent more inmates than in 1803.[22] The daily registers for 1807–8 indicate a similar increase: if the weekly average of 15.7 entrants held for an entire year, 816 paupers would have entered the asylum (not including the Patriotic School) over a twelve-month period, some 15 percent more than the 707 who entered in 1803. This upward trend was soon reversed, however. The inmates declined from some 685 paupers plus students in 1808, to only 551, including students, in 1811. After a brief and modest expansion, the Poor House had returned to its shrivelled prereform size.

The main reason for its stagnation was financial. When the Poor House undertook its ambitious expansion, it counted on two new sources of funding. The first was the two new endowments from Zúñiga's estate. The Patriotic School endowment, wisely invested in the Commercial Tribunal, produced a steady annual income of 11,250 pesos. Unfortunately, the donation earmarked for the rest of the asylum became worthless when Zúñiga's Real de Catorce mine stopped producing a profit.[23] The second source was the fundraising campaign initiated by the Poor House board in 1806 and kicked off with a contribution of 500 pesos from the viceroy, which similarly fizzled.[24] In addition to soliciting individuals and corporations, the board reiterated a request made by Ortiz Cortés in 1764 that a tax of 4 reales on each hog butchered in the city be applied to the asylum. The request was never granted, and substantial private donations failed to materialize.[25] Moreover, the asylum was robbed of some 13,500 pesos, skimmed off the regular contributions by its alms collector over many years. The effects of this embezzlement, which only came to light in the written records in 1811 when the Poor House attempted to recover the money, must already have been felt when the new reforms were being implemented.[26]

TABLE 10 Poor House Inmates by Category, 1795–1811

	1795	1803	1808	1811
Students	—	—	—	
Boys				131
Girls				53
Corrigendos (male)	—	—	2	—
Secret births (fem)	—	—	2[a]	—
Vergonzantes		—		—
Men	3			
Women	19[b]		4[b]	
Boys	4			
Girls	9			
Pobres				
Men	277	191	355	182
Women	206	254	195	118[b]
Boys	77	71	39	27
Girls	67	39	37	15
Matrimonios		—	—	—
Men	11			
Women	11			
Boys	3			
Girls	4			
Mecas		—	51	
Males	27			
Females	62			25
Desertores	40	—	—	—
ALL	820	555	685	551

Note: men and women are fifteen years of age or older, except that in 1795 some of the mecas may have been children. Boys and girls are under fifteen, except that in 1811 twenty-five students are fifteen or older.

[a] The two women listed in the secret births section were inmate employees rather than women using these services; a third appears to have been their maid.

[b] One additional woman listed as a vergonzante in 1795 (a mulatta slave), two in 1808, and one in 1811 appear to have been maids of the vergonzante inmates. They are not included in these statistics.

In the face of diminished funding, the Poor House board had to choose which services the institution would provide, and which people would receive them. Despite the lip service paid to resuscitating the original Poor House experiment, they let it die quietly. Instead, they intensified the trends already visible by the opening of the nineteenth century, when the asylum focused on an increasingly dependent clientele, which was also predominantly of Spanish descent. The records of this period demonstrate that the reformed Poor House functioned to prevent the downward mobility of whites, a goal that was not even written into the carefully drafted "Prospecto."

The Stillborn Department of Correction

The first program to be scaled back was the Department of Correction, which had been begrudgingly copied from the Cádiz model. Citing a scarcity of funds, the board postponed its opening until July 15, 1807. Even then (and contradicting the preference for orphans stated in the "Prospecto"), they decided to accept only boys whose parents could pay the pension—a small subset of juvenile delinquents. The pool was further restricted by limiting the age of eligible youths to between 10 and 20 years rather than up to 25 years as prescribed in the bylaws. The girls' section appears never to have opened.[27]

The 1808 Communion list shows a department barely functioning. It had one employee, Don Rafael González, with only two corrigendos under his charge: José María Arce, a 20-year-old Indian from Santa Fe, and Don Ignacio Peña, an 18-year-old Spanish youth from Mexico City. The daily registers show that Don José Ignacio Peña was the son of the widowed Doña Manuela Domínguez and the deceased Don Juan de Dios Peña. He stayed three months in the asylum, from November 30, 1807, until March 3, 1808. A 20-year-old Juan José Aperchea y Arce (perhaps the same José María Arce?) entered on December 15 and left on March 3. Both his parents, Don Juan José Aperchea and Doña María Gertrudis Arce, were still alive.[28] These were the only two youths identified as corrigendos during the seven-month period covered by the entrance records. I have found only one additional reference to the department. On October 24, 1808, the "incorrigible" youth José Delgadillo was transferred to the department from the Court Prison where his father had twice placed him "for being lazy, dissolute, and insubordinate."[29] The correctional facility was thus rarely used even during the first year of its existence.

By 1811 the Department of Correction no longer existed. Not only was it absent from the 1811 census, but its director had been let go. Still counted by the 1808 census as living in the asylum with his wife, child, brother, and a maid, Don Rafael González did not appear in the 1811 enumeration of live-in employees. The next available information, for 1822 and 1824, confirms that the Poor House no longer had a correctional facility.[30]

Although the board blamed financial constraints for preventing the Department of Correction from functioning as envisioned, similar constraints did not keep them from moving ahead with the other two new departments. Moreover, the reformatory filled a real need, for there was no comparable institution in Mexico City. Juveniles fell through the cracks of the prison system, the penalties for vagrancy applied mainly to draft-age males, and the sole remaining retirement home, the Recogidas, had become a women's prison.[31] Nonetheless, the board was reluctant to have the Poor House serve a formal carceral function. Indeed, on June 25, 1807—three weeks before the correctional department opened—González Carbajal, the board vice president, cautioned against admitting individuals "of bad conduct" because this "house of mercy will become odious to the public if they come to view it as a house of punishment."[32]

Despite the disappearance of the Department of Correction, the Department of Worthy Paupers may have provided an occasional correctional service, just as it had in the past. The daily registers show that Doña María Marta Ulloa, a 19-year-old Spanish girl, was placed in the asylum for six weeks by her mother, who paid six pesos for her room and board and retrieved her on December 1, 1807. Doña María Josefa Gutiérrez was returned to her mother "because her term is completed." María Micaela, a 22-year-old Indian servant, was placed there by her mistress with instructions that she not leave without written permission. The 26-year-old mulatta María Candelaria Vega from Tehuacán was Don Tomás Morfi's slave.[33] These notations are but a miniscule proportion of the 835 entries in the daily registers. Thus, the reformation of juveniles, though not totally abandoned, was the weakest aspect of the reformed institution.

The Marginal Department of Secret Births

The opening of the Department of Secret Births in 1806 was marked by a solemn ceremony in which Dr. Juan Antonio Bruno, the board member and priest in charge of supervising it, praised its important role in preserving "the honor of many marriages, the decorum of families, and the peace and tranquility of society."[34] Despite the board's enthusiasm for this new department, it remained a marginal part of the Poor House because the demand for its services was limited and sporadic. Owing to the secrecy to which it was sworn, no census taker was ever allowed to count its inmates. Yet in 1808 it was well staffed, with two inmate *amas de confianza* and a maid. Its director, the 52-year-old single Doña Ana Medina, had been enumerated as a vergonzante in 1795. The 36-year-old single Doña Josefa Vidaurri y Medina, who had accompanied the older Medina in 1795, was probably her niece and assistant.[35] The 1811 census did not list the department at all—although it provided separate listings for the Hospicio and Patriotic School—and included Medina and Vidaurri among the Hospicio's inmates. Republican documents noted its continued existence. Yet no inmates were present when inspectors visited the institution in 1824 and 1835.[36] The department had such a low profile that the social reformer Tadeo Ortiz de Ayala was unaware of its existence in 1832 when he proposed establishing just such a *casa de maternidad* in Mexico City to prevent infanticides by desperate mothers.[37] The department still existed in 1863 when García Icazbalceta observed that the facility, presided over by an elderly inmate, had always been "viewed with aversion" by the rest of the staff, which was barred from entering it to protect the anonymity of its clients.[38]

The Department of Secret Births thus fared better than the Department of Correction, which barely outlasted its first year. In part, the former perdured because, with no regular clientele, it was relatively inexpensive to maintain. Yet it did represent a drain on the asylum's resources. It took up space, including an "apartment of the Señoras Medina" referred to in the exit register on October 1, 1807. According to García Icazbalceta, this two-room apartment was completely isolated from the rest of the asylum and had its own door to the street. In addition, its inmate director, first Doña Ana Medina and by 1832 the younger Vidaurri y Medina, drew the substantial annual salary of 157.5 pesos with an additional food ration worth 151.5 pesos.[39] The Poor House board apparently allowed this department to continue because they believed that protecting Spanish women in their time of need was more in keeping with the asylum's mission than disciplining unruly juveniles. The only section of the reformed Poor House that did not follow contemporary European trends, the Department of Secret Births responded to a colonial environment in which white elites wanted to shore up crumbling racial hierarchies.

The Thriving Patriotic School

The Patriotic School, the board's favorite new department, prospered from the start. In 1811, the first date for which information on the school is available, it was close to the optimum size of two hundred students envisioned when it was founded.[40] Its 184 students, attended by 20 live-in employees, represented one-third of those served by the Poor House. Thus, five years after its inauguration, the school was a large and thriving operation. It served a highly selected group of children, however, 89 percent of whom were white and 71 percent male. This group cannot have represented a cross section of the capital's orphans. Indeed, it contrasted sharply with the orphans in the Foundling Home, only 43 percent of whom were white and 58 percent male.[41] Entrance in the school therefore appears to have been considered a privilege best reserved for whites—especially boys—who could (or more precisely, from the staff's perspective, should) rise above the level of menial jobs.

Boys were favored by the school's admissions policies because of its emphasis on training artisans, as clearly outlined in the "Prospecto." When the school opened in 1806 it had beds for 140 boys and 60 girls.[42] The enrollment in 1811 reflected a nearly identical sex ratio. This preponderance of boys did not characterize the capital's elementary schools, which enrolled boys and girls nearly equally.[43] It was the concern with "improving popular industry" that led the Poor House to take in more boys, for (unlike elementary schools) the Patriotic School substituted for apprenticeships, which girls rarely entered. The better-defined curriculum for boys likewise indicates the board's partiality toward male orphans.

The board's preference for assisting whites is even more notable, although less stark than in the segregated maternity wing. Only 4 percent of the students in the Patriotic School were listed as Indian and 8 percent as *casta* (thirteen mestizos and one mulatto). Most of the few nonwhite children were boys, perhaps because they showed a special talent that was considered important to develop. The girls in the school, though fewer in number, were even more highly selected than the boys, with all but two listed as Spanish, or 96 percent compared with only 85 percent of the boys. It is as though the authorities viewed Indian and caste girls as unworthy of the investment since they could easily work in domestic service, spinning, sewing, or food preparation without further training from as young as nine or ten years.[44] It is far from coincidental that the principal vocational skill prescribed for girls in the "Prospecto" was embroidery, a refined craft appropriate for "respectable" women, instead of the more common skills that would prepare girls for lowly jobs.

The differing age ranges for the male and female students likewise suggest that the Patriotic School believed it had a special duty to safeguard white girls. In 1811 the average boy was 11, and the average girl was 10. Yet the age range for girls was broader. The male students were between the ages of 6 and 18, by which time they were ready to set themselves up in a trade. By age

15 & 16 STREET CHILDREN. Homeless children filled the streets of the Mexican capital. Indian youngsters like these, photographed around 1865 by Maximilian's court photographer, might begin working at the age of eight or nine years. Yet few of them entered the Poor House school because the institution, although originally founded to control the multiracial populace, had become a safety net for impoverished whites.

17 all the male youths had, in the contemporary phrase, "found their destiny." This professional identification began as early as 9 or 10 for some; by age 13 half the boys had chosen a career, as had three-quarters by 16. Of these, 69 percent declared themselves to be weavers, 15 percent tailors, 15 percent cobblers, and one, 17-year-old José Legorreta, a barber. In contrast, the female students included two 5 year olds as well as three girls aged 19, 21, and 23. Although the older girls had presumably finished their schooling, they remained under the school's protective wing. Instead of graduating, the older girls were apparently waiting to be called for in marriage; indeed, none of the female students identified herself to the census taker according to a trade.[45] To some extent the weaker placement record for girls reflected their limited options on the job market rather than a deficiency in the training they received. Yet the Patriotic School did not transfer them to the Department of Worthy Paupers or send them out to fend for themselves because of the need to preserve their status.

The school's partiality toward respectable white orphans may explain why many inmate children remained in the Department of Worthy Paupers instead of being transferred to the Patriotic School, as mandated by the "Prospecto." Some clearly were transferred, for the proportion of children under 15 dropped from 20 to 26 percent of the inmates between 1795 and 1803 to 12 percent of those in the Hospicio in 1808 and 1811.[46] Yet—in clear violation of the 1806 bylaws—sixty-seven school-age children (between the ages of 5 and 14) remained in the asylum in 1808, as did thirty-three in 1811. In addition, the entrance registers show that none of the thirty-nine school-age children who entered the Poor House between August 3, 1807, and March 9, 1808, was sent to the school.

Perhaps some of these children remained in the Department of Worthy Paupers because they came in the company of relatives who planned only short stays in the asylum. Half the school-age children listed in the daily registers for 1807–8 entered with relatives, sixteen with their mothers, and two each with their fathers or grandfathers. A few children would not have been considered potential students because they suffered from some physical or mental deficiency, as did three handicapped boys of Spanish descent in the Hospicio in 1811. The 11-year-old Francisco Luna was mute, and the 12- and 14-year-old Urbano Sánchez and Crecencio Robles were *insultado* (a term that literally means "insulted" and denotes people paralyzed by a stroke or blow).[47] While the Department of Correction lasted, deficiencies of character kept the corrigendos out of the school; their dissolute behavior made them undeserving—though equally in need—of an excellent education, and further made them a potential corrupting influence on the other students.

Other children were apparently kept out of the Patriotic School because of their lowly social backgrounds, of which their race provides a rough indication. Those who remained in the asylum had a markedly different racial profile from those in the school: only 63 to 64 percent of school-age children in the Hospicio in 1808 and 1811 were listed as Spanish, compared with 89 percent of the students in the school. Among the school-age inmate children 21 percent were caste and 15 to 16 percent were Indian, compared with only 8 and 4 percent of the students. Thus, the school discriminated against caste and Indian children as well as against girls. It did not take in all the eligible white children from the Department of Worthy Paupers, either, perhaps because it was already approaching the maximum number of students it could accommodate.

The school's admissions policies reveal the prejudices of the Poor House board and staff. Although racial criteria were never spelled out in the "Prospecto," the orphans considered most deserving of a good education were overwhelmingly of Spanish descent. Indeed one Indian boy, the 10-year-old orphan Leonardo Montenegro, was transferred from the school to the asylum on December 3, 1807, even though, as a school-age child who had lost both parents and had no relatives to take him in (he remained in the asylum until placed with a Don Francisco de la Torre five months later), he met the stated eligibility requirements for the Patriotic School.

The privileged students were deemed worthy of a substantial investment. According to the *Gazeta de México* their spacious school building was amply furnished with beds, bedding, and tableware imported from Spain.[48] By 1811 at least twenty new employees had been hired to serve the students, in addition to the existing employees like the administrator and chaplains who served the entire asylum (table 11). Available information on wages, food, and other expenditures for 1803 and 1824 indicates that the Patriotic School cost over 13,000 pesos a year to run, thereby exceeding the 11,250 pesos it received as interest on its endowment.[49] Thus, even though the Department of Correction was phased out and corners were cut in the asylum, the board funded the Patriotic School generously.

The students were treated better than the rest of the Poor House inmates. Their superior status is reflected in the high proportion of employees that served them: while there were only seven live-in employees for the 368 inmates of the asylum in 1811, there were twenty live-in employees exclusively for the 184 students. The fact that eleven of them were servants is significant, for they shielded the students from the menial household chores that the other inmates performed for themselves.

In keeping with the aim of improving the taste and manners of the stu-

TABLE 11   Poor House Employees, 1803 and 1811

Occupation	1803	1811
Asylum		
Administrator	1	[1]
Assistant	1	—
Mayordomo	1	1
Rectora	1	—
Chaplain	2	2
Secretary	1	—
Scribe	1	—
Accountant	1	—
Surgeon	1	—
Doctor	1	—
Bleeder	1	—
Master artisan	1	1
Warden	—	2
Secret births		
Ama		[2]
Patriotic school		
Teacher		1
Assistant teacher		2
Warden		1
Rectora (also teacher)		1
Master artisan		1
Portero		3
Cook		4
Atolera		4
Laundress		3

Note: The 1811 census only counts live-in employees. Although bracketed employees are not listed in the 1811 census, they are referred to in other documents. It is likely that all the asylum positions existed in the 1811 Poor House as well.

dents, the nine "professional" employees of the Patriotic School were selected to provide exemplary role models. The schoolteacher, master artisan, two assistants, warden, three porteros, and the rectora de niñas were all of Spanish descent and, except for the two male porteros, were listed as dons or doñas. Two of the seven men were from Spain, an origin that conferred some status and an aura of "civilization" in a colonial society: the warden,

Don Pascual Portillo, a 56-year-old father of four, came from Cádiz, and the assistant of halls, Don Francisco Corsa, a 30-year-old bachelor, came from Seville. His single status distinguished Don Francisco from the other male employees, who were respectably married and living with their wives, children, other relatives, and servants in rooms provided by the Poor House. The rectora and portera, the only two female employees of the "better sort," were both honorable white ladies who, like most women of their class, took up formal employment only when they had no male relative or inheritance to support them. Doña María Colunga, the rectora, was a 30-year-old single woman living in a room with her widowed mother; Doña María Camacho, the portera, was a 50-year-old widow living alone. The female servants, who did not supervise or instruct the students, presented a marked contrast. With the exception of the white María Pérez, the four cooks, three washerwomen, and four atoleras were Indians or castes. Moreover, none of them merited an honorific title.

The opening of the Patriotic School thus brought an impressive expansion in the Poor House personnel. The number of staff members serving the entire institution grew from 12 in 1803 to more than 30 in 1811, for, although the 1811 census only enumerated the 26 employees who resided on the premises, the Poor House undoubtedly continued to hire an administrator, 2 chaplains, a doctor, a secretary, an accountant, and a scribe. The tripling of the number of employees occurred even though the total number of inmates was approximately equal to what it had been in 1803. This dramatic increase in personnel represented a far larger investment for the institution than merely increased wages. Every new live-in employee added an average of 3.8 people to the building because their family members, dependents, and servants moved in as well. In fact, the 1811 census counted 106 people residing in the Poor House in addition to the 552 students and inmates. (The ecclesiastical census of 1808, which excluded the Patriotic School, only counted 26 noninmates in the Hospicio.) The growth in the Poor House staff thus represented a hidden drain on its resources. Not only did the employees' families and dependents take up considerable space in the institution, but (as later documents indicate) they used food, medicine, and other institutional resources. Consequently, they created a new set of obligations that would be hard to shake.

The Declining Commitment to Adult Beggars

While the Poor House was thus strengthening its commitment to the Patriotic School, it was weakening its commitment to the Department of Worthy

Paupers. Although the 368 inmates in this department still constituted a majority of the Poor House clients in 1811, they were becoming a secondary priority for the institution. Table 10 shows that the number of worthy paupers (combining the categories of pobres, vergonzantes, and mecas) increased by approximately one-fifth two years after the Poor House reform but then declined by nearly half in the next three years—during which time the enrollment in the Patriotic School remained close to the 200-bed capacity. The result was that by 1811 the asylum took in very few of the capital's destitute. At a time when Mexico City's population had mushroomed from some 113,000 residents in 1790 to roughly 169,000, the Hospicio housed only 42 children and 301 adults (in addition to 25 mecas forcibly brought from afar).[50] Thus, the Poor House had a decreasing impact on the capital's poor. Rather than trying to discipline its street people, the smaller institution reverted to its prereform focus on the city's most vulnerable—or perhaps most "deserving"—paupers.

The reformed Poor House still confined some indigenous war captives, though their numbers steadily declined from eighty-nine in 1795 to fifty-seven in 1808 and twenty-five in 1811. Moreover, by 1811 the male mecas had disappeared—one of them, Puamano Caxeri, having committed suicide in the asylum in 1807.[51] To be sure, the continued presence of female mecas apparently violated the 1798 and 1806 bans on placing criminals in the asylum for punishment; as late as January 14, 1808, a group of eighteen mecas was delivered to the Poor House by the *sargento mayor de la plaza*.[52] Yet it appears that the asylum's staff may have considered them to be needy women who could not be turned away. By 1811, when complete information is available for the mecas, all twenty-five were single adult women. (The designation "single" may be misleading, for, since they were gentiles, any marriage outside the Catholic Church would not be recognized.) They had resided in the Poor House long enough for 40 percent to have been converted to Catholicism, compared with only 10 percent of the mecas in 1808. Their place of origin was listed as Apache (21), del Pitie (2), and Chihuahua (2). They ranged in age from 18 to 70, with an average age of 41.8. They retained strong traces of their earlier background. Even the baptized lacked last names—which was rare, though not unheard of, among the other inmates. Over half the mecas (56 percent) gave their age as a round number, compared with only 13 percent of the other female inmates. These characteristics suggest that even the baptized mecas may not have been acculturated enough to fend for themselves outside the asylum. Alone, far from home, and illiterate, they may have come to be viewed less as prisoners of war than as vulnerable women worthy of compassion.

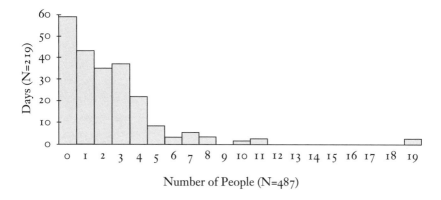

FIGURE 2   Entrances per day, August 3, 1807, to March 9, 1808

As mandated by the 1806 decree, the reformed Poor House at first also took in beggars who had been apprehended soliciting alms. The entrance registers for 1807–8 provide occasional indications of coercion. María Gertrudis Robles, a 16-year-old mestiza "brought by *un soldado Dragón* after Father Don Pedro Cortés y Gálvez denounced her for soliciting alms," was unusual because most of those forcibly interned were men. For example, Manuel Serrano, a 50-year-old Indian leather currier, was returned to the asylum after having escaped three times. Clemente Serbín, a 46-year-old widowed Spanish weaver, was brought back half naked after he fled, "taking with him a shirt and pants." Juan Astorga, a 35-year-old married Spanish man, punched the sentinel who conducted him to the asylum. And a 49-year-old Spanish cigar maker, Pablo Santa Marina, was "injured on the left arm by the commissioner who brought him to the Hospicio."

Yet the number of Mexico City paupers who were forcibly confined was relatively low. The entrance register only records one, two, or three paupers entering the asylum on most days and none on approximately one quarter of the days (fig. 2). Assuming that only the inmates brought *por la tropa* were forcibly interned, then half of them came voluntarily. Thus, only seven or eight beggars, on average, were rounded up each week.[53] This number represented a minuscule fraction of the crowds of beggars that observers repeatedly noted in the huge metropolis.

The impact of these confinements on reducing mendicity was further limited because few paupers were permanently removed from the city streets. The 1807–8 registers show, for example, that Doña María Aguilar del Castillo, a 43-year-old Spanish widow, was released on the same day she was brought to the asylum despite being labeled a *limosnera perpetua*. The 61-year-old Indian weaver Guadalupe Ramírez was only held for a few hours, following orders from the Marqués de Guardiola (the board member in charge of rounding up beggars) to "place him in the stocks until evening vespers." Among those who were officially admitted, one of seven inmates left within a week and half were out within four months, free to beg again. Many were merely listed as "released," without having been claimed and vouched for as required. A surprising 21 percent of those recorded in the exit registers simply walked out. Well-behaved inmates were allowed Sunday outings, and every Monday the administrator noted that one or two, or five or ten—and as many as fourteen on one warm April day in 1808—failed to return, taking with them the usual shirt, pants, shawl, skirt, or blanket belonging to the asylum. Trusted inmates sent out to run errands sometimes bolted. And those denied the privilege of outings occasionally found other ways to escape, like the 45-year-old Spanish José Almazán, who fled through the chapel. Altogether, 2 percent of those listed in the exit registers escaped.[54] Thus, just one year after the 1806 decree, beggars were not being systematically arrested, forced into the Poor House, and detained until they mended their ways.

The persecution of beggars may have been briefly revived after a decree of May 25, 1809, reiterated the 1806 directive—thereby suggesting by its very existence that the earlier decree was no longer being enforced.[55] In the weeks immediately following the new decree, the correspondence between the Sala de Crimen (a chamber of the Audiencia of Mexico) and the secretary of the Poor House board contains two examples of paupers placed in the Poor House against their will. The embroiderer José Andrés Zamano, who had been held in the Royal Jail for a minor infraction, was transferred to the asylum because he was known "as a perpetual beggar in the Church of Santa Teresa la Antigua" who "because he is crippled cannot exercise his profession and will surely beg again." The elderly María Josefa Pumareta, a Spanish woman from Cádiz, had been imprisoned numerous times by the *guardas del alumbrado* (night guards) who found her "lying in the street drunk." Since "repeated jailings had failed to reform her" and her "advanced age and impediments exposed her to an unhappy death," she was likewise sent to the Poor House.[56] Since neither pauper had been arrested for soliciting alms, however, it would appear that the regular roundups of beggars did not resume. Although beggars were still occasionally placed in the Poor House against their will,[57] the 1809 decree did not succeed in resuscitating the original vigorous campaign against Mexico City's street people.

The Changing Face of Worthy Paupers

As the Poor House increasingly catered to its willing clients, it came to enclose less of a cross section of the capital's poor. During its initial postreform expansion the Department of Worthy Paupers attempted to serve the varied clientele that came to it voluntarily. However, as the adult inmates decreased from 554 in 1808 to only 300 by 1811 (excluding mecas in both years) the Poor House staff became much more selective.

In 1807–8 the Hospicio still took in needy families who sought help in dealing with temporary crises. Among the 487 people who entered the asylum from August 3, 1807, to March 9, 1808, were 4 couples, 26 mothers and 5 fathers with children, 2 grandfathers with grandchildren, and 2 sets of siblings. For example, the widowed Mariano Franco, a 60-year-old Spanish tailor, sought shelter with his son for one month so that he could recover from an illness and return to work. The very pregnant Indian María Gertrudis Domínguez arrived with two young children, delivered a third child the next morning, and left with her brood three weeks later. Another Indian, the 20-year-old María Felipa Mesa, was placed as a wet nurse after spending three months in the Poor House recovering from the birth of her second child. These women were two of four who gave birth in the Poor House during the seven-month period and who undoubtedly appreciated the institution's assistance during a particularly difficult time. Indeed, "single" mothers (all of whom claimed to have been legally married) remained a substantial group of the asylum's short-term clientele in 1807–8: 18 percent of the women age 15 or over listed in the entrance registers were mothers with infants or young children.

By 1811 few families resided in the asylum. Mothers with young children were now only 4 percent of the female inmates age 15 or older, down from 18 percent three years earlier. Their decline may partly reflect the differences between the two documents: the 1811 census only recorded those living in the asylum on a single day, while the entrance registers included many whose stay was brief.[58] The contrast with the similar 1795 census more accurately reflects the shift. Unlike 1795, when there were at least sixty-eight identifiable family groups among the inmates, by 1811 there were only six: five mothers with children and one set of orphaned brothers. Inmates in family groups had consequently dropped from 16 to 2 percent of adults (excluding mecas). Indeed, the diminution of married inmates was so steep, from 24 to 10 percent of both male and female inmates, that the category of matrimonios was omitted from the censuses of 1808 and 1811 (table 10). Thus, by 1811 the Poor

House served less as a shelter for homeless families, single mothers, and abandoned wives than it had in the past.

Table 12.D shows that, to the extent that it still took in adults, the Poor House predominantly catered to the unmarried and widowed facing their advancing years alone. By 1811 the dwindling adult population had become increasingly elderly. The proportion of inmates age 60 or older increased from 19 percent in 1795 to 27 percent in 1811, a sharp contrast with Mexico City residents, only 8 percent of whom had reached that age. In particular, the average female inmate had gotten older, largely because of the decline of mothers with children. While the mean age of men remained at some 47 years, for women it rose by 11 years to reach 45.8 years. Some of the inmates were surprisingly old, given that average life expectancies at the time were less than 40 years.[59] The 1811 census listed the 87-year-old Indian merchant José Antonio Romero and the 95-year-old Indian carder Juan Victoriano. The 1808 Communion list included two men who claimed to be 104 and 108 years old. The 1807–8 registers listed the Spanish widow Petra Martínez, who claimed to be 105, as well as the Spanish silversmith Don Antonio Hurtado y Mendoza, who claimed to be 100 and entered with his 60-year-old wife because his "trembling" prevented him from earning a living. Several elderly paupers apparently entered the Poor House to die, as did the 60-year-old José Vergara, who entered on August 3, 1807, and died ten days later.[60]

The young adult paupers who remained in the Department of Worthy Paupers were increasingly disabled. This trend must be teased out of the data, which is not directly comparable in different years. (The 1795 census does not systematically list disabilities, and the 1803 statistics do not provide the ages of disabled inmates.) An initial glance at table 13 actually suggests the opposite trend, for the disabled (excluding the category of "habitually sick" in 1803 because it is not given for 1811) declined from 24 percent of the inmates in 1803 to 20 percent in 1811. Yet this apparent decline merely reflects the aging of the inmate population, for the elderly were the least disabled of any age group. Table 14 shows that the proportion of adult inmates with a physical or mental disability decreased progressively with age. Fully 38 percent of those between the ages of 15 and 29, and 32 percent of those between 30 and 44, were either blind, epileptic, crippled, deaf, mute, paralyzed, demented, or retarded. After the age of 60, only 7 percent of the inmates were handicapped, all of them blind or crippled. To be sure, some may have suffered from chronic illnesses, a category that was not included in 1811 but applied to 4 percent of the inmates in 1803. For most of the elderly it was the infirmities of old age rather than any specific handicap that hindered their ability to live independently. As those 60 or older increased from 10 to 23 per-

TABLE 12 Inmate Characteristics by Sex, 1811

| | MALE | | FEMALE | | ALL | | Population Mexico City, |
	Number	%	Number	%	Number	%	1811 %
A. Race							
Español	106	51	82	62	188	55	50
Casta	56	27	24	18	80	23	17
Indio	47	22	27	20	74	22	33
ALL	209	100	133	100	342	100	100
B. Title							
Don/Doña	11	5	19	14	30	9	
Untitled	198	95	114	86	312	91	
ALL	209	100	133	100	342	100	
C. Place of Origin							
Foreigners	4	2	2	2	6	2	2
Mexican migrants	85	41	44	33	129	38	37
Born in Mexico City	120	57	87	65	207	61	61
ALL	209	100	133	100	342	101	100
D. Marital Status (age 15 and over)							
Single	98	54	51	43	149	50	37
Married	19	10	12	10	31	10	44
Widowed	64	35	55	47	119	40	19
Unknown	1				1		
ALL	182	99	118	100	300	100	100
E. Age Groups (age 15 and over)							
15–29	36	20	19	16	55	18	43
30–44	42	23	39	33	81	27	33
45–59	52	29	32	27	84	28	16
60 plus	52	29	28	24	80	27	8
ALL	182	101	118	100	300	100	100
F. Mean Age (age 15 and over)							
	47.7		45.8		46.9		

Note: Totals exclude 184 students in the Patriotic School and 25 indias mecas who never begged on the streets of Mexico City. The statistics for Mexico City in 1811 come from my sample of the 1811 census, described in Arrom (1985), 271–76.

TABLE 13   Disabled Inmates by Type of Handicap and Sex, 1811

	Males	Females	All
Blind	20	6	26 (36%)
Epileptic	7	1	8 (11%)
Crippled	6	6	12 (16%)
Paralyzed	4	1	5 (7%)
Demented	2	7	9 (12%)
Deaf/mute	7	1	8 (11%)
Simple	4	1	5 (7%)
ALL	50	23	73 (100%)
Total inmates	209	158	367
Percentage of total	24	15	20

Note: Excludes students in the Patriotic School.

cent of all inmates between 1803 and 1811,[61] it is natural that the proportions disabled would decrease. Indeed, it would have decreased much more than 4 percent between 1803 and 1811 unless the young adults had simultaneously become more infirm.

To some extent, the changing profile of pauper inmates reflects the decline in forcible confinement, since the dependent elderly inmates and the disabled youths were precisely those who sought refuge voluntarily. Yet the Poor House staff did not merely respond to the demands of its willing clients. The dramatic decline of related inmates by 1811 suggests that destitute families were turned away. So were the temporarily unemployed, like the "examined master tailor," Mariano Sagardo, who unsuccessfully petitioned for admittance along with his family because "the scarcity of work has reduced me to the greatest misery."[62] Thus, the Poor House staff was favoring certain groups of paupers over others in granting admission to the asylum.

Their definition of what made paupers eligible for assistance was highly gendered, as can be seen in the profile of the disabled inmates (table 14). As in 1803, the institutionalized men were more likely to be disabled than the women: 25 percent of the adult male inmates in 1811 listed a physical or mental handicap compared with only 18 percent of the female. This disparity was particularly marked between the ages of 15 to 29, where half of the men listed a handicap compared with only 16 percent of the women. It was this handicap that qualified these young male inmates for institutionalization, for otherwise they were expected to work to support themselves and their families.

TABLE 14   Disabled Inmates by Age and Sex, 1811

Age	MALE		FEMALE		ALL	
	Number	%	Number	%	Number	%
1–14	4/27	15	2/15	13	6/42	14
15–29	18/36	50	3/19	16	21/55	38
30–44	17/42	40	9/39	23	26/81	32
45–59	8/52	15	6/32	19	14/84	17
60 plus	3/52	6	3/28	11	6/80	8
ALL	50/209	24	23/133	17	73/342	21

Note: Excludes students and mecas.

In contrast, many young women were considered worthy of asylum despite their apparent good health because of their limited opportunities in the labor market and the vulnerability they suffered because of their sex.

In addition, the Poor House staff preferred serving only well-behaved paupers. The 1807–8 exit registers listed twelve inmates expelled for misbehavior. Since residence in the Poor House was not originally designed as a privilege, expulsions for misconduct were not envisioned in any of the by-laws prior to 1866; instead the Poor House statutes detailed the punishments that could be administered to the unruly and listed a very restricted set of conditions under which inmates could leave. Yet the release records of eight women carried notations to the effect that they would "not be accepted back under any circumstances." For two men the notation read "will be whipped if he returns." A third, Mariano Valverde, was admonished "not to set foot in this house again." A fourth man, José María Ponze, was expelled by the Poor House board with "a cruel punishment" promised should he ever come back. The exit registers did not describe their transgressions. One of the women may have been caught having an affair with a male employee, despite the prescribed separation of the sexes. On August 20, 1807, after at least twelve years spent in and out of the asylum, Doña María de La Luz Frexomil was sent to live with an aunt and ordered not to return, "not even to visit." She later turned up in the 1811 census as the 26-year-old-wife of Don Francisco Borja, a 36-year-old master artisan in the Patriotic School.[63]

In turning away disorderly paupers, the Poor House director and board secretary repeatedly affirmed that their responsibility was only to "those truly of this institute, such as the blind, the crippled, and the lame."[64] Yet this claim rings hollow in view of the fact that 78 percent of the adult inmates in 1811 listed no disability, while 45 percent were in the prime of their lives (between 15 and 44 years of age) and 65 percent of these were able-bodied. It is also contradicted by examples of certain paupers who were granted admittance, like Doña María Osores, who was sent by Viceroy Iturrigaray to protect her from the beatings of her husband Don Ignacio Avendaños.[65] Without fitting any of the stated criteria for admission, Osores found space in the asylum because of her high status and connections.[66] Although the staff never admitted it, as the asylum was forced to allocate increasingly scarce resources, race and class became ever more important factors in the selection—as well as self-selection—of the Poor House clients.

The available records provide occasional glimpses of how white paupers were given preference in the reformed Poor House. Although it continued to be racially integrated, its inmates by 1811 were less representative of the capital's population than in 1795. By 1811 the Indian inmates (excluding mecas) declined from 25 to 22 percent, while those of Spanish descent increased from 52 to 55 percent.[67] The castas remained about the same, at 24 and 23 percent (table 12A). Although these shifts are small, they contrast with the changing ethnic profile of Mexico City as documented by the censuses of 1790 and 1811. Despite the margin of error in these figures,[68] the trend is clear. While Indians increased from some 24 to 33 percent of the city's residents, they declined among the inmates. Meanwhile the Spanish inmates became more prevalent, representing 55 percent of the inmates but only 50 percent of the capital's population. The presence of distinguished white paupers who merited the title don or doña remained nearly constant at 9 percent.

It is difficult to know whether the Department of Worthy Paupers actively discriminated against Indians by defining them as unworthy poor, as did the Patriotic School and the Department of Secret Births. The total absence in the 1811 census of Indian women between the ages of 15 and 19 compared with their prominence in the 1807–8 exit registers among those placed as servants in private homes,[69] suggests that when a young Indian woman arrived at the Poor House door, the staff found her a job rather than letting her stay in the asylum. The Indian men would be similarly treated unless there were extenuating circumstances. Of course, it may also be that Indian paupers avoided the Poor House if at all possible. The entrance registers for 1807–8 indicate, for example, that among the Indian women between the ages of 15 and 29, fully 60 percent were single mothers compared with only 15 percent of the Spanish women. The 1811 census shows that among the men, 29 percent of the Indian inmates were disabled, compared with only 21 percent of the Spanish. It may therefore have taken considerably more adversity for Indian paupers to seek shelter—or for the asylum to take them in.

The criteria for accepting white paupers, especially dons and doñas, were apparently much looser. The demographic profile of the eleven Spanish don inmates in 1811 suggests that most were actually vagrants who should never have been in the Poor House at all. These dons were younger and healthier as a group than the other male inmates, with a mean age of only 43.7 years, compared with 47.3 for the other men. Only one, a 21-year-old insultado, was listed as handicapped, which made only 9 percent of the dons disabled, compared with 25 percent of the other men. Moreover, the dons were more than four times more likely to be married than were the other male inmates (45 percent in contrast to 10 percent), perhaps because some were dissolute men who abused their wives or abandoned them—the very vagrants denounced in repeated decrees. Indeed, the only three dons under age 50 listed in the 1807-8 entrance registers were able-bodied married men who were forcibly interned without their wives. One, the 43-year-old Don Ignacio Morelos from Guadalajara, entered the Poor House on March 3, 1808, with his brother promising to pay 5 pesos a month for his sustenance. The next entry, for his 37-year-old wife, Doña Francisca Pinto, is crossed out as though she had refused to follow her husband. Unfortunately, there is no explanation of what he had done to make his family want him shut up in the asylum even though he was healthy and his relatives could afford to support him. According to the Poor House bylaws he should not have been admitted. Likewise, the healthy draft-age Don José Bernardo Gutiérrez, an 18 year old from Colima who listed no trade, or Don José María Castro, a 22 year old from Cádiz who declared himself to be a merchant, should have been sentenced to serve in the army or public works. Yet both were living in the asylum when the census enumerator came in 1811.

Apparently these men were too distinguished to be treated in the same manner as the "ordinary" vagrants. To be sure, race and class were never mentioned in the detailed legislation defining vagrancy or in the Poor House bylaws as factors differentiating the deserving from the undeserving poor. In practice, however, their superior social background shielded these Spanish dons from the legally mandated penalties for vagrancy and gained them the institutional assistance for which they were technically ineligible.

In practice, the criteria for accepting "distinguished" white women was also broader than those set forth in the "Prospecto." Many young healthy women of Spanish descent were considered worthy of asylum because the staff did not want to see them suffer the indignities of public destitution. In fact, among the inmates age 15 or older, 62 percent of the women in 1811 were Spanish, compared with only 47 percent of the men—a marked change from 1795, when whites were equally represented among women and men.

The prevalence of doñas suggests that the more "respectable" pauper ladies took advantage of public welfare more often than did other groups. As in 1795, there were far more doñas than dons, with 16 percent of the women age 15 and older using the honorific title compared with only 6 percent of the men. Moreover, by 1808 all the vergonzantes were female, unlike the situation in 1795. By 1811 the majority of the doñas were single: 53 percent compared with only 33 percent of the other women. On average, they were somewhat younger than the others (42.3 years instead of 45.8). None listed a handicap. Lacking immediate family to rely on, and with their employment options more restricted than those of women from humbler backgrounds, these ladies apparently welcomed the shelter the Poor House offered and were in turn welcomed by the institution.

Compared to the other female inmates, these distinguished white ladies were more likely to make the institution their permanent home. The doñas had a higher persistence rate than the untitled women, for 25 percent of those listed in the ecclesiastical census of 1808 were still in the Poor House in 1811, compared with only 8 percent of the other women.[70] The rate of persistence was 100 percent among the few distinguished vergonzantes. Although the 1811 census did not include this category, the four pobres de solemnidad listed in 1808 as living "upstairs" (two of them with their maids) were still there three years later. So were the inmate supervisors of the Department of Secret Births. Doña Ana Medina lived there for more than twenty-nine years, from at least 1795 until 1824; the younger Doña Josefa Vidaurri lived there for more than thirty-seven years, from at least 1795 until 1832. Doña María Ignacia Olmedo, who first appeared in 1811, would still be there in 1824.[71]

The disproportionate presence of Spanish women means that, apart from their tendency to be elderly or handicapped, the male inmates came much closer than the female to being representative of the city's poor. This was true not only in their racial composition but also in their rate of migration, for the largely city-born Spanish women skewed the female group (table 12C).[72] In addition, the men represented a broad spectrum of the city's occupational groups. The 1811 census is the only document in Poor House history to provide systematic data on the male inmates' previous employment (table 15). Only one women listed an occupation: the 30-year-old Indian María Cesaria Ramírez, who served as a maid to her vergonzante mistress Doña María Manuela Sierra y Tagle, just as she had in 1808 (and whom I have not counted as an inmate). In contrast, most men listed either an occupation (67 percent of those 20 and over) or in its place a handicap (23 percent), most often blindness, that explained why they did not have a trade. Only 10 percent listed neither, mostly elderly men who had long since retired. Prior to entering the

TABLE 15   Occupations of Male Inmates, Age 20 and Over, 1811

	Number	%
Artisans	69	41
Weavers	15	
Spinners	9	
Carders	8	
Tailors	13	
Cobblers	11	
Food	3	
Wood	3	
Metal	2	
Hat makers	2	
Other	3	
Commerce	6	4
Cooks	5	3
Soldiers	3	2
Scribes	3	2
Masons	3	2
Others	24	14
Infirm	39	23
No trade	17	10
TOTAL	169	101

Poor House 41 percent of the men had been artisans, particularly weavers, spinners, carders, tailors, and shoemakers, but also a few silversmiths, gilders, blacksmiths, carpenters, and bakers (the latter two were considered artisans because they belonged to organized guilds). The decline of the textile sector is mirrored in their occupations, since textile workers were twice as numerous among the artisan inmates (68 percent) than in Mexico City at large.[73] Yet men from many walks of life ended up in the Poor House, including servants, water carriers, masons, laborers, butchers, a muleteer, a miner, an embalmer, and a sacristan. Among the eleven Spanish dons were two of the three men listed as "in the military," the three scribes, two of the six *comerciantes* (merchants, or perhaps "in business," a category that covers as wide a range of occupations as the Spanish term), one of the two barbers (at this time still in the lower echelons of the medical profession),[74] and the one portero. It is a testament to the precariousness of the economy that so many men with skills could be reduced to pauperization—and not only among the elderly.

Although those in their twenties were nearly evenly split between those who were handicapped and those who had a trade, two-thirds of the men age thirty and over listed a trade, which evidently did not prevent their indigence.

Yet, even for the able-bodied men from the declining textile sector, the reformed Poor House made little attempt to prepare them for new jobs, for education and vocational training had become almost exclusively the province of the Patriotic School. The emphasis on religious instruction remained strong. As in 1795, two chaplains served the Poor House (although their efforts may have been increasingly devoted to the students). In 1811 only one master artisan, a *maestro de medias*, is listed among the employees serving the 368 inmates of the Department of Worthy Paupers. As a sockmaker, he was ironically in the battered textile sector, where competition from foreign goods was making it increasingly difficult to earn a living, especially after the protected market ended with the outbreak of the Napoleonic Wars in 1804.[75] By 1811 the Poor House had largely given up on rehabilitating its adult inmates—or even keeping them busy—as the newly revised bylaws required.

Conclusion

The much-heralded revival of the original Poor House experiment in 1806 was a dismal failure. After a brief initial expansion, the asylum again contracted. Although an occasional beggar was still forcibly confined, the systematic roundups of beggars had ceased. By 1811 the adults in the Department of Worthy Paupers were mostly those who chose to enter; and they received little training or discipline. The new Department of Correction was stillborn, and the Department of Secret Births never amounted to much. Only the Patriotic School thrived. Not only were its students one-third of all inmates by 1811, but they soaked up a large portion of the institution's employees, space, and budget. Thus, a mere five years after the school opened it was well on its way toward becoming the core of the reformed Poor House.

Although the 1806 restructuring had committed the institution to enlarging its clientele, it in fact became narrower. By 1811 the Poor House was serving a far more dependent group of paupers than it had in 1795. When the two functioning departments are considered together, 36 percent of the inmates were under the age of 15, up from only 21 percent in 1795. The adults were increasingly elderly and handicapped. Moreover, 67 percent were white (again combining departments), for the staff of the Patriotic School, the Department for Secret Births, and to a lesser degree the Department of Worthy Paupers gave privileged access to paupers of Spanish descent. Although the asylum was still racially integrated, it was less so than in 1795 when the institution still attempted to control the capital's poor and only 52 percent of the inmates were white.

Historians of Mexico usually attribute all changes of the early nineteenth century to independence and the ensuing economic decline (just as twentieth-century historians attribute everything to the Revolution). The transformation of the Poor House clients and purpose began, however, even before it felt the impact of these events. Straitened resources, already a problem before the insurgency of 1810, help explain why the reformed asylum remained small, but it is only one of several reasons why the original project was modified. Indeed, at the very time that the financial pinch began to be felt, the Poor House added a school, which was much more expensive to run than an asylum for adults, and maintained its commitment to it throughout the difficult independence period.

The wishes of the new donor were one factor diverting the Poor House from its original goals. The Patriotic School was Francisco Zúñiga's pet project and, between its building expenses and endowment, the one to which he devoted the largest portion of his estate. The sound performance of his bequest to the school (in contrast to the unforeseen extinction of his contribution to the asylum) made a difference, too, for the school's endowment continued to produce enough income to cover most—though not all—of its expenses, while the other departments of the Poor House had to share revenues that by the turn of the century were already insufficient.

The partiality toward the Patriotic School also reflects the new sensibility toward children and the accompanying view that this precious human resource needed schooling. Like many enlightened reformers, Zúñiga and González Carbajal (the board member who persuaded the wealthy miner to fund the school) saw orphans as a potentially valuable asset that should be salvaged for the nation.[76] The two gentlemen were said to have worried about the predicament of children who lacked the beneficent influence of the family and were exposed to the vices of the community.[77] They wanted their school to separate the students from the adult paupers so that the children would not become tainted with deficient lower-class mores.[78] Consequently they pushed the Poor House toward concentrating on preventing the corruption of the next generation rather than on reforming adults who were already set in their ways.

The Patriotic School project struck a responsive chord among its contemporaries. The viceroy, for one, apparently shared the special concern for children. On his visit to the newly inaugurated school in 1806, Viceroy Iturrigaray is said to have "shed tears" as the "innocent" orphans surrounded him and "called him their protector."[79] Indeed, when the asylum was in danger of closing in 1817, the argument considered most likely to obtain viceregal support was to emphasize its services to children. A petition from the board quickly brushed aside "the blind and crippled" but waxed eloquent about the "tender and miserable children" who would be exposed to danger, vice, and prostitution unless they could be saved by the Patriotic School.[80]

The renewed campaign against beggars did not receive a similarly warm reception. The city's elites failed to rally in support of the fundraising drive launched in 1806. Although the new Poor House board requested that priests in the Mexican archbishopric instruct their parishioners to donate alms to the asylum instead of giving them directly to "the poor who beg from door to door,"[81] the request had little effect. "Voluntary alms" never recovered their early volume, and the continuing plague of mendicity shows that rich people did not cooperate with the reformers' exhortations. If some propertied Mexicans maintained traditional charitable giving to buy their own salvation, others opposed the detention of paupers on principle. Jacobo de Villaurrutia gave voice to this position in an article in the *Diario de México* on November 19, 1805.[82] A prominent member of Mexican society, Villaurrutia served on the Audiencia and helped found the *Diario* that same year.[83] Although as a young man he had shared a long voyage to Spain with Archbishop Lorenzana,[84] he did not agree with the prelate's policy of institutionalizing beggars. Under the pseudonym "El Proyectista" Villaurrutia argued that it was a mistake to "deprive them of their liberty." Instead, it would be far more humane and cost effective to offer them home relief or, if they were homeless, to pay a neighbor to take them in. Evidently, there was no consensus among the capital's elites about the confinement of beggars.

Another factor thwarting the reform was resistance from Mexico City's paupers. During the years when beggars were still being rounded up and sequestered, many paupers contested the plan. Just as Araujo noted that people who did not want to go to the Poor House bought their way out, the daily registers for 1807–8 show that many who had been confined simply walked away or escaped—or misbehaved so badly that they were expelled. Consequently, the institution largely came to serve those who welcomed its services: orphans, unemployable single women and widows, and the elderly, blind, crippled, idiotic, epileptic, and infirm. Increasingly, its inmates were also whites who felt a special sense of entitlement to receive public aid. Thus, pressure from paupers helped shape the kind of asylum that emerged.

The Poor House staff and board members also contributed less than enthusiastically to the persecution of paupers. The quick demise of the Department of Correction and the expulsion of unruly inmates suggest that those responsible for implementing the plan had little taste for imposing discipline.

They were happy to educate vulnerable orphans—especially the most "deserving" children of Spanish descent. They took in some disabled adults and feeble elderly. Yet even after the asylum shrank in size, making it impossible to accept as many needy beggars, they still managed to make room for numerous white dons and doñas who were neither elderly nor handicapped, while restricting access to paupers at the bottom of the social scale. Indeed the Department of Worthy Paupers appears to have accepted vagrant dons, just as the Department of Secret Births accepted "libertine" white women with illegitimate children. Comparably profligate behavior would have barred those from the lower classes or resulted in their dismissal.[85] Thus, because of their ingrained prejudices, the staff distorted the institution's stated mission.

A hidden agenda of the reformed Poor House (probably present since the institution opened, though not as obvious) was to strengthen the declining caste system by preventing the downward mobility of white paupers. The Patriotic School served to uplift white orphans. The Department of Secret Births promoted white births and preserved the honor of white women. The Department of Worthy Paupers protected the impoverished whites, especially women, from the indignities of public poverty and provided lenient punishment for "distinguished" white vagrants. Indeed, by ensuring that white orphans did not grow up to be professional beggars, and by keeping idle dons off the streets, the asylum combated white vagrancy, a dangerous precedent in a colonial society. Far from challenging the stratified social system, the Poor House thus reinforced white privilege and validated the racial distinctions that prevented the poor from becoming an undifferentiated mass. Although a few particularly pitiable Indians and castes were still admitted, the staff had modified the definition of worthy poor so carefully spelled out in the "Prospecto." To the list of orphans, elderly, and disabled, they added whites—especially dons and doñas—in danger of losing status. Thus, even before it was buffeted by the crisis of independence, the Poor House had strayed far from the original experiment in social control.

{ 5 }

INDEPENDENCE AND DECLINE,

1811–1823

Although patriotic histories claim that independence was a major step toward the modernization of welfare institutions, this periodization has little meaning for the Poor House. On the contrary, the experience of the asylum challenges the triumphalism of nationalistic accounts because independence caused it to decline dramatically. Its misfortunes were not the result of conscious policies or legal changes. Instead, it was the outbreak of the independence wars in 1810 that precipitated the worst financial crisis suffered by the asylum in its four decades of existence. By the time Mexico became independent in 1821, the Poor House had suffered a drastic retrenchment that took it even further away from its original goals.

To be sure, the Poor House was affected by some of the jurisdictional changes that accompanied the end of colonial rule. The confusion about which government entity was responsible for the asylum began in 1812, when the new Spanish constitution placed all welfare institutions under the supervision of the municipalities.[1] During Agustín de Iturbide's short-lived Empire it reverted to the central government, with the imperial vice president serving as the president of the Poor House board.[2] In 1824 the new Mexican republic placed the asylum (along with other welfare institutions) under the direction of the city council, with the capital's governor serving as board president.[3] Thus, the powerful viceroy, who had presided over the colonial Poor House board, was replaced by weaker administrators, who, given the political instability of the early republic, rarely remained in their posts long enough to provide continuous supervision.

The asylum emerged from the independence years bereft of two other powerful patrons, the Church and the Poor House director. Although priests continued to sit on its governing board, top ecclesiastical officials were no longer serving as advocates of the asylum by 1806 and regular ecclesiastical funding had disappeared. Moreover, its wealthy and well-connected director, Don Simón María de la Torre, who had helped sustain it for decades, vanished from the records, never to be replaced by another director. His position was apparently abolished during the 1806 reform, but he had stayed on as an active member of the board until 1809.[4] The Poor House therefore confronted the crisis of independence solely in the hands of the much lower status salaried administrator, who, for the first time since the asylum opened, was essentially on his own. Although these twin losses did not initiate the institution's woes, they did signify a loss of protection at a time when it was badly needed.

The Poor House produced few records during this turbulent period, a pattern that would recur whenever it weathered trying times. The surviving documents show a steady reduction in its revenues beginning in 1811 and a precipitous decline (followed by a documentary vacuum) after 1817. A report submitted in February 1824 by a committee of aldermen painted a grim picture of the Poor House in 1823, when members of the committee inspected the asylum and collected their data.[5] By then it had shrunk nearly beyond recognition. The separate school and asylum had been merged. The remaining inmates—mostly elderly women and children—were enduring considerable deprivation. As the institution struggled to survive, it had abandoned all pretense of controlling the poor. It offered bare-bones assistance to a highly selected group of paupers without attempting to impose discipline. And it devoted an increasingly large portion of its resources to protecting the livelihood of its employees. Indeed, to a large extent what kept the asylum open during these difficult years were the vested interests its employees had acquired in the institution. When it was founded the Poor House had inadvertently created a new constituency that could not be abandoned, even though it did not contribute to the asylum's stated mission.

The Crisis of Independence

Although Manuel Rivera Cambas, the late-nineteenth-century chronicler, states that the Poor House endowment was lost in the Consolidación de Vales Reales of 1804, there is no evidence to support his claim. Only the institutions under ecclesiastical jurisdiction, such as the Hospital de San Andrés, were directly affected by this measure,[6] just as they were the only ones affected by the 1820 decree of the Spanish Cortes (parliament) suppressing the hospitaler orders.[7] Indeed, the Patriotic School endowment of 250,000 pesos survived the period intact. The leaders of independent Mexico took over the

Commercial Tribunal's obligation to pay the asylum interest, although they reduced it from the original 5 to 4.5 percent. The government fell behind in its payments for three months during the transition from imperial to republican rule, but then payment of the monthly interest quickly resumed.[8]

Correspondence between the viceroy and the city council for 1817–18 and two reports from 1824 and 1826 clearly date the onset of the decline to the aftermath of the Hidalgo Revolt of 1810. As Viceroy Juan Ruiz de Apodaca explained on September 30, 1817, "Since that fatal moment in which the atrocious fire of rebellion ignited on this handsome soil, all abundance disappeared. The corporations, houses, and rich families have been reduced to extreme want, and the asylums of piety, which subsisted mostly on voluntary donations, have been left without funds to support their unhappy inmates."[9] His perception was shared by Lt. Col. José Bernardo Baz, the syndic of the city council, who on December 29 explained that the independence wars, "which have destroyed this precious and opulent kingdom, now threaten this sanctuary of poverty, . . . which for so many years has been the shelter of disabled paupers, the school for destitute youths, and the asylum for people who with some punishment can improve their customs."[10]

The reduction in the Poor House revenues was gradual, as various government subsidies evaporated and businesses, properties, and government bonds in which its capital was invested ceased producing income. Table 16 shows that the first defaults came in 1811, as an hacienda, a pulque ranch, and the estate of a donor stopped meeting obligations totaling 177.5 pesos a year. Three more defaults followed in 1812. One of these was substantial: on January 1, 1812, the Tribunal de Minería stopped paying annual interest of 701.7 pesos on the principal of 14,035 pesos. Another loss followed when in May of 1813 the Tribunal del Consulado stopped paying interest of 237 pesos on funds secured on the Renta de Tabaco. In April of 1816 the estate of Captain Antonio Piñeiro stopped honoring its much smaller commitment of 90 pesos a year.

In 1817 the situation took a sharp turn for the worse. A devastating loss came in May with the suspension of the asylum's single largest source of funding, the lottery income of 1,000 pesos a month.[11] In October the city council announced that, since its own municipal funds were in arrears, it could not keep up its monthly contributions of 100 pesos (which it had resumed paying sometime after 1804, perhaps when the 1812 Constitution placed welfare institutions under municipal jurisdiction).[12] The situation deteriorated further in 1819 when the Poor House stopped receiving payments from the Temporalidades of the ex-Jesuitas. There is some discrepancy in surviving records about how much revenue these funds had been produc-

TABLE 16   Poor House Income, 1823 (in pesos)

	Principal	Interest (annual)	Date
Producing income			
Tribunal del Consulado (Fondo de Avería)	250,000	11,250	
Rental properties[a]		800	
Alms		468	
Pensioners (7)		504	
TOTAL	250,000	13,022	
Payments suspended			
Temporalidades (cajas nacionales)	25,355.3	1,267.7	1819
Tribunal de Minería	14,035.0	701.7	1812
Conde de Xala (property of San Cosme)	6,000.0	300.0	1812
Tribunal del Consulado (Renta de Tabaco)	4,740.0	237.0	1813
Estate of Don José P. Cobian	2,918.3	145.9	1811
Obrapía Don Juan Ruiz Aragón (consolidación)[b]	2,406.0	102.3	1812
Capt. Antonio Piñeiro	1,800.0	090.0	1816
Doña María Guadalupe Verdeja (Hacienda de Huizastitlan)	452.6	022.6	1811
Don José Ximenez Arenal	202.3	010.1	?
Doña María Gertrudis Villanueva (rancho de pulques, Zempoala)[b]	177.5	008.9	1811
Estate of Don Fernando Zorrilla	unknown	unknown	
TOTAL	58,087.0	2,886.2	

Source: 1824 report. The date on which payments were suspended is from "Informe," 1826, AHCM, Beneficencia, vol. 423, exp. 2, ff. 2v–3.

[a] Rental properties consist of three *fincas* (Calle del Relox, San Pedro y San Pablo, and Callejón de Dolores); a house called La Panadería, with its *acesorias;* and the acesorias of the Patriotic School.

[b] The 1826 report gives their last names as Arangoite and Villavicencio.

ing, with the 1824 report placing the annual loss at 1,267.7 pesos and the 1826 report claiming it was 3,725.9 pesos.[13] Either way, the Temporalidades had provided substantial revenues for the asylum. To make matters worse, the lucrative tablas de carnicería (the taxes assigned to the Poor House on the butchering of cattle in Mexico City and Querétaro) were no longer mentioned in any of these documents, probably because tax remissions declined during the independence struggle.[14]

Contributions from private benefactors, already waning by the turn of the century, apparently decreased even further. As the Poor House board explained in 1817, voluntary alms could not be relied on because they "so easily decline either due to the donors' deaths or the decadence of their fortunes or because they finally tire and resist giving any more."[15] Juan Abadiano, author of a late-nineteenth-century history of Mexican welfare institutions, echoed this analysis: almsgiving was insignificant by the time of Mexican independence, he claimed, "either because the spirit of charity had cooled or because donors no longer had the means to continue making contributions."[16] Thus, the crisis of the mother country took its toll as the colonial economy, already strained by Spain's ambitions in the late eighteenth century, buckled under the weight of new upheavals and demands. In addition, the long-standing embezzlement of some 13,500 pesos by the asylum's alms collector, which probably became public when the Poor House tried to recover the money in 1811,[17] may have made potential donors reluctant to give money to its fundraisers.

Ecclesiastical contributions also diminished. Although it is difficult to date their decline, it was quite dramatic by 1823 when the Poor House only received private and ecclesiastical "alms" of 468 pesos. By comparison, in 1803 the regular ecclesiastical alms alone had totaled 2,160 pesos: 1,200 from the archbishop, 600 from the cathedral chapter, and 360 from the Convent of Santo Domingo.[18] Surprisingly, no contemporary remarked on the reduction of ecclesiastical funding, perhaps because by the nineteenth century public welfare was considered the proper domain of the state or because it was obvious that the Church had been impoverished by the multiple blows it had suffered at the end of the colonial period, including the 1804 Consolidación and the 1820 loss of the hospitals it had administered.

By the fall of 1817 the institution was in serious jeopardy. In response to pressure from the Poor House board, the city council petitioned the viceroy for assistance. Their proposals came to naught, however. The city first requested permission to reduce by 600 pesos the amount it spent on the fiestas of the city's patron saints so that it could continue monthly payments of 50 pesos to the Poor House. The viceroy did not grant his approval, citing the "harm to third parties" that might arise if these festivities were not celebrated "with the accustomed solemnity." Apparently aware that ceremonial functions bolstered the legitimacy of the colonial state, he must have feared that abandoning symbolic rituals at this delicate time would undermine public consent in the colonial regime. The city fathers then proposed increasing parochial fees for burials and marriages by 1 peso and for baptisms by 4 reales in order to raise an estimated 500 pesos per month for the asylum. This plan also failed because it was felt that the "many miserable people" who could barely afford the current fees might therefore be discouraged from marrying

TABLE 17   Poor House Inmates by Category, 1811–23

	1811		1817		1823	
	No.	%	No.	%	No.	%
Adults						
Women	143				69	
Men	182				22	
ALL	325	59	?		91	66
Children	42	8	?		—	
Students						
Boys	131				37	
Girls	53				9	
ALL	184	33	?		46	34
TOTAL	551	100	289	100	137	100

and baptizing their children. The next proposal, to follow Madrid's example and tax each caballería of land 2 reales a month and each notarized will 1 peso, was likewise rejected by the viceroy because in the midst of a struggle against insurgents this was not the right time to ask the public to pay new taxes.[19] By March of 1818 the Poor House board was pinning its hopes on a request already made twice in the past (in 1764 and 1806) that the asylum be granted a tax of 4 reales on every pig slaughtered in Mexico City. The board members waited in vain for an answer. The viceroy's alternative—a printed fundraising letter sent on September 30, 1817, to selected individuals, trusting that Almighty God as "Protector of the Poor" would inspire them to contribute to this worthy cause—did not produce the desired result, either.[20]

The Poor House managed to remain open only with great difficulty. By December of 1817 it had 289 inmates, including the students in the Patriotic School—approximately half the number living there just six years earlier (table 17). The employees were reduced from twenty-six in 1811 to nineteen by 1817.[21] As the inmate population plummeted the Poor House began to rent out unoccupied portions of its huge building. By 1819 there were so few students that they were moved out of the Patriotic School quarters into the original part of the edifice. From then on the school and the asylum remained joined in the old building, with the students mixed in with the adult paupers—a cause of perennial problems.[22] The Royal Cigar Factory temporarily moved into the Patriotic School wing, and a porcelain factory took over a section adjacent to the chapel. By the time Mexico became independent, two-thirds of the establishment had been rented out for income, eventually to be lost during the Reforma.[23] Not only had it shrunk to one-third its previous physical size, but it had also become vulnerable to the disentailment of corporate rental property.

According to Abadiano the institution reached its nadir in 1820. Its employees endured several years without receiving a salary.[24] Rations were reduced to bread, beans, soup, and atole. There was no money for medicines or clothing. The inmates were in rags. The workshops were closed, and with them went the meager profits they had produced. Suppliers refused to provide food and materials on credit. Tenants fell behind in paying their rent. And the building, as well as three of its rental properties, deteriorated to the point of ruin.[25]

The first two years of independence, under the ill-fated Regency and First Empire, brought small relief, as the government approved some funding for the Poor House[26] and appointed a new Junta de Caridad composed of twenty of the capital's leading citizens (see appendix 4). There was considerable continuity with the colonial board. Eight of its members had served since at least 1806, including its "protector and president," the imperial vice president Don Francisco de Paula Luna Gorraez Malo Medina y Torres, Mariscal de Castilla, Marqués de Ciria, and Señor de Borobia. He had probably led the Poor House board in 1817–18 as well, when he signed its correspondence with the viceroy. As before, several board members used noble titles or (like the Fagoagas) came from noble families.[27] They divided their responsibilities in the same manner as the earlier junta, with individual members assigned to act as secretary, treasurer, and accountant; to supervise the departments of the Hospicio, Secret Births, and Patriotic School; and to be in charge of gathering contributions, admitting paupers, and caring for the linens and physical plant.[28] The imperial board had hardly begun functioning, however, when Emperor Iturbide was toppled.

The demise of the Empire in February of 1823 did not bring immediate changes. Since a new republican board was not immediately constituted, many of the old board members continued at their posts. Four who are mentioned in the 1824 report (the Marqués de Ciria, Don Domingo de Lardizával, Don Esteban Vélez de Escalante, and Don José María Fagoaga) had served on the board since at least 1806, their presence cushioning the Poor House from the three governmental changes of the period and their financial support keeping it afloat. The asylum also relied on old connections to suppliers such as the House of Yermo, which still provided food on credit as it had in 1803.[29] These patronage networks helped avert total disaster, but

TABLE 18 Poor House Expenditures, 1803 and 1823

	1803[a]		1823	
	Number	%	Number	%
Food	17,590.7	50	11,025.0	67
Medicine	1,221.6	3	208.6	1
Salaries[b]	3,667.2	10	4,416.0	27
Inmate wages	869.8	2	754.1	5
Divine cult	335.4	1	—	
Office	98.2	0	—	
Materials	6,855.5	20	—	
Tailors	285.9	1	—	
Tools	1,082.2	3	—	
Building	3,020.2	9	—	
TOTAL	35,026.7	99	16,403.7	100

[a] Expenses for 1803 omit 13,782.2 pesos in debt repayment.
[b] The 1824 report specifies that salaries include the value of food rations given to five of the twenty-two employees. The 1804 report only mentions supplementary rations for the rectora and does not specify their value.

they could not counter the loss of more than half the institution's income as well as of its two most powerful protectors, the viceroy and the director.

The "Lamentable" Poor House of 1823

The new republican government found the asylum in "lamentable" condition.[30] Poor House income for the fiscal year ending June 30, 1823, was 13,022 pesos, most of it from Zúñiga's endowment (table 16). Even though all expenditures except food, medicine, and wages had been eliminated (table 18), its revenues fell 3,381 pesos short of its expenses. Any unreported income, such as the earnings from accompanying funerals (which in 1803 had totaled 2,100 pesos), could not close the gap. Consequently, the asylum was heavily indebted. Employees were owed 11,898.9 pesos in back wages. Food suppliers were owed 1,382.1.[31] The institution had amassed a debt of 24,917.9 pesos to five board members who had served as treasurers and paid its bills out of their own pockets.[32] To make matters worse, the physical plant required 17,935 pesos worth of urgent repairs. The Poor House population had dropped to its lowest level ever, with only 137 inmates—and this number probably represents an expansion from a much lower point, since the 1824 report specified that eight of the nine girls had entered within the past year.

The Poor House that emerged from the independence crisis was not just a smaller version of the colonial asylum. During those dozen difficult years it finally abandoned the forcible confinement of beggars. Already moribund by 1811, this policy received its death blow in 1812. Meeting on February 3, 1812, the city council candidly admitted that the goal of interning beggars had been chimerical. The city fathers decried—in language reminiscent of earlier rhetoric—"the multitude of people of both sexes" who begged on the city streets, including many robust individuals who defrauded the deserving poor of alms. This time their solution was to appoint two aldermen to examine the capital's beggars, arrest the vagrants among them, and grant the "truly poor, useless, and disabled" licenses, printed at their own expense, which they could show whenever soliciting alms.[33] Although this system of licensed begging does not appear to have been implemented, it indicates that by 1812 city officials were resigned to tolerating mendicity; indeed, they would issue no more bans on begging until 1830.[34] The 1824 report confirmed that the rounding up of adult beggars had long ago ceased.

Homeless children were still occasionally apprehended and interned, at least before the fiscal crisis deepened in 1817. Correspondence with the secretary of the Poor House board in 1812 shows that the paupers placed in the asylum by city officials that year were mostly orphaned minors. For example, the two "vagrants" Anacleto Naba and Vicente Galeote, 11 and 7 years old, were interned "because they have no trade, spend their days selling lottery tickets in the streets, and have no knowledge of Christian doctrine." The 7-year-old Gregorio Mena was interned after his father was executed for murdering his mother, which left the child helpless and alone. And—in a case showing how the independence wars increased the population of orphans— the 14-year-old José María Naranjo was interned because he was an "orphan with no relatives or career who came from San Luis Potosí with the column of grenadiers."[35]

Despite the widespread need, however, the Poor House in 1823 had only forty-six youngsters in its school, a far cry from the 184 of 1811. In choosing among the many potential students, the staff showed a distinct preference for boys, who accounted for 80 percent of the students compared with only 71 percent in 1811. The staff also showed a preference for orphans whose relatives could afford to pay their way: seven of the thirty-seven boys were "pensioners" whose families provided a small stipend for their schooling.[36] Although the 1824 report supplies no demographic information on the male students, it gives detailed information for eight of the nine girls. These were

TABLE 19　Disabilities of Inmates, 1823

	Men	Women	All	%
Blind	3	10	13	14
Epileptic	0	5	5	6
Crippled	3	7	10	11
Chronically ill	5	16	21	23
Healthy	11	31	42	46
ALL	22	69	91	100

the 20-year-old María Encarnación Luna, who had been in the Poor House for eleven years; the 20-year-old Juana Francisca Cayón, who had been there eight years; the 16-year-old Juana Carlota Marañón, who had been there four years; and five other girls ranging in age from 9 to 18 who had entered in 1823.

The Poor House did not assist many adult paupers, either: only 91 compared with 326 in 1811. As the institution contracted, its adult inmates became even more highly selected than they had been twelve years earlier. Their profile is that of people who sought shelter voluntarily. The mecas whom the Poor House still incarcerated and attempted to acculturate in 1811 were gone. The remaining inmates were more elderly and infirm than before. Table 19 shows that 31 percent of the adult inmates were handicapped in 1823, compared with only 22 percent in 1811. Another 23 percent suffered from a chronic illness, compared with only 5 percent of the adults in 1803 (the only previous date for which that category was listed).[37] The striking increase in the chronically ill suggests that the adult population was older, since chronic infirmities increase with age. A higher proportion of blind inmates (14 percent of the adults in 1823 compared with 9 percent in 1811) likewise indicates aging, for nearly all the blind in the past had been elderly. For the first time in Poor House history a majority of the inmates (54 percent) were either disabled or chronically ill. As the 1824 report explained, they were the "truly needy who absolutely could not work for a living."

In addition to intensifying the early-nineteenth-century tendency to favor elderly and disabled paupers, most adult inmates were now women. By 1823 they represented 76 percent of the adults, compared with only 43 percent in 1811. Although the female population had fluctuated considerably during the last two decades (reaching 57 percent once, in 1803), women had never before come close to representing three-quarters of the inmates. Despite continued fluctuations in the sex ratio, they would never again slip back to the earlier levels. The feminization of the Poor House became a permanent characteristic of the institution. As the adult population remained a small part of the republican asylum, it would continue to concentrate its aid on the female paupers whom its staff considered most in need of protected seclusion.

The proportion of vergonzantes had increased as well. Although impoverished women of genteel background were already prominent in the late colonial Poor House, they had only accounted for 6 percent of the women in 1795. By 1823, ten of the sixty-nine women were listed as the solemn poor, a proportion that rises from 15 to 17 percent if the inmate-employees Medina and Vidaurri are counted among the vergonzantes, as they were in 1795. As in 1808, all of these distinguished paupers were female. One of them, the 80-year old widow Doña María Ignacia Olmedo, had negotiated considerable privileges within the asylum in which she had lived for at least thirteen years. She received her own rations of beans, rice, salt, lard, chile, meat, and bread worth 75 pesos annually, apparently because she took her meals separately from the rest in her upstairs apartment.

Thus, as it drastically restricted its inmate population, the Poor House favored the "respectable" poor even more than it had in the past. Not only was one of every seven women a vergonzante but one of every five male students was a pensioner whose relatives could afford to board him. They were probably white paupers, too. Although the republican documents, complying with the doctrine of legal equality, did not record the inmates' race, we can assume that, like most students and all vergonzantes in the past, they were of Spanish descent. By 1823, then, a substantial portion of the institution's resources were directed toward clients who were better off than the street people it was originally designed to serve.

Although these inmates may have felt fortunate to have a roof over their heads, they no longer lived in the "luxury" noted by Viera and Villarroel. The quality of the meals had deteriorated. According to the authors of the 1824 report, lamb—a large expenditure in 1803—had been eliminated in the diets of all but the sick, and healthy inmates ate meat (in the form of beef) only once a week, on Sunday. Most of the food budget in 1823 was spent for beans, chickpeas and other legumes, rice, and bread. Medical care had also degenerated, as the three positions of doctor, surgeon/pharmacist, and bleeder had been telescoped into one surgeon by 1823 (table 20).[38] In fact, the per capita expenses for medicine had dropped from 2.5 pesos per year in 1803 to 1.5, even though the inmate population had become considerably less healthy.

By 1823 the Patriotic School was scarcely worthy of that name, although its students still represented one-third of the Poor House inmates, as in 1811.

TABLE 20   Poor House Employees and Salaries, 1823 (annual salaries in pesos)

Employees	Salary
Asylum	
Administrator	1,000[a]
Rectora	256.9[b]
Chaplain	500[a]
Second chaplain	80 (part time)
Doctor	180
Patriotic School	
Assistant administrator	500
Teacher	500[a]
Warden	322.9[b]
Assistant warden	310.9[b]
Rectora (also maestra)	240.4[c]
Secret Births	
Ama	309[c]
Other	
Portero	12
2d portero	12
3d portero	12
Portera	30
Maestra amigas	18
Cook	36
Cook	24
Cook	12
Cook	9
Atolera	15
Sacristan	36

[a] Includes room only.
[b] Includes room and ration.
[c] Includes ration.

Since the separate school building had been rented, the students lived alongside the adult paupers in the old wing, thereby violating the prescribed separation of adults and children. The authors of the 1824 report lamented the disappearance of the workshops, which formerly had provided vocational training. Their loss is evident in the list of employees, which no longer in-

TABLE 21   Inmate Positions and Wages, 1823 (annual payment for each in pesos)

Women (N = 36)	Wages	Men (N = 18)	Wages
1 presidenta	9.0	1 portero street[a]	190.1
1 portera grate	9.0	1 assistant portero	18.0
1 assistant portera	6.8	1 lamplighter	15.0
1 portera upstairs door	6.8	1 plumber	9.0
1 portera chapel	6.8	1 refectolero	13.5
1 head atolera	24.0	1 catechism instructor	4.5
4 grinders	9.0	1 butcher	13.5
2 juicers	4.5	1 head nurse	48.0
2 strainers	9.0	1 assistant nurse	13.5
1 refectolera	6.8	1 cleaner	9.0
1 reader	4.5	1 apothecary servant-boy	9.0
1 catechism instructor	9.0	1 nurse epileptics	9.0
1 cook	18.0	1 watercarrier	4.5
2 assistant cooks	6.8	1 barber	9.0
1 dishwasher	6.8	2 stretcher carrier	11.3
1 primary schoolteacher	13.5	1 market porter	13.5
1 sewing teacher	9.0	1 attendant	4.5
1 mending teacher	4.5		
1 nurse	13.5		
1 assistant nurse	13.5		
1 ointment spreader	6.8		
1 supervisor	9.0		
1 cook	18.0		
1 nurse epileptics	9.0		
1 portera	6.8		
1 laundress	27.0		
1 assistant laundress	18.0		
1 night supervisor	6.8		
1 patio supervisor	4.8		
1 general supervisor	4.8		
Total wages	349.1		406.2

[a] Salary of 84 pesos plus extra rations.

cluded the master artisan who had been hired in 1811 (without his being substituted by a knowledgeable inmate; see table 21) and in the lack of a budget for buying tools or materials for the looms (table 18). The students were learning little more than the three Rs taught by their schoolteachers (the girls' was an inmate *maestra de amiga*) and the religious instruction provided by a priest and two inmate *doctrineros*, one female and one male. The girls may have learned to sew and mend from an inmate compensated as a *maestra de costura*, but the boys received minimal training for a viable career. The "school" had therefore been largely reduced to providing refuge rather than educational services. In particular, the two 20-year-old girls who had lived there for many years seem to have been merely protected rather than prepared for a life outside the asylum. Indeed, María Encarnación Luna, who was listed as "dull," could not have been a bona fide student.

The adult inmates were likewise sheltered rather than disciplined. Despite the straitened material conditions, they appear to have obtained assistance with dignity. Table 21 shows that a surprising number were paid for their services to the Poor House, though these payments, like those to employees, were in arrears. Although the practice of compensating selected inmates already existed in the colonial asylum, only 11 percent of the adult inmates had been so rewarded in 1803.[39] In contrast, the fifty-four inmates who received gratuities in 1823 (up from forty-eight in 1803) represented 52 percent of the women and 82 percent of the men, and must have included all the able-bodied adults as well as twelve of the ailing. Most of their "tips" were small, ranging from 6 to 9 pesos a year for such services as cooking, drawing water, washing, or caring for the sick and epileptic. Yet a few inmates who performed particularly important functions were paid better than some employees: thus, the inmate portero received a ration worth 106.1 pesos in addition to his 84-peso salary, the head nurse earned 48 pesos annually, and the head atolera earned 24 pesos a year. In addition, Doña Ana Medina (who is not included in these statistics) received a salary and rations worth 309 pesos for her job as *ama de confianza* in the Department of Secret Births.

The high number of inmate-workers underlines the degree to which residence in the asylum had become a privilege. The Poor House not only offered room and board, with care for the ailing, but also provided all capable paupers with useful work and an income to spend on amenities. Their services must have earned them the trust, and in some cases the respect, of the staff. As an administrator commented many years later, the inmate cooks were far superior to "the cooks from the street," who were often "vicious thieves or the kind who protect runaways and lovers."[40] As so many inmates took on positions of responsibility that helped the asylum function, the line between inmates and employees—already thin for a fraction of them—became increasingly blurred.

Just as many adult inmates had become employees, many employees had become clients. The most astonishing finding of the 1824 report, which its authors labeled "absurd," was the excessive number of staff members retained by the Poor House despite its fiscal woes. Even as the institution administered draconian economizing measures, it did not reduce its personnel commensurately. Although seven employees were let go between 1811 and 1817, the Poor House thereafter refused to cut more staff despite the declining number of inmates. Indeed, the 1824 report listed twenty-two employees (table 20), three more than in 1817 when the inmate population was twice the size.

To be sure, the number of employees is not necessarily an accurate reflection of how many of the Poor House resources went to its staff. The new positions might have been at lower wages or part time; we cannot tell who was cut in 1817 or added by 1823 because the 1817 reference to nineteen employees does not list them separately. A comparison with the 1811 census list shows five fewer maids, no mayordomo or master artisan, and one less teacher and warden by 1823, although a part-time chaplain and sacristan had been added to compensate for the loss of the second full-time chaplain. The substitution of these two employees for one actually saved the institution 284 pesos per year.

Yet the Poor House budget confirms the pattern of disproportionate spending on personnel. A comparison with the Poor House wage lines for 1803 (the last year for which financial records are available) highlights the magnitude of these costs. Table 18 shows that, as the inmate population plunged by 75 percent, outlays for food dropped by 37 percent and for medicine by 83 percent. In contrast, outlays for wages rose by 20 percent. Proportionally, the resources spent on employees thus increased from 11 to 27 percent of the asylum's budget. Indeed, by 1823 the cost of employees—had they been paid—would have been 32 pesos per year per inmate, compared with only 6.6 per inmate two decades earlier.

The growth in wages cannot be explained by inflation. Salaries, in the instances where we have comparable information, had remained flat for fifty years. As shown in table 20, the administrator still earned 1,000 pesos per year, as he had in the 1770s; the chaplain still earned 500 pesos and the rectora 120, plus rations of beans, peas, rice, salt, lard, chile, lamb, bread, candles, and charcoal. The 1824 report gave the value of these rations as 136 pesos, more than the rectora's entire salary, but that had probably been the case earlier as well. A few wages had actually been reduced over the last two decades. The rectora's wage had risen to 160 pesos in 1803, only to return to 120 by 1823. The retainer paid to the surgeon was also reduced from 300 to 180 pesos, perhaps reflecting the smaller number of patients he saw as the inmate population dwindled.[41]

Instead, the increase in wage expenditures reflects a dramatic expansion in the number of salaried employees, from twelve in 1803 to twenty-two in 1823. Most of this growth had come in 1806 when the Poor House added the Patriotic School. Thus, the ratio of employees to inmates had already risen from one employee for every 42 inmates in 1803 to one for every 20 inmates in 1811. Thereafter, as the number of inmates decreased, the ratio of employees to inmates did not decline proportionately. On the contrary, by 1817 there was one employee for every 15 inmates, and by 1823 there was one for every 6.5. Needless to say, the higher ratio of employees to inmates did not improve the services the institution offered.

The failure to release any staff member after 1817, even as the number of inmates plummeted, puzzled the authors of the 1824 report. By their calculation, which included among the employees the 54 inmates who were on the payroll, the Poor House employed 1 person for every 2 inmates. Although they recommended that the asylum immediately reduce the number of employees as well as their salaries, their suggestion appears to have had little effect. The next available list of employees, in a city guide of 1829, lists eleven "professional" employees for 202 inmates.[42] Assuming that the "nonprofessional" employees (the assistant porteros, sacristan, and servants), who had accounted for half the employees in 1823, remained in the same proportion as before,[43] then the Poor House had the same number of employees in 1829 as in 1823. Since the inmate population had risen to 202, there would have been 1 employee for every 9 inmates — only a minor improvement over the ratio of 1823. The reluctance of the Poor House to release personnel after 1817 suggests that the asylum had become an institution of patronage. As resources evaporated, it put caring for its own staff before caring for the indigent paupers it was designed to serve.

Its commitment to employees is also evident in the apartments the Poor House provided, not only for current staff members but also for two former employees' widows. These upstairs apartments were quite spacious. The administrator's apartment had seven rooms, including a living room, kitchen, three bedrooms, and a maid's room. Each widow had a two-bedroom apartment.[44] This arrangement may not have burdened the asylum unduly when it had space to spare, but that was no longer the case after the Patriotic School wing was rented. On the contrary, the 1824 report complained that the asylum was short an apartment to give to the assistant administrator, even though the job required his presence at all times. Since the institution did not charge its employees rent, it also forfeited potential rental income, which it badly needed.

In addition, the employees and their families soaked up other resources such as food and probably medicine as well. The surviving records only hint at these perquisites. The 1824 report lists five employees and one inmate-employee as receiving separate rations. But many others undoubtedly borrowed from the institution's stocks or joined the inmates for meals in the refectory, as the chaplain was required to do. Indeed, the employees' access to food is the only plausible explanation for the huge increase in per capita food expenditures from 32 pesos in 1803 to 80 in 1823. The relatively high amount spent on food in 1823 bought far less than in 1803, not only because of wartime inflation but because much of the food was not consumed by the inmates. The increased per capita food expenditures are thus a function of the large number of employees relative to the small number of inmates on which per capita calculations are based.

The asylum's largesse to its employees, and to the families of former employees, symbolizes the degree to which it conceived of itself as a responsible employer rather than a minister to the poor. In a sense, the employees had become clients entitled to job security, salaries, free apartments or rooms, meals, and probably medicine and medical care, too. Their access to free room and board provides an important clue as to why the asylum did not close during the terrible years of 1819–20. Even the staff members who did not receive their salaries for several years would have stayed to avoid having to pay these expenses elsewhere. The benevolent institution allowed them to remain rather than forcing them out into a difficult labor market where they might have faced pauperization. By doing so it extended the role it had already been performing for respectable but penurious white inmates who resorted to living in the institution to prevent their downfall.

Conclusion

The expenditure of scarce resources on employees rather than inmates suggests that the founders' dream of "well-administered charity," which would channel alms to an efficient central asylum, was not attained. The Poor House had created an entrenched bureaucracy whose goals had come to include self-preservation. This experiment therefore embodies the now-familiar pattern of welfare systems eventually benefiting the middle class that runs them as much as they benefit the poor. When push came to shove, the asylum economized by reducing the number of inmates and cutting corners on their food, training, and medical care, but it protected its employees. Although the favoring of staff only became obvious when the independence crisis forced the institution to reveal its priorities, it had likely been established long before. And it apparently persisted for many decades, since an 1863 report complained of how well the Poor House employees lived at public expense, taking the best part of the dilapidated building for themselves.[45] This factor must be added to those discussed in the previous chapters to explain why the asylum strayed from its original goals. Once they came to depend on institutional employment, the self-interest of the staff members helped undermine the Poor House experiment.

The channeling of alms to a central asylum also created a target for "white-collar" crime, though it rarely surfaced in the records. The pilfering of food and supplies is a universal problem in institutions. The embezzlement of 13,500 pesos obliquely referred to in an 1811 document may have been unusual, but it was unlikely to have been the only one in Poor House history. Corruption surfaced again in 1833 when government officials allegedly forced the asylum to buy spoiled corn and in 1841 when the administrator was accused of maladministering funds.[46] An 1869 report charged that employees were stealing linens and tableware and that suppliers were selling the asylum food at above-market prices.[47] These incidents suggest that Manuel Payno's colorful depiction of the early republican Poor House in his novel *Bandidos de Río Frío* was not entirely fictional. When the unlucky protagonist Juan unwittingly landed in the asylum, he encountered filthy, lice-ridden boys, merchants who regularly delivered inferior goods, employees who daily took home portions of the food meant for the inmates, and a kindly administrator, Don Epifanio, who when alerted to these practices chose to overlook them because he feared that if the truth came out he would be fired for incompetence.[48] Although it is impossible to estimate how much of the asylum's resources were wasted or skimmed off in this fashion, the petty corruption embedded in institutional life—as well as the occasional outright theft—undoubtedly added to the unreasonably high cost of providing services that is so starkly reflected in the per capita expenditures.

Despite these abuses, the authors of the 1824 report still believed in the original colonial idea. They proposed that the asylum once again intern all beggars by force, "receiving and teaching the helpless youths, vagrants, and all those whom laziness has disseminated on our streets as beggars" as well as the legitimate beggars who required shelter and assistance. They called for the workshops to reopen. They wanted to retrain "those who pretend to be disabled" as well as to care for "those who are truly unable to work." They argued that the confinement of beggars would "increase the alms from powerful individuals in this capital, who have always clamored against this kind of scourge, impossible to exterminate without recourse to these measures." [49] In other words, they felt that the initial purpose of the Poor House—combining shelter, repression, and reform—would still appeal to donors because it continued to fill a need in the republican capital.

Their dream was never realized, however. Although the asylum eventually recovered from its low point, it would always bear the imprint of the independence years. It emerged from this difficult period firmly in the hands of the state, which was hardly an advantage given its instability and penury. The Patriotic School and the Department of Worthy Paupers would continue to be joined (though the school retained its name), thereby undermining the goal of offering specialized services to separate clienteles. The adult paupers would remain few and primarily female and elderly. Moreover, the Poor House would never regain the punitive and rehabilitative thrusts it shed during the crisis. Half a century after it began, the long moribund experiment in social control was finally dead.

{ 6 }

REPUBLICAN DIFFICULTIES,

1824-1855

The recuperation of the republican Poor House was slow and faltering. As the Mexican state entered an era of unprecedented turbulence and the economy spiraled into depression, the asylum experienced brief periods of improvement alternating with backsliding. Republican leaders may have wished to restore the experiment designed in the mid–eighteenth century, but their sporadic attempts to confine and rehabilitate beggars (in 1830, 1833–34, 1843–44, and 1851) quickly fizzled. Instead, the institution devoted itself primarily to educating orphaned youth and secondarily to sheltering a few dozen elderly paupers, mostly women, who entered voluntarily. Indeed, by increasing its focus on children the republican asylum intensified the trend of the early nineteenth century.

The study of the Poor House during the first three republican decades sheds new light on some of the governments of the period, especially the early Santa Anna administrations. Yet what is most striking is its internal continuity amid the surrounding turmoil. These years witnessed frequent turnovers in government as well as three separate constitutions (1824, 1836, and 1843). Mexico was invaded three times from abroad, and for nine months during the Mexican-American War (from September 1847 to June 1848) U.S. troops occupied the capital city. These standard political markers had little meaning for the Poor House, however. It was barely affected by the transition from a federal republic (1824–35) to a central one (1836–47) and back again, because it remained under the jurisdiction of the city council under both systems. Moreover, while the Mexican presidency changed hands some forty times between 1824 and 1855, the asylum was apparently administered by only five individuals (appendix 3). One of these, José María Gómez Eguiarte, served the better part of two decades.[1] The board members also provided much continuity. Yet this stability could not protect the asylum from the successive crises that dampened republican dreams.

The Poor House Founders, 1824–33

In 1823, even before the enactment of the first republican constitution, the new government showed its good intentions toward the Poor House by mandating the appointment of a new board of directors and commissioning an inquiry into its situation.[2] The committee's report, submitted on February 8, 1824 (and analyzed at length in chapter five), detailed the deplorable state in which the asylum emerged from the years of the independence struggle. Republican leaders clearly meant to turn this situation around. The Acta Constitutiva of the Mexican Republic of January 31, 1824, assigned the responsibility for the Poor House to the city council.[3] The new administration accepted the earlier commitment of the Constituent Congress to pay the colonial state's debt to the asylum, which had invested 294,130 pesos of its endowment in various government agencies.[4] Early in 1826, when the Minister of Relaciones failed to see sufficient progress, he appointed another committee, the Comisión de Beneficencia, to investigate the condition of the Poor House, Foundling Home, and Retirement Home for Women.[5] Both in its name, which used the secular term *beneficencia* rather than the religious term *caridad*, and in its mandate to report on the three institutions together, this commission showed that the republican government was already thinking in terms of centralizing the management of welfare institutions.

The asylum began to recover, although its improvement was not always obvious to contemporary observers. Its situation was so bad in 1826 that Edward Thornton Tayloe, a member of U.S. Minister Joel Poinsett's staff, believed that the Poor House had closed "for want of funds, these having been exhausted by the government during the Revolution."[6] Tayloe apparently confused the Poor House with the Foundling Home, which did close for four years.[7] There is no evidence that the Poor House ever ceased functioning. The committee that submitted its report in April of 1826 found it in much better shape than the institutions for foundlings and recogidas. Indeed, the Poor House was considerably better off than in 1823. Although much of its income was still "paralyzed," the interest on the Patriotic School endowment was current. Most of the outstanding wages owed to employees had been paid.[8] Moreover, the school had expanded to take in 111 students, more than double the number served in 1823 (table 22). Still, the asylum could hardly be described as thriving.

TABLE 22   Poor House Inmates by Category, 1823–35

	1823	1826	1828	1829	1834	1835
Adults						
Men	22	?	15	?	—	29
Women	69	?	61	?	—	73
ALL	91 (66%)		76 (38%)		80 (25%)	102 (28%)
Students						
Boys	37	84	89	?	—	165
Girls	9	27	29	?	—	83
ALL	46 (34%)	111	118 (59%)		240 (75%)	248 (67%)
Juvenile delinquents	—	—	—	—	—	18 (5%)
Super-numeraries[a]	—	—	6 (3%)	—	—	—
TOTAL	137 (100%)	?	200 (100%)	202	320 (100%)	368 (100%)

Source: For 1826, 1826 report, AHCM, Beneficencia, vol. 423, exp. 2, f. 2.
[a] A term used in Spanish institutions to denote paying pensioners. Tikoff (2000), 11.

In 1827 the city council formally accepted jurisdiction over the Poor House and pledged 200 pesos a month for its maintenance.[9] This was an important step because, despite the instructions in the 1824 Constitutive Act, the oversight of the institution had been neglected in a conflict between the governor of the Federal District and the city council. As late as July 19, 1827, municipal leaders claimed that, with its independent governing board, the asylum was "subject to the governor, who is president of its junta," but not to the *ayuntamiento*.[10] To be sure, the city council had a long connection with the Poor House: two of its members had regularly served on the Poor House board, and it had provided regular funding for two brief periods (from 1774–87 and for several years ending in 1817). It had petitioned the viceroy on the asylum's behalf during the crisis of 1817–18. Yet its assumption of full responsibility for the institution was new, as was its substantial financial commitment. After 1827 the city council regularly appointed a *regidor comisionado*, an alderman assigned to the Poor House to replace the colonial director who had ultimate authority over the live-in administrator.[11] This arrangement did not, however, end the conflicts with the governor of the Federal District (known as the Department of Mexico from 1836 to 1847) who continued to preside over the Poor House board.[12] Although jurisdictional quarrels periodically flared, the Poor House benefited when an activist governor took charge, as it did under José María Tornel in 1828 and 1833–34, Miguel Cervantes in 1830, and Juan José Baz in 1869.

Only three days after taking office in February 1828, the first of these activist governors took measures to revive the asylum. Tornel appointed a Poor House board, finally fulfilling the 1823 mandate to create a completely new republican body. The Junta de Caridad had twenty-four members who, for the first time in Poor House history, were assisted by a fourteen-member Junta de Señoras, which oversaw the departments of women and girls (see appendix 4).[13] Soon thereafter, Tornel applied municipal taxes to the asylum[14] and the ayuntamiento asked the capital's vinaterías to make donations toward its expenses.[15]

The creation of a female board demonstrates Governor Tornel's commitment to improving that institution. It also reflects the expanding role of elite women in helping to deliver public assistance, for membership on a board went far beyond the role that the capital's ladies had played in the past when, as in 1806, thirty of them had served as godmothers for the girls in the Patriotic School. Like the male board, the ladies elected officers and divided among themselves the responsibility for various areas. Their vice president was Doña Luisa Vicario de Moreno, their treasurer was Doña Petra Ternel de Velasco, and their secretary none other than Doña Leona Vicario de Quintana Roo, the famed heroine of the independence wars. The other members included several wives of the male board members. The ladies had no elected president, probably because they served under the male board. Despite their formal status, legitimized by the gubernatorial appointment, this organization seems to have perdured less than a year—apparently failing to outlast Tornel's short tenure in office. An 1829 city guide makes no mention of the female junta when listing the twenty-six members of a Poor House board appointed by the interim government that ruled that year. Although there would not be another female board in the Poor House until 1865, this ephemeral organization was the first of several ladies' boards that supervised welfare institutions in the Mexican capital from the 1830s on.[16] It thus planted a seed that would blossom some four decades later.

The membership of the male board also shows the importance accorded the Poor House. Although the boards of 1828 and 1829 did not overlap in membership with those of the colony or the First Empire, they continued to attract leading citizens of the capital—and included two priests, as before. Even when Tornel was forced out of office in 1829, fifteen members of the 1828 board (62 percent) remained. In both years the vice president was

José María Bocanegra, a well-known statesman who held, among other positions, those of congressional deputy, Minister of Justice, interim president for a week at the end of 1829, and governor of the D.F. (and therefore president of the Poor House board) in 1841–42. Other well-known board members included Isidro Rafael Gondra, the writer, president of the Chamber of Deputies in 1828, and for many years director of the National Museum; José Manuel de Herrera, the famed engineer and professor at the School of Mines; and Anastasio Zerecero, the prominent federalist (and later Liberal) politician who eventually served as a magistrate on the Supreme Court of the Federal District during the Restored Republic. The appearance of foreign businessmen on the junta also mirrored changes in republican society (see appendix 4).

It is not clear what the presence of so many luminaries on its board signified for the Poor House. When Bocanegra later wrote a two-volume history of the period, he mentioned the asylum on whose board he had twice served only once, in a terse paragraph noting that Tornel had appointed him vice president of the Junta de Caridad on February 19, 1828.[17] Likewise, José Ramón Malo, appointed to the board in 1847, only mentioned the Poor House once in his diary, noting that twenty youths from the asylum had carried his sister's coffin to her final resting place on March 1, 1843.[18] Zerecero would write a history of the independence period without mentioning the Poor House at all.[19]

For many, membership on the Poor House board may have been an honorary position that mainly served to enhance their prestige. For a few, it became a serious commitment. Although full lists of board members are unavailable again until 1865, the partial information that survives (appendix 4) shows that some members served for decades, like the director of the Aduana, Mariano Domínguez (at least 1828–61), and the priests Dr. Agustín Carpena (at least 1844–56) and Presbyter Pedro Fernández (at least 1830–44).[20] Many others donated generously to see the asylum through difficult times. Francisco Fagoaga, who served on the board from at least 1833 to 1851, contributed so much to the republican Poor House that he was honored by burial in its chapel when he died in 1851.[21] Moreover, he was one of four Fagoagas to serve on the board, since for some prominent Mexicans patronage of the institution apparently became a family affair, passed on from father to son.[22]

The Poor House was reinvigorated under the leadership of the new boards of 1828 and 1829. Table 22 shows that the inmate population grew by 46 percent, reaching 200 in 1828 and then holding steady, at 202, the following year. The increase from only 137 inmates in 1823 was entirely due to the growth of the school, for 15 fewer adult paupers were served in 1828. By then 59 percent of the inmates were students, the highest proportion since the Patriotic School was founded in 1806.

Despite the increasing focus on children, the city fathers had not lost their desire to sweep beggars and vagrants off the city streets. In pledging a monthly contribution to the Poor House in 1827 the city council expressed its hope of thereby helping to eliminate the "swarms of vicious beggars that infest the streets of the first city of the Mexican Republic."[23] By 1828 the municipal authorities recognized that the Poor House could not fulfill this function "until [its] funds are brought up to date and new ones raised to maintain this establishment so interesting to the public morality." Thus, they devised alternatives to deal with two categories of male beggars. On March 3, 1828, President Guadalupe Victoria established the Vagrants Tribunal to expedite the trial and sentencing of healthy men to the armed services or colonization. Youths under sixteen years of age were ordered to learn a trade, not in the Poor House but under the direction of master artisans selected by the city council, so that they would not grow up to a life of "idleness and, consequently, vice." As an additional measure to discourage mendicity, a March 7 decree (which applied the presidential decree to Mexico City) prohibited, under penalty of a 25-peso fine, "the giving of alms to those who beg in churchyards and doors, plazas, portals, theaters, the Alameda and other parks, bars, cafes, restaurants, and shops."[24] This was a bold move that attempted to confront the pillar of traditional Catholic charity, almsgiving, head on.

These efforts were interrupted by two successive coups d'états. In the wake of these political crises, which included the Parián riot of December 4, 1828, in which an uprising of five thousand "plebes" terrified Mexico City elites,[25] the government of Anastasio Bustamante attempted to renew the roundups of beggars.[26] On August 9, 1830, seven months after Bustamante came to power, the governor of the Federal District, Miguel Cervantes, prohibited begging in Mexico City and ordered all caught soliciting alms to be confined in the Poor House.[27] This first reiteration of the colonial ban in independent Mexico clearly reflected diminished confidence in democratic rule and a renewed concern with public tranquility.

In order to accommodate all paupers who might be sent to the asylum, the Poor House board concurrently launched a fundraising drive, which was announced to the public in the 1830 decree. Soliciting donations from individuals and commissioning five of their members to collect voluntary subscriptions from local businesses, they expressed confidence that the effort would succeed if most people who already "assigned a monthly sum for alms" designated it for the Poor House instead, thereby "serving to provide succor for the truly needy while freeing themselves of the constant clamor of beggars."[28] This statement recognized that the 1828 ban had failed to change the patterns of almsgiving, thus necessitating a return to repression of mendicity.

A month later, in an article published in the September 4, 1830, issue of *Voz de la Patria*, the journalist Carlos María de Bustamante prematurely proclaimed the campaign a success. He claimed that the annoying "throngs of beggars" were gone from the streets and plazas of the capital. "Robust men," who had previously feigned illness to avoid work, now labored assiduously in the restored Poor House workshops. Bustamante attributed this accomplishment to the energy of the *junta patriótica* of the Poor House and principally to the zealous governor of Mexico City. Cervantes, the ex-Marqués of Salvatierra (noble titles having been abolished in 1826), had an old association with the Poor House on whose board he had served in 1822. As the head of its board in 1830 (by virtue of his position as governor), he personally led the roundups of beggars—much as Llanos y Valdés had done before he left the asylum in 1791. According to Bustamante, Cervantes "went out in person to round up this scourge of the republic, surprising many rogues in the act of begging."[29]

Since Bustamante realized that the confinement of beggars would require a substantial increase in the asylum's funding, the goal of his article was to appeal for donations to bankroll the effort. His exhortations emphasized the benefits of putting to work unworthy beggars who deceived the charitable public to obtain easy handouts. Repeating what appears to be an early version of modern "urban legends," which become widely accepted without much factual base, he exposed an alleged scam by Indians living in nearby towns who were blinding their children a few days after birth so that they could earn an easy living as beggars. This despicable practice would end, he claimed, once parents saw that their offspring would be shut up in the Poor House to card wool and perform other work that did not require sight. Indeed, although the title of Bustamante's article is "Poor Beggars," he portrayed them entirely as mendacious vagrants and urged his readers to contribute generously to extirpate this plague.

The response must have been disappointing, however, because the roundup and disciplining of beggars was short-lived. By 1831, the administrator was complaining that overcrowding and underfunding had forced him to expel eight boys for misbehavior, although they had nowhere to go.[30] The next available report on the Poor House, in February 1833, after another change in government, revealed that the asylum was again in a "state of abandonment." Its board had ceased functioning. Part of the cause was apparently a previous Minister of Relaciones's decision to reduce the board to ten members until so few were left that—since "some missed meetings because of their work and others because of impediments"—the board "never or very rarely" met.[31] A subsequent report of November 27, 1833,[32] revealed that the government had fallen behind on paying the interest on Zúñiga's endowment to the Patriotic School, even though it had been reduced from 4.5 to 4 percent.[33] The inmates were "miserable." The food—when it was delivered at all—was "scarce and of poor quality."[34] The workshops had again disappeared, and without vocational training the youths spent their days in idleness. Finally, a cholera epidemic had swept through the asylum in August.[35]

At this point, it is no wonder that even ardent republicans looked back on the colonial period with nostalgia. The author of the November 1833 report, his memory greatly enhancing the accomplishments of the past, remembered 1806 as a Golden Age when the well-funded Poor House had been able to "establish workshops in various trades, train orphaned youths, assist a multitude of beggars, confine all those wandering the streets, banish vagrants from the capital, and correct many vicious and corrupt youths who consequently became useful citizens." These worthy aims, though often compressed into the single goal of survival, had never been forgotten. Indeed, the two reports from 1833 are themselves manifestations of renewed government interest in the asylum.

Recovery under Santa Anna's First Administration, 1833–34

Upon taking office in June 1833, the new administration of President Antonio López de Santa Anna energetically tackled the Poor House problem. José María Tornel, already governor of the D.F. by February and again responsible for the asylum, ordered its board to be increased to fifteen and to meet twice a month. He obtained the government's commitment to pay the Poor House the equivalent of what it had received from the colonial lottery, 12,000 pesos a year, last paid sixteen years earlier. He approved the board's petition to collect directly from the Aduana 25,067.2 pesos, a total representing the interest due on Zúñiga's endowment, the lottery funds, and the rental income from a few properties.[36] On December 8, 1833, he granted the Poor House the fines levied against tavern owners for dispensing prohibited liquors, and on December 9 he granted it the fines on houses allowing the forbidden game of *bagatela*.[37] On August 5, 1834, the governor further favored the Poor House by ordering that various fines levied by the Jueces de Letras be remitted to the asylum.[38]

This infusion of funds brought a brief respite to the Poor House. Reporting on the condition of the Mexican poor in 1834, the British consul Richard Packenham noted a remarkable "recent" improvement since the Poor House corrected the problems caused by "its funds hav[ing] from time to time been taken possession of by the government" as well as its having been "for some years very badly managed."[39] Table 22 shows that it expanded to take in 320 inmates in 1834 and 368 in 1835—the highest number since 1811.

In a report submitted in May 1835, the Poor House administrator boasted of how well the inmates were treated, a claim corroborated by Packenham's brief description of the previous year as well as by internal records. The asylum was clean and orderly. The physical plant had been repaired. The inmates were neatly dressed, the men and boys in uniforms originally purchased for the army. The sick were daily visited by the doctor and received all necessary medicines. The inmates ate well, at least by the standards of the Mexican poor of today. For breakfast they received a cup of atole, half a torta of bread, and a piece of pan dulce—with "those who need it" enjoying a cup of chocolate as well. For lunch they ate a dish of beef or lamb, with a ration of six to eight ounces, depending on their age, "well condimented" rice, and a six-ounce loaf of bread. For supper they ate beans or stewed peas with bread. Apparently tortillas were not served—further evidence that the institution was no longer catering to Indians by that date.[40]

Packenham also found the school in excellent shape. Praising the vocational education provided to the students, he wrote that the boys and girls "are taught trades, domestic industry and find no difficulty in providing for themselves when of an age to leave the establishment." Several "ancient" looms had been restored, including one that manufactured socks. A new workshop may have been temporarily added in response to a proposal by Mariano Galván Rivera. A well-known publisher and member of the Poor House board, he offered to install a printing and binding shop in the asylum to simultaneously "teach the boys a useful and honest occupation" and produce revenue for the institution—and, presumably, since he did not have to pay rent or market wages, earn a profit for himself as well.[41] Indeed, the school in this period produced a famous alumnus, the paying pensioner José María Marroquí. After going on to obtain a secondary school and university education, Marroquí became a distinguished statesman, linguist, and chronicler of Mexico City's history.[42]

Finally, the Poor House reopened the Department of Correction, which had closed within two years of its establishment in 1807. In doing so, it fulfilled a request from the city council, which in 1829 had proposed that the asylum revive the disciplining of juvenile delinquents so that they would not have to be placed in prison with hardened criminals.[43] The asylum's staff apparently acceded to this proposal under some pressure from Governor Tornel in 1834. As recently as 1831 the administration had expelled eight unruly boys, proof of its continuing reluctance to have the institution serve as a reformatory. The eighteen corrigendos detained in 1835 were far fewer than the hundred for whom Tornel had requested places the previous year. Again this department soon shriveled, to close sometime before 1841.[44]

With renewed growth came an intensification of the trends that had accompanied the earlier retrenchment of the Poor House. Its concentration on youth had increased dramatically. The majority were students, who represented 67 percent of all inmates in 1835, compared with only 34 percent in 1823. Another 5 percent were juvenile delinquents kept in the new correctional department. Thus, the asylum was increasingly devoting its resources to training—and, while the correctional department lasted, reforming—needy young people. The proportion of adult inmates had dropped to its lowest level ever, only 25 percent of the inmates in 1834 and 28 percent in 1835, compared with 66 percent in 1823. The Department of Secret Births, though it still existed, had no inmates at the time of the 1834 or 1835 inspections.[45] The few adult paupers were even more elderly and infirm than before. Indeed, Packenham described all the adult inmates as "aged-infirm persons." The 1835 report labeled all men *ancianos* rather than *hombres*—a shift in terminology that came to apply to the women, too, in subsequent reports. Furthermore, one-fourth of the adults were sick enough to be in the infirmary when the list was made. As in 1811, the male inmates appear to have been less healthy than the female, for 38 percent of the men but only 18 percent of the women were in the infirmary. The republican staff thus continued to apply the same gendered notions of eligibility as had their colonial predecessors. Elderly women, who now represented 72 percent of the adult inmates, were considered the neediest of the capital's adult paupers, although very few of them found a home in the republican asylum. Elderly men had to be considerably more infirm to merit institutional assistance. Orphaned children, however, were now considered the worthiest of all.

The revival of the asylum was accompanied by new measures intended to restrict begging. Two decrees of October 24, 1834, ordered the confinement in the Poor House of blind beggars "who harangue the public" and youths "who mob parish churches" to beg for the volo at baptisms.[46] These were but two small subsets of Mexico City beggars, for the municipal authorities realized that the asylum's capacity, though recently expanded, was still limited. The timing of the edicts nonetheless serves as a reminder that efforts to restore the Poor House went hand in hand with efforts to eliminate mendicity.

The dramatic recovery of the Poor House under Santa Anna's presidency reflected a broad effort to improve the delivery of public services. The administration experimented with a centralized system of supervising the capital's welfare establishments: the Poor House documents of 1833 and 1834 (and, again, during Santa Anna's later administrations until 1847) are filed, for the first time, together with those of other welfare institutions under the title Negociado de Caridad: Hospicios.[47] This attempt to unify the oversight of public welfare—already presaged in the appointment of a Beneficence Commission in 1826—deserves further scrutiny, for it may have served as a precedent for Juárez's creation of the central Office of Public Beneficence in 1861. A related shift is that during this period the Poor House board was often referred to as the *Junta de Beneficencia* rather than the *Junta de Caridad* (see appendix 4). Although the new name may only reflect changing fashions (and was inconsistently used in any case), it might also symbolize the desire to replace the traditional assistance provided in disparate institutions with a system directed by the government from a central office.[48]

It is unclear who should receive credit for the reforms of this period. Perhaps it was Vice President Valentín Gómez Farías, to whom Santa Anna delegated power while he remained on his Veracruz estate and who enacted an ambitious program of liberal reforms from April 1833 to April 1834.[49] Perhaps it was Governor Tornel, who protected the Poor House in both 1828 and 1833–34 and who, as founder of the Lancasterian schools in Mexico, is known for his concern with public education.[50] Or perhaps some credit should go to Santa Anna himself. The positive experience of the Poor House during three of his early administrations—1841–42 and 1843–44 as well as 1833–34 (though not 1839, 1847, or 1853–55)—suggests that this much maligned figure may be due for a reassessment.[51]

Renewed Penury and Scandal, 1835–41

The brief flourishing of the Poor House ended soon after Santa Anna's resignation in January of 1835. The 1835 report was written four months later to inform the governor that, since the national treasury had failed to meet its obligations to the Poor House for two months in a row, it was 9,000 pesos in debt. Although the government responded by granting the asylum new fines on vinaterías and casillas de pulque,[52] the asylum's financial problems persisted. The government's hands were tied by its deepening penury, especially as customs revenues plummeted by 68 percent between 1834 and 1838.[53] As creditors with direct rights to these funds proliferated, the Poor House repeatedly lost out. Its plight was aggravated after 1836, when the adoption of a new centralist constitution gave rise to a dispute over the proper relationship between the Poor House and the governor of the newly created Department of Mexico, which replaced the Federal District.[54] The jurisdictional confusion thickened in January 1841 with the creation of a municipal Board of Health (Consejo Superior de Salubridad), which included among its duties the regular inspection of "hospitals and houses of beneficence."[55]

It is difficult to document the extent of the asylum's deterioration during these years because detailed record keeping ceased from 1835 to 1841, resuming only when Santa Anna returned to power in the fall of 1841. Brantz Mayer, the secretary of the U.S. Legation, believed that the Poor House had closed for lack of funds,[56] but a later report confirms that only the Departments of Correction and Secret Births had shut their doors (the former permanently, the latter temporarily).[57]

The records of the new Santanista administration provide a glimpse into the depths to which the Poor House had sunk during the past six years. Daily inmate counts, available for ten months beginning in November 1841, show that the number of inmates had dropped considerably from the high of 368 in 1835. In November and December of 1841 the asylum's population (perhaps already reflecting an improved situation) hovered between 251 and 271, some 30 percent less than during the first Santanista revival.[58] An 1844 report referred to the "sad times" when the "orphans of both sexes lived as if paralyzed, without occupation and reduced to learning only Christian doctrine, reading and writing, and some sewing and embroidery because the dearth of funds meant there were no workshops, teachers, tools, or materials for learning useful trades."[59]

The writer and statesman Guillermo Prieto, who accompanied Santa Anna's Minister of Hacienda Ignacio Trigueros on an inspection of the Poor House, found it in a shocking state of decay—despite the "efforts and spirit of evangelical charity of its chaplain, Don Agustín Carpena."[60] Prieto melodramatically described "patios full of sand with weeds growing to the banks of the drain pipes, loose and dangling gratings, broken bricks in the corridors, pieces of crumbling roof tiles. In the dining room, hunger; in the kitchen, smoke, grime, and bones replacing meat. In the department of beggars, filth, cold, and living skeletons."[61]

Two scandals that erupted in the fall of 1841 illustrate the usually well hidden underside of institutional life. Allegations of sexual molestation and cruel punishment reveal dangers that always existed for the students in the school, even if they did not make it into earlier written records. Although Santa Anna's ministers carefully investigated the charges and then attempted to correct these abuses, the documents indicate that the Poor House tried to shield its employees from serious public oversight.[62]

The first report was occasioned by a charge of cruelty leveled on November 4, 1841, by a citizen who had observed a group of Poor House boys marching in procession down the street of San Francisco to attend a funeral "escorted by a pedagogue with a whip in his hand and the appearance of a herder of beasts, bringing shame on the people of Mexico." The accusatory letter launched a full-scale investigation that lasted two months, for the punishment of whipping had been outlawed in schools by a decree of August 17, 1813.[63] Although the teacher and other staff members were exonerated, the questioning of the employees and inmates (individually and in private) provides insight into the daily routines of the republican Poor House.

The administrator, Francisco Barroeta, claimed that the students followed a daily schedule similar to that prescribed in the eighteenth-century bylaws. The students rose at 6 A.M., and "at this hour all but the littlest ones are given brooms to sweep the corridors." Afterward they went downstairs to the refectory for breakfast and then attended school (or were trained in the workshops) until noon. They had recess and lunch from noon until three, when they returned to school until their second recess at five. At evening vespers they prayed the rosary in the chapel and then returned to the refectory for supper before repairing to the dormitories, with the boys and girls kept separate at all times. The students thus spent seven hours a day in school. Their strictly regimented schedule combined study, work, religion, and play. Barroeta's portrayal of this orderly regime was called into question, however, by the remarks of 13-year-old Juan Cervantes. Having arrived in the asylum only five days earlier, he had been shocked to see that "the boys behave like beasts and are often injured."

The living conditions of the elderly paupers also show remarkable continuity with the late colonial Poor House, for adults were not subject to the rigid discipline once envisioned for all inmates. The 1841 report did not describe their daily regimen at all, and scattered evidence from the period suggests that the ancianos came and went freely, often without permission, received visitors at their pleasure, had access to alcoholic beverages, and were not required to work in the asylum's manufactories, which were exclusively for the youths. Indeed, the daily head counts for 1841 and 1842 show that anywhere from six to sixteen inmates were out *con licencia* (with permission) on a typical day. And pulque was a regular item in the Poor House budget.[64]

The degree to which the Poor House continued to be an institution of patronage can be glimpsed from occasional information on the vergonzantes (although the term was no longer used in the documents of the 1830s). These ladies still demanded special privileges such as the separate upstairs room requested in 1833 by Doña Ana María Benítez, widow of Lt. Col. Don Manuel

Páez. Having entered the asylum several years earlier when the government defaulted on her husband's pension, she had been living with her sickly daughter in a private room in the infirmary. In January of 1833, when the director tried to move her downstairs into the common dormitory, she tried (though the records do not state with what success) to have Maestro Cordero removed from his room, "which does him no good," because she felt it would benefit herself and her daughter more.[65] A petition from Doña María Josefa Urías, a descendant of one of the asylum's founders, shows a similar privileging of selected "respectable" paupers. Until she left to take care of a sick aunt, she had been one of the "solemn poor" who enjoyed a private room, double rations, "and other comforts." Denied readmittance when she attempted to return in 1833, she then contacted a high official in the Ministry of the Interior, who supported her petition, "considering the rights she has as a descendant of the founders." [66] Of course, her ancestor was thinking of the capital's beggars, not of genteel ladies fallen on hard times, when he helped establish the asylum. As in the colonial period, however, some distinguished ladies used their connections and pedigrees to live at public expense. During the republican years they had to be quite desperate, however, since living conditions in the asylum were considerably less pleasant than in its colonial heyday.

Despite the good order supposedly established for the students and the indulgence accorded the adult paupers, the shortage of funds forced the Poor House to cut many corners. The inmates interviewed in 1841 complained that the food was terrible and never included meat. The breakfast atole was "either raw or burned"; the bread was cold, and the frijoles were badly seasoned. Only a few ailing señoras ancianas were given hot chocolate in the morning. Although the sick received the medicines ordered by the doctor, they too complained that they lacked the meat or even the healthy broth "that in better times they had always enjoyed." Blankets were so scarce that the youths had to sleep huddled together on a few *petates* to stay warm—with the exception of the leprous, who were kept apart, and of the lucky few who "worked on the machines" and had their own mattresses, presumably because they bought them with the wages they earned. The Poor House administrator confirmed the inmates' complaints. He explained that the asylum could no longer afford the rations it had once provided. With only twenty-eight mattresses, thirteen blankets, and seventeen wool throws for more than two hundred children, they were indeed forced to sleep together, a situation that was "highly prejudicial to their morals as well as to public hygiene." He insisted that the budget did not allow any improvement because the Poor House income was sometimes as low as 200 pesos a month, while its monthly expenses totaled at least 2,000.[67]

Another cause of the inmates' suffering was the punishments regularly doled out to the students. One new boy's testimony—that he had heard of month-long lockups—was not corroborated by the other inmates. But the boys reported that they often received "slaps and blows" for misbehaving at meals and that they were locked up as a penalty for stealing or trying to escape from the asylum. Several girls complained that the rectora had beaten them or made them stand "in the manner of a crucifix with their arms tied against a stick." The administrator concluded, however, that the punishments, when administered, were justified and moderate, with short detentions only applying to the hours of recess. He further claimed (although his statement seems exaggerated to defend his employees) that the majority of the students were actually juvenile delinquents (*vagos y corrigendos*) either interned in the asylum by the government to be rehabilitated or sent by widowed mothers who could not control them. "This class of youths requires some vigor," he explained. He added that the teachers and rectora were generally well liked by their charges, and closed his report by praising the "good order, sufficient cleanliness, excellent organization of the hours of the day and of the work of the inmates, and painstaking care with their instruction"—as well as the kindness, morality, and Christian piety of his employees.

The Poor House troubles did not end here, as is revealed in a concurrent investigation of the administrator himself.[68] Barroeta was accused of embezzling the institution's funds and trying to rape two female inmates on a balcony, one of whom allegedly died when she jumped to the street to evade him. Barroeta denied both charges. He explained that the girl had jumped from the balcony to escape the asylum—for she was a corrigenda "of bad conduct" who wanted to "dedicate herself to profligacy"—and that she was back in the asylum, alive and well, after being apprehended. It is difficult to know whether the charges had any substance to them, for the Poor House board fired Barroeta without a full investigation. The accusations do suggest, however, that sexual abuse was considered a real threat to institutionalized women—at least by the citizen who leveled the charge. Barroeta's defense also indicates that, although the separate correctional section had been closed by 1841, some delinquents were still mixed in with the students. Along with many of the deserving orphans, they were boarded in the school against their will.[69]

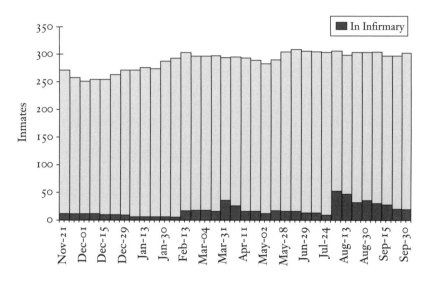

FIGURE 3   Weekly inmate counts, November 21, 1841, to September 30, 1842

The Second Santanista Revival, 1841–44

In the late fall of 1841 Santa Anna's new administration moved boldly to end these problems. The Poor House board dismissed Barroeta on November 18, claiming it had never been pleased with his work. Indeed, the directors may have been looking for an excuse to fire the administrator, for he had been much resented since Vice President Gómez Farías appointed him in 1833, in a blatant exercise of patronage, without consulting the board. Barroeta's appeal was denied, with the board members insisting that under the 1806 bylaws it was they, not the vice president, who had the right to name and remove all Poor House personnel. The government ordered Barroeta's compliance, "to keep the peace and good order of the Poor House,"[70] and the case was closed.

During the next few months the asylum again began to recover. Governor José María Bocanegra restored some of its funding and reopened the Department of Secret Births.[71] Figure 3 shows that the inmate population grew steadily throughout the winter and spring of 1842 until reaching a high of 309 inmates on the fifth of June. It then stabilized at an average of 301 inmates through September, when the daily registers end. The population apparently continued to grow, for a report of May 1, 1844, stated that the asylum regularly cared for some 400 inmates.[72]

The daily head counts available for November 1841 to October 1842 are an excellent source for studying fluctuations in the inmate population. The daily variations were slight and show no seasonal pattern, except that the summer rains seem to have brought recurrent epidemics. Just as in August of 1833 the Poor House in August 1842 was struck by what appears to have been another bout of cholera, which sent 52 inmates to the infirmary and caused one to die "of diarrhea."[73] The epidemic did not, however, reduce the total population of the asylum. There were an average of 277 inmates during the cold winter month of January, when we might expect more paupers to seek shelter; the numbers rose to 295 during the hot summer month of May, and then averaged 301 during the rainy months of July and August as well as the dry month of September. Of course, since most of the inmates were no longer adult paupers coming in from the city streets, it makes sense that seasonal variations would be minimal. Instead, the majority were students who lived in the school year-round, thereby contributing to the stability of its population.

The one significant trend during those ten months, the 18 percent growth in the inmate population, appears to correlate solely with Santa Anna's return to the presidency. The dates of the daily records (November 1841 to September 1842) correspond almost precisely with one of his terms in office (October 1841 to October 1842). The resurgence of other types of documentation also coincides with this presidency as well as his next one, from March 1843 to October 1844. Indeed, the renewed support received by the Poor House appears to have been part of a larger effort to improve the living conditions of the populace, which is evident in the creation of the Junta de Fomento de Artesanos in October 1843 and its related mutual aid society, the Sociedad de Beneficencia, in March 1844.[74] An attempt to improve the care delivered in public hospitals can also be seen in the October 1843 decree authorizing the establishment in Mexico of a French nursing order, the Sisters of Charity of St. Vincent de Paul.[75]

Again, it is unclear whether credit should be given to Santa Anna directly or to a member of his administration, as Guillermo Prieto does for the improvement of conditions in the Poor House. In his *Memorias de mis tiempos*, Prieto praises Ignacio Trigueros, the Santanista Minister of Hacienda from November 1841 to December 1842 and March 1843 to October 1844, for single-handedly turning the asylum's fortunes around. According to Prieto, Trigueros used his considerable personal wealth as well as the power of his office to renovate the building (including donating the statue of Captain Zúñiga) and "with extraordinary energy" to annul onerous contracts, to end the corrupt practice of "*giving* the children" to textile factories to serve as sweatshop labor, and, though "confronted with hatred and calumny," to correct the many "abuses to which this important establishment had become hostage."[76] Apparently initiated during Santa Anna's 1841–42 term of office, these changes bore fruit mainly when he returned, after five months' absence, in 1843–44. During this second period Trigueros, in addition to resuming his post at the Ministry of Hacienda, became a member of the Poor House board, on which he served until at least 1859 (appendix 4).[77]

Governor Bocanegra may also deserve some of the credit for the Poor House reforms. He spearheaded the first revision of the institution's by-laws since independence by appointing a drafting committee in November of 1841. The committee's completed *Ordenanza para el régimen y gobierno del Hospicio de Pobres de esta capital*, approved by Santa Anna in June 1843, was promulgated in November.[78] These bylaws were the culmination of a project that had been initiated by Tornel fifteen years earlier but twice shelved when he was ousted from power. A draft produced under his first governorship in 1828 and revised during his second one in 1833 formed the basis for the *Ordenanza* of 1843.[79] Since Bocanegra had been Tornel's appointee to the Poor House board in 1828 (and his close collaborator in editing the *Amigo del Pueblo*),[80] he may have provided some of the continuity that spanned the various Santa-nista administrations.

In November of 1841 Governor Bocanegra had charged the Poor House board with drafting bylaws "more in keeping with the enlightenment of the century" to guide an asylum that "provides to all classes in society the advantages they should expect from a paternal government wishing to elevate the republic to the level of the civilized nations of the world." Yet the *Ordenanza* fell short of this goal. Responding primarily to the recent jurisdictional quarrels, they dealt almost exclusively with the governance of the asylum and the duties of its employees. Indeed, the statutes were so brief that in most aspects of the internal regime the colonial bylaws continued to apply.

The new bylaws unequivocally asserted the independence of the Poor House board. Although the "Supreme Government" was named the "perpetual patron of the institution," its board was given the exclusive authority to nominate its members, hire and fire employees, set salaries, and generally determine how to "assist the inhabitants of the house with all charity . . . and provide them with moral instruction as well as a good civil and religious education." Putting to rest any uncertainty about his authority, the governor of the Department of Mexico was confirmed as president of the Poor House board.

The board mandated by the 1843 bylaws, though now simply called its junta (rather than the *Junta Real*, as in the eighteenth century, *Junta de Caridad*, as in the early nineteenth century, or *Junta de Beneficencia*, as in the 1830s), resembled those that had governed it previously. Members, who served life terms, were to raise funds for the asylum and closely supervise its affairs. Their division of assignments was similar to that of the past. Two of them were still priests. Confirming the reform put into place by Tornel in 1833, the board was smaller than the late colonial one, with fifteen rather than twenty-four members.[81]

The Poor House described in the bylaws consisted of only three departments: the Hospicio, the Escuela Patriótica (also called Casa de Huérfanos, or House of Orphans), and the Departamento de Partos Ocultos. The Department of Correction had been definitively abolished, for it had become superfluous with the creation in 1842 of a new institution, the Casa de Corrección.[82] This reformatory fulfilled the government's long-standing desire to have a separate facility to rehabilitate juvenile delinquents. Although it was first located next to the Poor House in part of the original building that was being rented out, the reformatory was separately funded and administered. It moved to the Tecpam in 1850 and was expanded (and renamed the Colegio Correccional de San Antonio) in 1853. In 1863, when García Icazbalceta wrote his report on the capital's welfare institutions, it housed fifty youths of both sexes.[83] The financially strapped Poor House was thereby relieved of the burden of serving as a correctional institute as well as a boarding school and asylum for elderly paupers. After 1842, when delinquent youths were no longer mixed with the deserving students, the Poor House could offer its pupils a better education as well.

Thus, the Poor House after 1843 functioned as a highly specialized institution dominated by the Patriotic School and sheltering a few dozen elderly inmates on the side. The Department of Secret Births, though maintained in the 1843 bylaws, was largely inactive and quite peripheral to the asylum. It continued to be staffed by an elderly inmate. In 1861 she was Doña Feliciana Desés, who received room and board plus an annual salary of 60 pesos.[84] By the time García Icazbalceta visited the asylum in 1863, she had presided over the dilapidated facility "for many years." The fact that her salary was less than half what its first director earned shows that the department functioned at a level much reduced from what its founders had expected.[85]

Yet Mexico City authorities still wanted the Poor House to do more. The 1843 bylaws instructed the board to reestablish workshops in the school so as to train the orphans to be "useful to society." Moreover, although there was no longer any mention of rehabilitating adult paupers, the municipal government briefly tried to revive the confinement of beggars. A month after the publication of the new bylaws, on December 20, 1843, the governor of the Department of Mexico ordered the city's alcaldes auxiliares and celadores to round up beggars and remit them to the asylum.[86]

A report of May 1, 1844, described an institution flourishing after Santa Anna—"once again" in the presidency and "desiring the progress of the country"—"saw to it" that the state met its obligations to the asylum. His government assigned the Poor House 4 percent of the customs revenues[87] and established a weekly lottery for the Poor House to replace the lapsed colonial lottery.[88] The inmate population reached four hundred after the asylum's "doors were opened to all beggars rounded up by the police on the capital's streets and to vagrants who were fomenting the vices that accompany idleness." The aging building was repaired and modernized "in contemporary style," with the addition of hot water piped from the roof to renovated kitchens and baths. Workshops trained the boys to be weavers, tailors, carpenters, and shoemakers and the girls to be spinners and embroiderers. The asylum again "provides aid to the indigent, who will there find succor, and to orphans, who will there find subsistence and training . . . to become artisans who are . . . well educated in the rights and responsibilities of citizens." In short, "this House of Beneficence has improved so much that it astonishes those who see it now and know how it was before."[89]

A private benefactor, Lt. Col. Manuel Ayllón, contributed to this revival by establishing a workshop to produce linen and canvas in 1843. According to Alfaro, this enterprise was so successful that the Poor House quickly dominated those industries. Indeed, Alfaro claimed (though it is doubtful that he could have known this from the vantage point of 1906) that the profits were high enough to pay the student-apprentices well and that with the training they received they easily found jobs upon leaving the asylum. In his 1881 survey of welfare institutions, Juan de Dios Peza reported that both boys and girls had once worked on the 150 spinning wheels and had earned tidy sums that they saved and took with them when they left. These workshops had been short lived, however, due to the "political revolutions" of the time.[90]

The disciplining of adult street people was not evident to contemporary observers, however. Travelers continued to remark on the crowds of beggars in the Mexican capital. In 1844, for example, Brantz Mayer described the professional beggars who overran the capital, importuning passersby "incessant[ly] from morning to night," using "blindness, a sore leg, a decrepit father or mother, or a helpless child" as "capital" to set up a lucrative business "for life." Mayer saw no evidence that they were being confined; indeed, he affirmed that "there is no 'poor-house' in Mexico, to which such vagrant wretches are forced to go."[91] At about the same time Waddy Thompson, writing the memoirs of his stint as U.S. envoy from 1842 to 1844, assured his readers (incorrectly) that mendicity was not forbidden in Mexico.[92]

The second republican attempt to revive the original Poor House experiment met the same fate as in 1830. Already faltering after Santa Anna left office in September 1844, it collapsed in the "fearful" earthquake of April 7, 1845, which destroyed much of the Poor House building. As usual, the asylum lacked the necessary funds for repairs, even though the Herrera government on May 5, 1845, restored the proceeds from the Temporalidades of the Jesuits, which had helped support it during the colonial period.[93] Although board member Francisco Fagoaga came forward with a sizable contribution for building repairs,[94] the confinement of beggars was not reinstated.

The next decade brought the renewal of a pattern that had plagued the Poor House since the early republic: government defaults on its payments followed by renewed petitions for assistance. These petitions invariably led to brief attempts to shore up Poor House income, including a decree of October 15, 1846, directing the Lottery of San Carlos to pay the Poor House the 1,000 pesos a month it had regularly received during the colonial period.[95] Unfortunately, in an era when the government was over its head in debt, and in any event changed regularly, such measures rarely outlasted the outgoing president. Public support, in the form of the small daily alms the junta had hoped for in 1830, once again proved disappointing. Over the next few years there were periods when only the generosity of individual board members, especially Francisco Fagoaga, kept the Poor House open.[96]

The documentation on the Poor House largely vanished during this decade, as had occurred during its previous periods of decadence. A petition from 1847, in the midst of the Mexican-American War, again alleged insolvency.[97] The situation must have deteriorated after September 14, when U.S. troops occupied the capital for nine months and imposed an onerous war tax on the ayuntamiento. Moreover, two city councils governed simultaneously —or, perhaps, as far as the Poor House was concerned, none governed.[98] In 1849 the Board of Health inspected the asylum and encountered "filthy conditions," which reflected the asylum's straitened circumstances.[99] The resignation of city councils in 1850 and 1852 cannot have helped matters.[100]

The municipal census of 1848 provides some information on the Poor House, although it only counted employees and skipped the inmates. The census taker found sixteen live-in staff members. This list shows that, even without the additional employees who lived outside the asylum, the various departments were reasonably well staffed—though perhaps, as in 1824, the employees had been retained at the expense of the inmates. The administrator had two assistants. The boys had two wardens and a schoolteacher;

the girls had a rectora, *vicerectora*, and embroidery teacher. The men's infirmary had a nurse, but none was listed for the female infirmary—perhaps because she was an inmate, as in previous years. Although the ancianas had a warden, none was listed for the elderly men who were now but a handful of the asylum's inmates. Finally, there were three live-in atoleras working in the kitchen.

As in 1823, the staff took up a substantial part of the Poor House building. The sixteen employees lived in the institution along with forty-one family members and three servants. Some lived with their minor children. For example, the administrator, the widowed José María Gómez Eguiarte, lived with his 9-year-old daughter Teresa and two servants (or perhaps female relatives).[101] The male nurse, the widowed Francisco García, lived in a room with his 6-year-old daughter Trinidad. The widowed vicerectora, Guadalupe Urbichari, lived with her two teen-age daughters. Other employees lived in complex extended families. The portero, José Benítez, lived with his wife, her brother, his sister, and his sister's two small children. The widowed rectora, María Cisneros Ordiera, lived with four sisters and her (or a sister's) two children. The largest live-in family was that of the embroidery teacher, the widowed Doña Dolores Arauz, who lived in an apartment with one servant and seven relatives: her married daughter with three children and her widowed sister with two.[102]

In addition to receiving free housing, these employees had considerable job security. At least six of them (the administrator, assistant administrator, rectora de niñas, rectora de ancianas, embroidery teacher, and girls' teacher) would still be there thirteen years later.[103] As before, the line between employees and inmates was somewhat fluid: both the girls' teacher, Doña Concepción Borja, and the rectora de ancianas, Doña Eusebia Durán, would be referred to as elderly inmates by 1861. Their shift from employees to inmates is only an extreme manifestation of the dependence that the staff (like many inmates) developed on the institution. The Poor House provided a particularly supportive environment for widows as well as some of the very few "respectable" jobs available for middle-class women in Mexico City. The proportion of widowed employees was high: eight of the nine women and two of the ten men. The many benefits they received is hinted at in an 1841 document. Requesting that the government pay the Poor House "what we are owed," the administrator had cited the difficulty of supporting 322 individuals—a figure that included some two dozen employees and their families, as well as the inmates, as part of the asylum's clientele.[104] As in 1823, however, these perquisites were provided at a time when the Poor House could ill afford them.

Although the asylum remained impoverished, after 1848 it was aided by a new Department for Curing Eyes. This clinic was the brainchild of Francisco Fagoaga, who donated 30,000 pesos for its establishment. Located in the Poor House building, it was isolated from the asylum itself and was entirely paid for out of a separate endowment. Directed by the famed Dr. José María Vértiz, it offered the first cataract operations in Mexico.[105] It still existed in the 1860s and 1870s, with its own staff and budget.[106] It may thus have improved the services the Poor House offered its blind inmates, who had always represented the largest proportion of the disabled.

By the middle of the nineteenth century the Department for Curing Eyes was but one of many enterprises functioning in rooms adjacent, but not formally connected, to the asylum. In addition to several apartments rented out as residences (including one where Guillermo Prieto lived),[107] there was a tavern, public bath, porcelain factory, cashmere manufactory, beer distillery, passementerie, and coachmaker's shop. These businesses operated in rented rooms that had once been part of the huge but now partially dismembered asylum.[108] In 1851 the street of Providencia was put through a rented section of the building, definitively isolating the republican Poor House from part of its former edifice (fig. 4).[109]

A financial report compiled on the eve of the Disentailment of 1856 sheds further light on the state of the asylum. By then the Poor House could only function with continuous penny pinching. Although its income of 29,000 pesos was approximately the same as in 1833, it was much worse off than in 1803, when its annual income (without including the loans and supplements from the director) was over 35,000 pesos—and when 65 percent of these funds (21,500 pesos) were steadily provided by the government. In 1856 the Poor House received only 45 percent of its income from the government: 12,000 pesos from the Lottery of San Carlos, and 1,200 from taxes on public entertainment. Nearly half its income (12,916 pesos) was derived from the revenues produced by what remained of its assets. These came from bequests, most made long ago in the form of real estate or monetary donations invested in real estate.[110]

By 1856 the bulk of the asylum's endowment, Zúñiga's 250,000 peso bequest to the Patriotic School, had disappeared, for the government had spent the principal and stopped paying the interest. The endowment may have been used to defray the costs of war with the United States in 1847. While interest was still being paid irregularly in 1844,[111] it had ceased by December 1, 1850. As late as October 22, 1851, the government still recognized its obligation to the asylum: on that date it ordered the lapsed interest due since December 1, 1850, to be paid out of "funds of the interior debt."[112] But at

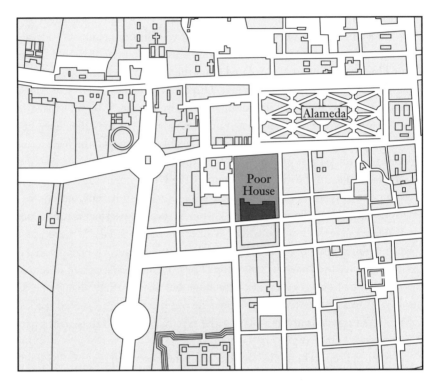

FIGURE 4   Poor House engulfed by growth of the city and intersected by Providencia Street, 1851

some point between 1851 and 1856 the attempts to meet the interest payments stopped altogether.

Thus, the government's usurpation of the Poor House endowment, often blamed entirely on the Disentailment, had in fact begun before the liberal Reforma. A half century later Miguel Macedo, surveying the history of Mexican poor relief, correctly dated the first confiscations to the early republic when "the urgent needs of our governments during that long and sorrowful period of internal revolts resulted in their following the example of the Spanish government and seizing a large part of the funds of public welfare, although almost always in the guise of a temporary loan, which, however, was rarely repaid." [113]

The Poor House generated very few of its own funds. The workshops no longer earned profits because the asylum did not run them directly, instead allowing the owners to keep the profits in exchange for training the students and paying them small wages.[114] Since the students used these gratuities to buy their own clothing and mattresses, or to accumulate savings for leaving the asylum,[115] the workshops provided only indirect savings for the Poor House.

Only the boys accompanying burials brought in income, for after keeping one real of the peso each earned, they were required to turn the other seven over to the institution.[116] A surviving ledger book shows that an average of twelve boys attended six to ten funerals a week during 1853–56. A familiar sight in the republican capital were the mourning youths in black frock coats and top hats, depicted by both Manuel Payno in his *Bandidos de Río Frío* and Antonio García Cubas in his *Libro de mis recuerdos*.[117] García Cubas described how eight older boys usually carried the coffin, while eight younger boys went ahead carrying burning candles. In large funerals, additional boys followed behind in a solemn procession. The mourning service was a lucrative business, providing 2,500 pesos, or 8 percent, of the asylum's total income in 1856.[118] An occasional lavish burial could be a windfall, as when one hundred *hospicianos* accompanied Don Lucas Alamán to his final resting place on June 3, 1853, as they did again for Doña María Guadalupe González de Salado three months later. Funeral processions that went outside the city gates paid double.[119] Such profitable burials were rare, however, and were balanced by those of benefactors and past employees, which had to be attended without compensation. For example, on April 19, 1853, five boys attended the funeral of Don José Severo Rocha without charge because he had taught drawing to the students for many years without accepting payment.[120]

The ecclesiastical funding lost by 1823 was never restored, unless its contributions were hidden in the small category of private donations. It was not that the Church had totally lost its connection to the institution. Two priests regularly served on the postindependence boards. Indeed, when the number of board members was set at fifteen in 1833, the two religious represented a larger proportion of the junta than they had on the much larger late colonial board. The republican priests often exercised considerable power, as when Félix Osores, the dean of the cathedral chapter, served as board vice president in 1841 and 1842 (appendix 4), or when longtime board member Canon Agustín Carpena served as rector of the asylum in 1856. Both of these priests contributed generously from their personal funds to keep the Poor House open.[121] But the Church no longer considered itself a partner in financing the institution, a sign that the republican secularization—notably including the abolition of mandatory tithes in 1833—had reduced the funds available to the Church for public assistance.

Regular private donations never returned to late-eighteenth-century levels, either. Although "alms" had doubled since 1823, they were but a mere 900 pesos—only 3 percent of Poor House income—in 1856. These contributions paled beside the 19,200 pesos received when the asylum was founded and the 3,817 received in regular pledges and alms in 1803.[122] The dampening of the charitable impulse that began during the asylum's second decade therefore became a permanent feature of Mexican life.

After three decades under republican rule the Poor House was deeply troubled. It could barely support a reduced number of inmates. Its own earnings were meager. Donations from private benefactors were erratic. Regular ecclesiastical contributions had disappeared. Funding from a perpetually penurious government that repeatedly raided—and finally dissipated—the institution's endowment, was precarious. The continual crises, both external and internal, that buffeted the asylum did not help.

Conclusion

Despite the sorry state of the asylum, republican leaders kept proclaiming their desire to revive the original Poor House experiment. Some of the impetus for that initiative had lessened after independence. The staggering growth of the colonial capital, which had prompted a fear of destitute migrants milling about on the city streets, abated briefly when refugees from the independence war returned to the countryside. Although a steady influx of migrants soon resumed, in a reversal of late-eighteenth-century patterns, Mexico City grew more slowly than the nation as a whole for the entire half century after independence.[123] In addition, the need to direct people into the labor force was much reduced because of the economic recession that plagued the early republic. Yet the large population of homeless, beggars, and vagrants remained a perennial problem. When the new republic failed to achieve prosperity and progress, its leaders fixated on the lower classes as part of the cause. Both federalists and centralists were embarrassed by the throngs of ragged paupers, a daily reminder that Mexico had failed to join the ranks of the "civilized nations" of the world. They worried about the difficulty of instilling the work ethic when so much of the population lived in idleness. They despaired of building a democratic government based on an ignorant public. They were particularly distressed that pauper children "in their most tender years" were exposed to the "vices and bad examples" of their elders—clear proof of the prevailing belief in the culture of poverty that prevented the development of "healthy morals, or . . . a knowledge of the duties of men in society." [124] They feared that crowds of street people could become unruly mobs threatening social order, as occurred in the Parián riot of 1828. In addition, they found the clamor of beggars a constant annoyance. Just like the Bourbon officials, the federalists and centralists were convinced that the only way to eliminate vagrancy was to remove all who begged from public spaces. Like them, too, they wanted to find a solution that would not "deprive the truly needy of the aid provided by charity." [125]

Like Don Quixote tilting at windmills, Mexico City officials tried four times to revive the original Poor House experiment. The 1830 decree of the Bustamante government ordered beggars confined to the asylum because their "incessant" solicitations had become "so excessive and bothersome that it forces us to dictate measures to remedy this abuse." [126] A decade after that attempt failed, the government tried again. An 1841 memo from the Minister of Relaciones to the governor of the Department of Mexico expressed provisional president Santa Anna's concern with "the innumerable beggars who throng the city streets, sleeping on benches at night and bothering the public on the avenues and at the door of churches." The minister inquired whether the Poor House could take them in along with "the dirty and naked youths" who "assault" respectable citizens entering cafes and bars with their requests for alms and "who need to be given a trade." The minister also expressed concern that the children of prisoners were "abandoned and corrupted" while their parents were in jail. Another group, "drunk and scandalous women, who offend public morals with their indecent nakedness and who wound the ears with their obscene words," he hoped could be confined in the Recogidas. The governor replied that unfortunately the last Retirement Home had closed in 1835 and the Poor House could not afford to fulfill "the obligations of its founders." He agreed, however, to accept prisoners' children over six years of age for as long as their parents were in jail.[127] Other attempts to round up paupers in December 1833 and the winter of 1843–44, both likewise under Santa Anna, similarly failed.

Although the government eventually gave up on detaining beggars in the Poor House, it continued to seek alternative methods for dealing with troublesome paupers. The Vagrants Tribunals of 1828 were designed to force able-bodied men into military service and place unemployed youths as apprentices or servants. The same decree that established the Mexico City tribunal attempted to reduce mendicity by outlawing the alms that made it profitable. Then, in 1842, a separate reformatory was established to rehabilitate juvenile delinquents. Finally, when city officials again attempted to prohibit begging, on December 18, 1851,[128] they relied on a new institution, the Casa de Asilo de Pobres Mendigos de San Miguel Arcangel, to confine the capital's beggars. The proposed bylaws for the House of Asylum, published by the Society to Promote Material Improvements in Mexico, echo those of the colonial Poor House. The new asylum was to take in "true" beggars only, excluding vagrants. It was to transform as well as shelter them, with workshops designed to provide vocational training and keep them busy and with religious instruction to provide a moral education. Men and women were to be strictly segregated. Regimented daily schedules were to instill the virtues of punctuality and discipline. The Casa de Asilo was to perform a carceral function since inmates could only leave after proving they had a means of earning a living. Those who fled and again solicited alms, as well as those who misbehaved, would be punished. And the inmates' plain uniform would daily remind them that they were cared for "thanks to charity."[129]

These alternative attacks on begging had no more success than the original Poor House experiment. The prohibition on almsgiving immediately became a dead letter. The Vagrants Tribunals convicted few men. Studies of the capital's tribunal by Frederick Shaw and Sonia Pérez Toledo show that it did not meet for months on end, even though it was supposed to meet twice a week. When it did convene, it released most of the men brought before it.[130] The aldermen who served on the tribunal apparently did not share the pressing desire to staff the army or northern colonies that had led Congress to create the national system of Vagrants Tribunals. Despite their broad mandate, they defined vagrancy narrowly in their deliberations and only convicted the unemployed who were making trouble, not those "of good character." A month after the Mexico City tribunal was founded, Councilman Isidoro Olvera protested its procedures as "odious . . . espionage" and "illegal inquisitorial questioning." He insisted that there were no vagrants in his two wards but only honest citizens who were unemployed because of "the lack of manufactures in which our artisans can be occupied."[131] Thus, conflicts between national and local authorities, as well as compassion bred by daily contact, spared idle men the full impact of the measures intended to combat mendicity. Moreover, since male paupers could vote until literacy and property requirements for suffrage were introduced in 1836,[132] the capital's aldermen had nothing to gain and something to lose by persecuting the destitute men in their wards.[133]

The Casa de Asilo did not last long, either. By June 1855 the city council noted an alarming "drop in the donations that help to sustain the Casa de Asilo de San Miguel Arcangel."[134] It subsequently disappeared from municipal records.[135] García Icazbalceta's report on the city's welfare establishments in 1863 did not mention any such institution.[136] The main reason for its quick demise, hinted at in the introduction to the reglamento for the Casa de Asilo, was that by the time it opened in 1852 the original Poor House experiment no longer had wide appeal. Private donors, such as those who created the Society of Beneficence in the 1850s, preferred to fund day schools, which provided breakfast for indigent children.[137] Wealthy foreigners supported new institutions, the Asociación de la Beneficencia Francesa, Suiza, y Bélgica and the Sociedad Española de Beneficencia (both established in 1842), which provided services to indigents from those nations.[138] Neither did the destitute appreciate the initiative. The editors of the *Revista Mensual de la Sociedad Promovedora de Mejoras Materiales* admitted as much when they wrote: "We will have to work very hard to persuade the needy paupers . . . to enter the House of Asylum, which is being opened for them."[139]

Even after the new beggars' asylum closed, the foundering Poor House did not take back the functions it had gradually spun off to other institutions — the punishment of vagrants, reform of juvenile delinquents, and confinement of beggars. Its services were now destined for a very limited subset of the Mexico City poor. As it recovered from the depths of the independence crisis, it concentrated its resources on orphaned children. By taking in half orphans, as well as those who had lost both parents, it also continued to provide assistance to widowed parents, especially widowed mothers. The few elderly inmates entered voluntarily and received humanitarian aid without being subjected to punishment or discipline. Efforts to mold paupers focused entirely on the education of children. Yet we should not judge the republican asylum as having failed simply because it did not resuscitate the original Poor House experiment. It successfully restored — and expanded — its boarding school under difficult conditions. The school served to raise and educate more orphans than ever before. In addition to this benevolent function, it contributed to the asylum's original mission in a very specialized way by salvaging selected children from a future of paupery, thereby sparing the capital a potential source of social disorder.

{ 7 }

LA REFORMA, REORGANIZATION,

AND CRISIS, 1856–1863

From 1856 to 1876 the Poor House was convulsed by the Reforma, two chaotic decades of liberal reforms, civil war, and foreign intervention. The Reforma began with a period of liberal control highlighted by the promulgation of the Constitution of 1857. This document unleashed the bloody Three Years' War (1858–60), as Conservatives refused to accept the new "heretical" Constitution. Winning the capital city in January 1858, Conservatives held it until the Liberals regained it in December 1860. Then, with the help of French troops, Conservatives routed the Liberals in June 1863 and established an empire under the Austrian Archduke Maximilian from 1864 until his defeat and execution in 1867. The Liberals then returned triumphantly to power during the Restored Republic of 1867–76. This chapter examines the tumultuous first stage, before the foreign intervention, when the famed liberal Reform laws began to be applied.

The best known of these laws was the 1856 Ley Lerdo (Lerdo Law) that decreed the disentailment of corporate property, including the property of civil corporations like the Poor House. Another much touted reform was the restructuring of the welfare system. In a series of decrees issued in 1861 President Benito Juárez completed the secularization of welfare institutions and created a central office to administer them. This attempt to develop a government-run system of public assistance has led historians to credit Reforma Liberals with transforming *caridad* into *beneficencia* by replacing the traditional model that emphasized religious duty with a modern system that makes public welfare the responsibility of the secular state.[1]

Mexican historiography is divided over whether these reforms were salutary. Conservatives denounced them as destroying the welfare system. As

Joaquín García Icazbalceta charged in 1864, through the Reforma "the state completely absorbed the wealth of the poor, and destroyed the work that the clergy and the faithful had accomplished with such constancy and disinterest."[2] In 1917 Victoriano Salado Alvarez concluded that "the Jacobins . . . dilapidated and destroyed that treasure" of charitable works accumulated over three centuries and enacted laws that only served to "fatten their own pocketbooks and those of their families and friends"—as well as those of the foreigners who bought the disentailed properties at bargain prices.[3] In 1940 Father Mariano Cuevas condemned the Ley Lerdo as an "immoral" act that caused "the fall of the principal orphanages and asylums for the destitute, which for many years afterwards the government did not replace with anything."[4]

Liberal historians, in contrast, heralded the reforms as a glorious turning point in Mexican history. In 1935, for example, Rómulo Velasco Ceballos praised the 1861 decrees with which "the vigorous hand of the Indian president, señor Juárez, swept away the decrepit, miserable and misguided old beneficence, . . . and gave it to the government, which accepted the obligation to convert it into public assistance," thereby "chang[ing] the fortunes of the needy forevermore."[5]

The Positivist scholar Miguel Macedo offered a more measured judgment in 1900. Although accepting the Reforma as necessary to Mexico's "further development," he conceded that the Reform laws that nationalized the assets of welfare institutions "were profoundly unfavorable for the existing charitable institutes and hindered the foundation of new ones" by scaring away potential donors, who feared the confiscation of their gifts.[6] Less polemical contemporary scholars have favored the latter view. For example, Armida de González noted in passing that the Reforma caused "transitory chaos" in the welfare system, a conclusion borne out by Josefina Muriel's research in the archives of Mexican hospitals.[7]

The experience of the Poor House during the Reforma supports the views of Macedo, González, and Muriel. If the Poor House was not destroyed, as Conservatives charged, neither did it benefit from the Liberal reforms. On the contrary, the "transitory chaos" they unleashed was quite painful. The dizzying changes of the period affected the asylum's relationship with the government, its board of directors, its real estate holdings, and its revenues. Yet they did not affect its basic character. The profile of its inmates and the services it offered remained much the same as during the early republic. Indeed, there is little evidence in the asylum's records of a transformation in welfare philosophy or practice before 1863.

The stability of the asylum is surprising, given the frequency and magnitude of change during the reform decades. For the Poor House, change began with the Law of Disentailment of June 25, 1856 (the Lerdo Law), which abolished corporate property. Although primarily aimed at weakening ecclesiastical corporations, the law applied to civil corporations like the Poor House as well.[8] By prohibiting civil and ecclesiastical institutions from owning real property not directly used in their day-to-day operations, the Lerdo Law forced the asylum to sell its income-producing real estate. This consisted of thirteen haciendas and urban buildings that had been donated to the asylum over the years, as well as the various rooms in the portion of the Poor House building that had been rented out since 1819.[9] These properties were producing an annual income of nearly 11,000 pesos before the Disentailment (table 23).

The effect of the Lerdo Law was initially muted because it did not confiscate these properties. Its goal was merely to put them on the open market, "considering that one of the greatest obstacles to the prosperity and greatness of the nation, is the lack of movement or free circulation of a large portion of its real estate, the fundamental basis of public wealth."[10] The Law of Disentailment therefore allowed the corporations to keep the proceeds from sales, minus a 5 percent tax paid to the government. In theory, revenues from the alienated properties would remain the same as before, for the law assigned ownership to the tenants (or, if they declined, allowed the property to be auctioned) and the buyers could make gradual purchases by paying mortgage interest equivalent to the rental income previously paid.[11] Thus, the Poor House was to have been converted from a proprietor into a mortgage bank and should have experienced little change in its real estate income.

In practice, the Poor House did suffer as a result of the Disentailment. Its disarray is mirrored in the dearth of documentation for the years 1856–60. We do know that (unlike many ecclesiastical corporations that refused to obey the law) the Poor House immediately sold at least six of its properties, one of them to Hugo Wilson for 33,333 pesos. These sales were approved by Minister Miguel Lerdo de Tejada on September 20, 1856.[12] Most of its remaining assets were sold over the next few years, although it is unclear whether the sales occurred before the Liberals were ousted from Mexico City in late 1857, during the three years when the Conservatives ruled the capital, or after the Liberals regained control of the central government in 1861–63.

The disposition of Poor House property shows that there is some truth to Salado Alvarez's charge that liberals and foreigners were the main beneficia-

TABLE 23   Poor House Income, 1856 and 1859 (annual income in pesos)

	1856	1859[a]	% Change
Real estate	10,608	5,541	−48
Interest on investments	2,308	3,076	+33
Lottery	12,000	9,725	−19
Municipal taxes	1,200	700	−42
Private donations	900	232	−74
Funerals	2,500	2,930	+17
TOTAL	29,516	22,204	−25

Sources: For 1856, Alfaro (1906), 19; for 1859, "Extracto de papeletas diarias," AHSSA, BP-EA-HP, leg. 1, exp. 1.
[a] The figure for 1859 is calculated from the information available for the first eleven months. All figures are rounded to the nearest peso.

ries of the disentailment. Well-known liberals such as Guillermo Prieto, Juan José Baz, and Manuel Romero Rubio were among the buyers of the asylum's property, along with José M. Gómez Eguiarte, the Poor House administrator who would be fired by the Liberals in 1862. The foreign buyers Hugo Wilson, Robert Blackmore, and Pedro Beauchamps ran successful businesses (a coach-making shop, beer distillery, textile factory, and foundry) on their new premises in former sections of the Poor House complex.[13] Salado Alvarez also appears to have correctly concluded that the disentailed properties were sold too cheaply in view of the rising price of real estate on the eastern side of Mexico City. Formerly on the outskirts of the city, the asylum was now engulfed by urban development. In 1861, only five years after the original sale, the terms of the contract with Robert Blackmore (and others) were challenged by the Poor House because the value of these properties had escalated so phenomenally.[14]

The conservative government of General Félix Zuloaga, which replaced that of the Liberals from January 1858 to December 1860, must share some blame for the loss of Poor House assets because it endorsed and encouraged their sale. Although Zuloaga annulled the disentailment of ecclesiastical property in January of 1858, he validated the sales of municipal properties. Indeed, by ordering the buyers to redeem their mortgages within three months—and pay the government a much stiffer tax of one-third rather than the originally stipulated 5 percent of the sale price—the conservative decree would have accelerated the alienation of Poor House property.[15]

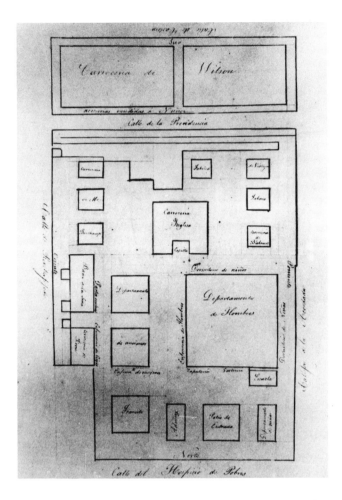

17 SECTIONS OF THE POOR HOUSE LOST DURING THE REFORMA. This diagram shows how approximately half the original building was taken over by coach-making shops, beer distilleries, a textile factory, a foundry, a tobacco shop, and public baths. The Lerdo Law of 1856 forced the asylum to sell these sections of the building, which had been rented out since the asylum contracted in the independence period. Most of the buyers were foreigners. The *carrocería inglesa*, probably Robert Blackmore's coach-making shop, abutted the chapel and deprived the Poor House inmates of a lovely patio.

The Poor House foundered under Conservative rule. On September 7, 1859, the Zuloaga government piously declared that all institutions of welfare and public instruction were to be "maintained and improved."[16] It appointed a high-profile supervisory board for the Poor House (appendix 4). Demonstrating its desire to support the asylum, it placed the board directly under the supervision of the president of the republic rather than the governor of the D.F. as before. Yet the institution was in crisis by the time the Liberals returned to power.

By 1859 Poor House revenues had dropped more than 7,000 pesos below the already meager 1856 level (table 23). Most of this decline came from a 48 percent reduction in its income from real estate. The loss of some 5,000 pesos must have resulted from tenants who did not pay their rent or buyers who did not pay mortgage interest, for the Disentailment produced such opposition and uncertainty about ownership that the economy became paralyzed.[17] By 1863 seven buyers, including Guillermo Prieto, had fallen over 23,000 pesos behind in their payments.[18] Although its interest on capital rose slightly between 1856 and 1859, probably because of newly invested proceeds from the sale of real estate, this was not enough to offset the dramatic decline in what had once been a major source of Poor House funding. The relatively small increase in interest income (only 718 pesos) suggests that most of the real estate payments were in monthly installments rather than one lump sum, just as Salado Alvarez claimed.[19] Any one-time profits from the disentailment must have been used up to pay daily operating expenses rather than being invested for future income.

Other sources of revenue had diminished as well, perhaps because of the hardships caused by the civil war. During 1859 the income from the Lottery of San Carlos fluctuated wildly from month to month, from a high of 1,148 pesos in July to a low of 414 in August; overall it dropped 19 percent between 1856 and 1859. Revenues based on 25 percent of the impost on entertainment also diminished by 42 percent. Here the monthly fluctuations reveal a clear downward trend throughout 1859. Tax earnings dwindled from a high of 195 pesos in January to a low of 25 in September and then disappeared altogether.[20]

The largest single percentage drop in revenues, however, came from the drying up of private donations. Regular limosnas were already so low in 1856 that they only accounted for 3 percent of the Poor House income, for contributions to institutionalized charity had never replaced direct individual almsgiving. Yet private donations dropped another 74 percent after the Disentailment. This time no great benefactor appeared, as had always occurred in the past. This trend reflects the phenomenon Macedo described half a century later, when he wrote that one of the effects of the Reforma was to discourage the "best-hearted and most pitiful men" from supporting welfare institutions.

The one bright spot was the funeral business. Perhaps as a bonus of wartime, the practice of accompanying burials had become more lucrative than ever. Annual earnings rose by some 430 pesos between 1856 and 1859 and came to provide approximately 13 percent of the institution's income—compared with only 8 percent three years earlier. Still, these earnings remained modest. Moreover, they were reduced by the costs incurred in providing the mourners' uniforms and candles and by the gratuities of one real paid to each boy who performed the service. These tips alone lowered net profits by some 13 percent, so that the revenue from funerals in 1859 was approximately 2,500 pesos, only enough to sustain the asylum for a month and a half.[21]

Despite the overall reduction in revenues from 1856 to 1859, the Poor House was hardly crippled. It had survived the first three years of the Disentailment with only a 25 percent loss of revenues. It still had an operating budget of approximately 22,267 pesos—nearly twice what it had earned during the nadir of the independence crisis. While its debts were steadily accumulating, from 1,919 pesos on January 1, 1859, to 3,833 by December 1, suppliers evidently continued to provide goods on credit. The asylum supported an average of 282 inmates per day in 1859, as it had done during most of the 1840s. Even as its debt grew throughout 1859 the number of inmates rose slightly, fluctuating between 276 and 280 from January to April and rising to between 289 and 293 from August to December.[22] The inmate population held steady during the winter of 1860 and reached a high of 297 in March.[23]

Still, the Poor House was operating under increasingly straitened circumstances. Table 24 shows that per inmate expenditures in 1859 were barely above 1803 levels—and then only because of the proportional increase in the wage line. The monthly food outlay of 2.3 pesos per inmate was lower than half a century earlier. Some of the savings came from creative strategies such as closing its kitchen and buying meals from a nearby prison. Unfortunately, by November of 1859 the prison was insisting on full payment before it would provide any more food. The city council refused to cover the debt, explaining that the Poor House "was not the responsibility of the municipality, only the responsibility of the Junta Protectora of that establishment."[24] Lottery revenues continued to decrease as well: they produced only 5,788 pesos in 1860,[25] a little over half of what they had provided the previous year. The mounting fiscal crisis inevitably caused a reduction in the number of inmates. By October of 1860 the Poor House sheltered only 240 inmates, 19 percent fewer than

TABLE 24 Monthly Expenditures per Inmate, 1803, 1859, and 1861

	1803 (N^a = 555, DEC.)			1859 (N = 282, MAY)			1861 (N = 244, MAY)		
	Pesos	%	Per Inmate	Pesos	%	Per Inmate	Pesos	%	Per Inmate
Wages	306	11	.6	491	28	1.7	274	15	1.1
Food	1,466	50	2.6	634	36	2.3	1,319	72	5.4
Other	1,147	39	2.1	620	36	2.2	250	14	1.0
TOTAL	2,919	100	5.3	1,745	100	6.2	1,843	100	7.6

Source: For 1803, 1804 report (calculated by dividing annual expenses by twelve); for 1859 (based on averaging expenses for May through August), "Papeletas diarias" AHSSA, BP-EA-HP, leg. 1, exp. 1; for 1861 (December), "Cuenta de entrada y salida. . . ," AHSSA, BP-EA-HP, leg. 3, exp. 38, ff. 2–4.
$^a N$ = total number of inmates.
Note: These categories may not be exactly comparable across the three years. Inmate wages are excluded from the 1803 and 1861 wage totals but may be included in 1859. Inmate wages for 1803 were only 72 pesos per month, or 2 percent of the total; estimated inmate wages for 1861 (based on a proposed June budget) were 188 pesos or 10 percent. The food per inmate ratio is probably too high (and the wage line correspondingly low) because some of the food was given as rations to live-in employees and others took occasional meals at the Poor House. Finally, since the 1861 figures are based on expenses for one month rather than on a several-month average, they may be distorted by unusually high expenditures during the holiday month of December.

seven months earlier. Thus, the brief Conservative restoration had failed to stem its decline.

The Juárez Presidency, 1861–63

The situation deteriorated still further in 1861 when the Liberal government returned to power, secularized the remaining ecclesiastical welfare institutions (the Foundling Home and Hospital of San Andrés), and centralized the administration of the capital's welfare establishments. The famed Reform Laws of July 12–13, 1859, which expropriated ecclesiastical capital and real estate without compensation, did not apply to civil corporations like the Poor House.[26] It was Benito Juárez's decree of February 28, 1861, that, in setting up the Dirección General de Beneficencia Pública, led to the eventual confiscation of their assets by the government.[27]

That was not Juárez's intent, of course. On the contrary, he hoped to strengthen the system of public assistance by making it the state's responsibility and creating an efficient central office to administer the welfare institutions of Mexico City. The decree placed the city's eleven hospitals, asylums, and prisons directly under the control of the Minister of Gobernación,[28] thereby removing them from the jurisdiction of the city council.[29] Their management rested with the new General Office of Public Beneficence, which was assigned a staff of twelve employees and an annual budget of 18,600 pesos.

The reform may have been on the right track in replacing the institutions' various governing boards with a professional, full-time staff. The decree gave the General Office the duties previously performed by the boards of directors, including those of inspecting each establishment regularly, raising funds, managing their endowments, and appointing and removing employees. It also gave the Dirección new duties, mainly to sell off any remaining properties subject to the Disentailment and to make sure that each inmate was properly vaccinated.[30] García Icazbalceta, who generally condemned Juárez's reforms, applauded the abolition of the old boards. "The juntas rarely met," he claimed, "and their members, with few but honorable exceptions, forgot about the establishment at the conclusion of one meeting and only remembered it again on the morning of the next."[31]

Although the restructuring may have improved the oversight of the city's welfare institutions and eliminated some duplication, it did not achieve the desired savings. The high salaries assigned to the twelve staff members of the General Office belie the stated aim of reducing expenses through centralization. The director earned 4,000 pesos a year, the *contador interventor* (accountant) and *abogado defensor* (attorney) 3,000 each, the treasurer 2,500, the secretary 1,500, and the inspector 1,200.[32] These were unusually generous salaries at a time when, for example, the best-paid Poor House employee, the administrator, earned 1,000 pesos. (In fact, these salaries were much higher than those paid sixteen years later to the six staff members of the equivalent Porfirian institution, the Dirección de Beneficencia. Since the Liberal office was much larger than its successor, its total budget was nearly five times greater than in 1877.)[33] Moreover, in the Poor House at least, neither the administrator nor his two assistants were removed to release funds for these new expenditures (see table 25). If anything, the additional layer of administration in the central office added to the cost of delivering assistance and created an entrenched bureaucracy, which, as García Icazbalceta charged in his 1864 report, would have absorbed (had it lasted) an increasing proportion of the funds set aside for public assistance.[34] Thus, when the regent of the next government in 1863 blamed the "*empleomanía* of the Republic" (its jobseeking frenzy) for reducing it to bankruptcy, he was not far off the mark.[35]

The fatal flaw in the centralization of public welfare institutions, however,

TABLE 25   Poor House Employees and Salaries, 1861

Position	Annual Wage (in pesos)
Administrator	1,000
Assistant administrator	500
Chaplain	600
Clerk	192
Doctor	240
Barber	120
Boys' instructor	330
Boys' music teacher	180
Boys' drawing teacher	120
SUBTOTAL	3,282
Inmate Employees	
Supervisor of boys' department	240
Supervisor of women's department	240
Rectora of girls' department	258
Vicerectora of girls' department	216
Girls' teacher	168
Rectora of women's department	144
Men's nurse	60
Women's nurse	72
Women's cook and four assistants	96
Girls' cook	48
Infirmary cook and two assistants	48
Atolera and two assistants	144
Patio guard	12
Lamplighter	12
Laundress	60
Refectolera	28.4
Ama of childbirth department	60
Pantryman	96
Portero and master tailor	240
SUBTOTAL	2,242.4
Unsalaried employees	
Embroidery teacher (room and rations for entire family)	
Master carpenter (room and workshops)	

was that the General Office now managed the endowments of the individual establishments. In theory, the office was to collect each institution's debts and pay each the interest income due. But, as Jan Bazant pointed out in his classic study of the Disentailment, "their endowments now belonged to the government which could, in case of need, appropriate them."[36] That is exactly what happened when the Liberal government was faced with fighting the French invaders who joined the Conservatives in January of 1862. Alluding to "the most sacred of duties, which is the salvation of the *patria*,"[37] Juárez issued three decrees gradually transferring to the government the funds controlled by the General Office of Public Beneficence. The process was completed by August 30, 1862, with the abolition of that office. The capital's welfare institutions (and their assets) reverted to the jurisdiction of the city council, which was instructed to sell off any remaining properties, redeem all mortgages worth more than 4,000 pesos within three days, and contribute the proceeds to the war chest.[38] Despite this aid, Mexico City fell to the forces of Napoleon III in June of 1863.

The Poor House faced a financial crisis even before the outright confiscation of welfare funds in August of 1862. An eloquent report by the distinguished liberal Ponciano Arriaga, who served as Defensor de los Fondos de Beneficencia, shows how vulnerable the asylum had become barely three months after being placed under the jurisdiction of the General Office. Arriaga's report depicts the pathetic condition of the Poor House by June 12, 1861. While he presumably collected his 3,000-peso salary, the asylum lay in "ruin and decadence," its inmates suffering "horribly." The boys and the elderly paupers were "barefoot, dirty, and in rags." They ate badly, slept on "repugnant" bedding, and "altogether lived in dreadful misery." The girls fared only a little better.[39]

Arriaga attributed the "pitiful" situation entirely to the "absolute absence of funds." He blamed the General Office of Public Beneficence for not paying the interest it owed on the asylum's endowment. The Juárez government recognized a debt of approximately 400,000 pesos to the Poor House. Arriaga placed this figure in quotation marks, as though it were an estimate, but he was very specific in stating that 81,120 of it was the back interest owed the establishment—even after the asylum "forgave" half of the outstanding unpaid interest of 162,400 pesos, partly accrued under previous governments.[40]

The Poor House's skyrocketing debt shows that its financial situation had worsened under the Juárez government. By June of 1861 debts to suppliers and employees had grown to nearly 11,000 pesos, up from 3,833 eighteen months earlier. Aside from the nearly 2,000 pesos of back pay owed its employees, money was owed for basic necessities: 4,700 pesos for bread, 1,852 for grain, 1,100 for meat, 500 for firewood, 200 for candles, and 600 for clothing and medicine. Arriaga wrote that the Poor House would have been forced to close had it not been for the heroic efforts of its treasurer, the chaplain and longtime board member Don Agustín Carpena, "who spent all he had, compromised his credit, pulled strings, begged for moratoria, . . . and thus managed to maintain it in the critical situation in which it finds itself." The creditors could no longer be put off, however, and they were taking the asylum to court.

Even the lottery revenues were threatened, for in May of 1861 Juárez abolished the Lottery of San Carlos as part of an effort to create a single national lottery to replace several smaller ones. Although the reform was well intentioned, it jeopardized a substantial source of Poor House income—even though lottery earnings had declined from a regular 1,000 pesos a month before 1856 to only 294 by April of 1861.[41] Juárez's decree assigned the proceeds of the new lottery mainly to the Academy of Fine Arts and the School of Agriculture, with any surplus assigned to the General Fund of Public Beneficence.[42]

Fortunately for the Poor House, this measure was never implemented. The Minister of Gobernación and the director of the Fund of Public Beneficence appealed to President Juárez, requesting that the Poor House, Foundling Home, and Hospital for Demented Women be permitted to continue their weekly lotteries previously administered by the Academy of San Carlos. One petition argued (among other things) that without the lottery income upon which it depended the Poor House—"an establishment of primary necessity in this capital, which maintains . . . a large number of youths of both sexes, whom it educates and moralizes as best it can given its scarce resources"—would have to close immediately. In view of his desire to foster "the public good," Juárez on May 17, 1861, authorized "the continuation of the *rifas menores* (minor lotteries) of this capital" until new funding could be found to sustain "the establishments of public charity."[43] Internal records show that the Poor House continued to receive a small and highly variable income from the weekly Rifa del Hospicio de Pobres for the rest of 1861 and 1862; in June of 1863 it still counted on a regular lottery income of approximately 250 pesos a month.[44] Although a single national lottery was not realized during this period, the reforms were wreaking havoc with Poor House finances.

After receiving Arriaga's report in June of 1861, the government tried to return the asylum to solvency. Arriaga had proposed several solutions to the fiscal crisis. One was for the government to pay off the Poor House debts with the proceeds of a recent loan or with the sale of some of the nationalized properties it still held. Another was for it to assign 2,000 pesos a month to the asylum from the proceeds of the customs house and municipal tax collections, the revenues from stamped paper, or the taxes paid to the Office of Disentailment. Some of these proposals must have been put into effect because reports from the fall of 1861 indicate that the asylum's situation had improved slightly. The overdue staff salaries had been paid, as had many debts to suppliers.[45] Table 24 shows that in December per inmate expenditures, especially those for food, were higher than in 1859 (although food purchases may have been greater than usual in that holiday month). The number of inmates had increased slightly, from 244 in May of 1861 to 256 in January of 1862.[46] Yet spending for "discretionary" items such as clothing and building repairs had been sharply curtailed. The asylum was still running monthly deficits, and by November of 1861 it was again falling behind in its obligations to employees and suppliers.[47] Thus, although the liberal government tried to honor its commitment to the Poor House, it was only temporarily successful in doing so. All efforts ceased after President Juárez suspended payment on the national debt in July of 1861.[48]

The asylum's deficits continued to mount throughout 1862. By September 19, when the Poor House was transferred from the by-then defunct General Office of Public Beneficence back to the city council and most of its remaining assets nationalized, it was 1,698 pesos in debt to its employees and suppliers.[49] It accrued another 1,471 pesos of debt in the next ten weeks, for a total of 3,169 by December 31, the last date of Juárez's presidency for which such information is available.

By the time the Liberals fled the capital in May of 1863, the Poor House was in abysmal shape. It had lost more than half its extensive colonial building.[50] The section it still inhabited was so dilapidated that some of the rooms were no longer usable. Beams and doors were rotting, and the roof had many holes. The chapel was in ruins. A flood had left several downstairs rooms filled with stagnant water. To add insult to injury, a temporary military hospital had been installed in the boys' dormitories to treat casualties of the civil war.[51] And the asylum was suffering the worst financial crisis in its history because the Juárez government had expropriated most of its assets.

In July of 1863 the next government found the Poor House reduced to penury. Its monthly revenues from real estate were only 126 pesos from the rent or mortgage of several downstairs rooms. It received an additional 20 pesos from the interest on 4,000 pesos in capital deposited with Don José González de la Vega, perhaps an investment of the remaining proceeds from real estate sales.[52] The rest was gone. Its projected annual revenue for 1863 from capital investments and real estate was 1,752 pesos, dramatically lower

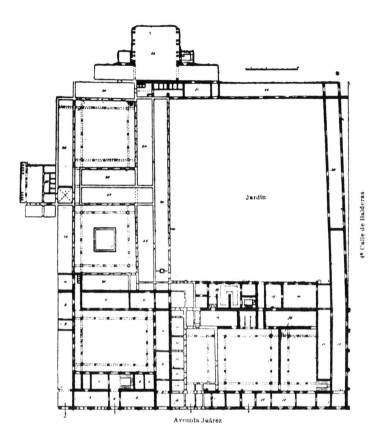

Jardín

4ª Calle de Balderas

Avenida Juárez

18 THE POOR HOUSE AFTER THE DISENTAILMENT. By the time the Liberals fled the capital in May of 1863, the asylum had been reduced to less than half its extensive colonial physical plant. The remaining section, depicted in this diagram, was so dilapidated that parts of it were close to ruins. The Poor House was also suffering from the worst financial crisis in its history because the Juárez government had expropriated most of its assets.

than the 12,916 earned from both these sources before the Disentailment and the 8,617 it still received in 1859, when the Conservatives were in power (table 23). Even when supplemented with earnings from funerals, the lottery, and erratic municipal contributions, this income was far less than the minimum required to sustain the asylum.[53]

From Charity to Beneficence?

Detailed records kept by the General Office of Public Beneficence during the eighteen months the Poor House was under its jurisdiction permit an assessment of President Juárez's reform of the welfare system. Just as the record fails to show any financial benefit from the reorganization of Mexico City's welfare institutions, it fails to support interpretations of the Reforma as a period that witnessed a shift in welfare philosophy. Even though the Liberals had little time to implement their plans before they were removed by the French invaders, their discourse shows that they still retained many traditional notions about charity.

Arriaga's arguments in attempting to persuade the government to fulfill its financial obligations demonstrate the degree to which the old and new ideas about poor relief—and the old and new terminology—commingled in the mind of one of Mexico's leading Liberals. With impeccable liberal credentials, Arriaga is known as the venerable "Father of the [1857] Constitution" and is buried in the National Rotunda.[54] Yet his 1861 report used the terms *charity* and *beneficence* interchangeably; indeed, he used the older term more frequently and ascribed a religious and moral significance to the supposedly secular term of *beneficence*. For example, he described the Poor House as "a house of true charity and Christian beneficence." He encouraged the government to turn its attention to this "important and sacred matter of public administration," namely, "the succor of the needy, the exercise of charity, the sublime virtue of Christianity." He wondered how the asylum could be suffering so much when it enjoyed a credit of 400,000 pesos against a government that was "liberal, humanitarian, philanthropic, and charitable." He exhorted the president to support the Poor House to prove the "refined Conservatives" wrong in charging that Liberal control of welfare institutions would leave them destitute. We must "practice charity to show that we are also Christian and civilized," he concluded.[55]

Arriaga's report suggests that Reforma Liberals had hardly replaced the religious discourse of charity with the secular discourse of beneficence. Indeed, the pious tone of his document did not seem anomalous to his fellow Liberals. In forwarding the report to the administration, the director of the Office of Public Beneficence effusively praised Arriaga's "enlightenment, zeal, and patriotism" and insisted on the glory and "blessings of posterity" that President Juárez would win by supporting this most deserving institution.[56]

It cannot even be said that Reforma Liberals consistently favored the term *beneficencia* over *caridad*, as was claimed by a recent study.[57] Arriaga was not the only one to use the terms interchangeably. President Juárez himself used them as synonyms in the decrees that created and then abolished the General Office of Public Beneficence. To be sure, he always referred to the central office as the *Dirección General de Beneficencia Pública*. But he labeled the individual establishments as houses of both *caridad* and *beneficencia* and empowered the General Office to create *juntas de caridad* to supervise each establishment.[58] A textual analysis of the landmark decree of February 28, 1861, shows that Juárez favored the term *caridad*, which appeared eleven times, over *beneficencia*, which appeared only five times.[59] Indeed, the president apparently saw no contradiction in the term *caridad pública*, which he used in the May 17, 1861, decree restoring the lotteries for welfare institutions.[60]

Sweeping claims about the transformation of the character of public assistance during the Reforma are not borne out by internal records of the Poor House, either. Article 16 of the February 28 decree stated that the bylaws of each institution were "not to be altered for now," and that was the way things remained. In July of 1861 the General Office of Public Beneficence requested that each institution revise its statutes. In response, the Poor House administrator, José María Gómez Eguiarte, sent a short list of proposed amendments to the 1806 and 1843 bylaws.[61] Given the prevailing instability, however, the new reglamento was never completed. In any case his draft, which mostly regulated inmate outings and visits to the Poor House, did not propose any changes in the asylum's mission. Gómez Eguiarte's cover letter, as well as a memo of October 21, 1861,[62] makes it clear that the staff still considered themselves bound by both the earlier statutes.

Surviving financial records suggest that the asylum's daily regimen did not change under the Liberals' stewardship. Even the daily religious observances continued. The budget for June of 1861 included 50 pesos for the chaplain's monthly salary plus 20 for the chapel.[63] The December budget, which again included 20 pesos for the chapel, specified that these were to purchase incense, wine, wafers, oil, and candles—as well as flowers and colored paper to celebrate the feast day of the Virgen de la Purísima on December 8.[64] At this point, then, the secularization of welfare institutions only consisted of putting them under government control and funding, not of eliminating the religious practices that Reforma Liberals evidently considered essential in shaping the moral character of Mexican paupers.[65]

Few changes are evident in the clientele served by the Poor House. On May 31, 1861, there were 244 inmates, about the same number as in 1860. Of these, 73 percent were listed as niños and niñas in the Patriotic School and 27 percent were ancianos and ancianas.[66] These proportions were almost identical to those of 1835, the last date for which such information is available.

An unusual group of surviving petitions for admission provides further details on the inmates accepted under the sponsorship of the General Office of Public Beneficence, which required notification every time a new pauper was admitted. Petitions from elderly applicants suggest that the Poor House continued to favor the "worthy," but not necessarily the poorest, paupers in its small section for ancianos. Several elderly paupers accompanied their applications with letters from respected citizens testifying to their special merits. For example, Doña Margarita Figueroa presented a letter in November of 1861 certifying that she was "pobre de solemnidad, without relatives, and honorable but, because of her advanced age and chronic illnesses, unable to earn a living."[67] The half-blind Doña Juana Ojeda, who requested admission along with her son, similarly presented a letter attesting to her indigence and "very good conduct."[68] Two retired soldiers argued that they were entitled to public assistance because of their services to the nation. One, the elderly and chronically ill Citizen Germán Esparza (the more egalitarian *citizen* having replaced *don* among ardent republicans), requested—and received—shelter in the Poor House as an alternative to a government pension, with permission to leave whenever he wished to conduct his business.[69] In approving the admission of veterans the government not only conceded its inability to honor its pension obligations but also continued the decades-old practice of using the Poor House as an institution of patronage for its favored clients.[70] Although republican documents did not provide racial identifications, the prevalence of honorific titles among those accepted indicates that—despite the Liberals' egalitarian creed—the Poor House still served a predominantly white clientele that continued to include the solemn poor.

Most petitions on behalf of children likewise argue that the applicant was no ordinary pauper but rather was especially deserving due to an upstanding family background. For example, the orphaned siblings Antonio and Concepción Solórzano, aged 12 and 9, were admitted after presenting a letter attesting to their "good conduct and well-known health."[71] The 6-year-old orphan Francisco Fajardo, who had been raised since infancy by his uncle, was accepted after Citizen Manuel María Soria, the inspector of Ward 8, explained that the uncle, "Citizen José Fajardo, has convinced me of his honesty and indigence due to the dearth of work in his field, which is bookbinding."[72] Only a few urgent requests omitted the certificate of poverty and probity. One was from 11-year-old Carmen Licona, who was admitted on November 27, 1861, after "she presented herself in tears, explaining that, since her mother had died the day before, she had no place to go nor any person to take her in."[73] Unlike the helpless Carmen, however, the majority of the students appear to have been selected from the penurious middle classes to prevent their downward mobility. Thus, the Liberal Poor House continued to validate distinctions among the poor based on social background.

These records also attest to the difficulties of growing up in an orphanage. To begin with, many children faced the emotional trauma of being separated from a widowed mother or relative who had taken them in years earlier but could no longer keep them. For example, the 6-year-old Francisco Fajardo, nephew of the unemployed bookbinder, was forced to leave the uncle who had raised him since infancy and whom "he had always considered a father."[74] The children appear to have been warehoused rather than nurtured. At the very least, the atmosphere of the institution, where approximately 180 students were cared for by some two dozen employees (see table 25) and where they slept in two huge dormitories with beds lined up in rows, was very different from that of the families or the streets from which most children came. (Only two students with the last name of Lorenzana, Vicente and Dolores, had come from the Foundling Home.)[75] Moreover, the students were supposed to follow a strictly regulated schedule and remain locked in the building except for Sunday outings and occasional visits to the homes of relatives.

Some children evidently hated the Poor House regime. One was Don Gregorio Palacios, whose "distinguished" parents had both died, leaving him with an impoverished aunt, Doña Francisca Villaroel. She had first placed her nephew in the Poor House in 1855, when he was 6. The child stayed only five months before escaping, apparently back to his aunt. She returned him when he was 13 in August of 1861. Two months later he again fled, this time taking a 9-year-old boy with him and disappearing from the records.[76] He was only one of many who ran away from the institution, or, as the records noted tersely—and frequently—se fugó. Thus, although the Poor House no longer confined adult beggars by force, some children were evidently interned against their will.

A few young inmates complained of mistreatment, often at the hands of other children rather than the staff—not surprising in an institution where the ratio of students to employees was high and older children were relied on to care for younger ones. For example, the orphaned sisters Gregoria and María Angeles refused to return to the Poor House after leaving to visit relatives "because the other girls had attacked the former, cutting her hair and stealing the only petticoat she owned." [77] A little girl, Rosalía Angeles, was pushed into a fire and burned on the buttocks by four older girls as punishment for repeatedly wetting her bed. (After an investigation, the older girls were reprimanded for their "barbarous" deed and sent to serve as maids to the ancianas.) [78]

In a petition to Ponciano Arriaga requesting that he find an adoptive family for her, 12-year-old Concepción Ríos told of being neglected and exploited. Her case illustrates the dangers that could befall girls who spent their lives in and out of public institutions. She had originally been brought to the Poor House in 1850 as a 1 year old soon after both her parents died. She left when she was adopted by Don Miguel Aguirre and his wife Doña Manuela Hargüen but was returned a year later after she was found "abandoned in the street." The girl charged that her adoptive father had raped her, and because the Poor House staff feared she was pregnant they placed her in the department for elderly women to await the child that never came. She remained there serving the old ladies while the Poor House took her adoptive father to court. The girl now complained that she had been taught nothing in the past eight or ten years. The Poor House administration defended itself by explaining that even though she was "somewhat of an imbecile, she has been treated with all the consideration due to the memory of her illustrious father," Don Andrés de los Ríos. She was not placed in the Patriotic School because she was "incapable of learning, made up tall tales, . . . and stole repeatedly." Her story may have had a happy ending, though, for a month later, on November 28, 1861, a Doña Josefa Landrove came forward to adopt her.[79]

Although the cases that appear in the records may have been the most unhappy ones, they are numerous enough to suggest that the Poor House was a harsh and unpleasant place for many orphans. Thus, despite the reorganization of the welfare system, Reforma Liberals did not eliminate the abuse and neglect that were endemic in poorly funded and understaffed public institutions.

Neither did they improve the education offered by the Patriotic School. The 177 students received instruction in the basic elementary subjects plus drawing and music. The boys studied with professional teachers, while the girls learned the three Rs from an inmate teacher (table 25) and took music lessons from a priest, Don Agustín Caballero, who taught them without compensation.[80] A third of the students also received vocational training in three workshops, where 13 boys were studying to be tailors or carpenters (leaving 36 boys bereft of vocational training) and 48 girls were learning to sew and embroider (leaving 80 without instruction). A fourth workshop, which trained

TABLE 26   Female Students in the Patriotic School, by Age, 1811–61

Age Group	1811		1823		1861	
	Number	%	Number	%	Number	%
40–44	0		0		3	2
35–39	0		0		1	1
30–34	0		0		2	2
25–29	0		0		2	2
20–24	2	4	2	25	33	26
15–19	6	11	4	50	31	24
10–14	28	53	1	13	36	28
5–9	17	32	1	13	19	15
0–4	0		0		1	1
ALL	53	100	8	101	128	101
Mean age	11		16.2		16.6 years	

boys as weavers, appears to have been added sometime in 1862, for García Icazbalceta's 1864 report mentioned that it had been operating for about two years.[81] As before, the workshops produced modest earnings for the most advanced students but little for the Poor House itself. During the week of September 23, 1861, 28 of the student apprentices were skilled enough to receive wages totaling 18.5 pesos, all of which they were allowed to keep.[82] The boys also continued to accompany burials. In December of 1861, a fairly typical month, between 8 and 18 boys attended twenty-four funerals, thereby earning 260 pesos for the Poor House and 37 for themselves.[83]

The persistent weakness of the vocational education is evident not only in that the majority of the students failed to receive it but also in the poor placement record for the girls. The General Office of Beneficence must have been concerned about the future of the female students because it requested a list of their ages. Table 26 shows that they were much older than when the Patriotic School opened. Although the youngest girl in 1861 was 4 years old, they averaged 16.6 years, compared with only 11 years in 1811. Fully 33 percent of the 128 female students were over the age of 20, compared with only 4 percent in 1811. These included 6 "girls" in their thirties and forties who had stayed on in the school. Not yet old enough to join the elderly, these women were unprepared to be self-supporting. Instead of graduating to make room for younger children, they had become lifelong dependents of the asylum. Their presence limited the number of needy orphans the school could take in. It also suggests that to some extent the Poor House continued to perform the old function of the defunct recogimientos, which had kept single women in protected seclusion. The asylum's staff thus apparently retained traditional notions about which paupers deserved institutional assistance.

The General Office of Public Beneficence did, however, make some changes in the asylum's personnel. It appointed a new Junta Directiva to oversee the Poor House in 1861, with the politician Marcelino Castañeda as provisional president.[84] Including longtime board members such as the vice president, Mariano Domínguez, who had served since at least 1828, the board may not have operated as a force for change.[85] At some point after 1848 the number of employees declined. Table 25 shows that by 1861 there were only 11 professional employees (compared with at least 16 in 1848) and 27 inmate employees (compared with 54 in 1823). Although it is unclear whether the board deserves credit for these staff reductions, it did preside over one dramatic shift in personnel. In 1862 the junta recommended that the General Office fire José María Gómez Eguiarte, the 50-year-old widower who had managed the Poor House for at least two decades.[86] He may have been dismissed for attempting to hide Poor House assets to prevent their loss, a charge brought against him in March of 1861 (which he roundly denied when petitioning the Second Empire, unsuccessfully, to get his job back in 1863).[87] Or he may have been dismissed because he suffered from an illness that kept him from his duties for most of November and December of 1861.[88] Gómez Eguiarte was replaced in 1862 by José Rafael Larrañaga, who served until the Sisters of Charity took over the asylum in October of 1863. Apparently a dedicated and competent administrator, Larrañaga worked hard to keep the Poor House open in difficult times.[89] Yet his short tenure in office marks the beginning of frequent turnovers in administration that would plague the asylum for the next decade and add to the "transitory chaos" that characterized that period.

Conclusion

The first decade of the Reforma dealt the Poor House a crippling blow. The Disentailment, coupled with the financial exigencies of civil war, destroyed most of its revenues. The creation of the General Office of Public Beneficence, though a step in developing a system of public welfare in which the federal government would replace ecclesiastical, private, and municipal institutions, was at best faltering and short-lived. Lasting only eighteen months, the General Office was never revived when the Liberals returned to power during the Restored Republic. Their experiment with centralized management failed to change the character of the asylum or improve the services offered. Its major impact was financial—and disastrous. Despite the best intentions, the institutions placed under the government's direct protection were penniless by the end of 1862. From the perspective of 1864, García Icazbalceta exaggerated little in claiming that the Liberal state had "completely absorbed the wealth of the poor."[90]

Juárez's reform of public welfare was hardly the resplendent watershed that the Liberal historiography proclaimed. The Poor House and General Office of Public Beneficence were not the only institutions to founder. Juárez's other widely heralded welfare initiatives met similar fates. For example, his projects to establish a maternity hospital and a school for the deaf mute, both decreed in 1861, were realized only under the next government.[91] The Liberals' ambitious agenda was in some ways misconceived since the creation of a large and well-paid bureaucracy added little to the provision of services. In addition, the bankrupt state could not fulfill the new responsibilities it undertook. In the Poor House, at least, the verdict of Conservative historians was accurate: instead of replacing *caridad* with *beneficencia*, the Reforma merely undermined the already faltering welfare system and left little in its place.

{ 8 }

RECOVERY DURING THE SECOND

EMPIRE, 1863–1867

Most histories of Mexico, written by ardent nationalists, skip over or denigrate the brief and ill-fated French Intervention. The purportedly definitive compilation of nineteenth-century law by Manuel Dublán and José María Lozano omits Emperor Ferdinand Maximilian's copious legislation altogether.[1] Twentieth-century historians like Armida de González dismiss his achievements because "most of what he accomplished during the Empire died with him."[2] Velasco Ceballos distorts the record to such an extent that he blames the Austrian archduke for confiscating the Poor House assets,[3] a deed that actually occurred under President Juárez in 1862. Historians have instead reserved their praise for the Restored Republic, during which the returning Liberals supposedly consolidated their glorious reforms.

Yet these histories are misleading. The welfare policies of the Second Empire merit a closer inspection than they have received, for even scholars sympathetic to Maximilian and Charlotte overlook them.[4] It is the Second Empire, not the Restored Republic, that deserves the credit for the recovery of the Poor House. Acting quickly to restore the ailing welfare institutions, the imperial government returned the asylum to the Liberals in 1867 in much better shape than they had left it. It was also, in some ways, a changed institution. During those four years it grew substantially larger. It shed even more functions so as to focus on an ever younger clientele. For the first time, it was placed in the hands of a religious order. Moreover, its staff for the first time was largely female and worked under the direction of a partly female board. Although Charlotte's contributions to feminizing social welfare have been unappreciated in the historiography,[5] she inspired Mexican women to expand their formal roles in caring for the poor.

The Regency Takes Stock, June 1863

The government of the Regency that took over Mexico City in June of 1863 wasted no time in turning its attention to the institutions that served the indigent. On July 9 it commissioned Joaquín García Icazbalceta, the renowned bibliophile and president of a Conference of the Association of St. Vincent de Paul in Mexico,[6] to investigate the state of the capital's prisons and welfare establishments. After conducting research during that summer and in subsequent months, he presented his beautifully bound report to Emperor Maximilian on July 18, 1864, shortly after his entrance into Mexico City. It devoted considerable space to the Poor House, which García Icazbalceta considered "undoubtedly the principal among our establishments of beneficence and one which should become more important in the future."[7]

The urgent condition of the city's welfare institutions could not, however, await the completion of García Icazbalceta's report or the arrival of the emperor. The city council, in charge of all hospitals, schools, and asylums since September of 1862, commissioned its own studies. Tomás Gardida, the alderman in charge of the Poor House, reported on its condition in December of 1863.[8] García Icazbalceta evidently saw this document, as he incorporated its findings and recommendations—as well as some of its prose—into his own report. This eyewitness account of life in the Poor House shows the large gap between the bylaws' prescriptions and the way the asylum was run in practice.

Gardida found the inmates living in considerable hardship, just as Ponciano Arriaga had described two years earlier. They suffered from shortages of food, clothing, and medicine as well as the discomforts of a crumbling and insalubrious physical plant. Only the theater, with its stage and benches used for school plays, was in reasonably good shape. But what vexed Gardida most was the lax discipline and deficient education he encountered.

The girls ostensibly studied *primeras letras*, Christian doctrine, music, drawing, and sewing. About half of them learned embroidery as well. But Gardida concluded that the instruction they received in all but the last subject was severely wanting. They had only twelve catechisms and eight textbooks. Their longtime teacher, the elderly inmate Doña Concepción Borja, was totally deaf—in addition to being "ignorant."[9] In contrast, the girls' embroidery was "exquisite." Yet the Poor House derived no financial benefit from their talents. Just as she had for at least fifteen years, the embroidery teacher ran an independent business using the inmates' labor and giving nothing to the institution in return. Paying the girls a pittance, Doña Dolores Arauz obtained rent-free rooms for her residence and business, received food rations for herself and her family, and kept the profits for herself.[10] According to Gardida, the girls used their earnings to buy beautiful dresses, some of silk, while the other inmates dressed in rags. This "abuse practiced for many years" not only created divisions among the students but violated the 1806 bylaws that stipulated that the Poor House keep part of the student earnings.

Gardida judged the situation of the boys to be even worse. Displaced from their dormitories by a military hospital and crammed into the former infirmary, they were barefoot and dirty. Treated like servants, they were forced to carry loads and run errands for the employees, the girls, and the elderly paupers. Although their teacher was responsible and hardworking, he knew so little that there was almost nothing he could teach his charges.[11] Even his handwriting was like that of a child. If a few boys received vocational training, it was of such poor quality and at so high a cost to the Poor House that Gardida did not think it worthwhile. In return for teaching seven boys, the weaving master occupied "seven or eight" rooms and one of the main patios free of charge. Gardida found the boys making such slow progress that they were still beginners after two years. The carpentry master had a workshop on the ground floor and a bedroom upstairs, yet he taught only eight youths. So rudimentary was their instruction that they could not even help in simple repairs to the building and the Poor House had to hire outside carpenters at considerable expense. Eight boys studied with a master tailor, but one admitted that he could not yet cut a jacket after eight years. In exchange, the master received a salary of 4 pesos per month and obtained three rent-free rooms. Furthermore, the boys were forced to work on Sundays and holidays in violation of the rules.

Gardida was also shocked by the "moral disorder" that reigned in the asylum. "Everyone" entered and left at all hours. Street vendors and food suppliers traipsed through "as if it were a public place." Visitors came and went with abandon. The alderman was particularly worried about the freedom enjoyed by the girls. Instead of being safely isolated from the outside world, they dealt directly with the salesmen who bought their embroidery and sold them various goods. They entertained members of the opposite sex who were not their relatives—and not just on Sundays, the one day set aside for visits.[12] They attended parties at the rectora's quarters on holidays, where they heard discussions of topics that were "alien to the character of this institution." They left the asylum on weekdays as well as the permitted Sundays, and they could be found returning at all hours. Finally, "following an ancient corrupt custom," the girls were taken out by the rectora and administrator on holidays such as the sixteenth of September (Independence Day) and were brought back late at night. The boys, too, were exposed to "corruption" when they mingled with artisans who labored beside them in the workshops. In addition, the children had terrible table manners, which revealed "little or no culture." Even the elderly, although most of them were "octogenarians" too old to work, spent their time in "complete idleness," without keeping to any daily routine and going in and out of the asylum at their pleasure, again in violation of the bylaws.[13] These remarks suggest that the republican Poor House followed a household model in which the orphans and paupers were treated more like family and dependents than inmates of a disciplinary institution[14] and their isolation from the outside world was weakly enforced.

Elaborating on these criticisms, García Icazbalceta portrayed the schooling of all students as severely deficient. The vocational training provided the boys was nearly useless, and the music and drawing they studied a frill. The girls' instruction was so frivolous, he claimed, that it was like that of a fine finishing school. "This is no longer an asylum," wrote García Icazbalceta, "but a school for *señoritas* privileged for life and waited upon by the poor boys." Well aware that the Poor House founders had never intended to provide upward mobility for its inmates, he chastized it for giving them "an education superior to their class, since the majority of the girls have no other future than domestic service, sad as this may be." He labelled it "cruel" to "give them aspirations and tastes which they will never be able to satisfy . . . [for] how can a girl who is used to dressing well, embroidering with delicacy, and playing the piano . . . humiliate herself to serve?" This was the reason, he explained, that so many girls stayed on "vegetating in that enclosure." They had been ill-prepared to function in the outside world, and there was no other institution that would take them in.[15]

García Icazbalceta recommended several changes to restore the original function of upgrading the labor force. One was to tailor the students' instruction to their future life as skilled artisans and servants—and to encourage them to leave quickly to join the work force and make room for new students. Another was to eliminate music and fine arts for both girls and boys, since the students were "almost exclusively from that class of society that works with its hands." The girls should be given the practical training required of a domestic servant, including instruction in gourmet cooking and pastry making. Although García Icazbalceta had no illusions that most female graduates would be able to support themselves with their sewing and embroidery, he suggested the introduction of lace making, which he believed would be profitable. The boys should learn industrial drawing to improve the quality of their products, and they should train in new workshops with the latest machines and technology. García Icazbalceta also felt that they should stop accompanying burials, which were a waste of time that took them away from their studies and taught them nothing except to view death with "hardened hearts." This loss of income could be offset, he insisted, by having the asylum share in the earnings of the workshops. In addition, he proposed instruction in gymnastics to improve the health of the girls and boys (who should use the gymnasium in alternation, in keeping with the required separation of the sexes).[16]

Although García Icazbalceta found the religious instruction of the inmates to be adequate, he wanted the Poor House to counter the culture of poverty more effectively. It should instill the work ethic by forcing all inmates to perform some useful labor since "work is the most powerful means to moralize man, steer him away from vice, give him self esteem, and create a path for him in the world." It should give the inmates new habits: "Above all they should become accustomed to the most rigorous cleanliness, thus combating one of the most common and repugnant vices of our people; to dress with decency, always wearing shoes; to sleep on a bed; and to eat at a table using silverware." García Icazbalceta wanted to Westernize the population by supplanting popular customs such as wearing sandals, sleeping on the floor with a petate, and eating with tortillas instead of forks and spoons. A beneficial side effect—of which García Icazbalceta was fully conscious—would be to force the urban poor into the cash economy. As consumers of manufactured goods, no matter how "humble their position in the world, they will have to work to cover their necessities." In this way, he concluded, "the Poor House will contribute . . . to the moralization of a people whose defects largely stem from the very little they need to survive."[17] Thus, the goals envisioned for the Poor House by Bourbon reformers like Archbishop Lorenzana, who railed against the willful idleness, bad manners, and depravity of the poor, were still alive and well in Mexico a century later.

What García Icazbalceta failed to realize (perhaps because he relied on Gardida's report rather than carefully inspecting the asylum on his own) was that most of the Poor House inmates were neither indigenous nor of the servant class. Many of its students were singled out to receive a refined education precisely because of their respectable backgrounds. Like the feeble-minded Concepción Ríos, whom the Poor House in 1861 "treated with all the consideration due the memory of her illustrious father," the orphaned children of distinguished parents were given special aid, with the girls allowed to stay on under the asylum's protective wing long after they should have graduated. The elderly dons and doñas did not need to become part of the cash economy either; they were already part of that world. Instead, they needed help to avoid sliding down the social scale where they would be in danger of mixing with those at the bottom. Not surprisingly, the reforms that were implemented over the next few years were only those that helped the institution fulfill its actual, rather than its original, mission.

The city council tried to correct the most glaring problems immediately, even before receiving Gardida's formal report on December 31, 1863. First, the aldermen authorized him to dismiss the boys' master artisans and hire new ones. Second, they accepted his recommendation, made on September 6, that the military hospital be removed from the Poor House. His arguments were compelling. Contact with sick soldiers exposed the students to typhoid fevers. It prejudiced their morals as well as the educational goals of the institution. And it limited the number of boys who could be taken in since they were deprived of their two spacious dormitories. By December, the military hospital had been moved out.[18]

Gardida's third recommendation, made on September 19 and likewise put into effect with celerity, was that the Sisters of Charity of St. Vincent de Paul be brought in to manage the asylum.[19] Gardida felt that the "abuses" in Poor House practices were of such long standing that they could only be remedied by a complete change in the staff. The sisters were preferable to lay staff, he argued, because they had been managing other welfare institutions successfully ever since the order was established in Mexico in 1843.[20] In two decades these "saintly ladies" had earned an excellent reputation for their abnegation, frugality, conscientiousness, unimpeachable morality, and the "desire to sacrifice themselves for God and for their fellow beings."[21]

The savings from staffing the asylum with nuns may also have been a consideration, for each nun was to earn only 60 pesos a year plus room and board.[22] These wages were little more than what many of the institution's servants made and far less than the lofty salaries earned by the professional staff (see table 25). Although the Poor House would continue to hire domestic servants as well as a chaplain, doctor, barber, male schoolteacher, and three master artisans for the boys, it stood to save on the other employees the sisters replaced. Indeed, García Icazbalceta's figures for the spring of 1864 indicate that the asylum reduced its wage outlays by 40 percent after the sisters arrived, saving about 1,600 pesos a year (table 27).[23] Still, since this sum only represented some 4 percent of its budget, it cannot have been as important a consideration as the desire to have an administration that was honest, efficient, and totally dedicated to serving its inmates.

Gardida's recommendation was immediately accepted by the city council, which on September 21, 1863, signed a contract with the Sisters of Charity giving them the direction of "all aspects of the administration and interior

TABLE 27   Monthly Expenditures per Inmate, 1863–66

Expenses	1863 (N^a = 276, AUG.)[b]			1864 (N = 590, JUNE)[b]			1866 (N UNKNOWN, JULY)	
	Pesos	%	Per Inmate	Pesos	%	Per Inmate	Pesos	%
Wages	336	16	1.2	200	4	.3	424	10
Food	1,582	76	5.7	3,375	67	5.7	3,076	74
Clothing/shoes	63	3	.2	650	13	1.1	—	—
Other	102	5	.4	800	16	1.4	669	16
TOTAL	2,083	100	7.5	5,025	100	8.5	4,169	100

Sources: For 1863–64, García Icazbalceta (1907), 213, 218, 220, 222; for 1866, AHCM, HP, vol. 2295, exp. 36, f. 6.
[a] N = total number of inmates.
[b] García Icazbalceta does not give the month for his figures. The 1863 figures are probably from the August report by José Larrañaga, the Poor House administrator, which he credits for the income statistics. García Icazbalceta presents the 1864 figures as "current" in the report he submitted in June.

economy of the House, as well as all facets of the moral, religious, and civil education" of its inmates.[24] On October 9 eight sisters moved in and took charge under the direction of the mother superior, Sor Melchora Yriarte.

This shift in administration may seem like a sharp reversal of Juárez's secularization of Mexican welfare institutions. Indeed, it was the first time in its eighty-nine-year history that the Poor House was staffed by a religious order. Furthermore, the Sisters of Charity remained in control of the asylum only during the four years of Maximilian's reign. They resigned in September of 1867, three months after the Liberals returned to power.[25] Yet this seeming parenthesis of religious control under imperial rule is not as anomalous as at first appears. Juárez himself had put the sisters in charge of the newly secularized Hospital of San Andrés in 1861.[26] In order to avoid any conflict with the Liberal goal of separating church and state, on May 28, 1861, he declared the Sisters of Charity "a civil society" without any recognized religious character.[27] And, when he suppressed the religious orders on February 26, 1863, he exempted the Sisters of Charity because of their "devotion to serving humanity."[28] Thus, the Juárez government had helped pave the way for the nuns to take over the Poor House.

Upon arriving on October 9, the Sisters of Charity energetically set about remedying the asylum's problems. Gardida reported that some students at first opposed the change because they feared being treated like the inmates of a strict reformatory. Indeed, ten girls immediately left. In the end, the nuns apparently won the others over. By the time Gardida submitted his report on December 31, they had already accomplished a great deal. They had arranged for the most dilapidated areas of the building to be repaired and painted (though García Icazbalceta still found it so shabby and ugly six months later that he recommended tearing it down and building a new asylum in a location farther from the city center).[29] They had moved the elderly women to dry upstairs rooms furnished with new beds and bedding. They had improved the rations so that inmates again received generous portions of meat and bread. They had ordered matching uniforms. They had obtained sufficient books and supplies for the students.[30] The sisters had presumably restored discipline as well. A report filed in March of 1869, less than two years after they left the Poor House, concluded that the asylum had run "perfectly" under their administration.[31]

Under this new regime the number of inmates grew dramatically. Within eight months of the sisters' arrival, there were 560 inmates, a number that rose to 590 by June 1864 (table 28). The inmate population had therefore doubled since the Liberal administration, with the Poor House for the first time serving as many paupers as before independence. By the spring of 1864 the asylum had grown so much that four more sisters joined the original eight who had come to the asylum that fall. Moreover, the Poor House managed to expand its physical plant by taking back a part of the building leased to a porcelain factory whose tenants had fallen behind in their rent.[32]

In addition to their dedication and inexpensive labor, the sisters' success reflected the return of adequate funding. The Poor House earned very little income of its own. It received only 126 pesos per month in payment for the alienated portions of its building and another 20 in interest from a 4,000 peso capital investment. It also received between 200 and 300 pesos a month from its weekly lottery (the Rifa del Hospicio de Pobres), and 150 to 200 from accompanying burials.[33] In August of 1863 some 73 percent of its income was coming directly from the government (table 29). Although García Icazbalceta did not provide a breakdown of this funding, he noted that the Regency had recognized a debt to the Poor House of 519,631.2 pesos (394,647.9 as the estimated value of the confiscated assets it had permanently lost during the Reforma and 124,983.6 in unpaid back interest owed by various govern-

TABLE 28 Poor House Inmates, by Category, 1861–64

	1861	1863	1864 March	1864 June
Ancianos				
Men	17	13	16	15
Women	50	35	40	55
SUBTOTAL	67 (27%)	48 (17%)	56 (10%)	70 (12%)
Students				
Boys	49	65	106	125
Girls	128	163	220	243
SUBTOTAL	177 (73%)	228 (83%)	326 (58%)	368 (62%)
Beggars				
Men	—	—	90	?
Women	—	—	88	?
			178 (32%)	152 (26%)
TOTAL	244 (100%)	276 (100%)	560 (100%)	590 (100%)

ments) and that the city council had supplemented the asylum's revenues with its own funds.[34] Besides reaping the rewards of sponsorship by a government with foreign financial backing, the Sisters of Charity also obtained private (and perhaps also ecclesiastical) donations to renovate the chapel and several upstairs rooms for the elderly women.[35] García Icazbalceta lauded their ability to solicit charitable contributions as one of the sisters' particular talents,[36] for private donors alienated by the Reforma were apparently still wary of opening their pocketbooks.

The Poor House again had enough money to care for its inmates "with decency." The available statistics on expenditures, although few and sometimes contradictory, suggest that basic expenses were amply covered until the middle of 1866, when the French withdrew their support. Even in the spring of 1864, when spending grew to 5,025 pesos a month (table 27),[37] the asylum was able to meet its obligations.[38] Part of the increase in expenditures reflects the doubling of the inmate population in the year between June of 1863 and June of 1864. Yet some of that increase also reflects the improvement in the services offered. Per inmate expenditures of 8.5 pesos a month were the highest they had ever been, with food outlays of 5.7 pesos more than double those of 1803 and 1859 (see tables 24 and 27).

So impressive was the improvement of the asylum that the municipal au-

TABLE 29   Poor House Income, August 1863

Income (in pesos)[a]	Monthly	Annual
Government	1,512 (73%)	18,144
Remaining assets	146 (7%)	1,752
Lottery	250 (12%)	3,000
Funerals	175 (8%)	2,100
TOTAL	2,083 (100%)	24,996

Source: García Icazbalceta (1907), 83–84, 217–18, 222–25, 227.
[a] All figures are rounded to the nearest peso.

thorities decided to try once more to round up the "swarms" of beggars who bothered its inhabitants and brought "discredit on our nation." [39] A decree of December 10, 1863, prohibited begging and ordered all adults caught soliciting alms to be sent to the Poor House, with the youths sent to the Reformatory for Juveniles at the Tecpam.[40] This renewed confinement of beggars accounts for part of the increase in the population of Poor House inmates. By March of 1864 ninety male beggars picked up on the city streets and eighty-eight women, "some with their children," comprised one-third of the inmates (table 28).

As before, the efforts to confine beggars did not last. By June the number of forcibly interned inmates was dropping (to 152 rather than the 178 housed three months earlier). In any case, that number was too small to make a dent in Mexico City's crowds of beggars. García Icazbalceta complained that by the spring of 1864 the attempt to discipline them had become only half-hearted.[41] Although he recommended renewing the systematic detentions of beggars, they apparently ceased soon after. Subsequent documents fail to mention any mendigos recogidos and list only the students plus a few aged ancianos and ancianas who had sought shelter voluntarily.

Even in the winter of 1863–64 little effort was made to reform the beggars in the Poor House. The Political Prefect of the Valley of Mexico, reviewing the state of the asylum in February of 1866, found the lack of workshops for adults to be a long-standing deficiency. The confinement of adults did more harm than good, he argued, because they "acquire the bad habits of a soft life of idleness." In his view, the asylum's "nearly monastic system" only served to "distance them from the active and diligent life of society." [42] His comment reflected a general disillusionment with enclosure as a policy of social control. Unlike eighteenth-century reformers, who had counted on the large disciplinary institution to rehabilitate paupers, the prefect believed that institutionalization often had the opposite effect.

One reason for the failure of the renewed roundups of beggars is that the Sisters of Charity opposed it. Several documents show that the mother superior, Sor Melchora Yriarte, regularly turned beggars away from the asylum, even when they were sent there by the municipal mayor. On August 21, 1866, the mayor protested her policy to the Minister of Gobernación by arguing that the Poor House, according to a recent order of the Political Prefect, had an obligation "as the only asylum for beggars" to accept all those who sought shelter. She defended herself, insisting that the Poor House did not have the room or funds to take in beggars and that they would corrupt the students because the adults were "scandalously loud, set a bad example, . . . and teach the children vicious habits." The imperial government backed her up, ruling that "without receiving more funds from the city council the *superiora* is not obliged to maintain so many people, especially when there is no room for them."[43] Thus, the sisters were able to resist municipal efforts to confine adult paupers.

The sisters' preference was to take in more orphaned children. They apparently agreed with Gardida, who likewise saw no reason to bring beggars into the Poor House. His report of December 1863 had made a strong case for serving orphans exclusively. "Because of the very frequent revolutions that have buffeted the country," he wrote, "there are a considerable number of orphans in the capital who, without the assistance of this establishment, will be reduced to mendicity. Without moral or civic education these unfortunates are destined to a future as vagrants who, far from being useful, will become a heavy burden on the society of which they are members."[44] There was no shortage of destitute children such as "Niño Enrique," found on the streets January 7, 1864, and still unclaimed ten days later despite the prefect's efforts to locate his family through an advertisement in the newspaper *Pájaro Verde*.[45]

Thus, immediately upon taking over, the Sisters of Charity expanded the asylum to accommodate more of these children. Even while beggars were being confined in the winter of 1863–64, much of the increase in the inmate population came from the growth of the primary school. Between July 1863 and June 1864 the number of students rose by 61 percent. With 368 students, the school was larger than ever before, for it had never surpassed 200 students in its pre-independence heyday and had reached only 248 during its brief rehabilitation in 1835 (table 30). Moreover, for the first time since it was founded in 1806, the students accounted for more than four-fifths of the inmate population.

TABLE 30   Students in Poor House School, by Sex, 1806–71

	BOYS		GIRLS		
	Number	%	Number	%	All
1806 (July)[a]	50	63	30	38	80
1811	131	71	53	29	184
1823	37	80	9	20	46
1826	84	76	27	24	111
1828 (Jan.)	89	75	29	25	118
1835 (May)	165	67	83	33	248
1861 (June)	49	28	128	72	177
1863 (July)	65	29	163	71	228
1864 (March)	106	33	220	67	326
1864 (June)	125	34	243	66	368
1868 (October)	169	31	368	69	537
1869 (February)	223	50	220	50	443
1870 (January)	266	46	316	54	582
1870 (July)	313	47	348	53	661
1871 (December)	317	49	330	51	647

Sources: in addition to those in Appendix 1. For 1806, Suplemento a la Gazeta (July 2, 1806), 523; for 1826, AHCM, Beneficencia, vol. 423, exp. 2, f. 2; for 1864 (March), Valle (1864), 423; for 1868, La Gaceta de Policía (October 11, 1868), 4; for 1869, AHCM, Hospicio de Pobres, vol. 2295, exp. 65, ff. 24v, 25v; and for 1870 (January), AHCM, Hospicio de Pobres, vol. 2295, exp. 113, f. 4.
[a] The figures for 1806 are low because they are for the opening day. The school was outfitted with beds for 200 students, 140 boys and 60 girls.

As students were favored over adults, the presence of elderly paupers steadily declined from 27 percent in 1861 to 17 percent in 1863 and only 12 percent in June 1864. Although the proportion of adults had already begun declining in the late eighteenth century, the process was hastened under the Sisters of Charity. Thus, the brief attempt to revive the roundup of beggars in the winter of 1863–64 had little lasting impact on the character of the imperial Poor House. By the time the asylum returned to its pre-independence size in the spring of 1864, it had also narrowed its mission to focus on the education of orphans—although they were probably less highly selected than when the institution served only a limited number of children of more "distinguished" parents.

Increasingly, these orphans were girls. The concentration on girls was a sharp reversal of the Patriotic School's early preference for boys. As is shown in table 30, the percentage of boys had fluctuated between 62 and 80 percent of the students between 1806 and 1835. It dropped to only 28 or 29 percent from 1861 to 1863 largely because the military hospital had displaced the boys from their dormitories.[46] Yet by the spring of 1864, months after its removal, the proportion of boys had risen only slightly, to 34 percent, for 80 new girls had been taken in and only 60 boys. Over the next three years the sex ratio appears to have become increasingly unbalanced: when the Sisters of Charity left the asylum in October of 1867 there were 518 girls.[47] As long as the nuns controlled the asylum, female students predominated.

The Poor House records contain few hints as to why, even after the boys regained their dormitories, the institution continued to favor girls. Part of the increasing proportion of girls in the 1860s may reflect growing support for women's education, although boys and girls had long ago reached parity in the capital's primary schools.[48] Some of it may reflect the gendered notion that as the more vulnerable sex, female orphans were more deserving of assistance than their brothers, who could better fend for themselves. Much of the shift, however, may simply reflect the fact that the Sisters of Charity were female, for the sex ratio came back into balance after they relinquished control of the asylum.[49] The nuns themselves taught the girls in all subjects (academic subjects as well as drawing, sewing, and embroidery), while they had to hire male laymen to teach the boys. And they apparently felt more comfortable with children of their own sex.

The preferences of the Poor House staff were thus decisive in shaping the character of the asylum. Just as the colonial staff had favored paupers of Spanish descent and the republican staff had favored women and children, the Sisters of Charity favored the students, especially the girls. Under their direction the Poor House moved farther away from the varied clientele it was originally designed to serve. After Maximilian and Charlotte arrived in the Mexican capital, their extensive reorganization of the system of public welfare allowed the Poor House to continue narrowing its mission.

Maximilian and Charlotte Reorganize the Welfare System, 1864–67

The Poor House children were prominent participants in the ceremony welcoming Maximilian and Charlotte to Mexico City on June 11, 1864. At their first stop, at a festively decorated "Arch of Peace," they were greeted by a chorus of Poor House children who sang a hymn while two orphans presented wreaths to the imperial couple. That afternoon, as the emperor and empress rode through the capital in an open carriage, they graced the Poor

House with a visit.[50] Thus, as the institution changed from a beggars' asylum to an orphanage, its inmates had become a group to cherish and display rather than to hide away. The children apparently won the hearts of Mexico's new rulers, who immediately offered the asylum their protection, with Charlotte donating 2,000 pesos to the institution from her private funds.[51]

Their consistent support of the Poor House was part of a broader strategy to enhance public welfare. Maximilian explained that these policies grew out of the imperial couple's shock at the poverty they encountered in Mexico and their sincere desire to improve the lot of the needy: "Since we accepted the Throne of Mexico, to which we were called by the will of the people, the needy classes have been the object of our special attention; and in our voyage through the interior of the empire we have been able to see the necessities and sufferings of which they have until today been victims."[52] Their utopianism and sense of noblesse oblige must have been supplemented by a desire to gain legitimacy for their government in the face of nationalist opposition. Whatever their motives, Maximilian and Charlotte put considerable effort into strengthening the Mexican welfare system. The emperor produced a flurry of legislation on the subject and then delegated to his young wife—whom he officially declared the "Mother of Mexicans"—the responsibility for the well-being of Mexico's institutions of public assistance.[53] Their success was enhanced by the influx of foreign funds, both from the rulers' personal fortunes and from the loans that covered their government's deficits from June of 1863 until January 22, 1866, when Napoleon announced that he was pulling French troops out of Mexico.[54]

Maximilian proclaimed his most important initiatives for social welfare on April 10, 1865, to mark the first anniversary of the Liberal defeat. The best-known decree created the Junta Protectora de las Clases Menesterosas (the Commission to Protect the Needy Classes) under the jurisdiction of the Ministry of Gobernación.[55] The five-member junta was to serve as an ombudsman to receive complaints and requests from the Mexican poor. It was specifically charged with promoting free schools for adults and children—also a favorite project of the Liberals—and distributing public lands to landless peasants—a step that was far ahead of its time.[56] Two less well known decrees of April 10, 1865, directly affected the Poor House. One granted 1,000 pesos to the asylum (as well as equal amounts to the hospitals of Divino Salvador, San Hipólito, San Pablo, San Andrés, and San Juan de Dios).[57] The second created a centralized Consejo General de Beneficencia to oversee welfare institutions throughout Mexico. This Council of General Beneficence was under the jurisdiction of the imperial government, with the empress as president of its ten-member board. The "Reglamento Interior" of the council, issued the next month, granted her wide powers, which show that her post was far from honorary.[58]

The General Council of Beneficence at first had mainly supervisory and fundraising functions, without any direct administrative authority over individual welfare institutions. It could not (unlike Juárez's General Office of Public Beneficence) hire or fire employees or alter the nature of the institutions—until a new decree of June 20, 1866, gave it these duties as well.[59] The original council was primarily charged with founding subsidiary councils in provincial cities, regularly visiting and supervising the institutions under its care, making proposals for their improvement, and protecting and increasing their assets. The latter function was particularly crucial, the decree explained, because "the civil war, which for many years has desolated the country . . . [and] the lack of security for capital and of work for the needy classes, daily augment the number of the indigent . . . [who] demand the urgent attention of the government because the welfare institutions in existence today lack the indispensible funds" to function adequately.[60]

The council quickly acted to improve the hospitals and asylums under its control. It appointed ten-member *comisiones de vigilancia*, or boards of overseers, to supervise each institution.[61] It sent a subcommittee to visit the capital's nine welfare establishments. In May, just one month after the creation of the General Council, this subcommittee presented a report recommending a comprehensive plan to have different institutions specialize in delivering services to separate age groups. The Foundling Home was to care only for infants, a new asylum was to be established for young children, the Poor House was to take in only children of elementary school age, and the Tecpam and other new institutions were to train adolescents.[62] Although the General Council of Beneficence approved this plan for a well-ordered regime of public assistance, it was not implemented during the Second Empire for lack of alternative institutions. Yet the imperial government moved deliberately in this direction.

One step toward specialization, taken on June 20, 1866, removed prisons and reformatories from the jurisdiction of the General Council of Public Beneficence, thus ending the traditional conflation in one administrative body of the institutions for the worthy poor and those for criminals and delinquents.[63] With the disciplining of the poor now separated from the function of sheltering and educating the indigent, the General Council could concentrate its efforts on public assistance rather than punishment.

Besides improving the oversight and funding of Mexico's existing welfare institutions, Maximilian and Charlotte founded two new institutions to serve previously unmet needs. On June 7, 1865—in honor of Charlotte's twenty-fifth birthday—Maximilian decreed the establishment of her pet project, a Maternity Hospital for the capital city. This hospital helped the Poor House focus on its school: by including a section for secret births, it allowed this department to be removed from the Poor House once and for all. The Casa de Maternidad flourished into the twentieth century, eventually expanding its charge to treat ailing children.[64] Thus, it was Maximilian and Charlotte who realized Juárez's dream of modernizing Mexico's obstetrical services. Indeed, in 1869 the returning Juárez government—in a rare acknowledgment of its debt to the Second Empire—recognized the empress's contributions by naming the hospital the Casa de Maternidad e Infancia de San Carlos after her patron saint.[65]

A similar pattern occurred with a new School for the Deaf-Mute, which opened the next year. Although originally proposed by the Liberal Congress in 1861 as part of its April 15 Law of Public Instruction, it came to life only during the Second Empire. The Escuela de Sordo Mudos opened in 1866 with funding from the city council and a private philanthropist, Don Urbano Fonseca.[66] Like the Maternity Hospital (and the 1848 Department for Curing Eyes), the new institution reflected the specialization of care services that was taking place as new techniques of treatment were developed. The Poor House, which had once sheltered—but never educated—deaf-mutes, was now relieved of that responsibility.

Another imperial innovation was to create an organized system of home relief to enable the capital's poor to avoid institutionalization. This was an important contribution to the Mexican welfare system, for, unlike Europe, Mexico had few formal organizations for outdoor relief before this time.[67] In addition to facilitating the provision of direct aid to the poor in their own houses, the imperial government took measures to help impoverished citizens subsist independently, for example, by selling meat to the poor at cost to combat the high price of living.[68]

A major step in building the infrastructure of home relief came on April 10, 1865, when Maximilian decreed the establishment of a Casa de Caridad in Mexico City. Managed by the Sisters of Charity, it was charged with distributing food, clothing, medicine, and "spiritual assistance" to needy families and pobres vergonzantes (a term that reappears in the documents of the period after having disappeared for several decades).[69] Although the decree funded the House of Charity with 14,000 pesos, it is unclear how well—or how long—it functioned. The only reference to it I have found shows that it was still operating in June of 1866.[70]

In June of 1865 Charlotte expanded the provision of home relief by establishing a network of Associations of Ladies of Charity, modeled after those of Paris. The members were wealthy ladies who volunteered their time to help the less fortunate members of society. The associations were independent from the General Council of Beneficence, for they were organized around parish churches and directed by Archbishop Pelagio Antonio Labastida. In June of 1866 the secretary of the Central Council of these Asociaciones de Señoras de la Caridad, Doña Agustina Castillo, published its first annual report. She noted that in the past year thirty-four associations had been established throughout Mexico with 2,860 members. The ladies raised large sums of money and distributed aid to the indigent, especially the sick, through their parishes. They saw to it that indigent children were baptized and their parents married. They practiced traditional Catholic charity, such as inviting twelve paupers to dine on Maundy Thursday and "having the president and other ladies kiss their feet." In addition, the home relief agencies in Mexico City often referred orphaned children to the Poor House.[71]

These new organizations reflect Charlotte's mobilization of elite women to improve the system of public welfare. Not only were elite ladies the backbone of the home relief system, but—in a major departure from previous practice—they constituted half the members of each comisión de vigilancia that supervised the individual welfare institutions after June of 1865. The ladies were apparently effective in their new roles. Indeed, the señoras of the Hospital de San Pablo's Board of Overseers published their own separate report in August of 1865, boasting of their accomplishments.[72]

In expanding the role of elite women in organized philanthropy, Charlotte drew on both her European experience and Mexican precedents. By the middle of the nineteenth century elite ladies in Europe had become actively involved in a myriad of philanthropic organizations. The empress had several pamphlets printed in Mexico that described the Parisian welfare system in order to instruct and inspire the Mexican elites.[73] Mexican ladies were receptive to playing a charitable role. Since the late eighteenth century, women had been assigned an enhanced role in nurturing children and the poor, a result of improvements in women's education combined with a new idea of women's social utility. A small group of educated middle-class women, often widows, had occupied professional positions in schools and welfare institutions. (The Poor House had hired a few female staff members from the beginning, though none was as powerful as the Sisters of Charity.) After independence, elite women anxious to serve a wider sphere than their families found new avenues for their talents in at least four *juntas de señoras* established from 1828 to 1844, including the 1828 ladies board of the Poor House itself. With the exception of the Junta de Señoras of the Foundling Home,

19 EMPRESS CHARLOTTE, POOR HOUSE BENEFACTOR. Upon arriving in the Mexican capital, Maximilian and Charlotte immediately began to strengthen the system of public assistance. The young empress presided over the General Council of Beneficence, which was created to oversee all of Mexico's welfare institutions. She helped mobilize elite women to enhance the delivery of poor relief by appointing women to half the places on each institution's governing board and creating the Associations of Ladies of Charity. Under her protection the Poor House recovered from the disastrous effects of the Reforma.

which lasted two decades, these were short-lived.[74] Thus, Charlotte breathed new life into women's organizations that had long ago expired.

On April 10, 1866, the empress submitted a glowing report on the first year of the General Council of Beneficence. The council met regularly. It set up thriving councils in the provinces, several of which established asylums for youths much like the Mexico City Poor House. It raised funds for the institutions under its jurisdiction, mostly from private donations, which the government supplemented with 19,267 pesos. The empress also claimed that the deficit of Mexican welfare institutions had been eliminated or greatly reduced.[75] A week after she submitted her report, Maximilian praised his wife's accomplishments in an effusive letter that was published on the front page of the *Diario del Imperio*.[76] Mixing the discourse of modern beneficence and traditional charity, he thanked the members of the "charitable" Council of Beneficence for their good works and lauded "the august and sacred mission . . . of beneficence." A month later he further secured the funding of welfare institutions by establishing a lottery for "beneficence" in each departmental capital.[77]

The imperial welfare initiatives merited this praise. The creation of a systematized infrastructure for public welfare, with home relief agencies complementing asylums and hospitals, church and private volunteers supplementing paid public servants, and well-educated ladies of the leisure class assisting busy men, permitted the imperial government to aid far more needy people than under the previous system. Moreover, from the perspective of the Poor House, the specialized functions assigned to each institution helped relieve the multiple pressures to which it had always been subjected. The home relief agencies reduced the need for it to shelter indigent adults. The new Maternity Hospital and School for the Deaf-Mute allowed it to cease caring for pregnant women and deaf-mute children. By moving ever further away from being a multiage and multipurpose asylum, it was increasingly able to concentrate on its school.

The Poor House under the General Council of Beneficence, 1865–67

The Poor House flourished during its two years under the General Council of Beneficence. Indeed, the asylum was the largest beneficiary of the council's funding. Between April 1865 and April 1866 it received 6,000 pesos directly from that body.[78] In addition, it enjoyed steady funding from the city council, although the ayuntamiento no longer supervised the institution after the General Council was created.[79] According to Charlotte's report of April 10, 1866, the Poor House also received considerable sums from private donors.

The new Board of Overseers was energetic and effective. Its five male and five female members (appendix 4) included leading Mexican supporters of the Second Empire. Three of the ladies, Señoras Guadalupe Y. de Siliceo and Catalina Barrón de Escandón and Señorita Carlota Escandón, were related to members of the General Council of Beneficence. In addition, Señora Barrón de Escandón was one of Charlotte's ladies-in-waiting.[80] Other board members, like Aniceto Ortega and Juan Sánchez Azcona, went on to play important roles during the Restored Republic. Indeed, Ortega would be the alderman assigned to the republican Poor House in the fall of 1868. Miguel Cervantes, probably the son of the ex-Marqués of Salvatierra, provided continuity with the past, for his father had served on its board in 1822 and 1830, when he led a drive to round up beggars. Thus, the asylum's experience was less discontinuous than would appear from the frequent changes of administration. One notable change, however, was that clerics no longer served on the Poor House board.

On February 24, 1866, the Board of Overseers issued new bylaws for the Poor House, which were signed by its president, José María Godoy, and by board members Aniceto Ortega and Antonio de Mier. The "Proyecto de reglamento para el gobierno del Hospicio de Pobres de esta Capital" was approved by the General Council of Beneficence on March 13.[81] Although later suppressed from the historical record by the returning Liberals, this reglamento was the crowning achievement of the Poor House board. The first bylaws since those of 1806 and 1843, these were the most detailed since 1777.[82] The "Proyecto" embodies some major departures from previous statutes. Yet, far from imposing a foreign model on the Poor House, these changes mostly codified shifts in practice that had already taken place.

Approximately one-fifth of the 123 articles described the new administrative structure, which placed the Poor House under the jurisdiction of the General Council of Beneficence. The bylaws modified the board structure through which the council exercised its authority. There were now to be two boards of overseers: a male board with nine members, the Junta Protectora, presided over by the Minister of Gobernación or the Political Prefect of the District of Mexico City as ex officio members; and a separate ladies' board with five members, the Comisión de Protección. Whereas the male junta was vested with formal authority over the Poor House employees and budget, the ladies' board was crucial to the smooth functioning of the asylum. The *señoras de la comisión* were charged with visiting the asylum at least once a week, taking special responsibility for overseeing the girls departments, and—in recognition of the importance of a patronage network—using their influence and connections to sell the students' handiwork and place them in suitable positions after they graduated. In addition, the ladies were to review the budget once a month and communicate regularly with the male junta, either in writing or by attending one of the two monthly board meetings.

The description of the employees' duties reflects the changes introduced when the Sisters of Charity took charge. In addition to delineating the duties of the sisters, the chaplain, and the doctor, the bylaws described the position of administrator, which apparently had been added sometime after the nuns arrived. Despite his similar title, this administrator was not the equivalent of those who had directed the Poor House before 1863. Rather, his position was somewhat like that of the *mayordomo* of a convent: he served as secretary to the junta, kept the Poor House books, and represented it in all transactions outside the asylum. Other than serving as the formal disciplinarian of the boys, he had little involvement with the internal affairs of the institution, which were to be managed by the sisters.

The most striking change was in the Poor House mission, which was much narrower than in the colonial bylaws. Although the 1866 bylaws list six departments, they only offered the services provided by two of the four departments outlined in 1806. The Departments of Correction and Secret Births were gone. The Department of Worthy Paupers still lingered, although it now consisted of two departments for the Disabled Elderly and Beggars, one for women and one for men. The Patriotic School was replaced by four new sections for children: the departments for young boys and girls (aged 5 to 12), and those for older boys and older girls (12 and over). Thus, the seeming expansion to six departments merely reflects a finer age and gender classification. The separation of the sexes was not new, of course, but the division of the children into two separate age groups reflects the trend toward providing specialized services for people of various ages. Using the age of twelve to divide the children into two groups, rather than the age of fourteen, which had been used since colonial times to mark the end of childhood, reflects a new conception of adolescence as a separate stage of youth.

The six departments were not equal, for the school was the centerpiece of the imperial Poor House. Indeed, the two departments for incapacitated adults were included almost as an afterthought because their closure would turn helpless paupers out on the streets. The Departamentos de los Ancianos y Mendigos Inhábiles merited only two rather vague articles out of 123. The statutes clearly envisioned the eventual elimination of all but the most elderly paupers: although the care of the elderly was listed as a goal of the asylum, other disabled adults were to be taken in only "for now" and "until another asylum is founded for beggars." The nomenclature of the 1866 bylaws symbolizes the reduced importance of the adult departments. In 1806 the department for adult paupers was listed as the *Hospicio de Pobres*, and the school was designated by the separate name of *Escuela Patriótica*. The 1843 bylaws still distinguished between the adult and children's sections by labelling them as the *Hospicio* and the *Escuela Patriótica, o Casa de Huérfanos*. By 1866, however, the *Hospicio de Pobres* encompassed all six departments and the Patriotic School had disappeared. The school no longer required a separate name because it had, in effect, become the core of the Poor House. Meanwhile the department of adult paupers—once the entire asylum—had atrophied. This trend was hardly initiated by the new bylaws, of course; and the name change merely reflected popular usage, for the last documents to refer to the Patriotic School date from 1861.[83]

By 1866 the Poor House's principal mission, set forth in the first section of the first article, was to shelter and educate children between the ages of five and twelve. These could be orphans who had lost one or both parents, children removed from "vicious parents" by the judicial authorities, those whose parents were too poor to provide for them, or pensioners whose families paid a small fee for their education.

Recognizing the lack of alternative institutions for youths twelve and over, the bylaws reluctantly provided for a secondary school as well. A second section of the first article added the goal of "perfecting the education" of girls over twelve by "teaching them useful skills and an honest way of living." The Poor House was not supposed to accept new girls age twelve and older, however, but only to keep those who graduated from its primary school. Given the difficulty young women had in fending for themselves, this article prudently refrained from setting an upper age limit for female inmates. The bylaws nonetheless insisted that the girls should eventually leave since "the establishment of its students in society is the most interesting and principal end of the Hospicio." Once they had completed their education they were supposed to find a job, set themselves up in their own shop, move in with a willing family (or their own, if its fortunes had varied), or marry. The asylum's commitment to the teenage boys was far more tentative. The second article of the bylaws explained that "for the time being" the Poor House would educate boys between the ages of 12 and 21. Their presence was clearly meant to be temporary. They were not supposed to stay past the age of majority, and the bylaws called for the department for older boys to close once a vocational school for teenage youth could be established.

The reduced emphasis on the secondary school followed the plan recommended by the General Council of Beneficence the previous year, when it envisioned the Poor House exclusively as an elementary school. It is therefore not surprising that the bylaws spelled out the educational goals and methods of the secondary school in considerably less detail than those of the primary school. The children between 5 and 12 were to be taught manners, morals, and Catholic doctrine as well as reading, writing, arithmetic, history, and geography. Sewing was part of the elementary school curriculum for the girls and gymnastic exercises for the boys. There were provisions for enriching the education of particularly talented children with French and drawing. And for the children "of scant intelligence" vocational training could begin before they had mastered the elementary curriculum. Otherwise, vocational training only began in the secondary school, making childhood a special period of academic rather than job-oriented instruction.

The bylaws instructed the Poor House board to improve the training provided to the older students so as to prepare them for a wide variety of careers. The existing workshops training boys to be carpenters, cobblers, and tailors should be supplemented by new ones in such areas as hatmaking, weaving, silversmithing, locksmithing, printing, bookbinding, and lithography. The girls' embroidery should be supplemented by additional workshops that made lace, artificial flowers, candles, and the like. In addition, all girls should be prepared for domestic service by learning to launder, cook, and make fancy desserts and confections. The bylaws further recommended that the Poor House establish a laundry and, incorporating a suggestion of the General Council's subcommittee report of May 1865,[84] that it open a store where the girls could sell their handiwork to the public and "learn the exercise of commerce."

Although the 1866 bylaws prescribed a rigorous boarding school regime meant to instill the work ethic and discipline, it was not spelled out in any detail. The schedule laid out in 1777 and described by García Icazbalceta in 1864 as still in force was apparently considered adequate. According to his report, the students rose at 5:30 A.M., cleaned their quarters, attended Mass and breakfast, and went to school or to train in workshops until noon. After lunch and a rest from 12 to 3 they returned to school until 7 P.M. At that time they said the rosary, took supper, and finally retired to their dorms at 9.

If the asylum's overall educational goals had changed little since the Patriotic School was established in 1806, its educational methods had changed considerably. Following the latest pedagogical theories, the school used positive rather than negative reinforcement to encourage learning. Achievement, demonstrated in public examinations, was rewarded with prizes—including money set aside for the students to take with them when they graduated. Punishments such as whipping, slapping, and placement in the stocks were explicitly prohibited, although short lockups (under three days!) were permitted as a disciplinary tool, along with the denial of recess, visiting privileges, prizes, and special desserts. Standardized requirements were introduced for graduation; indeed, the children were supposed to master the primary curriculum before moving on to more advanced studies in the secondary school.

The "Proyecto de reglamento" demonstrates that the Poor House had abandoned most of the repressive thrust outlined in the colonial bylaws. The asylum was no longer, as in the 1806 "Prospecto," envisioned as part of a plan to eradicate mendicity. The imperial statutes explicitly stated that "The Poor House shall always be an establishment of benevolence and not of correction or punishment." The section on permissible punishments corroborated this shift by mandating that inmates who required further disciplining must be transferred to another institution. The sections on adult paupers show that the Poor House no longer attempted to forcibly confine the city's beggars. It accepted only those paupers who were utterly unable to care for themselves— a narrowing of its mission reflected in the addition of the term *inhábiles*, or "disabled," to the name of the department. And there was little attempt to transform them, despite the lip service paid to providing them with "moral improvement" as well as material assistance. The adult inmates were to be read to from uplifting works and assigned light chores commensurate with their health and age. The Sisters of Charity were given considerable discretion in organizing a daily regime appropriate for people who were infirm and of advanced age, and the inmates' chores could be reduced as a reward for good behavior. Although their outings from the asylum were to be restricted, they were the only inmates allowed to leave on their own. The bylaws thus codified the treatment of adults over the past half century, when, as they became increasingly elderly and infirm, adult inmates were sheltered rather than disciplined.

The shift away from controlling the poor is reflected in the new requirement that all inmates be residents of the capital city. A practical move aimed at limiting the size of the potential clientele, this restriction was feasible in part because the General Council of Beneficence had established similar asylums for orphaned youths in provincial cities.[85] Yet it also shows the degree to which entrance into the Poor House was considered a privilege rather than a punishment. In one century the Poor House had come quite far from the original experiment, which made internment of any beggar, including migrants, compulsory.

To the extent that the goal of transforming the poor still existed, it was largely confined to educating children. In order to achieve this end, the reglamento imposed new restrictions on the students and their families. Once they entered the asylum, the children could not leave until they had graduated. They left the authority of their parents or guardians during those years, while the Poor House, "in representation of the political authority," held the legal guardianship of the child. Indeed, parents or guardians who brought children to the Poor House were required to sign a consent form relinquishing their authority and could not retrieve the children (except for paying pensioners) until their education was complete—an unprecedented restriction of parental rights.[86] The isolation of the students from the "corrupt" outside world—including their families if they had any—was reinforced in the articles that regulated permissible outings. The children could go out in supervised groups for holiday walks or to attend funerals. They could also receive visitors under close supervision. Otherwise, they could leave to visit relatives only on occasional Sundays or in cases of grave familial illness. The Poor House was consequently a boarding school with no vacations. The requirement that children remain there until their education was complete shows the desire of the authorities to isolate the students for several years to mold them into useful and upright citizens. Although the original Poor

House shared this mission, the bylaws had never before imposed such rigid boundaries between the asylum and the city or between the children and their families.[87]

It is impossible to know to what degree the new bylaws were implemented because of the dearth of records for 1866 and 1867. It appears that the Sisters of Charity were unable to solve the persistent inadequacies of the vocational training, an area that had long been the weakest part of the Poor House regime. A report of November 6, 1867, on the state of the asylum when the nuns turned it over to a lay administration, shows that most boys studied primeras letras exclusively. The sisters had managed to open a workshop to train cobblers, thereby fulfilling a proposal made in the 1866 bylaws (as well as by the Liberal administration in 1861),[88] but now the weaving workshop was gone. There were consequently only three workshops training tailors, cobblers, and carpenters. According to the 1867 report, few boys were apprenticed in these workshops and even fewer mastered their craft. Furthermore, these apprentices produced no profits because they only worked for the Poor House, by mending clothes, making shoes, and repairing the building.[89] As before, the girls' embroidery workshop was more successful. Under the sisters' management the Poor House—not the girls themselves—sold the products, and the profits (of 71.6 pesos for August and 81.6 pesos for September 1867) were split between the asylum and the workers, with the girls receiving 41 percent of the earnings during the two months for which such information survives.[90] Thus, the sisters had eliminated the worst abuses of the old system.

Although the imperial Poor House school provided only limited training for its students, the sisters had attempted to address the criticism leveled at them by the subcommittee of the General Council, which visited the Poor House in May 1865, that too many adolescents stayed on.[91] Their record in placing the older girls was mixed. In the fall of 1867 nearly half the female students were above the age of 13 (48 percent). These included 34 "girls" in their twenties and 2 who were 30 years old. Together these young women represented 7 percent of the female students.[92] There were far fewer than in 1861, however, when the 41 girls 20 or older had represented 33 percent. Thus, if the problem persisted, it had at least been ameliorated, either because the sisters successfully prepared the students for independent lives or because they merely forced some of the oldest girls out.

The Poor House appears to have survived the final, difficult year of the Second Empire in relatively sound condition. The last monthly meeting of the General Council of Beneficence, on June 2, 1866, was the last one presided over by the empress, who left for Europe on July 8 to plead with Napoleon to continue supporting the far-flung Mexican empire. The General Council met only twice more (on October 11, 1866, and January 9, 1867) under the presidency of José María Lacunza.[93] Yet even in the midst of the mounting crisis, as Maximilian's government fought for its life against the Liberal armies, the empress did not forget the Poor House. On June 22, 1866—in one of her last acts before leaving the Mexican capital—Charlotte personally ordered twenty-one beggars to be dismissed from the asylum so that twenty-one boys could take their place.[94] Then, only five days before departing, she instructed the city council to continue covering the asylum's expenses "with all possible regularity."[95]

Expense figures for the month of July 1866 (table 27) suggest that the number of inmates remained large, for the asylum spent 3,076 pesos for food. This was enough to feed 540 mouths if 5.7 pesos were spent on each inmate, as in 1864.[96] Indeed, in October of 1867, when the sisters turned the Poor House over to a lay administration, the girls' department alone had 518 students.[97] By 1866 the budget was tight. The 669 pesos spent in July 1866 on such items as medicine, lighting, shoes, clothing, and materials for the students' workshops were less than half the 1,450 pesos allotted to these items two years earlier. And the asylum was beginning to experience revenue shortfalls.[98] Yet the sisters must have found ways to make ends meet. For example, their figures omitted three variable sources of funds. One was the small profits from selling the girls' embroidery, which produced approximately 35 pesos per month for the asylum.[99] More substantial earnings of between 150 to 200 pesos a month came from accompanying burials. The third source was the private donations the sisters and board members were able to elicit from the capital's philanthropists.[100]

The last surviving record concerning the Poor House in the archives of the General Council of Beneficence noted that from June to December of 1866 the asylum spent 8,853.67 pesos on building repairs[101]—in addition to the impressive renovation of the Poor House building the empress boasted of in her April 1866 report.[102] This information suggests that the institution was functioning relatively smoothly, for it is doubtful that it would have spent so much on renovations unless it was covering its basic expenses. The Liberals therefore inherited a notably restored Poor House when they returned to power in June of 1867.

Conclusion: From Beneficence to Charity?

There is considerably more continuity between Juárez's and Maximilian's welfare policies than most Mexican historians are willing to admit. For one thing, Maximilian confirmed the disentailment of corporate property. For another, in setting up the centralized General Council of Beneficence the emperor successfully revived the short-lived Liberal experiment of 1861–62. The imperial organization improved on the republican one by being national in scope rather than limited to the capital city. Moreover, by appointing wealthy citizens who served without compensation the imperial council avoided the creation of an expensive bureaucracy, as the Liberal Office had not. (The General Council's entire annual budget, including an administrator, scribe, and porter, was only 2,350 pesos, compared with the 18,600 pesos for Juárez's central office.)[103] The imperial government also took up several of Juárez's projects, such as expanding public education and establishing the Maternity Hospital and School for the Deaf-Mute. Even the placement of the Poor House in the hands of the Sisters of Charity followed the precedent he had set by relying on this order to manage other welfare institutions.

The main difference was that the imperial authorities worked in partnership with the Church and private donors. As the empress stated at the first meeting of the General Council of Beneficence, the government's role was to "set the first example for private charity," that is, to encourage ecclesiastical and individual philanthropy, not to replace it.[104] This approach is symbolized in the membership of the General Council of Beneficence. In addition to Charlotte, it included two representatives each from the government and the Church: the Minister of Gobernación, José María Esteva; the Minister of Relaciones, Martín Castillo; the archbishop, Pelagio Antonio Labastida; and the *visitadora* of the Sisters of Charity, Sor María Ville.[105] The other six members were wealthy citizens, including members of the old Mexican nobility. This board is reminiscent of the colonial Junta de Caridad. Although the presence of two women would have been unthinkable in the late eighteenth century, the colonial board was similar in that it was presided over by the viceroy and contained representatives of the Church, the state, and private individuals among whom the nobility was prominent.

In a sense, then, Maximilian and Charlotte's formula for providing assistance to the destitute was similar to that of the Bourbon state that had founded the Poor House in partnership with the Church and private donors a century earlier. Indeed, the emperor fulfilled a Bourbon dream by placing the welfare institutions firmly under government auspices. Maximilian could do so, however, only because he built on the bold initiatives of the Reforma Liberals who had already secularized the remaining ecclesiastical establishments and made them totally dependent upon government patronage. In addition, Maximilian enjoyed the advantage of foreign financial backing, which helped him to bring several of Juárez's plans to fruition. Thus, the imperial welfare policies cannot be considered a step backward toward traditional charity. Despite the traditional overtones of their pious discourse, Maximilian and Charlotte brought modern ideas about social welfare from Europe and they advanced many goals put forward first by the Bourbon state and then, more boldly, by the Reforma Liberals. If they partially restored the role of the Church in providing poor relief, they by no means tried to eliminate the government. The imposition of a national rather than merely municipal level of organization in the General Council of Beneficence was a major step toward the centralization of power in the hands of the state. Realistically accepting the limits of government resources, the imperial regime enlisted the aid of the Church and private citizens as well as public servants, of volunteers as well as paid professionals, and of women as well as men. Still, in organizing these individuals and groups the imperial state reserved the central role for itself.

{ 9 }

THE LIBERALS RETURN, 1867–1871

The Poor House fared much better during the third Juárez presidency than during the first. Yet the luster of the great Liberal's final years in office diminishes when they are placed beside Maximilian's accomplishments in the sphere of public welfare. This time around, Juárez did not initiate bold projects in public assistance. In the Poor House his administration preferred to follow the smooth course set during the Second Empire. Yet it was soon forced to deal with a series of crises that beset the asylum: the resignation of the Sisters of Charity, a typhoid epidemic, a public scandal, incompetent staff, and chronic financial shortages. Indeed, things deteriorated so quickly that within a few months after the Liberals regained power members of the city council would nostalgically recall the days of the Sisters of Charity— roughly synonymous with the days of the Second Empire—as a halcyon time for the institution. By the time Juárez died in 1872, the worst of the Poor House problems were under control. But the asylum did not regain the prosperity it enjoyed under Charlotte's care.

Although he disbanded the elaborate imperial welfare structure, President Juárez did little during the Restored Republic to consolidate his earlier reforms in this area. The secularization of ecclesiastical welfare institutions was by now a fait accompli, as was the disentailment of corporate property. A few decrees making final adjustments in the disentailment[1] did not affect the Poor House, which had already sold off the property it did not directly use in operating the establishment. President Juárez did not even try to revive the centralized Office of Public Beneficence. After abolishing Maximilian's General Council of Beneficence, Juárez returned to the pre-Reforma organization, with the capital's welfare institutions under the jurisdiction of the city council. Otherwise, the Poor House retained many of the imperial innovations. The republican city council reissued the imperial bylaws with very few modifications. It continued to rely on women to supervise and manage the asylum, and encouraged it to continue specializing as a school. Indeed, although the Poor House recovered its huge eighteenth-century size, the adult inmates dropped to their lowest proportion in the asylum's history.

One of Juárez's few reforms actually hurt the asylum's funding. On February 28, 1868, the president abolished the "many small lotteries that are daily held in the capital . . . [and] whose profits are destined to the establishments of beneficence and public instruction." His decree explained that the Poor House (as well as the Hospital of San Hipólito, the Antigua Enseñanza, the Tecpam de Santiago, and the School of Agriculture) did not require any compensation for the cancellation of their lotteries because they were already funded by the city council; the Foundling Home and the Hospital del Divino Salvador were awarded a new municipal stipend to compensate them for their losses. Unlike six years earlier, Juárez did not attempt to create a single national lottery to replace those that were eliminated. Instead, he now condemned lotteries altogether as "among the immoral and prohibited games."[2] Three years later, in view of his administration's persistent penury, Juárez reversed himself again. Beginning in July of 1871 he authorized the reestablishment of several lotteries in favor of welfare institutions.[3] In the meantime, however, the Poor House had become more dependent than ever on municipal funding.

President Juárez's best-known achievements in the area of public welfare during the Restored Republic were in reorganizing and expanding the system of public education.[4] The Law of Public Instruction for the Federal District of December 2, 1867, mandated free secular primary education for children over five, prescribed a standardized curriculum, and proposed the establishment of secondary schools in Mexico City.[5] By 1871 numerous primary schools had been founded throughout the republic and the Mexican capital could boast several new secondary schools.[6] As a further boost, educational and welfare institutions were exempted from paying certain taxes.[7] Although these were laudable policies, they did not distinguish Juárez from his predecessors. The emphasis on public education had been shared by every administration since the 1780s. Moreover, in the Poor House at least, the quality of schooling under Juárez's stewardship, although it looked good on paper, left much to be desired.

The transition from imperial to liberal rule was an initially rocky one. The first headache came on September 17, 1867, when Sor Melchora Yriarte gave the city council one month's notice that the Sisters of Charity were withdrawing from the Poor House. Her only stated reason was "a disagreement with certain dispositions." Although she did not elaborate any further, this statement probably refers to the republican city council's attempt to remove her—in violation of her contract—in order to install a male lay administrator who would be directly beholden to the municipality.[8]

The city council named two laypeople to replace the nuns. Don Mariano Aguilar, appointed by August, was in charge of the entire asylum. In October a female director, Doña Rosa Espinosa de los Monteros, took over the huge Departamento de Niñas. They earned annual salaries of 1,200 and 600 pesos, respectively, plus food rations.[9] The administrator's salary was 20 percent higher than in 1863, the first salary rise in nearly one hundred years. The female director's position was new, combining the old rectora of the girls' department with the old male assistant administrator. If her salary was only half that earned by the administrator, it was nonetheless more than what the rectora and assistant administrator had earned in the past.[10] Now, for the first time in republican Mexico, a lay woman became the second most powerful—and second best paid—employee in the asylum. The Liberals can hardly take credit for the elevation of women in the asylum, however, since the precedent of powerful female administrators dated from the French Intervention, when the Sisters of Charity were in control.

These administrative reforms were not enough to keep the asylum running smoothly. The Poor House apparently deteriorated almost immediately after the Sisters of Charity left. By January 7, 1868—after only three months under the new lay management—the first of several committees of aldermen investigating the asylum recommended that the Sisters of Charity be brought back because of the "egregious hygienic conditions, abysmal system of education, and especially the lack of discipline and order."[11] On March 1, 1869, the capital's governor seconded this assessment, insisting that "everything was in perfect condition when the Sisters of Charity turned over the establishment."[12] The sisters never returned, and the next two years were extremely difficult. During that period the administrator changed at least four times,[13] as did the alderman assigned to the asylum.[14] The turnover in the girls' department was even more dramatic: in the first fifteen months following the nuns' departure, it had five directors, two of whom were fired.[15]

In addition, a typhoid epidemic broke out just as the Liberals were returning to the capital. It arrived at the Poor House on June 23, 1867, when one of the girls, Guadalupe Zermeño, came down with the fever. Within eight months it had stricken 229 of the approximately 700 inmates. Dr. Wenceslau Reyes, who had served as the Poor House doctor for at least twenty-eight years, considered it the worst epidemic ever to visit the asylum. It claimed the lives of the administrator Aguilar, the chaplain, 2 of the 13 elderly victims, and 9 of the 216 stricken students.[16] The Board of Health, which inspected the asylum in May of 1868, attributed the spread of the disease to faulty hygiene. It ordered the Poor House to remove the festering latrines in the boys' dormitories, reduce the number of beds per room, improve light and ventilation, remove stagnant water in the laundry room, clean the filthy infirmary, and wash the inmates' bedding and clothing at least once a week. The epidemic was over by the time the board submitted its report, however; it ended on April 15 when the Poor House stopped treating the sick in its own infirmary and sent them to the municipal hospitals instead.[17]

The other problems were more difficult to solve because they had become deeply embedded in the practices of the asylum. The aldermen's report of January 7, 1868, concluded that students were staying on in the school far too long without being prepared for "an independent and useful position in society."[18] Reviewing statistics submitted by Aguilar on November 6, 1867, the committee discovered that, while most boys quickly moved into the job market, many girls did not. Although most girls had left the asylum by the time they were eighteen, the 36 girls between 20 and 30 years of age would not be easy to place, for they lacked marketable skills and faced a job market in which "decent" opportunities for women were scarce. In addition, few had family members who could take them in. Ten who had come from the orphanage, as evidenced by their last name of Lorenzana, may not have known any life outside of public institutions. Only 13 percent of the 247 girls over 13 had two parents still living; 42 percent had lost both parents, and the rest were half orphans. (That so many more had lost a father than a mother—31 percent versus 14 percent—confirms what was only hinted at in earlier documents: that widowed mothers placed children in the asylum far more often than did their male counterparts.)[19] The older girls languished in the asylum, taking up space that was needed for younger orphans.

The aldermen's committee concluded—just as the imperial General Council of Beneficence had nearly three years earlier—that the Poor House should abandon its efforts to serve a wide range of orphans and instead concentrate exclusively on children between the ages of five and fourteen years. The children under five should be transferred to the Foundling Home and the older ones placed in the city's new secondary schools. The remaining children were to receive an improved vocational training that would permit them to earn a living. The committee was particularly concerned with the training of the girls, whose traditional embroidery skills did not ensure their future employment. It proposed new courses for the girls in lithography, photography, bookbinding, and topographical drawing. Evidently sensing the need to justify the training of women for these unconventional careers, the report explained that these tasks could be carried out "without prejudice to the labors and arts of their sex." The final recommendation was that two *juntas protectoras*, one of men and one of women, immediately be appointed to oversee the Poor House, thereby resurrecting part of the imperial supervisory structure. The boards' first duty should be to draft new bylaws for the more specialized institution that the aldermen envisioned.

The committee's report is just as revealing in what it left out as in what it included. It made no mention of the elderly, who were not to be part of the future asylum. It also omitted juvenile delinquents, even though municipal authorities were again pressuring the Poor House to take them in. Since the merger of the Tecpam Reformatory with the Vocational School for Boys, the government had begun transferring youths from the cities' prisons to the Poor House to be educated. The alderman who held the Poor House commission had already protested the policy in June 1867.[20] It may also have contributed to the resignation of the Sisters of Charity, who during the Regency had resisted municipal efforts to place such youths in the Poor House. The committee of Liberal aldermen evidently opposed this policy as well, since imprisoned youths were usually older than their proposed age cutoff of 14 years. Like most Poor House staff members during the past half century, the aldermen wanted the asylum to focus on the education of deserving orphans rather than the disciplining of delinquents. Their proposals thus continued the decades-long trend of narrowing the function of the institution and of delivering services to ever younger groups of paupers.

The city council acted quickly.[21] Within six months new bylaws were in place and a new ladies' board had been appointed. Its president was none other than the first lady, Señora Margarita Maza de Juárez.[22] Her appointment followed the precedent set when Empress Charlotte had presided over the General Council of Beneficence. It also demonstrates that under the Restored Republic the federal, as well as municipal, government took an active interest in the asylum, another viceregal pattern reestablished during the Second Empire.

The 1868 Bylaws

The "Reglamento para el Hospicio de Pobres" set forth in one hundred articles the rules that should guide the institution. It was signed by Juan Abadiano and Aniceto Ortega, who succeeded Abadiano in the position of regidor comisionado in the fall of 1868; was approved by the city council on June 15, 1868, and by the governor of the Federal District on July 29; and was disseminated to the public on October 11 in the official *Gaceta de Policía*.[23] As the only bylaws produced by Reforma Liberals, the "Reglamento" provided an opportunity for them to put their mark on the asylum. Indeed, it was presented to the public as a purely republican initiative. Yet, although the Liberals hid their debt to the imperial bylaws, the 1868 "Reglamento" in fact copied most of the 1866 document verbatim. One link between the two was Aniceto Ortega, who signed both the republican bylaws (as regidor comisionado) and the imperial ones (as a member of the Poor House board). Thus, returning Liberals owed much more to their imperial predecessors than they were willing to admit.

The main differences between the two sets of bylaws were in the sections describing the governance structure, for the city council had replaced the General Council of Beneficence in supervising the Poor House and a lay administration had supplanted the Sisters of Charity. The republican bylaws clarified that only the city council and the governor of the Federal District, as its president, could intervene in Poor House affairs. The *comisión* of the city council (it is unclear whether this meant the commissioned regidor alone or a committee of aldermen) was to supervise the asylum directly, visiting it at least twice a week. The city councilmen were to be assisted by a ladies' board, referred to as the Junta Protectora and Junta de Protección, with the same size, structure, duties, and even name as the imperial ladies' board. Confident that supervision by the aldermen and ladies would be sufficient, the city council eliminated the separate male board.

The 1868 bylaws codified the administrative changes that had been introduced the previous year. The male administrator who headed the asylum was assisted by a female director, and a new position of female subdirector had been created. The relationship between the male administrator and the female directors (always referred to in the plural) only slightly modified the relationship between the imperial administrator and the Sisters of Charity. Although the male administrator had more power than his immediate predecessor, he had far less than previous republican administrators had enjoyed. In addition to keeping the records and handling the Poor House finances, he had final authority over the entire asylum. But he shared his power with the two female directors, who were in charge of the asylum's *gobierno eco-nómico* (internal management). Required to consult the directors in preparing the budget and making policy, he was to give them "full freedom to govern the women's departments as well as to oversee the day-to-day workings of the asylum." The republican asylum thus maintained the imperial innovation of assigning important governing roles to women.

In comparison with the imperial bylaws, the republican ones downplayed the role of religion—but they did not eliminate it. The long section on the chaplain in the 1866 bylaws, which had given him identical duties as in colonial times, was omitted in the 1868 version. Yet subsequent documents show that the Poor House continued to employ chaplains.[24] Indeed, the section on the primary school in the republican statutes still specified that children were to learn "manners, morals, and religion." Thus, Catholic instruction persisted as an explicit part of the basic curriculum, even though it had been banned from public schools by the Law of Public Instruction promulgated for the Federal District the previous year.[25] The disappearance of priests from the governing board, a striking departure from the 1806 and 1843 bylaws, merely followed the imperial precedent.

Another revision of the 1866 bylaws increased the emphasis of the Poor House on its school. Whereas the imperial reglamento made care of the disabled elderly part of the asylum's permanent mission, the 1868 bylaws specified that (just like the secondary school) the departments for the elderly would remain in the Poor House only "provisionally, until the Supreme Government determines what to do with them." The disabled younger beggars, still eligible for assistance on a temporary basis in 1866, had disappeared by 1868. This focus on the elementary school was hardly a liberal innovation, however, since it had been recommended in 1865 by Maximilian and Charlotte's General Council of Beneficence.

The other modifications of the imperial bylaws were so minor as to be of little substance. For example, the minimum age for children was raised from five to six, further narrowing the client base. The older boys were now to be expelled upon reaching the age of majority instead of merely being encouraged to leave by the age of twenty-one. Physical education was prescribed for girls as well as boys, as García Icazbalceta had recommended. Following the recommendations of the January 7, 1867 report, a broader vocational training was mandated for the older girls. Finally, the bylaws specifically mentioned adoption as one of the ways in which children could leave the asylum. This option did not represent a republican innovation, either, since it had already existed in the 1806 "Prospecto."[26]

It would be misleading to portray the 1868 bylaws as a particularly Liberal blueprint for the Poor House. There were some major departures from the ordenanzas of 1806 and 1843, for the disciplining of adult paupers had disappeared, the school had largely taken over the asylum, priests had been dropped from the governing board, and women had reached a new prominence in its administration. Yet these changes built upon decades-long nonpartisan trends that had already been incorporated into the bylaws of the imperial regime. Moreover, there were striking continuities with the colonial Poor House, especially in the goals of the students' education. The most unexpected continuity was the persistence of Catholic instruction as a part of the basic curriculum, despite the much-touted Liberal secularization of welfare institutions. Catholic charity had not been removed from the Poor House, either. It was invoked in the closing section of the bylaws, which enjoined the employees and benefactors of the asylum to "exhibit compassion and charity" and show familial affection toward its "unfortunate" and "helpless" inmates. The new Poor House statutes therefore suggest that, in the area of public welfare, Reforma Liberals were not nearly as different from their predecessors—or from their Conservative enemies—as they claimed to be.

A New Crisis

As usual, there was a huge gap between the well-ordered vision embodied in the bylaws and the actual Poor House regime. After completing the "Reglamento" in the summer of 1868, the regidor, Abadiano, apparently satisfied that he had fulfilled his duty, asked to be relieved of the Poor House commission. So beloved was he (or possibly complicitous, as we shall see) that several hundred inmates and staff members signed a petition on August 7, 1868, begging him to reconsider.[27] Abadiano resigned anyway and must have left believing that the worst of the Poor House problems were behind him. But he was mistaken.

On January 8, 1869, the city council received an urgent memo from Governor Juan José Baz instructing the council to look into several allegations that had appeared the previous day in the newspaper *La Orquesta*. A short article entitled "The Poor House: Horrors" charged that the young ladies there were being corrupted. The anonymous piece alleged that several girls had been seen with the administrator, rectora, and alderman at the theater and promenading at the Cadenas and Zócalo. Others went out for Sunday coach rides, and the prettiest ones (all over sixteen) had separate bedrooms within the asylum, ostensibly so that they could receive visits from gentlemen.[28]

The city council lost no time in responding. The same day that it received the governor's instructions it sent a committee to investigate. After questioning the Poor House staff and students, the aldermen reported that nothing untoward had happened. The administrator and his family had indeed taken Paz Estrada—a 28-year-old girl "of high morals who is much esteemed in the establishment"—to the theater for her entertainment and cultural enrichment.[29] The other charges were roundly denied. Only groups of girls, not individuals, left the asylum for outings. The former regidor, Abadiano, had never taken girls out. When he visited the Poor House he was always accompanied by several employees and at Christmas, "during the time of the *posadas*," by his wife. Finally, the committee members found no separate bedrooms and observed that all the girls slept in communal dormitories.[30]

Despite this favorable report, the rumors persisted. Fearing that they would be implicated in the developing scandal, the new regidor comisionado and several members of the ladies' board resigned.[31] Before leaving, however, the ladies alerted the governor of the Federal District to serious problems in the asylum, and a new investigative committee was appointed. Its report, signed by Governor Baz himself on March 1, 1869, was published in the newspaper *Siglo XIX*, an unusual step, suggesting that the governor took the matter very seriously (or perhaps that he was publicizing the scandal to discredit a political opponent).[32]

The report shows how difficult it is to determine what really went on behind the asylum's thick walls. Although Abadiano was cleared of any active wrongdoing, Baz's committee concluded that "the bandage unfortunately covering his eyes" had blinded Abadiano to the disorder that plagued the establishment. According to the second investigating committee, the first one—"charged only with studying specific allegations . . . and speaking only to people who wished to hide the truth"—had missed the problems as well. The report proceeded to delineate the disastrous state of the asylum in eight areas: morality, discipline, work, instruction, hygiene, clothing, beds, and food.

Baz painted a lurid portrait of a Poor House totally lacking in discipline. He refused to give details about the sexual scandals beyond stating that the immoral acts were so "horrible" and "offensive" that modesty prevented their description. It is nonetheless clear that the mandated separation of the sexes was not enforced (nor, for that matter, was the separation of old and young, good and bad, sick and healthy). In addition, the shortage of beds in the boys' dormitories forced them to double up, which caused them to acquire "disgusting vices." Stealing was rampant. Employees took supplies home or threw them out of the windows to accomplices waiting outside. Inmates passed silverware, bedclothes, and utensils to relatives who came at all hours for unsupervised visits. They exchanged Poor House supplies for sweets, fruits, or other treats provided by vendors, who thronged the asylum in contradiction to the rules.

Baz was appalled by the children's poor education. They slept as late as they pleased, used foul language, and cut classes with regularity. The teachers often failed to show up, fought among themselves, and imposed no punishments on the unruly students. The girls learned little beyond making crude embroidery, playing a few notes on the piano, and "smudging some marks on paper, which they call drawing." Preferring to dress in rags rather than sewing for themselves, they spent their days lounging in the sun. The situation was no better in the boys' departments. The three workshops trained only thirty-two boys to be tailors (eleven), carpenters (twelve) or cobblers (nine), which left another two hundred "vegetating" and occasionally "shouting out their ABCs." A printing press and lithography machine bought with city council funds had never been used. And, despite the bylaws' mandate to focus on the younger children, 59 percent of the female students were over twelve— approximately as many as in November of 1867.[33]

The problems in two of the three workshops show that some of the asylum's woes stemmed from an entrenched system of patronage and corruption. Baz found only the carpentry workshop free from this affliction: the carpenter was "honest, hard-working, and intelligent," but his shop was so small and lacking in tools that few boys could learn the trade. The tailor was also competent, but he labored under a faulty contract (signed by an unnamed administrator) that forced his shop to make uniforms for the army at a price below the value of the cloth. Consequently, the Poor House was losing money. It also lost money in the shoemaker's shop. The cobbler was a lifelong inmate of the Poor House "with all the defects of these." In addition to being "ignorant," he was overextended, simultaneously accompanying boys at funerals and serving as the sacristan and "gossip monger" for the institution. The boys learned nothing, and the Poor House wasted on him a salary greater than the cost of buying shoes outside the asylum.

Baz likened the sanitary conditions to those of a "malodorous pigsty." The recommendations made by the Board of Health a year earlier had not been implemented, and new health hazards had appeared because the windows of the dormitories were kept locked to prevent theft. The children's sheets were filthy, wet with urine, and never hung out to dry. The floor of the girls' dormitory was fetid, since they had no bathroom to use at night. The boys still had open latrines in their rooms. The inmates rarely changed clothes because they only had one set. They averaged one bath per month because there were only eight bathtubs for more than 500 persons. Not surprisingly, the children were riddled with mange, which affected 170 of the 223 boys and 50 of the 220 girls. Mealtimes were likewise repugnant. There was little protein in the inmates' diet, and the rotting food frequently gave them indigestion—even though the Poor House paid more to purchase it than it would cost "in the plaza," another hint of the corruption and inefficiency of public institutions. Furthermore, the inmates were often forced to eat with their hands because the silverware and plates had disappeared.

Governor Baz placed the blame squarely on the Poor House staff. In the year since the Sisters of Charity had turned over the establishment "in perfect order," the new administration had lost control. The report exonerated the regidor comisionado and the ladies' board, explaining that despite their energy and zeal they were continually frustrated by the resistance of the "corrupt," "stupid," and "lazy" employees. In fact, Baz praised the good ladies for generously donating a complete set of table service, ninety-six bolts of cloth, and other necessities. But they lacked the authority to override the employees. According to the governor, the only solution to this deplorable situation was to replace the staff and spend more money on the asylum. Unless the city council was prepared to exercise "an iron will" and "spend a regular sum of money," he recommended that it close the Poor House for once and for all.

The Reformed Poor House

The situation was so urgent that Governor Baz personally intervened, visiting the Poor House daily and, "with his characteristic activity and energy," meting out "exemplary punishments to the promotors of the disorder." [34] By the time he submitted his report on March 1, 1869, he had already taken steps to end the crisis. He had fired the administrator, one director, the chaplain, master shoemaker, drawing instructor, one of the girls' teachers, and one supervisor. [35] He had separated the "good" inmates from the "bad" by dismissing twenty-three older girls who had families or who could earn a living and by transferring to other institutions twelve girls "whose presence was incompatible with the good order and morality" of the asylum. He had separated the sick from the healthy. Under his supervision, the building had been cleaned and stolen goods recovered from nooks and crannies throughout the structure. Additional beds, mattresses, and sheets had been purchased and a second set of uniforms ordered for each student. [36] Latrines were covered, a large bathing pool was installed for the children, and a sturdy new storeroom was constructed. The quality and quantity of food rations was improved. A sewing machine and a set of carpentry tools were acquired to enhance the

20 PRESIDENT AND MRS. BENITO JUÁREZ. The Poor House fared much better during the third Juárez presidency than during the first, when his bold initiatives in the sphere of public welfare nearly destroyed the asylum. Returning to power during the Restored Republic, President Juárez followed the precedent set during the Second Empire by appointing his wife, Margarita Maza, to preside over the Poor House board. Her active involvement in the affairs of the institution signaled a new role for first ladies in Mexico.

students' vocational training. Yet Baz admitted that "there is still much to do to improve their education."

Doña Margarita Maza de Juárez tried to help the asylum as well. We do not know how long she presided over the Poor House board, but she was active in early 1869 when she donated twenty-one bolts of cloth[37] and personally wrote Doña Juana Rodríguez de Herrera (the second lay director of the Poor House after the Sisters of Charity left, who had resigned to attend to family business in Chihuahua), imploring her to return "because . . . of the terrible state in which this establishment finds itself."[38] Señora Juárez's work in the Poor House has been ignored by her biographers. Although they have portrayed her as merely the ever-faithful wife who bore a dozen children and suffered exile and deprivations stoically, her role as her husband's helper also included her direct involvement in the management of the asylum and possibly of other public welfare institutions as well.[39] Apparently, elite women's philanthropic roles were unremarkable to their contemporaries. After her death in January of 1871 Señora Juárez's obituaries praised her "boundless charity" and concern for the poor but did not mention her special efforts on behalf of the Poor House.[40] The role of dutiful first lady had nonetheless evolved considerably since her husband's first presidency.

The wife of the governor of the Federal District (and a close friend of Señora Juárez) also played a key role in helping the Poor House through its period of crisis.[41] Until Señora Rodríguez could return to accept Mrs. Juárez's offer of employment, Governor Baz installed his wife, Luciana Arrázola de Baz, as administrator of the asylum. The Poor House records refer to this period as the time when "el señor Juan José Baz and his wife took charge."[42] Apparently Señora Baz served as her husband's trusted trouble-shooter elsewhere, too: she briefly served as the director of the Maternity Hospital and as the inspector of the ailing Foundling Home as well.[43]

The management of the Poor House stabilized with the arrival of Doña Juana Rodríguez in December of 1869. She filled the positions of administrator and director concurrently, and very capably, for many years. Under her direction, "good order and morality" were apparently restored.[44] A conscientious and hardworking widow, she lived in the asylum with her children, was on call day and night, and regularly assigned tasks to family members to keep the institution running smoothly. Her correspondence and reports, written in a beautiful flowing hand, are models of tact and clarity. Her service earned her the praise of the city council, which cited her excellent work and devotion when in January of 1872 it finally awarded her the salary of 1,200 pesos that had been assigned to the male administrator she replaced.[45] She nonetheless retained the title of director rather than assuming the title of administrator, which the men in charge had always enjoyed.

The administration of the Poor House had apparently become more efficient since 1861, the last date for which comparable information is available. The number of employees had decreased, from thirty-eight (including twenty-seven inmate workers) to twenty-seven, while the number of inmates had nearly tripled, from 244 to 703. Despite the reduction in employees, the annual salary outlay had increased by 16 percent because the staff was now composed entirely of professionals, as shown in table 31. The inmate employees had disappeared since the few adults who remained in the asylum were too infirm to work. Yet the average expenditure on wages per inmate had decreased from 1.1 pesos in 1861 to only .9 pesos, a sign that, if the Poor House was not run as cheaply as under the Sisters of Charity, it was nonetheless controlling costs much better than it did under the previous republican regimes. And the management of the Poor House was solidly in female hands. Although 63 percent of the employees were male, the top positions were all filled by women. The city council must have concluded that with a female administration in charge the danger of sexual impropriety would diminish.

In a report of July 6, 1870, the director described a thriving, orderly institution largely centered around its school. The number of inmates had doubled since the crisis of 1869 (table 32), and at 703 was approximately the same as in the spring of 1868.[46] Of these, 94 percent were students—the largest proportion ever—and only 6 percent were the "decrepit elderly." According to Doña Rodríguez, the inmates kept to a strict daily schedule that regulated their activities from the time they rose (at 4:30 A.M. in the summer

TABLE 31 Poor House Employees and Salaries, 1870

Position	Annual Wage (in pesos)
First directora	600
Second directora	360
Third directora	360
Fourth directora	360
Girls' teacher	360
Assistant girls' teacher	180
Boys' teacher	360
Assistant boys' teacher	180
Doctor	360
Clerk	360
Master tailor	360
Master carpenter	288
Master shoemaker	288
Pantryman	216
Barber	144
Male nurse	96
Supervisor, boys' department	240
Assistant supervisor, boys' department	72
Female nurse	96
Laundress	360
Assistant laundress	96
Cook	120
Male domestic	180
Gatekeeper	96
Firewood steward	36
Supervisor baths	15
Water carrier	48
TOTAL	6,231

and 5:00 in the winter) until they turned out the lights at 8 P.M. The students spent five and a half hours in classes or workshops each day. They ate nourishing, well-balanced meals, with extra rations of bread, lamb, chicken, or milk provided for the sick, the elderly, and the boys and girls who "dedicated themselves to hard labor."[47]

Yet this rosy situation—if it ever existed—did not last.[48] The vocational training remained extremely limited. Although in July 1870 the boys' workshops had twenty-four more apprentices than a year earlier, there were still

TABLE 32   Poor House Inmates, by Category, 1868–71

	1868 (October)	1869 (February)	1870 January	1870 July	1871 (December)
Ancianos					
Men	?	?	?	9	13
Women	?	?	?	33	36
ALL				42 (6%)	49 (7%)
Students					
Boys	169	223	266	313	330
Girls	368	220	316	348	317
ALL	537	443	582	661 (94%)	647 (93%)
TOTAL	?	?	?	703 (100%)	696 (100%)

Source: For students, see sources for table 30.

only three workshops: the tailoring shop had twenty-two boys making the uniforms for the male inmates; the carpentry shop had fifteen boys making the institution's furniture and repairing the building; and the cobbler's shop had nineteen boys making shoes for the asylum. The girls were learning to make artificial flowers as well as mending, sewing, and embroidering. A few also assisted in the kitchen (six) and laundry (twenty-two). But, as Doña Rodríguez lamented in her report, the asylum's funding had not permitted the introduction of lithography and printing workshops (or gymnastics, for that matter)[49] and drawing and music had been eliminated.[50] Furthermore, the workshops were antiquated. For example, the cobbler's shop still made shoes by hand rather than with "modern machines." Consequently, it could not produce enough shoes for all the inmates, especially since the handmade shoes only lasted four months on the hard floors.[51] Moreover, only the girls' handiwork provided earnings, which they split with the asylum.[52]

The quality of elementary instruction was likewise deficient. This became public knowledge when in May of 1871 many students failed to pass their exams. The director blamed the elementary school teachers, Gabriel Gelt and his wife Josefa Huguet de Gelt, who had been hired seven months earlier.[53] In her report on the incident, Doña Rodríguez claimed that they did not spend enough time at their jobs, for they were often tardy or absent due to illness. Citizen Gelt denied these charges and accused the director of interfering with his teaching and of wanting him out of the way so that her son, the assistant boys' teacher, could take over his job. Although the city council found no reason to dismiss Citizen Gelt, he left anyway and was replaced by Nicolás González (not the director's son) on July 26.[54] In the process of investigating the charges, the city council discovered abysmal conditions in the school. Both the boys and girls' classrooms suffered from a shortage of textbooks, blackboards, desks, and chairs, which made it exceedingly difficult to teach the children. Indeed, dozens of children sat through lessons on the floor, unable to work.

The acrimonious fight between the director and the schoolteacher Gelt had an ideological dimension that led him to threaten her position. He ridiculed the "pious practices" of the institution, which he felt violated the freedom of religion recently decreed by the Liberal government. She complained that his discussions with the children "manifesting his extravagant ideas about the religion they profess" were "an exhortation to insubordination." The conflict came to a head in June 1871 when Citizen Gelt, already under scrutiny himself, retaliated by requesting that the Poor House schools be removed from the director's authority and placed under the jurisdiction of the Commission of Public Instruction, which administered the other public schools in Mexico City. His request was denied after Doña Rodríguez assured the city council that all religious observances had been voluntary, thereby bringing the Poor House into compliance with the new regulations.[55] The director had managed to weather this crisis, one of several in which she received the strong support of the city council.

Yet the Poor House was still riddled with problems. The director constantly had to fend off delinquents sent to the Poor House by municipal authorities in violation of the bylaws. For example, in May of 1870 she challenged the governor's order to admit three older girls who had been expelled a year earlier for "pernicious acts." In this case she successfully argued that they should not be readmitted because they were over twelve years of age and the Poor House was not meant to serve as a reformatory.[56]

There were nonetheless many unruly—and often unhappy—inmates. On March 26, 1870, the city council investigated charges against the director for whipping some of the boys, a violation of the bylaws. Doña Rodríguez denied the accusations, insisting that she only administered the permitted short "lockups." The charges, she explained, were invented by dissatisfied students, for "it is quite usual for the inmates of this House, who are unhappy with the separation from their families or perhaps disgusted with the work and order imposed here, to invent complaints with the hope of gaining their liberty."[57] Misbehaving students were also punished with extra chores such as washing the floors.[58] One "incorrigible" girl was several times sent to serve as a maid in the Hospital for Demented Women, but since she returned more insubordinate each time she was finally expelled "to avoid scandals and the corruption of the other girls." [59] As before, the asylum's records continued to note an occasional runaway.[60]

Patronage bordering on corruption was still an integral part of the institution, as hinted at in Citizen Gelt's charges against the director. In fact, both her son and daughter were for a time on the Poor House payroll, he as assistant boys' teacher and she as the subdirector.[61] Although Doña Rodríguez was exonerated of charges of impropriety in 1871, similar charges of favoring relatives would result in her dismissal five years later.[62]

The Poor House employment records also contain clues to a different kind of patronage. Several cases show that certain favored inmates regularly stayed on as permanent dependents of the asylum despite the mandate of the bylaws to place them outside the institution. One was the infamous shoemaker fired in the winter of 1869. Another was Antonio Lorenzana, the *superior de niños* who resigned on July 12, 1870. His last name indicates that he had been transferred from the Foundling Home to the Poor House, where he remained as an employee after he completed his education. A third employee's history emerged only because he appealed for a salary increase on October 30, 1871. Gregorio Ortiz had been raised in the asylum, married a fellow inmate, and remained there with his wife and growing family as the *despensero* who doled out food and supplies from the locked storeroom. His well-written petition, accompanied by a glowing letter from the director, shows the successful workings of the patron-client system. His annual salary was raised from 216 to 300 pesos in recognition of his ten years of loyal service and his "special affection for the Poor House and immense gratitude to his benefactors." [63] A quarter century later, Alfaro's history of the Poor House listed Ortiz as one of many inmates who had stayed on as employees, although perhaps he was the one with most longevity, having worked there some fifty years at the time of his death.[64] These cases suggest that to some degree the Poor House was a self-contained institution that gave many orphans lifelong protection and employment but contributed less to improving popular industry or upgrading the labor force than was originally intended.

Finally, as always, the institution's finances were rocky. By the fall of 1871 its debts were so large that the director feared its food vendors would cut off supplies.[65] The budget shortfalls undermined the good order she claimed to have achieved only one year earlier. Despite the recommendations of the Board of Health, the sewer pipes from the adjacent Maternity Hospital still passed through the boy's dormitory, spreading a new typhoid infection.[66] The walls were in urgent need of repainting. There was a shortage of mat-

TABLE 33   Average Monthly Expenditures per Inmate, 1859-71

Year	Overall (pesos)	Food[a] (pesos)	Wages[a] (pesos)	Inmates
1859 (May–August)	6.2	2.3	1.7	137
1861 (May)	7.6	5.4	1.1	244
1863 (August)[b]	7.5	5.7	1.2	276
1864 (June)[b]	8.5	5.7	0.3	590
1871 (November)	4.8	3.6	0.9	696

Sources: Sources for tables 24 and 27; for 1871, AHCM, vol. 2296, exp. 145, f. 7.
[a] The food/per inmate ratio is too high (and the wages line correspondingly low) because some of the live-in employees received food rations, and others took occasional meals at the Poor House.
[b] See note to table 27.

tresses, blankets, and clothing. Many children were going barefoot and without meat in their diet. They hardly ever changed their clothes. Lacking school supplies, the students in the boys' department were "wasting their time, a lamentable situation especially since the exams are so near."[67] And many of the older girls were "merely sheltered and fed, without learning anything" that would allow them to earn "an independent and honorable living" in the future.[68]

The Poor House did not, however, revert to the financial crisis it had suffered during the first phase of the Reforma. With an income of 3,360.2 pesos in November 1871, the average per inmate expenditure of 4.8 pesos was the lowest in two decades. Yet the monthly food outlay—perhaps a better measure of the quality of life—was 3.6 pesos per capita. If this sum was less than the 5.7 pesos spent during the Second Empire, it was at least more than the 2.3 pesos of 1859 (table 33). In response to the director's repeated requests for "urgent" funding, the city council paid enough of the asylum's debt to keep its creditors at bay and to cover the most pressing repairs.[69] Although the budget was perennially tight and small deficits were chronic throughout 1870 and 1871, public funding was at least steady. Moreover, it was regularly supplemented with donations from leading citizens, usually granted for a specific purpose such as Señora Beistegui's 5,000 peso bequest to make new uniforms for the entire school or Citizen Yáñez's 1,113 peso contribution to buy belts for the boys.[70] Thus, the Poor House continued to recover from one of the worst effects of the Reforma, the alienation of private donors.

Another sign of at least minimal funding was that the Poor House finally eliminated the practice of renting out boys as mourners. Suggested by García

Icazbalceta in 1864, this reform was not implemented at that time, perhaps because the earnings from this service were too important. They continued to constitute a significant source of income throughout the first three years of the Restored Republic, especially because the asylum by then owned a coach and mules so that it could produce the entire funerary procession for an added fee. The governor nonetheless decreed the end of this practice on June 22, 1870, "to prevent the degradation the inmates suffer attending these events." In August the coach and mules were sold. Such a measure would not have been contemplated in the face of a dire financial emergency, for the funeral service had produced 1,800 pesos the previous year.[71] Neither would the Poor House have purchased eighty iron cots, as it did in June of 1871, or appointed a music professor, as it did in December, unless it had adequate revenues.[72]

The size of the Poor House also attests to its basic well-being. At the time when Governor Baz submitted his report on March 1, 1869, the departments for boys and girls had dropped to 443 students. By January of 1870 their numbers had increased to 582 and by July to 661 students plus 42 elderly inmates. The precipitous growth of the school explains many of its shortages in 1870 and 1871. Yet the number of inmates stabilized at the larger size, as the Poor House in December of 1871 again registered close to 700 inmates: 647 students and 49 elderly (table 32). This was the maximum size, according to its director, that the building could hold.[73]

Conclusion

The leaders of the Restored Republic could congratulate themselves on maintaining a large establishment that sheltered hundreds of children and a few dozen elderly paupers. After a difficult transition from the Second Empire, they saw it through the worst scandal of its first century. They issued the new bylaws called for during the first Juárez administration in 1861. They could even take credit for a few modifications of its internal regime. They could not, however, claim to have reshaped the institution in a new Liberal mold.

The Juárez regime may have reduced the presence of Catholic ritual in the Poor House in 1871, when it became voluntary rather than obligatory, though the director may only have made the claim in order to appear to comply with new municipal regulations. If true, this was a major departure from the institutional practices of the past hundred years, in which Catholic instruction, daily recitation of the rosary and attendance at Mass, the blessing of meals, and annual confessions were a required part of the Poor House regime. If true, it was also a very late reform. The 1868 bylaws explicitly mandated religious instruction as part of the curriculum. The firing of the chaplain in the winter of 1869 shows that the Poor House still had an in-house priest during the first two years of the Restored Republic. In fact, this chaplain had been hired just one year earlier, under the new Liberal administration, to replace the chaplain who had died during the typhoid epidemic of 1867–68. The well-stocked chapel inventoried on January 28, 1870,[74] likewise suggests that Masses were regularly held. Although the Poor House records for 1871 do not mention a chaplain or daily Mass, references to gala meals on All Saints' Day and Christmas, funded with special contributions from the city council, show that as late as December 1871 religious holidays were still celebrated in the asylum.[75] Indeed, later records suggest that after Citizen Gelt left the institution in July 1871 the Poor House reverted to its customary patterns, since its internal secularization was no longer a public issue. Even after 1874, when religious practices were prohibited in public institutions, the asylum apparently found ways to circumvent the law.[76]

The Liberal initiative to stop the renting of boys as mourners is also less than it at first appears. This reform embodies several major cultural changes. It signals the waning of the traditional Catholic view that assigned to the poor the function of helping the rich achieve salvation. It also reflects the decline of baroque public displays in favor of a new piety that privatized religious rituals.[77] In fact, the decreasing revenues from the funeral-accompanying business (from 2,500 pesos in 1859 to 1,800 in 1870) suggest that the demand for this service was diminishing. In addition, the end of this practice responded to the increasingly egalitarian belief that the children in the Poor House should be treated just like those in other municipal schools. Attendance at burials stigmatized the boys as paupers, which is why the governor's decree of June 22, 1870, described the practice as "degrading." Unlike the reduction of the role of the Catholic Church, however, it is difficult to consider this reform "Liberal" when it was first proposed by the Conservative García Icazbalceta. It owes at least as much to the nonpartisan sentimentalization of childhood and changing religious practices as it does to Reforma ideals.

The Liberals should not get the credit for abandoning the forced confinement of adult beggars, either. Although this was the principal departure from the colonial bylaws, it followed the 1866 statutes. If the relegalization of begging occurred under Juárez's administration, with the 1871 Penal Code, the Poor House experiment had perished long before. Furthermore, the new legislation did not reflect a Liberal conviction about paupers' right to beg. The Penal Code made it clear that the licensing of "true" beggars was a temporary measure of expediency "until there are enough asylums and workhouses" to institutionalize those who solicited alms. The restrictions on beggars in the new law code revealed a lack of respect for their civil liberties.[78] The Juárez government may not have detained beggars in the Poor House, but they were nonetheless persecuted under his regime. In 1868, for example, thirty beggars were incarcerated in the Belén Prison.[79] By using municipal prisons to substitute for the Poor House, Reforma Liberals merely recognized the transformation of the asylum into a school for deserving pauper children and to a lesser extent into a nursing home for a few dozen worthy elderly.[80]

Yet the Poor House had only limited success in achieving this narrower role. Reforma Liberals fared little better than the Sisters of Charity in improving the vocational education offered the older students. The workshops were too few to reach many youths and in the case of the girls only gave them traditional (and fairly useless) needle skills—despite the repeated calls for adding new training in printing, lithography, and the like. The basic academic instruction had deteriorated, causing the director herself to lament in 1871 that too many students were "wasting their time." The Poor House may have lodged and fed hundreds of children, thereby performing an important humanitarian role. But it contributed far less to the utilitarian project still mandated in the bylaws because so many students were warehoused rather than prepared for an independent, productive adulthood.

Moreover, the Poor House could not keep up with the demand for its services. Even though the 1866 and 1868 bylaws restricted its clientele to Mexico City residents, documents dating from 1870 and 1871 repeatedly reported that the Poor House was too full to take in any more paupers. Heartrending petitions continued to arrive from feeble paupers who lacked a family, like the penniless 79-year-old Petra Parra, who requested assistance "for the few days of life that are left me." Widowed parents asked that their children be taken in, as did the elderly Benito Portillo, who feared his two daughters would fall into prostitution, or the illiterate Angela Castro, who could no longer support her two sons on the small salary she earned as a domestic servant.[81] Yet the Poor House often had to turn away such "persons who frequently present themselves late at night and others who, ragged and hungry, solicit protection." [82]

It was not that the Liberal administration neglected the Poor House. President Juárez took a personal interest in the institution, even after his wife's death in January 1871. In December, for example, he solicited the director's ideas about what the inmates needed and how it could accommodate the growing numbers of paupers who sought refuge and deserved to be cared for by "public beneficence." [83] The governor of the Federal District and municipal aldermen—and their wives—were also actively involved in the Poor House. Despite their good intentions, however, they could not make the huge, underfunded orphanage an effective institution for nurturing and educating children.

The deficiencies in the system of public assistance during the Restored Republic were noted six years later when the Porfirian regime removed the Poor House and other welfare institutions from the city council's jurisdiction and placed them under a newly created central Dirección de Beneficencia. The first secretary of its junta, former regidor Juan Abadiano, explained that the old system had been unworkable because the aldermen in charge had too many other responsibilities and changed too frequently to provide adequate supervision and direction and because the mixing of revenues destined for public welfare with municipal funds had led to disastrous consequences.[84] Abadiano had considerable experience with these problems, for he had supervised the Hospital de Maternidad e Infancia as well as the Poor House before heading the Dirección de Beneficencia.[85] Alfaro's brief assessment of the Reforma Poor House from the vantage point of 1906 was even more damning: "In the years between 1870 and 1872 the Poor House suffered repeated modifications of its personnel and interior regime and was on many occasions on the verge of closing."[86] The study of Juárez's last administration—usually overlooked as though his last five years were "an appendix or an aberration"[87]—show the importance of probing beyond the affirmations of the official historiography. Just as during his first administration, the Indian president's record in the Poor House was hardly everything that it was trumped up to be.

$\left\{\text{ CONCLUSION }\right\}$

The original Poor House experiment in confining and transforming the beggars of Mexico City had a relatively short life. After being proclaimed with much fanfare in 1774, it remained "on the books" in the formal legislation until 1871. Yet it was only sporadically enforced during the nineteenth century. The impression conveyed by repeated decrees—of constant campaigns against street people, of the persecution of ever-expanding categories of the urban poor, and of increasing state encroachment on their lives, including attempts to change their character as well as behavior—is highly misleading. Although the asylum contained several hundred paupers within its walls, for most of that century it imposed little control on the beggars of the Mexican capital.

The Poor House succeeded in reducing mendicity mainly during its first two decades, when beggars were regularly rounded up and detained in the asylum. Even then the experiment did not work exactly as envisioned. From the start, city residents attempted to use the institution for their own ends. While propertied citizens and authorities turned to it for help in correcting unruly youths or subordinates, the destitute incorporated it into their survival strategies—proof that the urban poor were not marginalized from the institutions of the larger society. Under pressure from its willing clients, the Poor House admitted groups that were excluded by its bylaws: the "shame-faced" poor and delinquents who were never part of the target population because they did not beg on the city streets, and healthy unemployed men and women who should have been excluded as vagrants. Offering them shelter alongside the "true" beggars, the Poor House took in a cross section of the urban poor, including people of all races and ages and of both sexes. Among them were numerous single mothers and homeless families who welcomed temporary refuge. Thus, at the point of implementing policy, benevolence coexisted with the desire to repress the poor.

Although the inmates had to endure regimented daily lives and a loss of privacy, the Poor House was not as harsh as the carceral regimes described by Michel Foucault as the product of the Great Confinement of the poor. There was a huge gap between the prescribed routines and actual practices of the institution. The perfect order depicted in the self-serving reports of its directors is contradicted by occasional references to inmates sleeping late, engaging in boisterous entertainment and mealtimes, walking in and out of the asylum at leisure, receiving guests outside of visiting hours, and mingling with the opposite sex. Whether they came to it by force or voluntarily, few inmates stayed long. Those who did often became paid workers whose contributions to running the asylum earned them the respect of its staff. Others became enmeshed in clientelist bonds that softened the severity of institutional life. A few paupers, particularly genteel ladies, came to view the Poor House as their home. If some inmates were "disciplined" by being put to work in the asylum's workshops or placed in jobs as apprentices or servants, these were more often youths than adults. The vocational training offered by the institution was always weak. So was the moral correction of inmates, which largely centered on making them good Christians. The city's paupers brought with them, and often kept, their customs as well as their social hierarchies — and a few vergonzantes even brought their servants. Thus, the Poor House neither homogenized nor rehabilitated most of its inmates. The utopianism of its founders soon gave way to the realization that it was far easier to provide lodging, food, and medical care than to reform adults.

After its third decade the Poor House barely tried to discipline the paupers under its roof. As it abandoned the forcible confinement of beggars, the asylum shifted its priorities to aiding the elderly, disabled, unprotected women, and orphaned children who entered voluntarily. In a society in which poverty most often afflicted people of Indian descent, these inmates were disproportionately white, a sign that the asylum sheltered a highly selected (and self-selected) group of paupers and left the others alone. After its Patriotic School was established in 1806, the students increasingly became the focus of the institution. In 1884 a new set of bylaws confirmed its complete transformation into a boarding school for orphans.[1] Since the colonial statutes had excluded children (except those accompanying adult inmates), it no longer catered to its initial clientele. By the end of its first century the Poor House designed to control adult street people cared exclusively for destitute orphans instead (fig. 5). Despite the persistence of hostile rhetoric in the legislation on beggars, humanitarian policies — or perhaps only benign neglect — prevailed.

The broader attack on the "moral economy" of begging also failed. Throughout the nineteenth century beggars were as ubiquitous on the streets of Mexico City as they had been before the experiment was undertaken. (Indeed, as late as 1808 the Poor House itself sent selected inmates out with its alcancías to beg for the institution.)[2] Alms were just as freely given, despite attempts to rationalize their distribution and, when the repression of paupers alone was judged insufficient, to prohibit almsgiving outright. Modern "well-regulated" charity did not replace indiscriminate almsgiving. Encouraged by the generosity of the capital's propertied residents, paupers continued to dress in rags; display their disabilities, old age, and offspring; and station themselves strategically in heavily traversed sections of the city in order to enhance their earnings. As a result the work ethic that enlightened reformers wanted to instill continued to be undermined by the availability of alms.

There are many reasons for the demise of the bold project in social engineering. Official policy was not one of them. On the contrary, various regimes periodically (and unsuccessfully) tried to resurrect the original plan. Historians who rely on political markers or legislation to assess change emphasize independence in 1821 or the Reform Laws of 1856–61 as turning points in Mexico's social welfare history. Yet the asylum's practices rarely reflected external initiatives. Although these did affect its finances, and thus the number of paupers it could serve, they had very little impact on its mission. The Poor House records over a century show that most transformations occurred organically, as the institution's staff interacted with its willing

FIGURE 5   Poor House inmates, 1774–1886

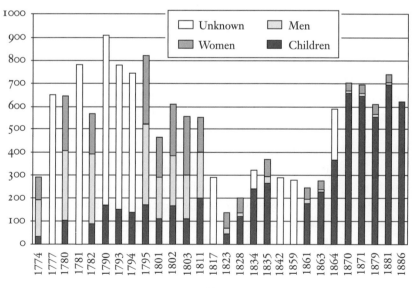

Year

CONTAINING THE POOR

21 BEGGARS THRONGING THE DOORS OF CHURCHES. The scene depicted in this
early-twentieth-century photograph of Mexico City is similar to those repeatedly described by eighteenth- and nineteenth-century observers. Although the Poor House experiment may have reduced mendicity during its first two decades, thereafter the crowds
of beggars were just as ubiquitous as when the project was launched in 1774. Despite a
century of repressive legislation, city officials failed to suppress the "moral economy of
begging" in which the needy had an undisputed right to demand alms and the affluent
considered it their duty to dispense them.

and unwilling clients and responded to the wishes of its donors. The major
long-term changes—the end of forcible confinement, the growing emphasis on women and children, the loss of ecclesiastical funding and support,
and the prominence of the school—were all well under way before independence. The only significant internal changes initiated afterward came during
the Second Empire, which introduced a religious order and elevated women
to positions of responsibility as both board members and upper-level staff.
Even these innovations (the former transitory, the latter permanent) merely
intensified the long-term trend of narrowing the asylum's services and clientele. Indeed, if we had to choose a turning point that changed the direction in
which the asylum was headed, it would be the opening of the Patriotic School
in 1806, a date with no political significance.

How, then, can we explain the withering of the project to which so much
lip service was paid in the three-quarters of a century following 1774? Finan-

cial constraints were one factor. It was prohibitively expensive to confine Mexico City's large population of homeless and destitute, many more of whom proved to be "deserving" than its founders had anticipated. As the demand for the asylum's services exceeded its resources, and as these resources dwindled—dramatically so in the independence years—the Poor House staff and board were forced to make hard choices about which clients to serve. These choices took it farther away from its foundational goals. Yet the abandonment of the original blueprint was much more than a financial decision, for the school that gradually supplanted the original asylum was more expensive to run, on a per capita basis, than the shelter for beggars had been.

The Poor House experiment proved impossible to impose because it met both active and passive resistance from many of the capital's residents. Even in the early years, when the asylum tried to confine bothersome beggars, many who did not want to be institutionalized bought their way out or, once sequestered, walked away or escaped from the asylum. The policemen charged with rounding up beggars often refused to cooperate or at least colluded with recalcitrant street people by accepting their bribes. In contrast, paupers who wanted refuge insisted on their right to assistance, even if they were not the beggars for whom the asylum had been intended. Thus, the institution increasingly catered to those who welcomed its services.

The Poor House administration contributed to this shift. Although we have very little information on them as individuals, it is clear that the asylum's personnel were important, though usually overlooked, agents of its transformation. Whereas the first director was committed to eradicating mendicity, those who replaced him after 1791 were not. Time and again the staff and boardmembers showed little enthusiasm for the original utilitarian project. Uncomfortable with combining aid with punishment and correction, they considered shelter a privilege, were reluctant to admit delinquents, and expelled those who misbehaved. They quickly abandoned the disciplining of beggars to concentrate on providing succor to the groups served in the past by charity: not only the elderly and disabled for whom the asylum was originally designed but also healthy women and children as well as whites—especially the "shamefaced poor" and, once the school was established, orphaned children from distinguished families. Thus, centuries-old notions about who deserved aid—shared by its clients as well as its staff—reasserted themselves to distort the asylum's mission. Contemporary concerns also shaped the choices of the staff. As they saw the caste system declining around them, they were less concerned with controlling the multiracial populace that thronged the streets of the capital city than with shoring up crumbling racial hierarchies. The individuals responsible for implementing policy therefore followed the hidden agenda of preventing the downward mobility and public begging of whites. Showing solidarity with others from the "middling classes," the staff particularly favored white paupers from respectable families.[3] By redefining who was eligible for scarce assistance, the Poor House employees and board turned an institution founded to deter vagrancy and suppress mendicity into one buttressing white privilege. In doing so they also followed time-worn patterns of philanthropy in the Hispanic world, where institutional relief often helped an advantaged sector struggling to maintain its status (such as the families of civil servants eligible for montepíos or the honorable maidens eligible for endowed dowry funds) rather than aiding the poorest of the poor.

The experiment in heavy-handed state intervention was also mitigated by the lukewarm support it received from the city's well-to-do residents. Since the original plan was jointly promoted by clerical as well as secular leaders, it appeared to have the backing of unified elites. In practice, however, there was little consensus about the desirability of confining beggars. By the beginning of the nineteenth century a few voices were openly arguing that it was wrong to deprive beggars of their liberty. By the middle of the century enthusiasm for institutionalizing healthy adult paupers had waned, with some critiquing it as counterproductive because it encouraged "monastic" idleness. Yet most opposition to the plan was far more subtle. After the first decade, few wealthy donors supported the asylum. Instead, they undermined the project by continuing to give alms directly to those who solicited them on the streets of the capital.

The divisions among elites that affected the Poor House were not always those emphasized in the literature, such as clerical/secular, federalist/centralist, liberal/conservative, or native/foreign. These groups shared many basic assumptions about the role of the poor in a modernizing society. The ineffective prosecution of sturdy male beggars, despite the mandate of the 1828 Vagrants Tribunal, suggests that divisions between national and local leaders are also worth examining. In this case, local authorities in daily contact with the presumed vagrants, jealous of their jurisdictions and anxious to defend city residents from the "despotism" of impressment to fight for causes far away from home, dragged their feet in convicting the unemployed men in their wards.[4] Between 1824 and 1835, when the constitution allowed for universal male suffrage, the possibility of making electoral alliances with poor male voters also dampened their desire to repress them. The perennial conflict between the city council and the governor of the Federal District, which hampered the recovery of the republican Poor House, likewise points to the importance of regional and jurisdictional, rather than ideological, divisions.

The final factor explaining why the Poor House experiment failed was the persistence of the "moral economy" that shaped the relations between rich and poor. Although the original project embodied the shift from traditional Catholic charity to modern poor relief, the fact that it could not be implemented shows that the new notions did not set deep roots. The reformers' disdain for paupers coexisted with customary tolerance—though perhaps no longer exaltation and sanctification—of the poor. There are many indications that mendicity was an accepted way to earn a living throughout the nineteenth century. Beggars followed timeworn conventions, including a ritual calendar that dictated that different saints be invoked for different seasons and days of the week. They appealed to religious piety with their pleas "for the love of God" or "for the love of the Blessed Virgin." They recited the catechism along with poems. Propertied citizens likewise incorporated almsgiving into their daily lives by continuing to distribute coins, especially on holy days and at special family occasions such as baptisms. Businesses continued designating one day a week (usually Saturday) for almsgiving. Whether they did it to save their souls, out of true compassion for those less fortunate, or to impress their peers with their generosity, these almsgivers did not consider begging pathological.[5] In a city where "the poor lived cheek by jowl with the rich in mixed residential neighbourhoods,[6] the old social contract of mutual obligation still operated.[7] Indeed, the Seven Acts of Mercy, which delineated the duties of the rich toward the poor, continued to be taught in Father Ripalda's catechism, which was used as an elementary school textbook until at least the middle of the nineteenth century.[8] Not even among the boldest anticlerical Liberals did the modern discourse of secular public welfare completely replace the traditional religious discourse of charity. As in so many other instances, the original plan folded in the face of what Eric Van Young has termed "the resilience of popular culture, and the recalcitrance of large segments of civil society in the face of statist projects."[9]

If the persecution of beggars did not strike a responsive chord among many residents of Mexico City, the Patriotic School did. The schooling of orphans built upon traditional charity that had always provided succor for abandoned children. It appealed to both the growing sentimentalization of childhood and the enlightened view that education was necessary to avert future paupery. The wishes of a major donor facilitated the creation of the school. Francisco de Zúñiga funded an addition that housed the school until 1819, and his generous bequest paid part of its expenses until approximately 1850. Yet even after the Poor House lost the separate school wing and endowment the school continued to thrive because it had the essential support of the public and the staff.

This case study suggests that the power of the Mexican state has been overestimated. Although the Bourbon regime initially conducted concerted campaigns against beggars, it was not strong enough to sustain these efforts. The penurious and unstable republican governments that followed were even less capable of imposing unpopular laws. In contrast to the widespread assumption that the reach of the state grew over time, in Mexico City its impact on paupers diminished notably during the first three-quarters of the nineteenth century.

The role of the state in public welfare did gradually expand between 1774 and 1871. The Bourbon regime took a leading role in supervising and financing the Poor House, while the role of the Church gradually declined—and precipitously so after the turn of the nineteenth century. Yet the strong partnership of state, Church, and private philanthropists that characterized the late colonial period did not give way to state control smoothly. The trend toward secularizing and centralizing public welfare proceeded in fits and starts, with periods of backsliding as the first short-lived attempt at centralization in 1861 ended in failure and as the Poor House was taken over by a religious order for the first time in 1863 after nearly a century as a independent lay institution. Moreover, the Poor House suffered enormously under municipal jurisdiction during the early republic and its transferral to federal jurisdiction under Juárez's General Office of Public Beneficence was an unmitigated disaster. In the end, the asylum's experience suggests that the Liberal state may have succeeded in wresting control of welfare institutions from the Church and from private philanthropists, but without delivering visible benefits to those institutions themselves. Recognizing its weakness, the Liberal government that returned during the Restored Republic backed down from such ambitious schemes.

If the paupers of Mexico City—with allies at all levels of society—successfully resisted the experiment in social control, it was a very limited victory. Sporadic police repression of beggars never disappeared. It was probably concentrated in brief spurts: for a few years after the 1774 ban on begging went into effect and thereafter in a few key months after the issuing of decrees reiterating that ban. It also continued after the legalization of begging in 1871; unlicensed beggars were periodically imprisoned,[10] and some drunkards, simpletons, and epileptics formerly confined to the Poor House were sent to the mental asylum instead.[11] Moreover, the poor were still subjected to the kind of social control imposed by race, culture, gender, and class, which restricted the options available to any given individual. Indeed, by favoring whites, especially the "shamefaced poor," and providing a gendered education, the Poor House reinforced the hierarchies and prejudices of Mexican society, thus validating the distinctions among paupers that kept them from forming ties of solidarity.

While spared the onerous aspects of the Poor House project, Mexico City's paupers were also denied institutional relief. Aside from informal networks of family, friendship, and patronage, there were few sources of aid for the destitute. After 1794, when the last recogimiento was turned into a prison, the Poor House was the only asylum in the Mexican capital providing assistance to indigent but healthy adults. Its metamorphosis into a school left a gap that was only partially filled by two new asylums in the 1870s. The municipal Casa de Corrección y Asilo de Mendigos, established in 1871, took in some elderly and disabled adults, but it was closed by 1874.[12] A private Asilo de Mendigos, established by Francisco Díaz de León in 1879, functioned into the twentieth century, finally allowing the Poor House to transfer out its few remaining elderly inmates. Yet the Asilo was too small to have much impact on the sizable group of Mexico City residents that had been reduced to pauperization.[13] Until the late-nineteenth-century creation of public dormitories and cafeterias,[14] most adult beggars were left to fend for themselves.

At the same time, it is probable that alternate sources of assistance dwindled. There is no evidence that republican governments continued the rudimentary "safety net" provided by the public granaries and meat monopolies of colonial times.[15] The prolonged recession that accompanied independence reduced the ability of extended families (including fictive kin, or *compadres*) to take in needy relations. The decline and eventual expulsion of conventual orders also limited the institutional options for orphaned children who in the past were often cared for by cloistered nuns. The lay confraternities that offered aid to their members were weakened during both the Bourbon and republican regimes.[16] The charitable works of the Church appear to have decreased even before the abolition of mandatory tithes in 1833 and the loss of most ecclesiastical property during the Reforma. The colonial tradition of private philanthropy (aside from petty almsgiving) also appears to have withered during the nineteenth century. The repeated confiscations of bequests by financially strapped governments, beginning with Spain's Consolidación de Vales Reales of 1804 and culminating in Juárez's nationalization of the assets of welfare institutions in 1862, must have dampened the generosity of the Mexican upper classes. So did the "daily" decline in "religious sentiment" noted by the French visitor Isidore Löwenstern.[17] Future historians should study the changing patterns of giving as well as the ways in which the poor adapted to these shifts. When and to what degree the private charitable impulse recovered is another puzzle worthy of further exploration, especially because—despite the Revolution of 1910—public welfare services remain woefully inadequate.

The Mexico City Poor House was not alone, of course, among asylums that failed to achieve their original goals. Scattered evidence on contemporary European institutions suggests that confinement projects were often unsuccessful. Although the scale of the French experiment was much larger—the French *dépôts de mendicité*, for example, detained 230,000 people from 1768 to 1790 alone—Robert Schwartz found the same pattern of active policing at first, which gradually subsided and then disappeared.[18] Kathryn Norberg found that the huge Hôpital Général in Grenoble, originally established for all beggars, with particular emphasis on disciplining the impoverished adult male, likewise narrowed its clientele over time to focus on the sick. Norberg noted that "The war against begging and the campaign for souls were so thoroughly obliterated from the Hospital's program that it is hard to believe that they ever served as the institution's foundation."[19] Reviewing the history of welfare institutions in the United States, Michael Katz concluded that "Mental hospitals did not cure; prisons and reform schools did not rehabilitate . . . and poorhouses did not check the growth of outdoor relief or promote industry and temperance. A preoccupation with order, routine, and cost replaced the founders' concern with the transformation of character and social reform."[20] In the case of Mexico City's Poor House its initial goals were so ambitious—nothing less than eradicating mendicity and preventing future poverty—that the Poor House experiment was bound to fail.

Neither did the institution entirely succeed in its more modest mission of raising and educating orphans during the years before 1871. In its new guise as a boarding school it undoubtedly provided a useful service in a city full of homeless street children, whose numbers swelled due to frequent warfare and civil strife. Despite the good intentions of many dedicated staff members, however, neglect, harsh punishments, and occasional sexual scandals were endemic in the perennially underfunded and understaffed institution. Children continually ran away to escape a regime they disliked. Even during its brief "glory days" under the Sisters of Charity, children were often warehoused rather than nurtured and the vocational training was so limited that many students, especially girls, were not effectively prepared for independent adulthood. Indeed, the asylum created a new group of permanent dependents unable to fend for themselves outside its walls. Moreover, the employees became an entrenched bureaucracy that took up an increasing portion of the Poor House rooms and revenues, thereby diverting resources away from its intended clientele. Institutional waste, patronage, and corruption also reduced the resources available for needy children. Thus, the dreams of achieving efficiency and improving services through centralization were not fulfilled. If the institutionalization of paupers saved some from starving on the city streets, it was no panacea under any of the regimes that ruled Mexico from 1774 to 1871.

$$\left\{ \text{APPENDIX 1} \right\}$$

STATISTICS ON THE INMATE

POPULATION, 1774–1886

Year	Total	Women (as % adults)	Children[a] (as % inmates)
1774[b]	292	38	11
1774	500	—	—
1777	650	—	—
1780	644	44	16
1781	780	—	—
1782[b]	568	37	15
1790	910	—	19
1793	777	—	19
1794	743	—	18
1795	820	46	21
1801	464	49	23
1802	609	51	27
1803	555	57	20
1808[b]	683	36	—
1811	551	43	36
1817	289	—	—
1823	137	76	34 (students)
1828	200	80	61 (students)
1829	202	—	—
1834	320	—	75 (students)
1835	368	77	72 (students)
1841	279	—	—
1842	291	—	—
1859	279	—	—

Statistics on the Inmate Population, 1774–1886, continued

Year	Total	Women (as % adults)	Children[a] (as % inmates)
1860	271	—	—
1861	244	75	73 (students)
1862	256	—	—
1863	276	73	83 (students)
1864	590	—	62 (students)
1870	703	79	94 (students)
1871	696	73	93 (students)
1877	537	—	—
1879	610	78	91 (students)
1881	741	81	94 (students)
1886	622	0	100 (students)

Sources:

1774 (March 24): Letter of March 27, 1774, in AGN, Cédulas Reales, vol. 108, exp. 81, f. 165.

1774 (August 16): AGN, Cédulas Reales, vol. 108, exp. 3.

1777: Viera (1952), 70.

1780 (April 15): "Nota de los Pobres que existen en este Real Hospicio oy 15 de Abril de 1780," in BNM, Lafragua Collection, no. 33.

1781 (March): Letter from Poor House director, March 3, 1781, in "Testimonio del expediente sobre arbitrios para la subsistencia del Hospicio," August 11, 1781, AGI, México, vol. 2791.

1782 (March 23): "Padrón para el cumplimiento annual de Nra. madre Iglesia de los Pobres de ambos sexos que contiene este Rl. Hospicio oy 23 de marzo de 1782," GDCLDS, Mexico D.F., microfilm roll no. 35978.

1793-94 (December 31): "Estado que manifiesta el Real Hospicio de Pobres en fin de Diciembre 1794," *Gazetas de México*, February 3, 1795, 33.

1795 (April 12): "Padrón de los Pobres de ambos sexos, que existen en este Real Hospicio de Pobres, para el Cumplimiento de N.a Santa M.e Yglesia, oy Dia 12 de Abril de 1795," GDCLDS, Mexico D.F., microfilm roll no. 35978.

1801 (December): "Estado General del Real Hospicio de Pobres de Mexico del año de 1802," AHCM, Hospicio de Pobres, vol. 2295, no. 15.

1802-3 (December 31): "Estado del Real Hospicio de Pobres de Mexico en 31 de diciembre de 1803 as.," AGN, Historia, vol. 441, ff. 7-12 (1804 Report).

1808: "Padrón . . . del Hospicio de Pobres," GDCLDS, Mexico D.F., microfilm roll no. 35978.

1811: Census of Mexico City, 1811, AGN, Padrones, vol. 72, ff. 39-58.

1817 (December), "Opinión del Síndico del Ayuntamiento," December 29, 1817, AGN, Policía, vol. 30, f. 268.

1823: "Estado general de la Casa del Hospicio de Pobres de Méjico, February 8, 1824," AGN, Archivo Histórico de Hacienda, Estadística, vol. 117, ff. 177-92 (1824 report).

1828 (January): Galván Rivera (1828), 101.

1829 (January): Galván Rivera (1829), 105.

1834 Report of R. Packenham, in Gilmore (1957), 219.

1835 (May 25): "Hospicio de Pobres. Estado que manifiesta las personas de ambos secsos que existen en este Establecimiento. . . ," AGN, Gobernación, tramo 1, vol. 130, exp. 36.

1841 (November 21): "Papeletas diarias," AHSSA, HYH-HP, bk. 10.

1842 (February 12): "Resumen general de las personas en el Hospicio de Pobres. . . ," in BNM, Lafragua Collection, no. 118, 8.

1859 (January 3 to February 26): "Papeletas diarias," AHSSA, BP-EA-HP, leg. 1, exp. 1.

1860 (May): "Papeletas diarias," AHSSA, BP-EA-HP, leg. 1, exp. 4, f. 55.

1861 (June): "Presupuesto gral. pormenorizado. . . ," AHSSA, BP-EA-HP, leg. 1, exp. 21, f. 2.

1862 (January 23): "Papeletas diarias," AHSSA, BP-EA-HP, leg. 4, exp. 2, f. 24.

1863 (August): García Icazbalceta (1907), 13-16.

1864 (June): García Icazbalceta (1907), 212.

1870 (July 6): "Informe que rinde la encargada del establecimiento acerca del estado que guarda actualmente," AHCM, Hospicio de Pobres, vol. 2295, exp. 119, f. 1 verso.

1871 (December 9): "Informe sobre el Hospicio," AHCM, Hospicio de Pobres, vol. 2296, no. 145, f. 2.

1877 (February 1): AHSSA, BP-EA-HP, leg. 5, exp. 19, f. 5.

1879 (February 31): AHSSA, BP-EA-HP, leg. 7, exp. 3.

1881 (November 8): "Hospicio: visita practicada por el Gefe de la Sección," AHSSA, BP-EA-HP, leg. 10, exp. 9, f. 1.

1886: (April): AHSSA, BP-EA-HP, leg. 13, exp. 18, cited in Blum (1998), 240.

[a] This category is not strictly comparable over the entire century. Until 1811, children are either those under 15 years of age or those classified as muchachos and muchachas in the documents (also usually under 15, the age normally used to distinguish children from adults). After independence, the category of niños and niñas includes all students, most (but not all) of them 18 or under. The 1835 figure includes eighteen juvenile delinquents who were not students.

[b] These figures are artificially low because (1) the 1774 count is for the fifth day after the Poor House opened; (2) the 1782 census, taken for ecclesiastical purposes, omits an unspecified number of unbaptized indios mecas; and (3) the 1808 Communion list omits students in the Patriotic School.

{ APPENDIX 2 }

POOR HOUSE BYLAWS

For full texts see this volume's website, http://www.brandeis.edu/~arrom/.

1764 (proposed): Included in petition from Fernando Ortiz Cortés to the king, April 2, 1764, AGI, México, vol. 2791, exp. 1.

1769 (proposed): "Ordenanzas de la Real Casa de Hospicio de Pobres Mendigos de México y su Arzobispado," October 22, 1769, AGI, México, vol. 2791, exp. 8.

1777 (approved in 1785 with modifications): "Ordenanzas para el govierno del Real Hospicio de Pobres de la Ciudad de México, erigido bajo el Patronato y protección del Rey Nuestro Señor Año de 1777," AGN, Bandos, vol. 10, exp. 18.

1806 (approved): "Prospecto de la nueva forma de gobierno politico y economico del Hospicio de Pobres de esta capital," AGN, Bandos, vol. 22, ff. 145–148v.

1843 (approved): *Ordenanza para el régimen y gobierno del Hospicio de Pobres de esta capital* (Mexico City: Imprenta de la Casa de Corrección, 1844). Copy in AHSSA, BP-EA-HP, leg. 2, exp. 5.

1866 (approved): "Proyecto de reglamento para el gobierno del Hospicio de Pobres de esta capital," February 24, 1866, AHCM, Consejo General de Beneficencia, vol. 420, exp. 119.

1868 (approved): "Reglamento para el Hospicio de Pobres," *La Gaceta de Policía*, October 11, 1868, 1–3. Copy in AHCM, Hospicio de Pobres, vol. 2295, exp. 50.

1884 (approved): "Reglamento del Hospicio," AHSSA, BP-EA-HP, leg. 12, exp. 11.

{ APPENDIX 3 }

POOR HOUSE ADMINISTRATORS

Directors

1774–91	Andrés Ambrosio Llanos y Valdés
1792–1806	Simón María de la Torre

Salaried Administrators

1774–77?	Joseph Elizalde y León
1778–91	Pedro Antonio de la Sierra y Lombera (died 1791)
1795?–1807?	Juan Antonio Araujo
1824?–1828	José María Pelaez
?–1829?	José María Gómez
?–1833	Vicente Garviso (died 1833)
1833–41	Lt. Col. Francisco Barroeta (fired 1841)
1848?–62	José María Gómez Eguiarte (fired 1862)
1862–63	José Rafael Larrañaga
1863–67	Sor Melchora Yriarte (superiora)
1867–68	Mariano Aguilar (died 1868)
?–1869	Señor Márquez
1869	Luciana Arrázola de Baz
1870–76	Juana Rodríguez de Herrera (fired 1876)

{ APPENDIX 4 }

POOR HOUSE BOARD MEMBERS

*Denotes priests. Names and noble titles appear as they are listed in each document.

1774 *Real Junta del Hospicio de Pobres*

1. President: Viceroy Bucareli
2. Juan Lucas de Lassaga
3. José Matheos
4. Domingo Balcarcel
5. Juan Ignacio de Rocha
6. Luis de Torres
7. Fernando González de Collantes

1785 *Junta*

1. President: Audiencia Regent Herrera
2. Villaurrutia
3. Azedo
4. Luyando
5. Guevara
6. Urizar
7. Galdeano

1805 *Junta de Caridad (partial)*

President: Viceroy Joseph de Yturrigaray
Secretary: Juan Francisco de Azcárate
Ciriaco González Carbajal
Francisco Xavier Borbón
Ambrosio Sagarzurieta
Juan Antonio Bruno*
Antonio Méndez Prieto y Fernández
Francisco Primo Verdad y Ramos
Simón María de la Torre

1806 *Junta de Caridad*

1. President: Viceroy Joseph de Yturrigaray
2. Vice president: Ciriaco González Carbajal
3. Juan Antonio Bruno*
4. Ignacio de la Peza y Casas
5. Ignacio Iglesias Pablo
6. Francisco Fernández de Córdova (Marqués de San Román)
7. Antonio Basoco
8. Simón María de la Torre y Albórnoz
9. Joseph Mariano Fagoaga
10. Juan Cervantes y Padilla
11. Pedro Azlor de Valdivieso (Marqués de San Miguel de Aguayo)
12. Antonio Zevallos Calderón (Marqués de Santa Fe de Guardiola)
13. Luis Gonzaga de Ibarrola y Candia
14. Luis Madrid
15. Bernardo Palacios
16. Juan Francisco de Azcárate
17. Juan Francisco Campos*

18. Juan Francisco Domínguez*
19. Pedro Romero de Terreros Trebuesto y Dávalos (Conde de Santa María de Regla)
20. Ignacio Obregón
21. Antonio Méndez Prieto y Fernández
22. Francisco Primo Verdad y Ramos
23. Domingo Ignacio Lardizábal
24. Francisco de la Cotera
25. Francisco de Paula Luna Gorraez y Malo (Marqués de Ciria, Mariscal de Castilla)
26. Joseph María Fagoaga
27. Juan Díaz González
28. Isidro Antonio de Icaza
29. Gabriel Yermo
30. Juan de Madariaga (Marqués de Casa-Alta)
31. Francisco Alonso Terán
32. Rafael Ortega
33. Francisco Escobosa
34. Juan Velázquez de la Cadena
35. Francisco Manuel Sánchez de Tagle
36. Juan Fernando Meoqui
37. Antonio Terán
38. Mariano Zúñiga y Ontiveros
39. Vicente Gómez de la Cortina (Conde de la Cortina)
40. Roque Valiente
41. Felipe Sabalza
42. Estevan Vélez Escalante
43. Marqués de Selva-Nevada
44. Juan de Sarría*
45. Juan Francisco de Castañiza (Marqués de Castañiza)
46. Juan Joseph Guereña*
47. Francisco de Echederreta*
48. Pedro Marcos Gutiérrez

1809 Junta (partial)

Ciriaco González Carbajal
Ignacio Obregón
Simón María de la Torre

Ciro de Villaurrutia*
Juan Fernández de Meoqui
Mariano de Ontiveros
Luis Gonzaga de Ibarrola
Esteveles de Escalante
José María Fagoaga
Conde de Peñasco
Francisco de Yglesias
Diego de Agreda
Francisco Sánchez de Tagle

1822 Junta de Caridad

1. President: Francisco de Paula Gorraez y Malo (Mariscal de Castilla, Marqués de Ciria)
2. Francisco Manuel Sánchez de Tagle
3. Antonio Medina
4. Ciro Villaurrutia*
5. José Antonio Cabeza de Baca*
6. Domingo María Pozo
7. Conde del Peñasco
8. Juan Antonio Cobián
9. Miguel Cervantes (Marqués de Salvatierra)
10. Marqués de Santa Fe de Guardiola
11. Juan Francisco de Azcárate
12. José Mariano Fagoaga
13. Mariano Zúñiga y Ontiveros
14. Juan de Cervantes y Padilla
15. José María Fagoaga
16. Manuel de Lardizábal
17. José Juan de Fagoaga
18. José Ignacio García Illueca
19. Agustín Iglesias*
20. Francisco de la Cuesta*

1824 Junta de Beneficencia (partial)

Domingo de Lardizábal
Estevan Vélez de Escalante
Mariscal de Castilla
José María Fagoaga
Antonio Velasco de la Torre

1828 Junta de Caridad

1. President: Governor José María Tornel
2. Vice president: José María Bocanegra
3. Estanislao Cuesta
4. Juan Pina
5. Joaquín Ladrón de Guevara*
6. Manuel Posada*
7. Isidro Rafael Gondra
8. Vicente Valdés
9. José María Cervantes
10. José Manuel Herrera
11. Mariano Sánchez Espinosa
12. Manuel Barrera
13. José Ignacio Paz de Tagle
14. Antonio Velasco de la Torre
15. Mariano Domínguez
16. José Domínguez
17. Ventura Miranda
18. Juan de Dios Rodríguez
19. Juan Manuel Elizalde
20. Rafael Alarid
21. Juan Gómez Navarrete
22. Ricardo Ester
23. José Collin
24. Manuel Lozano

1828 Junta de Señoras

1. Vice president: Luisa Vicario de Moreno
2. Treasurer: Petra Ternel de Velasco
3. Josefa Arrillaga
4. Josefa Marcela Ortiz
5. Guadalupe Sandoval de Espino
6. María Guadalupe Cardeña de Illueca
7. Ignacia de Agreda
8. Guadalupe Fernández de Filisola
9. Leona Vicario de Quintana
10. María Loreto Vivanco de Morán
11. Mariana Amezola de Echave
12. María Guadalupe Amezola

13. Ignacia Ternel de la Torre
14. Josefa Rodríguez de Uluapa

1829 Junta

1. President: Governor of the D.F.
2. Vice president: José María Bocanegra
3. Joaquín Ladrón de Guevara
4. Manuel Posada
5. Isidro Rafael Gondra
6. José María Cervantes
7. José Manuel de Herrera
8. Mariano Sánchez Espinosa
9. Manuel Barrera
10. Mariano Domínguez
11. José Domínguez
12. Juan de Dios Rodríguez
13. Juan Gómez Navarrete
14. Ricardo Exter
15. Manuel Lozano
16. Anastasio Zerecero
17. Juan José Flores Alatorre
18. Juan de Dios Lazcano
19. Lázaro de la Garza
20. Ignacio Sotomayor
21. Agustín Gallegos
22. José Ignacio Basadre
23. Francisco Robles
24. Manuel Martínez Vea
25. El Sr. Marchall

1830 (partial)

José María Rico
Santiago Aldazoro
Pedro Fernández*
Agustín Gallegos
Roberto Manning

1833 (partial)

Pedro Fernández*
Atilano Sánchez

Mariano Domínguez
Santiago Aldazoro
José María Echave
José María Cervantes Michaus
Mariano Galván Rivera
Francisco Fagoaga
José Fernández de Celis
José María Fagoaga

1836 (partial)

José Gómez de la Cortina

1841 Junta de Caridad (partial)

Vice president: Félix Osores*

1842 (partial)

Vice president: Félix Osores*
Mariano Domínguez

1843 (partial)

Vice president: Ignacio Inclán

1844 (partial)

Félix Osores*
Gregorio Mier y Terán
Juan Portillo
Treasurer: Diego Somera
Agustín Carpena*
Pedro Fernández*
Mariano Domínguez
Ignacio Trigueros

1847 Junta de Beneficencia (partial)

José Ramón Malo

1856 (partial)

Treasurer: Agustín Carpena*
Accountant: Vicente Carbajal

1859 (partial)

President: Miguel María Azcárate
Manuel Lizardi
Ignacio Trigueros
E. Mackintosh
Juan Goribar

1861 Junta Directiva (partial)

President: Marcelino Castañeda
Vice president: Mariano Domínguez

1865 Comisión de Vigilancia

1. President: José María Godoy
2. Antonio de Mier
3. Juan Sánchez Azcona
4. Aniceto Ortega
5. Miguel Cervantes
6. Guadalupe Y. de Siliceo
7. Catalina Barrón de Escandón
8. Francisca Pérez Gálvez
9. Carlota Escandón
10. Carmen Pesado

1866 Comisión de Vigilancia

Guadalupe Godoy de Echeverría
   (replaced Pérez Gálvez)
Alternates: Clara Segura and Aurora
   Batres

*1869–70 Junta de Protección
del Hospicio (partial)*

President: Margarita Maza de Juárez

{ SOURCES OF ILLUSTRATIONS }

1. "Las Cadenas en una noche de luna," drawing by Casimiro Castro, in *México y sus alrededores: colección de vistas monumentales, paisajes, y trajes del país*, rev. ed. (Mexico City, 1869). Reprinted courtesy of the Beinecke Rare Book and Manuscript Library, Yale University.

2. AGN, Bandos, vol. 10, exp. 18. Reprinted courtesy of the Archivo General de la Nación, Mexico.

3. Lithograph by Claudio Linati, in *Costumes et Moeurs de Mexique* (London, 1830), pl. 16. Reprinted courtesy of the Beinecke Rare Book and Manuscript Library, Yale University.

4. Lithograph by Claudio Linati, in *Costumes et Moeurs de Mexique* (London, 1830), pl. 31. Reprinted courtesy of the Beinecke Rare Book and Manuscript Library, Yale University.

5. "Trajes mexicanos," drawing by Casimiro Castro, in *México y sus alrededores: colección de vistas monumentales, paisajes, y trajes del país*, rev. ed. (Mexico City, 1869). Reprinted courtesy of the Beinecke Rare Book and Manuscript Library, Yale University.

6. Oil painting reproduced in Rómulo Velasco Ceballos, *El niño mexicano ante la caridad y el estado* (Mexico City, 1935). Reprinted courtesy of the Library of Congress.

7. Illustration in Martiniano Alfaro, *Reseña histórico-descriptiva del antiguo Hospicio de México* (Mexico City, 1906). Reprinted courtesy of the Tulane University Library.

8. Poor House Building, Exterior: Illustration in Manuel Rivera Cambas, *México pintoresco, artístico y monumental* (Mexico City, 1880). Reprinted courtesy of the Yale University Library.

9. "Antiguo Hospicio, Altar Mayor de la Capilla," photograph in Martiniano Alfaro, *Reseña histórico-descriptiva del antiguo Hospicio de México* (Mexico City, 1906). Reprinted courtesy of the General Research Division, New York Public Library, Astor, Lenox, and Tilden Foundations.

10. "Nuestra Señora de la Caridad," drawing in Francisco de Ajofrín, *Diario del viaje que*

por orden de la sagrada Congregación de Propaganda Fide hizo a la América Septentrional
... (Madrid, 1958). Reprinted courtesy of the Sterling Library, Yale University.

11. Early-twentieth-century photographs reproduced in Martiniano Alfaro, *Reseña histórico-descriptiva del antiguo Hospicio de México* (Mexico City, 1906). Reprinted courtesy of the Tulane University Library.

12. Loose slip included in "Salidas, 1774," AHSSA, BP-EA-HP, bk. 2. Reprinted courtesy of the Archivo Histórico de Salubridad y Asistencia, Mexico.

13. "Estado del Real Hospicio de Pobres de México en 31 de diciembre de 1803 as.," AGN, Historia, vol. 441, f. 7. Reprinted courtesy of the Archivo General de la Nación, Mexico.

14. Oil painting reproduced in Rómulo Velasco Ceballos, *El niño mexicano ante la caridad y el estado* (Mexico City, 1935). Reprinted courtesy of the Library of Congress.

15. Street Children, Boy. Photograph by F. Aubert, circa 1865. Reprinted courtesy of the Musée Royal de l'Armée et d'Histoire Militaire, Belgium.

16. Street Children, Girl. Photograph by F. Aubert, circa 1865. Reprinted courtesy of the Musée Royal de l'Armée et d'Histoire Militaire, Belgium.

17. Undated diagram entitled "Croquis de la Planta del Hospicio de Pobres," BNM, Documentos para la historia de México, in the collection of the Fototeca de Culhuacán. Reproduction authorized by the Instituto Nacional de Antropología e Historia, Mexico.

18. Undated diagram entitled "Plano del Hospicio de Niños Pobres," BNM, Documentos para la historia de México, in the collection of the Fototeca de Culhuacán. Reproduction authorized by the Instituto Nacional de Antropología e Historia, Mexico.

19. Photograph by Vallarte y Cia, circa 1865, in the Museo Nacional de Historia, Mexico City. Reproduction authorized by the Instituto Nacional de Antropología e Historia, Mexico.

20. Oil painting by José Escudero y Espronceda, 1890, in the Museo Nacional de Historia, Mexico City. Reproduction authorized by the Instituto Nacional de Antropología e Historia, Mexico.

21. Photograph taken circa 1930, reproduced in Beneficencia Pública del D.F., *La mendicidad en México* (Mexico City, 1931). Reprinted courtesy of the Tulane University Library.

$$\left\{ \text{NOTES} \right\}$$

Introduction

1 García Icazbalceta (1907), 140.
2 It would take a lifetime to exhaust the documentary traces left by the institution. After completing this book I discovered an unpublished undergraduate thesis on the Poor House by María Xóchitl Martínez Barbosa (1994), which uses additional documents in the AGN and BN. Fortunately, her presentation of the information in these documents suggests that they would not have altered my conclusions.
3 Haslip-Viera (1986); González Navarro (1985), 88–91. Since then the Poor House has been the subject of a brief discussion by Sacristán (1994b) and of more systematic study in unpublished theses by López Figueroa (1993), Martínez Barbosa (1994), and Blum (1998), chaps. 2–4.
4 An excellent sociological study of mendicity in revolutionary Mexico did not fall into this trap. Briefly surveying previous attempts to eradicate begging, its authors noted that none had functioned as planned. See Beneficencia Pública del D.F. (1931), 89–100.
5 I thank the anonymous reviewer of this manuscript for Duke University Press, who suggested that I apply E. P. Thompson's concept of the moral economy to the customary relations between rich and poor in the area of poor relief. For Thompson's original use of the term, which he defines as the constellation of "traditional social norms and obligations," see (1971), esp. 79.
6 On the shifting boundaries of the municipality see, for example, Gortari Rabiela (1994).
7 See Blum (1998), 158–61, 174–80; and Rivera-Garza (1995), 98–100. Two notable studies of other parts of Latin America examine earlier female philanthropic organizations, a Sociedad de Beneficencia established in 1823 in Buenos Aires and a Junta de Damas founded in 1859 in San Juan. See Little (1980); and Matos Rodríguez (1999), 114–24. Edith Couturier also demonstrates the important role of women in private charity during the colonial period (1990).
8 See González Navarro (1985), chap. 1, esp. 40–54; Velasco Ceballos (1935), 103; López Figueroa (1993), esp. 8–9; Rivera-Garza (1995), esp. 92, 366; McLeod (1990), chaps. 1–2; and Centro Mexicano para la Filantropía (1996). A similar chronology is posited for Puerto Rico by Martínez-Vergne (1989), Ecuador by Kingman Garcés (1999), and Guatemala by Hernández (1992). In contrast, Meyer dates pivotal

changes to the Bourbon period in her brief but excellent bibliographical essay (1975), as does Haslip-Viera in his single paragraph on poor relief in colonial Latin America (1986), 304.

9 See the discussion in Hamnett (1994), xii, 244–51.

10 Ajofrín (1958), 1:80.

11 Villarroel (1831), 107. Villarroel's comment probably dates from 1785. The first two volumes of his work are dated 1785; the fourth volume is dated 1787. This comment comes from the third, undated, volume. See Estrada (1979), ix–xii.

12 Humboldt (1966) 1:235, 2:82. On the prevalence of homelessness in the late eighteenth century, see also Sedaño (1880), 95.

13 Poinsett (1969), 48–49.

14 Vigneaux (1863), 508.

15 Elsewhere I have estimated that the upper class (people of independent wealth, prosperous merchants and miners, top-level bureaucrats and clergy, ranking military officers, and the titled nobility) represented no more than 4 percent of the population. Another 18 percent might be considered middle class, having one or two servants in their households, while the rest—some 78 percent of the city's residents— were the *populacho* or *plebe* which contrasted with the *gente decente*. See Arrom (1985), 7–8. For descriptions of the urban poor, see Haslip-Viera (1986), Shaw (1975), and Di Tella (1973).

16 Villaseñor y Sánchez estimated Mexico City's population in 1742 at 98,000 (1746), 1:35. Humboldt's calculation of 137,000 for 1803 is based on a 1790 census, which counted 112,926 inhabitants (1966), 2:81–82. By 1811, with the influx of refugees from the independence war, it had reached 168,846. See the census of the Juzgado de Policía cited in Davies (1972), 501.

17 Florescano (1969); Florescano and Gil Sánchez (1976), 2:183–301; Reher (1992); Cooper (1965); Van Young (1992), chap. 2; Ouweneel (1996), esp. 9–10, 252, 329.

18 Villarroel (1831), 110.

19 Further research may uncover similar experiments. Julia Herráez refers to a Chilean *hospicio*, which opened in approximately 1760, the Hospicio de Pobres, Hospital de Expósitos, y Casa de Recogidas of Santiago. Unlike the Mexico City Poor House, however, the one in Santiago apparently targeted several dependent groups at once and lacked the element of forced confinement so central to disciplining the poor (1949), 142–59. Kingman Garcés refers to one in Quito, established in 1785, which also served as a hospital for the sick and demented (1999), 289–91. Several hospicios were established in nineteenth-century Mexico, as in Veracruz in 1801 and Guadalajara in 1810. See Voekel (1997), 22; and López-Portillo y Weber et al. (1971). These Poor Houses appear to have been more like shelters and orphanages than disciplinary institutions, but at least two Brazilian beggars' asylums built in the midnineteenth century had the correctional dimension. See Holloway (1997); and Fraga Filho (1996), esp. 151–67.

20 See Foucault (1961) and (1979). His term for the Great Confinement is *grand renfermement* and for discipline is *surveiller.*

21 Rothman (1971); Piven and Cloward (1971). Also see Alexander (1980), Schwartz (1988), and Olejniczak (1990).

22 See, for example, Platt (1969), esp. chap. 4; and Scull (1979). Although less directly related to the social control school, a growing body of works have examined what philanthropy meant for its female practitioners. See Ryan (1981), Smith (1981), Ginzberg (1990), and McCarthy (1990).

23 Ross (1901); Weber (1930); Durkheim (1961); Elias (1978). For a discussion of their theories, see especially Rothman (1983), the introduction by Finzsch in Finzsch and Jütte (1996), and Garland (1990).

24 For critiques of the social control school, see Grob (1973), Cohen and Scull (1983), Trattner (1983), Haskel (1985), Garland (1990), and Finzsch and Jütte (1996).

25 Scott (1985).

26 See, for example, Brown (1987); Dwyer (1987), esp. chap. 4; Ransel (1988); Cray (1988); Pascoe (1990), esp. chap. 3; Lis and Soly (1990); and Porter (1993).

27 See, for example, Pullan (1971), Gutton (1974), Fairchilds (1976), Jones (1982), Katz (1983), Himmelfarb (1984), Norberg (1985), Woolf (1986), De Swaan (1988), Gordon (1988), and Mandler (1990). On Spain, see Rumeau de Armas (1944), Sarrailh (1953), Jiménez Salas (1958), Callahan (1971), Perry (1980), Soubeyroux (1982), Martz (1983), Carasa Soto (1987), Sherwood (1988), Caro López (1989), Flynn (1989), Michielse (1990), and Shubert (1991).

28 Aguilar and Ezquerro Peraza (1936); Chase (1975); Venegas Ramírez (1973); Howard (1980); Zedillo Castillo (1984); Suárez (1988).

29 Muriel (1946), (1956-60), and (1974).

30 For Mexico, see MacLachlan (1974); Gonzalbo Aizpuru (1982); Sacristán (1992), (1994a), and (1994b), 227-49; López-Portillo (1971); Padilla (1993); López Figueroa (1993); Avila Espinosa (1994); Rivera-Garza (1995); and Blum (1998). On other areas of Latin America, see Russell Wood (1968), Little (1980), Martínez-Vergne (1991), Salvatore and Aguirre (1996), Holloway (1997), and Kittleson (1997).

31 For Mexico, the Departmento de Acción Educativa, Eficiencia y Catastros Sociales commissioned the remarkable Beneficencia Pública del D.F. (1931). The creation of the Ministry of Health and Welfare in 1937 inspired a cluster of sketchy works on social welfare, with a few works by conservatives defending the Church and the colonial regime and serving as a counterpoint to the triumphalism of officialist histories. Interest in the topic was renewed only in the 1960s. See for example, Velasco Ceballos (1934a), (1935), (1938), and (1943); Cook (1940); Secretaría de la Asistencia Pública (1940); Alessio Robles (1944); Carreño (1942); Palavicini (1945); Herráez (1949); Laguarta (1955); Cruz (1959); Alvarez Amezquita et al. (1960); Borah (1966); Lamas (1964); Chávez Orozco (1966); Vázquez de Warman (1968); Meyer (1975); Couturier (1975) and (1990); Bazarte Martínez (1989); McLeod (1990); Pescador (1990); Chandler (1991); Centro Mexicano para la Filantropía (1996); and Megged (1997).

32 Although the first survey of welfare institutions, conducted in 1863-64 by Joaquín García Icazbalceta, was only published posthumously (1907), it was known to Juan Abadiano, who cited it frequently in his work (1878). See also Peza (1881) and Macedo (1900).

33 See, for example, Orozco y Berra (1867), Rivera Cambas (1880-83), Marroquí (1901-3), and Galindo y Villa (1901).

34 Alfaro (1906).

35 Armida de González's 1956 study of the urban poor (1974), part of Cosío Ville-
gas's project to write a complete history of Mexico, was unusual for its time. The
subject attracted sustained attention only two decades later. See, for example, Di
Tella (1973), Chávez Orozco (1977), Shaw (1975), Scardaville (1977) and (1994),
Moreno Toscano (1978), Haslip-Viera (1980) and (1986), Florescano et al. (1980),
González Angulo (1983), Pescador (1992), Cope (1994), Márquez Morfín (1994),
Warren (1994), Illades (1996), Pérez Toledo (1993) and (1996), and Arrom and Or-
toll (1996).

36 N. Martin (1957), (1972), and (1985). See also Pogolotti (1978), Arrom (1988a), Sacristán (1988) and (1994b), Pérez Toledo (1993), and Serrano Ortega (1996).

37 See Scardaville (1980), Viqueira Albán (1987), Deans-Smith (1992), Voekel (1992),
articles in Beezley (1994), Rivera-Garza (1995), and French (1996).

38 González Navarro (1985).

39 Tyor and Zainaldin (1979), 25.

40 Clarke A. Chambers echoed Tyor and Zainaldin's lament by stating that most historians of social welfare "focus on program and policy formulation to the neglect
of implementation by practitioners working at the point of service delivery" (1992),
495. Despite several excellent studies of orphanages and asylums for the mentally ill
(e.g., Ransel 1988 and Dwyer 1987), I have been unable to locate a comparable systematic long-term study of a poorhouse. A few authors provide useful information
in one chapter or article, as do Crowther (1982), esp. chaps. 3 and 8; Clement (1985),
chap. 4; Norberg (1985), chap. 8; and Park and Wood (1992). The only book-length
study of a poorhouse I have located is Palomares Ibáñez (1975). Unfortunately, the
spottiness of his information on the actual workings of Valladolid's hospicio makes
comparisons with the Mexico City Poor House difficult.

41 Mandler (1990), 14.

1 The Problem of Beggars and Vagrants, 1774–1871

1 AGN, Bandos, vol. 8, ff. 210–11.

2 Fernández de Lizardi (1942), 202–6.

3 Jiménez Salas (1958), 148.

4 The best studies of the colonial orphanage are Gonzalbo Aizpuru (1982) and Avila
Espinosa (1994). There is considerable confusion in the literature even about such
simple facts as the opening date of the Casa de Cuna. Gonzalbo dates it to 1766, as
does Sedaño in his contemporary diary of noteworthy events (1880), 169. The late-
nineteenth and twentieth-century sources usually date it to 1767, as do Peza (1881),
104; and González (1974), 376.

5 See Chase (1975) and Muriel (1956–60).

6 On the Pawn Shop, see Francois (1998), Villamil (1877), Darío (1947), and Couturier
(1975).

7 On the montepíos, see Lamas (1964), esp. chap. 5; and Chandler (1991).

8 See N. Martin (1972), 8–9; McWatters (1979); and Deans-Smith (1992) and (1994).

9 Tanck Estrada (1977), chaps. 1–2; González (1974), 374–80.

10 See Thompson (1967). On Mexican attempts to instill work discipline, combat San Lunes (St. Monday), and reduce religious holidays, see Potash (1983), esp. 137, 160; Fernández de Lizardi (1974), 136–37; and "Proyecto de Reglamento para la Casa de Asilo de Pobres Mendigos" (1852).

11 This phrase is used, for example, in the Spanish decree of October 1783 reproduced in the *Novísima recopilación* (1805–7), bk. 7, title 39, law 24, art. 7 (hereafter cited as *Nov. rec.*). As Jorge Nacif Mina correctly points out, the term *policía* is not synonymous with *police* but rather with the *good government* of the poor (1994), 9–11.

12 For more information on these efforts in Mexico City, see Viqueira Albán (1987), esp. chap. 3; Scardaville (1980); N. Martin (1972); Voekel (1992); Nacif Mina (1994); Sacristán (1994b); Hernández Franyuti (1994b); and Morales (1994). On the poor in the streets, see especially Haslip-Viera (1980), 10–32.

13 See Scardaville (1994), esp. 508–12; Haslip-Viera (1980); Sacristán (1994b), 198–220; and Viqueira Albán (1987). On the 1770s reorganization of the Tribunal of the Acordada (founded in 1719), see MacLachlan (1974), chaps. 4–5. The 1782 division of Mexico City persisted into the republican period. See "Ordenanza provisional del Ayuntamiento de México," May 2, 1853, in Dublán and Lozano (1876–1904), no. 3832, 6:386, art. 7 (hereafter cited as Dublán and Lozano).

14 The quote is from the 1786 Ordenanza de Intendentes, but similar instructions were given the Mexico City *alcaldes* in charge of the newly created cuarteles in 1782. See the discussion of these directives in Sacristán (1988) and in the 1785 comment of the Poor House director in AGN, Templos y Conventos, vol. 47, exp. 9, f. 1054v.

15 See Callahan (1971); Jiménez Salas (1958), 119–26; Rumeau de Armas (1944), 275–85; N. Martin (1985), 100–106; and Soubeyroux (1982).

16 Pérez Estévez (1976), esp. 227; Rumeau de Armas (1944), 399–400, 504–8; Callahan (1971), 6; Brading (1994), 9.

17 Jiménez Salas (1958), 195–203.

18 *Nov. rec.*, bk. 7, title 39, laws 18–21, 23–24, 26.

19 On the persecution of vagrants before 1766, see Pérez Estévez (1976), 165–173, 193–95. For an excellent discussion of the sixteenth-century precursors to eighteenth-century policy, see Jiménez Salas (1958), 79–118, 127–30, 195–98; Rumeau de Armas (1944), 167–80; and Michielse (1990).

20 N. Martin (1957), (1972), and (1985). On the seventeenth century, see also Israel (1975), 77–78.

21 Muriel (1974).

22 Megged (1997), esp. 3–6.

23 Venegas Ramírez (1973); Borah (1983).

24 Valdés (1978).

25 Population figures for this period are crude estimates, as pointed out by Haslip-Viera (1980, 32–40) and Pérez Toledo (1996, 39–49). Writing in 1770 and 1785, both Lorenzana (1770) and Villarroel (1831) considered the precipitous increase in migration to be a recent phenomenon. It further escalated in 1785–86, when tens of thousands of starving country dwellers left their homes to seek assistance in Mexico City. See Cook (1940), 533; and Humboldt (1966), 1:121. On the size of Madrid and Mexico City, see Humboldt (1966), 2:81–2, 89–90. The 1742 figure of 98,000 comes

from Villaseñor y Sánchez (1746), 1, 35. Humboldt revised the figures of the Revilla-gigedo census to correct for undercounting and estimated that there were 130,602 inhabitants in the Mexican capital in 1793. A police census of 1811 counted 168,846, while municipal censuses of 1813 and 1842 only counted 124,000 and 113,188. In the absence of census data after that, various observers estimated the population in the 1860s and 1870s at approximately 200,000. See Davies (1972), 501.

26 On price inflation, which occurred throughout the period from 1770 to at least 1814, and on wages, which appear to have remained flat since the middle of the eighteenth century, see Florescano (1969), 115–17; Garner (1985); Reher (1992), Ouweneel (1996); and Van Young (1992), chap. 2.

27 On this concept, see De Swaan (1988), 28–37.

28 On the traditional mechanisms of charity, see especially Borah (1966); Couturier (1990); and Lamas (1964), esp. chaps. 1–4.

29 Villarroel's treatise (1831) embodies elite worries about the "relajamiento de cos-tumbres." See also Viqueira Albán (1987); Scardaville (1980) and (1994), 508–12; Haslip-Viera (1980); and Voekel (1992).

30 Villarroel (1831), 110.

31 After Ward's *Obra pía: medio de remediar la miseria de la gente pobre de España* (1750) came Pedro Rodríguez, Conde de Campomanes, *Sobre los vagantes y mal entreteni-dos* (1764), followed by Ramón Cortines y Andrade, *Discurso político sobre el estable-cimiento de los hospicios en España* (1768). Most of the better-known works on the subject date from the 1780s, such as Gaspar Melchor de Jovellanos's *Informe sobre el libre ejercicio de las artes* (1785). For a discussion of these writers, see Callahan (1971), Jiménez Salas (1958), Rumeau de Armas (1944), and N. Martin (1985). The Poor House project also predated the establishment of the similar *dépôts de mendicité* in France beginning in 1768. See Schwartz (1988), 2.

32 A copy of this publication is enclosed in AGI, México, vol. 2791, exp. 10b. For a dis-cussion of Lorenzana's later career, see Callahan (1971), 9. Note that Lorenzana had earlier written a similar memorial (with different arguments) in support of the Foundling Home (or Casa de Cuna). See exp. 10a and the excellent analysis in Gon-zalbo (1982), 32.

33 Callahan (1971), 9.

34 Although Lorenzana used the term *pueblos*, it is clear from his examples of Holland and Flanders that he meant "peoples" in the sense of countries, not towns.

35 See especially Lewis (1966) and the critiques in Leacock (1971).

36 Cited in Haslip-Viera (1980), 70.

37 Orders to arrest vagrants date from 1774, 1782, 1785, 1786 (three decrees), 1788, 1792, 1796, 1797, 1800, 1806, 1809, 1810, 1820, 1822, 1827, 1828, 1830, 1834 (two decrees), 1842, 1843, 1845, 1846, 1848, 1849, 1850 (two decrees), 1851, 1853 (three decrees), 1857, and 1862. Two antivagrancy decrees of September 1766 and February 26, 1767, which preceded the formal launching of the Poor House project, correspond to the arrival of a new viceroy, the Marqués de Croix. See AGN, Bandos, vol. 6, exp. 45, f. 140, and exp. 57, f. 180.

38 These decrees, promulgated only for Mexico City, were of March 5, 1774 (AGN, Bandos, vol. 8, ff. 210–11); 1782, included within instructions for the new *alcaldes de*

barrios, "Ordenanza" (1969), 99-100; 1783 (AHCM, Hospicio de Pobres, vol. 2295, exp. 8); April 10, 1786 (AGN, Bandos, vol. 14, exp. 24, ff. 59-61v); September 26, 1794 (AGN, Bandos, vol. 18, exp. 52, f. 266); 1797 (AHCM, Hospicio de Pobres, vol. 2295, exp. 11); July 9, 1800 (AGN, Bandos, vol. 20, exp. 100, f. 209); June 25, 1806 (AGN, Bandos, vol. 22, f. 140); May 25, 1809 (AGN, Bandos, vol. 25, ff. 139-40); August 9, 1830 (Dublán and Lozano, no. 858, 2:278-79); December 20, 1843 (AHCM, Beneficencia y Asilos, vol. 416, exp. 1, ff. 10-10v; February 3, 1845 (AHCM, Vagos, vol. 4778, exp. 303), May 6, 1850 (Dublán and Lozano, no. 3435, 5:704-5); December 18, 1851 (Castillo Velasco [1874], 247); and December 12, 1863 (Valle [1864], 379). More restricted prohibitions against soldiers' begging and youths' begging for the *volo* at baptisms were repeated, for soldiers, on September 14, 1820, and February 28, 1834 (Dublán and Lozano, no. 216, 1:517-18 and no. 1372, 2:678) and for the *volo* on January 25, 1800 (AGN, Bandos, vol. 20, exp. 62, f. 162), February 7, 1825; October 24, 1834; and February 13, 1844 (Dublán and Lozano, no. 1472, 2:752; and no. 2758, 4:745). On confining blind paupers who harangued the public with their loud "relaciones" about religion, see the decree of October 24, 1834, no. 1471, 2:752.

39 The Bourbon state attempted to limit these alms collectors (*demandantes*), too. A decree of April 9, 1795, commanded the bishops to limit the issuance of such licenses, which henceforth required viceregal approval. See Brading (1994), 161-63.

40 These phrases are from Viceroy Gálvez's decree of April 10, 1786, AGN, Bandos, vol. 14, f. 61. Note that, in contrast to these prescriptions, Archbishop Lorenzana had proposed confining vagrants as well as beggars (1770) esp. vii, xi and xxi.

41 See, for example, the decree of July 12, 1781, in *Nov. rec.,* bk. 7, title 31, law 10.

42 *Nov. rec.,* bk. 7, title 39, law 24, combines decrees published in Madrid from 1783 to 1798.

43 See the royal order of December 24, 1779 (*Nov. rec.,* bk. 12, title 31, law 9); the viceregal decree of June 25, 1806 and the decree of the Spanish Cortes of September 11, 1820 (Dublán and Lozano, no. 59, 1:307, and no. 229, 1:528), redecreed for independent Mexico on July 12, 1822 (AHCM, Vagos, vol. 4151, exp. 2); and the presidential decree of March 3, 1828, in Dublán and Lozano, no. 552, 2:62, art. 16. A presidential decree of August 8, 1834, mandated a return to open-ended sentences by specifying that vagrants would be released from the armed services only if they could show that they were leaving for a stable place of residence and an "honest" job and that prisoners incarcerated for crimes other than vagrancy were not to be released until they could prove that they would not become vagrants (no. 1438, 2:717, arts. 7-8).

44 Arts. 2 and 23 of the 1777 "Ordenanzas para el gobierno del Real Hospicio de Pobres de la ciudad de México," in AGN, Bandos, vol. 10, exp. 18.

45 See *Nov. rec.,* bk. 12, title 31; Pérez Estevez (1976), chap. 3; and N. Martin (1972). In practice, however, vagrants may have continued to be "sold" to *obrajes* (textile workshops). See Greenleaf (1967), 247.

46 A law of May 7, 1775, set the draft age at 17 to 36 and excluded married men even if they were vagrants (*Nov. rec.,* bk. 12, title 31, law 7). An August 16, 1776, law waived the exemption for married men, and a law of January 11, 1784, raised the age limit to 40 years (laws 8 and 12). Republican laws drafted men from 18 to 40 years and added an exclusion for married men who were living with their wives or supporting

minor children. See *Nuevo Febrero* (1850–52), 2:763; and the law of January 26, 1839, in Dublán and Lozano, no. 2020, 3:583–84.

47 See especially the decree of June 25, 1806 (AGN, Bandos, vol. 22, f. 140), which specified that since Indian vagrants could not be conscripted they "shall be destined to a task appropriate to their status." Note that "los indios puros y sin mezcla" continued to be exempted from some republican drafts. See, for example, the decree of August 2, 1853, in Dublán and Lozano, no. 3983, 6:627.

48 On convict labor, see especially Haslip-Viera (1980), chap. 5; and Pike (1978).

49 "Real ordenanza para las levas anuales en todos los pueblos del Reyno," May 7, 1775, in *Nov. rec.*, bk. 12, title 31, law 7, art. 40. This provision was reiterated in a *real cédula* of January 11, 1784.

50 Decree of July 12, 1781, in *Nov. rec.*, bk. 12, title 31, law 10. See also the decree of October 3, 1834, in *Nuevo Febrero* (1850–52), 2:768.

51 Humboldt claimed that the great famine (accompanied by pneumonia, dysentery, and influenza) ultimately killed 300,000 people throughout New Spain (1966), 1:121. On the Year of Hunger, see also Cook (1940); Cooper (1965), chap. 5; and Florescano (1969), esp. 174–77.

52 The entire quote is from the decree of April 10, 1786, AGN, Bandos, vol. 14, exp. 24, ff. 59–61v. Although it may only have been meant as a temporary measure to alleviate the crisis, a similar directive was included in art. 60 of the *Real Ordenanza* (1984), 69, which ordered "Vagamundos . . . [y] gente sin destino y aplicación al trabajo" to be placed in hospicios if they were "inútiles" for the armed services or public works projects.

53 See the decrees of December 10, 1792, and July 7, 1810 (AGN, Bandos, vol. 16, exp. 90, ff. 222–24v; and vol. 30, f. 15); April 29, 1820; March 3, 1828; August 8, 1834; and October 24, 1834 (Dublán and Lozano, no. 216, 1:517–18; no. 552, 2:62, arts. 14–15; no. 1438, 2:717, art. 6; no. 1472, 2:752); February 3, 1845 (AHCM, Vagos, vol. 4778, exp. 303); October 15, 1850; August 20, 1853; and January 5, 1857 (Dublán and Lozano, no. 3482, 5:747; no. 4006, 6:648–51; and no. 4859, 8:341, arts. 87–88). Although these decrees do not specify either gender, their descriptions of persons ineligible for military service suggest that they were only meant to apply to men.

54 Decree of Spanish Cortes of September 11, 1820 (Dublán and Lozano, no. 229, 1:528), redecreed for independent Mexico on July 12, 1822 (AHCM, Vagos, vol. 4151, exp. 2).

55 Real Cédula of January 11, 1784, in *Nov. rec.*, bk. 12, title 31, law 12.

56 Compare the Real Orden of April 20, 1745, in footnote 6 of *Nov. rec.*, bk. 12, title 31, law 7, to chapter 4 of the Bando of February 3, 1845, in *Nuevo Febrero* (1850–52), 2:765–66 (also in AHCM, Vagos, vol. 4778, exp. 303).

57 For a fuller discussion of the 1745 decree, see Arrom (1988c), 72–77.

58 Article 2 of a law of March 13, 1778, in Pérez y López (1791–98), 20:56. See also the viceregal decree of April 10, 1787, that recognized that many were "ociosos por faltarles donde trabajar" (AGN, Bandos, vol. 14, no. 24, f. 59). Even they were to be treated as vagrants, however. The instruction for *corregidores* of 1788 likewise stated that laborers or artisans who did not work because of "vice or laziness" should be treated as vagrants. See art. 33 in the cédula of May 15, 1788 (Pascua [1935], 7:177).

Note that the 1828 decree that established the Vagrants Tribunal, apparently written in some haste, only designated as vagrants the unemployed and libertine (presidential decree of March 3, 1828, in Dublán and Lozano, no. 552, 2:61). By August 8, 1834, the underemployed had been added as well (no. 1438, 2:716).

59 Presidential decree of August 20, 1834 (Dublán and Lozano, no. 1444, 2:724). Fernández de Lizardi's disquisition against vagrants in *El periquillo sarniento* argued that their unemployment was almost always voluntary (1974), 312.

60 Bando of July 7, 1810, AGN, Bandos, vol. 30, f. 15. This decree also designated as vagrants those who resold lottery tickets for more than the official price. Those who "because of their age or circumstances" could not serve in the armed forces were to be confined in the Poor House.

61 Decrees of November 2, 1826, June 6, 1833, and October 3, 1834 in *Nuevo Febrero* (1850-52), 2:767-68. Those convicted of this crime were sentenced to one month of labor in public works, if male, or one month of prison if female—with double terms for repeat offenders. Youths under 18 were to be placed in the Poor House school "to learn the basics of a useful trade."

62 Real cédula of August 2, 1781, in Pérez y López (1791-98), 28:369-70.

63 On this point see also Scardaville (1980).

64 Bando of April 1, 1789, in Pérez y López (1791-98), 20:63. The Spanish terms are *cafés, botillerías, mesas de trucos,* and *tabernas.* A similar explanation of the role of recreation appeared as early as in a viceregal decree of September 1766, AGN, Bandos, vol. 6, exp. 45, f. 140.

65 Decree of February 4, 1842, in Dublán and Lozano, no. 2273, 4:108. See also *Nuevo Febrero* (1850-52), 2:766-76.

66 *Nuevo Febrero* (1850-52), 2:766.

67 A decree of January 25, 1800, specifically designated as vagrants youths who begged for the volo at baptisms, and it imposed a 50-peso fine on godparents who engaged in this almsgiving ritual (AGN, Bandos, vol. 20, exp. 62, f. 162). A decree of February 7, 1825, reiterated on October 24, 1834, and December 13, 1844, had sentenced to the armed services (i.e., again treated like vagrants) youths over 18 years caught begging for the volo, while those under 18 were to be placed in the Poor House to learn a trade. The 1844 decree also reiterated the fine on godparents who gave alms. This type of beggar was not specifically mentioned in the 1845 decree because it was encompassed by the article condemning those who begged outside churches. See the 1834 decree, which refers to the 1825 decree, and the 1844 decree, in Dublán and Lozano, no. 1472, 2:752; and no. 2758, 4:745.

68 Decree of October 24, 1834, in Dublán and Lozano, no. 1471, 2:752.

69 See Reglamento for a new police force, May 6, 1850, in Dublán and Lozano, no. 3435, 5:703, art. 10; and *Código penal* (1871), arts. 785-88.

70 Like the 1745 vagrancy code, the 1871 Penal Code gave only partial protection to the abused wife. For example, the husband could be prosecuted only if his wife brought charges or the beatings were public and then only if they were "unwarranted." See *Código penal* (1871), arts. 509-10, 531, 554, 789. Other delinquent behavior previously covered by the vagrancy laws was also explicitly defined as criminal, such as a man's adultery (arts. 816-17) or public drunkenness (art. 1148).

71 The separate category of beggars gathered outside the doors of churches was also dropped, possibly because it was included within the category of those who used religious images and collection boxes to solicit alms. See the presidential decrees of August 20, 1853, and January 5, 1857, in Dublán and Lozano, no. 4006, 6:648-51, esp. titles 1 and 2; and no. 4859, 8:330-43, esp. art. 84.

72 According to Orozco y Berra, this force of gendarmes, modeled after the French police, did not last long (1973, 187). See the decree of May 28, 1826, in Dublán and Lozano, no. 488, 1:798. A special, short-lived police force had also been established in 1811, as an emergency wartime measure, under the Junta de Policía y Tranquilidad Pública. See Ortiz Escamilla (1994); and Nacif Mina (1994), 32-50.

73 See Pérez Toledo (1996), 30; and Nacif Mina (1994), 43-44.

74 Decree of March 21, 1834, in Dublán and Lozano, no. 1385, 2:684-87.

75 Decree of May 23, 1837, in ibid., no. 1868, 3:392-407.

76 Decree of August 22, 1848, in ibid., no. 3118, 5:443-51.

77 Decree of May 6, 1850, in ibid., no. 2435, 5:701-8.

78 Decree of January 17, 1853, in ibid., no. 3740, 6:294-303.

79 The 1828 tribunals were created by Congress and promulgated by presidential decree (ibid., no. 552, 2:61-62). See also the decree of March 7, 1828, applying the presidential decree to Mexico City, no. 553, 2:62-63. The 1857 Tribunal de Vagos, created by a presidential decree of January 5, 1857, is in no. 4859, 8:341-43, arts. 84-106. For more information on the 1828-46 Vagrants Tribunal, including copies of original documents, see Arrom (1989) and Serrano (1996).

80 Although the vagrancy laws theoretically applied to women as well as men, Pérez Toledo found that only men were brought before the Vagrants Tribunal (1996), 249.

81 Decree of March 7, 1828 (José María Tornel), in Dublán and Lozano, no. 553, 2:62-63.

82 In an attempt to eliminate the ritual of distributing the volo at baptisms, a fine of 50 pesos was imposed on January 25, 1800. The ban was reiterated in 1825, 1834, and 1844. See note 38. For a description of the custom, see García Cubas (1986), 185.

83 See especially the decree of November 18, 1877, which only applied to Madrid and warned parents who begged that the state would place their children in poorhouses "no teniendo derecho los padres que abandonan a sus hijos, o que no los educan o mantienen sino con el vicio y ocio, a impedir al Soberano que tome sobre si este cuidado paternal" (*Nov. rec.*, bk. 7, title 39, law 18). See also the decree of July 12, 1781, which limited their right of appeal (bk. 12, title 31, law 10).

84 This decree, promulgated only for Mexico City, applied to the capital the presidential decree establishing the Vagrants Tribunal. Dublán and Lozano, no. 553, 2:63, arts. 10, 11, and 13.

85 Decree of August 8, 1834, in Dublán and Lozano, no. 1438, 2:716-19. See also the August 20, 1834, circular accompanying the decree (no. 1444, 2:724). Note that, due to a typographical error, the circular appears to be incorrectly dated as 1833.

86 On April 6, 1862, the governor of the Federal District again ordered that servants carry identification. Servants found to have been unemployed for one month were to be treated as vagrants. I have found no evidence that the system of identity cards was

actually implemented in either 1834 or 1862. It was decreed again by the governor of the D.F. on November 1, 1879. Castillo Velasco (1874), 134–37, 249–51.

87 Salazar calculated that servants were some 10 percent of the Mexico City population in 1811 (1978), 124. That meant that there were approximately twice as many servants as artisans. See González Angulo (1983), 11; and Pérez Toledo (1996).

88 On the decrees of 1842 and 1843, see Monroy (1974), 642. On the decree of August 28, 1843, see Dublán and Lozano, no. 2647, 4:554, art. 52.

89 See Jiménez Salas (1958), chaps. 2, 3, 6; Pérez y López (1791–98), 20:53–54; and Pullan (1971).

90 The quote is from Gregorio Baca de Haro's 1703 *Empresas morales para explicación de los mandamientos de la ley de Dios*, cited in Callahan (1971), 2.

91 See, for example, Lorenzana (1770), vi, 7, 27–28; and the "Circular de la Junta del Hospicio de Pobres," January 12, 1774, BNM, Lafragua Collection, no. 118.

92 The quote is from a Spanish religious manual by Antonio Arbiol, cited in Callahan (1971), 2.

93 Bando of May 22, 1799, in AGN, Bandos, vol. 20, exp. 25.

94 The campaign against desnudos is analyzed by N. Martin (1972). Quote is from page 279.

95 AGN, Bandos, vol. 20, exp. 25.

96 Ibid., vol. 24, exp. 7.

97 Ibid., vol. 20, exp. 25.

98 See the decree of September 29, 1800, AGN, Reales Cédulas originales, vol. 178, exp. 74, ff. 217–19; and the discussion in N. Martin (1972), 289–92.

99 *Instrucción del Virrey* (1960), 53. A discussion of the racial question may be found in Sacristán (1994b), 210–11.

100 Villarroel (1831), 106–7. The date of this statement is unclear because it comes from the third—and undated—volume. It was written at some point between 1785 (the date of the first two volumes) and 1787 (the date of the fourth). See Estrada (1979), ix–xii. I have followed Haslip-Viera's translation of these passages (1980), 11, 18.

101 "Discurso sobre la policía de México . . . ," quoted in Viqueira Albán (1987), 214.

102 Using medieval terminology, Revillagigedo also called them "las gentes miserables" in his *Instrucciones* (1873), 2:172.

103 On this point, see especially Warren (1996a), 39.

104 Castillo (1856).

105 The anonymous "Proyecto de policía para la ciudad de México . . . ," submitted by B.T. to the city council in 1821, is quoted in Hernández Franyuti (1994b), 128.

106 Zavala (1845), 2:102, 110. On the early romantic democracy, see Virginia Guedea (1994). On the hardening of elite attitudes toward the poor after the Parián riot, see Arrom (1988), esp. 266–68; and Warren (1994), esp. chaps. 4–5.

107 AHCM, Hospicio de Pobres, vol. 2295, exp. 21.

108 Bando de Policía, May 6, 1850, Dublán and Lozano, no. 3435, 5:704–5, art. 27.

109 This phrase appears in legislation from the 1850s on, as in *Código Penal* (1871), art. 620.

110 Francisco J. Santamaría describes this usage as peculiarly Mexican (1942), 2:181–82.

111 Humboldt (1966), 1:235.

112 Although the Spanish friar Ajofrín used the term *lépero* to refer to Mexico's "rabble" in the 1760s (1958, 1:81, 87), the first Mexican usage I have found is in Fernández de Lizardi (1974), 305. The next Mexican usage I found is in Ibar (1829), 5. The term was consistently used in travel accounts written by foreigners in the early 1820s such as Poinsett (1969), 49, 65, 77; Lyon (1828), 2:127–28; Linati (1956), plate 11; and Tayloe (1959), 53. Norman Martin similarly dates the use of the term *lépero* to republican Mexico (1972), 294.

113 See, for example, Muriel (1974), 47.

114 For a humorous discussion of the meaning of *lépero*, see Prieto (1906), 2:292–97.

115 Note that the denial of suffrage to women was never explicitly stated because it was considered so obvious. See Tena Ramírez (1973), 39, 207–8, 409, 472, 612; *Constitución* (1973), esp. 65–66; *Legislación electoral* (1973); and Dublán and Lozano, vol. 2, no. 858 (1830); vol. 3, nos. 1668 (1835), 1796 (1836); vol. 4, nos. 2232 (1841), 2576 (1843), 2581; vol. 5, nos. 2887 (1846), 2982 (1847); vol. 7, no. 4545 (1855); vol. 8, nos. 4700 (1856), 4888 (1857), 4890 (1857); and vol. 9, nos. 5340 (1861), 5795 (1862). On the tightening of voting requirements after 1828, see Arrom (1988b), 266–68; and Warren (1994), esp. chap. 5.

116 Warren (1996a), 40.

117 See Serrano (1996); and decrees such as those of June 13, 1838, and January 26, 1839, in Dublán and Lozano, no. 1958, 3:533–34, and no. 2020, 3:582–9.

118 Decree of April 23, 1846, in Dublán and Lozano, no. 2867, 5:122.

119 The Vagrants Tribunals were partially reestablished by a presidential decree of July 20, 1848, but only as an appeals board for convicted vagrants. See the discussion in Arrom (1989); and the decrees of July 20, 1848; August 20, 1853; and October 18, 1853, in Dublán and Lozano, no. 3098, 5:427; no. 4006, 6:648–51; and no. 4063, 6:711.

120 *Nuevo Febrero* (1850–52), 2:767. See also decree of August 21, 1848, which states the government's desire to "discipline and moralize the troops." Dublán and Lozano, no. 3117, 5:442. A decree of January 26, 1839, had already disqualified from the armed services those convicted of defamatory crimes (no. 2020, art. 15, 3:583). This clause could conceivably have included vagrants, but the government's explanation in abolishing the Vagrants Tribunals in 1845, that they were not providing enough soldiers for the war effort, makes it clear that vagrants continued to be drafted (no. 2867, 5:122). Vagrants were, however, barred from serving in the civic militias established on March 21, 1834 (no. 1385, 2:684).

121 Decree of August 20, 1853, in Dublán and Lozano, no. 4006, 6:648–51. The sentencing of vagrants to the armed services was repeated on October 18, 1853 (no. 4063, 6:711). A decree of May 24, 1854, facilitated the sentencing of vagrants by mandating that their "destiny" would be decided in a verbal trial by the governors and *jefes políticos* of their respective areas rather than by an alcalde, *juez de paz*, or *juez menor*, as was mandated in 1853 (no. 4251, 7:203–4).

122 Decree of January 5, 1857, Dublán and Lozano, no. 4859, 8:341–43, arts. 84–106.

123 See, for example, republican decrees against foreign vagrants of March 3, 1828; August 8, 1834; December 13, 1843; August 20, 1853; and January 5, 1857, Dublán and

Lozano, no. 552, 2:62, art. 18; no. 1438, 2:718, art. 11; no. 2720, 4:668–69; no. 4006, 6:651; and no. 4859, 8:342.

124 Decrees of August 3, 1849, and October 15, 1850, in Dublán and Lozano, no. 3310, 5:598, art. 9; no. 3482, 5:747. Decree of August 9, 1849, in *Nuevo Febrero* (1850–52), 2:766–77. See also the vigorous prosecution of vagrants mandated in the instructions for jueces menores of January 17, 1853, in Dublán and Lozano, no. 3740, 6:294–303, esp. chap. 1, art. 18, and chap. 4, which is entirely on vagrants; and the decree of May 11, 1853, no. 3846, 6:399.

125 See viceregal decrees of December 10, 1792, and August 1797 in AGN, Bandos, vol. 16, exp. 90, ff. 222–24v, and vol. 19, exp. 51, f. 81; and presidential decree of April 12, 1846, in Dublán and Lozano, no. 2867, 5:122.

126 Viceregal decree of February 26, 1767, in AGN, Bandos, vol. 6, exp. 57, f. 180.

127 Viceregal decree of June 25, 1806, in Dublán and Lozano, no. 59, 1:306–7.

128 Presidential decree of August 8, 1834, in ibid., no. 1438, 2:718, art. 11.

129 Decree of the governor of the D.F., October 15, 1850, in ibid., no. 3482, 5:747.

130 Viceregal decree of July 7, 1810, in AGN, Bandos, vol. 30, f. 15.

131 Viceregal decree of August 7, 1786, in ibid., vol. 14, exp. 36, f. 103. See also the viceregal decrees of March 8 and April 10, 1786, in vol. 14, exps. 16–17, 24, ff. 50–51 verso and 59–61. See, in addition, the 1786 *Real Ordenanza* (1984), 66–70; and Villarroel (1931), 107–8, 110–11.

132 Decree of October 19, 1799, in AGN, Bandos, vol. 20, exp. 54, f. 145.

133 Real orden of October 23, 1783, in *Nov. rec.*, bk. 7, title 39, law 24.

134 Decree of June 25, 1806, in Dublán and Lozano, no. 59, 1:306.

135 Decree of August 8, 1830, in ibid., no. 858, 2:278–79.

136 Reglamento de Policía, May 6, 1850, in ibid., no. 3435, 5:704–5, art. 27.

137 The licensing proposal was made by Fernández de Lizardi in 1816, when he suggested interviewing potential migrants at the city gates and only permitting entry to those who could prove they had the means of earning a living. See the discussion in Sacristán (1994b), 236–37.

138 These trends have been noted for Mexico by Patricia Seed (1988), esp. 143; Sacristán (1994b), 239; González Navarro (1985), 19–53; and Gonzalbo Aizpuru (1992), 365. For a discussion of these trends in Spain, see Carasa Soto (1987) and Shubert (1991).

139 See excellent analysis in Viqueira Albán (1987), esp. chap. 3.

140 Decree of March 30, 1836 attempting to reform the popular celebrations of Holy Week (Dublán and Lozano, no. 1718, 3:138).

141 Villarroel (1831), 71, 106–7.

142 Voekel (1992).

143 Payno (1973), 25.

144 Memo of November 30, 1841, in AGN, Gobernación, Tramo 1, leg. 130, exp. 4.

145 *Código penal* (1871), arts. 854–62; also in Dublán and Lozano, no. 6966, 11:686–87.

146 Good examples, representing the years of 1822, 1839, and 1856, may be found in Poinsett (1969), 49; Calderón de la Barca (1966), 91, 106; and Mathieu de Fossey, cited in López Cámara (1973), 228–29.

147 Evans (1870), 369–70.

148 Decree of December 12, 1863, in Valle (1864), 379; decree of August 19, 1879, in Castillo Velasco (1874), 246–47.

149 See Arrom (1989), 217–21; Arrom (1988a), 10–14; Scardaville (1977), chap. 6; Shaw (1975), 280–92; Pérez Toledo (1993), 36–38; and Serrano Ortega (1996).

150 On late-nineteenth-century attempts to control prostitutes and the insane, see Rivera-Garza (1995). On the impressment of drunkards, see Turner (1969).

2 The Foundation of the Poor House

1 On the *chantre*'s position, see Taylor (1996), 121.

2 Writing in the 1860s García Icazbalceta (1907, 6–7) and in the 1870s Rivera Cambas (1880–83, 1:242–43) put this story in their descriptions of the Poor House. Alfaro presents it with a disclaimer that he cannot vouch for its accuracy (1906, 13–15). The story does not, however, appear in early documents on the founding, such as the report from the viceroy to the king of August 14, 1776 (AGN, Cédulas Reales, vol. 108, ff. 363–64v); the 1777 bylaws (AGN, Bandos, vol. 10, exp. 18, title 7); or Lorenzana's lengthy *Memorial* of 1770 arguing for the need for such an asylum. Neither is it recounted in the hagiographical biography of Ortiz Cortés on the painting that still hung in the Poor House in 1906, which Alfaro copied into his history (52).

3 See, for example, descriptions of the founding of the Casa de Cuna in Peza (1881), 106; and of the Colegio de San Ignacio in Orozco y Berra (1867), 190.

4 The Poor House was by then known as the Hospicio de Niños. Alfaro simultaneously served as the superior of its boys' department (1806), 12.

5 See viceroy's letter to king, April 3, 1763, in Herráez, who presents a long summary of these events, though with occasional errors (1949), 120–34.

6 Various authors disagree on his age at death. For example, Abadiano says Ortiz Cortés was born in March 1701, making him 66 years old when he died in April 1767 (1878), 25. Alfaro claims he was 75 years old when he died (1906), 15, 52, citing as his source the biography on the painting of Ortiz Cortés that hung in the Poor House.

7 This point is made only by Alfaro (1906), 15.

8 The generous executor Andrés Ambrosio Llanos y Valdés has been slighted by history. Rivera Cambas mistakenly called him Ambrosio Ramos (1880–83), 1:243. Alfaro called him Antonio Llanos Valdés (1906), 15. For a sketchy biography, see *Diccionario Porrúa* (1964), 857.

9 For a discussion of these shifts in Spain, see Callahan (1971); Sherwood (1988), esp. xi; Shubert (1991); Sarrailh (1953); Soubeyroux (1982); and Carasa Soto (1987).

10 See, for example, Farris (1968) and Brading (1994).

11 The colonial welfare system since the sixteenth century had consisted of a mix of private, ecclesiastical, and royal foundations under royal patronage. See Borah (1966), Muriel (1956–60), and Chase (1975).

12 The mistake apparently originated in 1878 with Abadanio (1878, 25) and was copied by such writers as Alfaro (1806, 14). Muriel, who examined the voluminous Poor House files in Seville, got it right, though (1956–60, 2:170).

13 This cédula real is reproduced in Laguarta (1955), 108–9.

14 The royal order of July 9, 1765, explicitly reminded the viceroy that "os ordené que

suspendieseis qualquiera providencia que huvieseis tomado para el establecimiento del Hospicio de Pobres," AGN, Cédulas Reales, vol. 87, exp. 4, ff. 7–9.

15　See Real Cédula of April 24, 1772, which contains a reference to the order of April 2, 1769, ibid., vol. 100, exp. 132, ff. 245–47; and the file on the foundation of the Poor House, AGI, México, vol. 2791, esp. exps. 9, 12.

16　Opinion of the Fiscal, May 18, 1765, and Real Cédula of July 9, 1765, in AGI, México, vol. 2791, exp. 1. On the jurisdictional squabble, see also letter from Llanos y Valdés of March 26, 1770; the opinion of the Fiscal del Consejo on July 18, 1771, ibid., exps. 9, 11; and "Extracto de los Autos sobre el Hospicio de Mendigos," ibid., vol. 1681.

17　Petition from the archbishop to the king, August 12, 1769, ibid., vol. 2791, exp. 7.

18　Archbishop Lorenzana's petition of August 12, 1769, ibid., vol. 2791, exp. 7.

19　This quote and the details are from art. 7 of the 1764 bylaws proposed by Ortiz Cortés, in ibid., vol. 2791, exp. 8.

20　See the discussion in the royal order of April 24, 1772, in AGN, Cédulas Reales, exp. 132, f. 246.

21　Explained in letter from Llanos y Valdés to the king, Mar. 26, 1770, and cited in Herráez (1949), 131.

22　"Ordenanzas de la Real Casa de Hospicio de Pobres Mendigos de México y su Arzobispado," October 22, 1769, AGI, México, vol. 2791, exp. 8.

23　The junta was to be composed of the archbishop of Mexico, the *oidor decano* of the Real Audiencia, the *fiscal de lo civil*, the dean of the Metropolitan Cathedral, the corregidor, the city attorney (*procurador*), one *regidor* from the city council, and the prior or consul of the Tribunal del Consulado. See art. 22 of Lorenzana's "Ordenanzas," ibid., vol. 2791, exp. 8.

24　Opinion of the Fiscal del Consejo, July 18, 1771, ibid., vol. 2791, exp. 9.

25　See royal order of April 24, 1772 (AGN, Cédulas Reales, vol. 100, exp. 132, f. 245) as well as the letter from Llanos y Valdés of March 26, 1770 (AGI, México, vol. 2791, exp. 11); and the "Extracto de los autos sobre el Hospicio de Mendigos" (AGI, México, vol. 1681).

26　Explained in the viceroy's letter of December 27, 1773, AGI, México, vol. 2791, exp. 12; and the royal order of August 14, 1776, AGN, Cédulas Reales, vol. 108, exp. 81, ff. 163–66v.

27　Letter from Junta del Hospicio to city council, January 15, 1774, AHCM, Actas de Cabildo, vol. 94-A, f. 7; letters from the viceroy to the king of December 27, 1773, and March 27, 1774, AGI, México, vol. 2791, exp. 12. Viceregal decree of March 5, 1774, AGN, Bandos, vol. 8, f. 211.

28　See the Real Cédula of August 14, 1776, AGN, Cédulas Reales, vol. 108, exp. 81, ff. 163–66.

29　Even without formal approval, Viceroy Mayorga decreed on February 27, 1781, that the 1777 statutes should be observed until further notice. Viceroy Azanza formally disseminated the revised version on February 23, 1799, AGN, Bandos, vol. 10, exp. 18. See the 1785 "Testimonio de las constituciones formadas para el regimen y govierno del Hospicio de Pobres de México," AGI, México, vol. 2791, exp. 16a, ff. 37–40; and correspondence between the city council and the viceroy, December 29, 1817, AGN, Policía, vol. 30, f. 268.

30 *Diccionario Porrúa* (1964), 1023.

31 The lower figure is an estimate based on the total of 111,903.6 pesos given by the 1804 report for "building costs," including the 1776 expansion and subsequent improvements. See "Estado general del Real Hospicio de Pobres de México en 31 de diciembre de 1803," AGN, Historia, vol. 441, exp. 1, f. 9 (hereafter cited as 1804 report). The higher figure comes from Alfaro (1906), 18. In a December 12, 1765, letter to the king, Ortiz Cortés said he had originally planned to spend only 24,000 pesos, but had already spent 60,000 by that date (quoted in Herráez [1949], 127).

32 In his letter of March 3, 1781, to the Poor House board, Llanos y Valdés claims to have spent 28,806 pesos from his own pocket, AGI, México, vol. 2791, exp. 13. Rivera Cambas gave a similar figure of 28,000 pesos (1880–83), 1:244. Alfaro estimates the alms collected by Llanos y Valdés at 59,580 pesos, 7 reales (*Reseña*, 18), but this is the figure given in the 1804 report as the funds raised by Viceroy Bucareli for the 1774–76 expansion. The 1804 report, a century closer to these events, would appear to be more reliable.

33 Petition of April 2, 1764, AGI, México, vol. 2791, exp. 1, secs. 16–19.

34 On this point, see esp. Borah (1966).

35 The 1804 report states that Llanos y Valdés contributed 10,720.5 pesos to the Poor House during the 17 years and $9^{1}/_{3}$ months that he served as director. It is unclear whether this sum includes the first year's contribution or other expenses that he met out of his own pocket (such as the retainer he paid the doctor until 1792), ff. 8–9.

36 See letters from the viceroy to the king of December 27, 1773, and March 27, 1774; Real Cédula of August 14, 1776, in AGI, México, vol. 2791, exp. 12, 16; and AGN, Cédulas Reales, vol. 108, exp. 81, ff. 163–66v, 363–64.

37 Abadiano (1878, 27), copied by Rivera Cambas (1880–83, 1:244). Alfaro (1906, 16) states that the *cabildo eclesiástico* (cathedral chapter) eventually contributed at least 50,000, but it is unclear what time period is covered by this figure. The 1804 report (f. 9) lists its total contribution from 1774 to 1803 as 15,000 pesos, which is probably the source of Abadiano's figure of 50 pesos per month.

38 Abadiano (1878, 27), copied by Rivera Cambas (1880–83, 1:244) and Alfaro (1906, 16). There must have been some delay or interruption in the archbishop's contributions, for the 1804 report lists the total over twenty-six years as only 59,408 pesos rather than the 62,400 he would have paid over that time span if he had contributed 200 every month since the Poor House opened, f. 9.

39 The 1804 report lists Lizana's contribution for the previous nine months as 846 pesos, but the ninth month may not have been completed, f. 9.

40 See arts. 38 and 44 of 1777 bylaws.

41 See petitions of 1774 and 1794 in AGN, Ayuntamiento, vol. 107.

42 Alfaro (1906), 19.

43 Abadiano (1878, 26) put the cost of the addition at 77,000 pesos, citing the inscription below Bucareli's portrait in the Poor House. Citing the same inscription, Alfaro (1906, 53) placed the cost of construction at 67,000 pesos. One of these sums must have been a typographical error, probably Abadiano's, since the 1804 report lists the "alms" collected by Bucareli for the expansion as 59,580.9 pesos, which adds up to

approximately 67,000 pesos when the viceroy's 8,000 peso "donation" is included. The 1804 report omits most capital costs from its figures.

44 It is similarly difficult to know where to put the contributions the viceroy made periodically for special treats, such as when Bucareli donated "2 reales per plaza and 200 pesos more" to pay for a special dessert on the Day of the Dead in 1776. See Alfaro (1906), 36.

45 See Abadiano (1878), 27; AHCM, Actas de Cabildo, vol. 94-A, f. 61; and AHCM, Hospicio de Pobres, vol. 2295, exp. 2, ff. 2-3.

46 The date of the first tabla is from AHCM, Hospicio de Pobres, vol. 2295, exp. 3. The date of the Querétaro concession is from the 1804 report, which lists twenty-nine years of the Tabla de San Pedro y San Pablo and twenty-eight years for that of Querétaro (f. 8). The 1777 bylaws list the other three as well (art. 39).

47 The income from these tablas had been lost by 1803. The 1804 report says that the two Puebla tablas produced an income of 6,869.4 pesos for nineteen years and that of San Luis Potosí produced 333.3 pesos over three years and four months. It does not mention the Zacatecas tabla at all, f. 8. Despite the city council's approval of applying these taxes to the Poor House (AHCM, Hospicio de Pobres, vol. 2295, exp. 3), there is some question as to how long the Poor House continued to enjoy this income, for it was not mentioned by the fiscal in his listing of the Poor House's finances in 1781 ("Testimonio del expediente sobre arbitrios para la subsistencia del Hospicio," August 11, 1781, AGI, México, vol. 2791, exp. 13).

48 Art. 40, 1777 bylaws.

49 A 1785 document reported that the *Temporalidades* produced 3,725.3 pesos that year; an 1826 report that they produced a steady 3,725.9 pesos until 1819. Yet the 1804 report only lists returns for one year, 1794, although earnings for other years may be hidden in the "income from other legacies" category. Revillagigedo claims they only produced 2,525 pesos, probably in 1793 (*Instrucciones*, 1873, 2:131). These properties are not mentioned by the fiscal in a long presentation of Poor House finances of August 11, 1781, perhaps because he did not consider it necessary to specify the origin of Poor House assets. AGI, México, vol. 2791, exps. 13 and 16; "Informe de la comisión" (1826), AHCM, Beneficencia, vol. 423, exp. 2.

50 Abadiano (1878, 27) and Rivera Cambas (1880-83, 1:244) add that on March 14, 1777, Viceroy Bucareli assigned the *bienes mostrencos* (unclaimed property) to the institution, but this is not corroborated by other sources. In art. 42 of the 1777 bylaws Bucareli did propose that the crown require notaries to remind testators to remember the asylum in their wills. Apparently nothing came of this proposal.

51 The 1804 report lists the cumulative cost of printing tickets as 399 pesos by December 31, 1803, f. 9.

52 Valle Arizpe (1943), 22-25; Velasco Ceballos (1934), 61-66. Orozco y Berra claims that the Poor House did not receive lottery income until September 1783 (1867), 204. There is also some question about what portion of the lottery went to the Poor House. Rivera Cambas (1880-83, 1:244) claims it was 3 percent, and Alfaro claims 2.5 percent (1906, 17). However, the 2 percent cited by the first three studies appears to be correct, since it is supported by primary documents. See city council review

of the institution's finances in AHCM, Beneficencia, vol. 423, exp. 2 (1826), f. 2; and memo from the city council to the viceroy, December 29, 1817, AGN, Policía, vol. 30, f. 268.

53 According to city council records the monthly commitment was approved for three years on January 3, 1775, and then renewed twice more, on September 3, 1777, and September 14, 1781, so that it would have lasted only until 1784, AHCM, Hospicio de Pobres, vol. 2295, exp. 4.

54 The Poor House continued to petition the city council for a renewal of its commitment, as on October 4, 1798, ibid., vol. 2295, exp. 4, f. 30.

55 Letter from Llanos y Valdés to the Junta del Hospicio, March 3, 1781, in "Testimonio," AGI, México, vol. 2791, exp. 13.

56 Alfaro, who may have seen the original financial records when he cleaned out the institution's archive in the early twentieth century, states that the second director, Simón de la Torre, gave 30,000 pesos and that the administrator during the 1780s, Pedro de la Sierra y Lombera, also gave a hefty sum (1906, 58). Alfaro lists other donors by name without indicating who gave during the colonial and who during the republican years. The list of colonial donors reproduced in table 16 likewise gives no indication of the date of their contributions.

57 Note that the 1804 report lists the year as 1776, which must have been a mistake (f. 8). Although unseasonably cold weather caused illness and suffering in Mexico City during the winter of 1776 (Chase 1975, 8), the great year of hunger was 1786. Nothing in the Poor House records for 1776 suggests anything unusual about that year; moreover, prior to its expansion in November 1776, the building would not have been able to house so many people (see the discussion in chap. 3). Note that the printed summary based on the 1804 report, which appeared at the end of the *Suplemento á la Gazeta núm. 53* 13, no. 65 (July 2, 1806), inexplicably omitted this line (and several others) altogether. This issue is hereafter cited as *Suplemento*.

58 *Diccionario Porrúa* (1964), 857.

59 The 1804 report claims that Llanos y Valdés paid the doctors and surgeons privately; it is partially contradicted by the 1777 bylaws, which state that the doctors and surgeons "de la corte" served the asylum "without charge" (art. 7). The 1777 bylaws set the director's salary at 1,500 pesos, although this high salary appears never to have been paid. The 1804 report lists a salary for the administrator only, not the director, and notes that the doctor had been earning 180 pesos per year since 1792 and the "cirujano y Boticario" 300 since 1781, ff. 9, 11.

60 See letter to the Junta del Hospicio, in "Testimonio," AGI, México, vol. 2791, exp. 13.

61 1804 report, f. 5.

62 *Suplemento*, 514. The end of the 100-peso municipal contribution and the reduction of the archbishop's "alms" by 100 pesos per month would account for 21 percent of the decline referred to by Araujo. That still leaves a monthly decline of 1,400 pesos in private contributions.

63 See, for example, Macedo (1900), 713.

64 Alfaro lists 27,000 pesos for various repairs and 10,000 to build new infirmaries on the second floor (1906), 16–18.

65 The income from surplus sales may only have begun in 1780, the date when the *Gazeta* article claims the first workshops were established. *Suplemento*, 513.

66 In 1781 the royal ministers recommended that art. 47 of the 1777 bylaws be modified to reflect the 1-peso rate, "as is currently charged." See "La Junta remite Testimonio de las constituciones al Consejo," March 21, 1785, AGI, México, vol. 2791, exp. 16, f. 38v.

67 See Abadiano (1878), 27–28; and Alfaro (1806), 44–45, 51–53.

68 Report from the fiscal, August 17, 1781, AGI, México, vol. 2791, exp. 13.

69 Correspondence from city council to viceroy, October 24 and November 11, 1817, AGN, Policía, vol. 30, f. 258.

70 AHCM, Hospicio de Pobres, vol. 2295, exp. 6, f. 1 verso.

71 On the "enlightened piety" spearheaded by clerics, see Voekel (1997) and Brading (1994).

72 Ortiz Cortés was born in Pachuca, Hidalgo, in 1692. See López de Escalera (1964), 804.

73 Petition of April 2, 1764, AGI, México, vol. 2791, exp. 1.

74 Note that the General Hospital of San Andrés, founded in 1779, likewise treated members of all races. See Chase (1975), 17–18. On U.S. asylums, see, for example, Lebsock (1984), esp. 211–12; Clement (1985); and Bellows (1993).

75 See the letter of December 12, 1765, quoted in Herráez (1949), 127.

76 The descriptions of the dungeon and chapel are from Alfaro (1906), 23, 25–26, 28; and the 1777 bylaws, art. 65. The descriptions of the rest of the building are from the 1764 petition by Ortiz Cortés, AGI, México, vol. 2791, exp. 1.

77 The terms for the female manufactures are *colchas, medias y calzetas, mantas*, and *todo género de paños de rebozo;* the male manufactures are *paños de la tierra, bayetas, fresadas, lanillas, palmillas*, and *sayales.*

78 Alfaro described the room as a *cobacha* used as a *calabozo* (1906), 25–26.

79 García Icazbalceta (1907), 182; Rafael de Zayas Enríquez, preface to Alfaro (1906), 7–8.

80 Ortiz Cortés gave its dimensions as 92 varas in the front, and 145 in the back. See the December 12, 1765, letter to the king, quoted in Herráez (1949), 127.

81 They also dropped any explicit mention of the sentinel paid for by the asylum to round up beggars, although the 1804 report indicates that it continued to pay one. The total wages paid by December 31, 1803, were 2,192.5 pesos. 1804 report, f. 9.

82 The Royal Council recommended two clarifications and two minor changes in the bylaws. First, the statement in art. 1 (that the Poor House take in "all paupers of both sexes, elderly, infirm, needy, and vagabonds who go about begging") should clarify that the true vagrants could not stay, as specified in art. 11. Second, art. 26 should clearly state that youths who became masters of textile production should not be compelled to stay in the Poor House to work and that any youths who voluntarily chose to stay on past age 14 to work the looms should be paid a fair wage. Third, art. 47 should raise the fee for each inmate attending a funeral from 4 reales to 1 peso, "as is currently charged." Fourth, instead of the junta outlined in art. 57, the existing junta named by Viceroy Bucareli in 1772 and approved by the king in 1776 should

continue to serve. "Testimonio de las constituciones formadas para el regimen y govierno del Hospicio de Pobres de México," 1785, AGI, México, vol. 1791, exp. 16a, ff. 37-38v, reproduced by viceregal decree on February 23, 1799, AGN, Bandos, vol. 10, exp. 18.

83 The 1777 bylaws mentioned only two seasons: winter, defined as running from September 14 to May 3, and summer, running from May 3 to September 14 (arts. 29-30).

84 On this point see Sacristán (1994b), esp. 239.

85 The 1777 bylaws listed only eight salaried employees of "known" virtue, zeal, and charity. One, the director, was assigned an annual salary of 1,500 pesos, although Llanos y Valdés filled this position without compensation. The two live-in chaplains' salaries were unspecified. Three employees received annual salaries (plus room and board) of 1,000 pesos for the administrator, 300 for the mayordomo, and 120 for the rectora. It is noteworthy that the mayordomo, who supervised the men, received more than twice the salary of the rectora, who supervised the women, although she was at least a salaried employee rather than an inmate, as Ortiz proposed. She was, however, to receive a double portion of lamb each day, which she could presumably sell to compensate for her low wages (art. 100). Finally, a scribe and secretary received 300 and 200 pesos, respectively, but no room and board. Since the doctors and surgeons were paid by Llanos y Valdés, no salaries were assigned to them.

86 On this point, see D. Valdés (1978).

87 See Foucault (1979), esp. 141, 149, 178-79, 183, 198, 224, 235.

88 The archbishop's bylaws included two provisions that further eroded the boundaries between the asylum and the city: the 1769 statutes permitted indigent men to come into the Poor House by day to earn money in its workshops and then return to their homes and families at night (art. 4); and they stipulated that six inmates should be assigned to go out into the city each day to solicit funds for the asylum (art. 75). Both of these provisions were omitted from subsequent statutes. The 1777 bylaws specified that the junta should have its own quaestors to solicit alms for the asylum (arts. 45, 83).

89 See, for example, Weber (1930), 177-78; and Bremner (1958-59), 377.

90 See esp., Davis (1975), 17-64; Pullan (1971); and Gutton (1974).

91 See Callahan (1971); Flynn (1989), esp. 98-99, 110-11; Sherwood (1976); Martz (1983); Jiménez Salas (1958); Sarrailh (1953), 371-80; Pérez Estevez (1976); Soubeyroux (1982); Carasa Soto (1987); and Shubert (1991).

92 Martínez-Vergne (1989); Hernández (1992).

93 González Navarro (1985), chap. 1, esp. 40-54; López Figueroa (1993), esp. 7-9, 50-65.

94 See esp. González, who noted that the Bourbons widened the system of welfare to reach new groups (1974), 377-80; Borah (1966), 55-56; N. Martin (1972) and (1985); and Haslip-Viera (1986), 304-8. The only colonialist to follow through on these hints is Chandler, in his study of the pensions established for civil servants (1991).

95 Letter of January 12, 1774, in BNM, Lafragua Collection, no. 118.

96 The Spanish phrase is "las naciones mas cultas." See the notation of September 3, 1777, AHCM, Hospicio de Pobres, vol. 2295, exp. 4, f. 19.

97 See the December 4, 1786, Ordenanza cited in an 1817 memo, AGN, Policía, vol. 30, f. 268v; and the decree of September 27, 1816, exp. 261.

98 Carr (1982), 62. See also Callahan, who concludes that the eighteenth century witnessed the first stage in the secularization of public assistance (1971), 21.

99 On enlightened piety, see Góngora (1957), Brading (1983), and Voekel (1997).

3 The Experiment in Practice, 1774–1805

1 Letter from viceroy to king, March 27, 1774, AGN, Cédulas Reales, vol. 108, ff. 164v–165v.

2 AHCM, Hospicio de Pobres, vol. 2295, exp. 2, f. 2; AHCM, Actas de Cabildo, vol. 94-A, f. 6.

3 AGN, Cédulas Reales, vol. 108, exp. 3.

4 AHCM, Actas de Cabildo, vol. 94-A, ff. 2v–3; Abadiano (1878), 26.

5 Letter of August 11, 1781, from Llanos y Valdés to the Junta del Hospicio, in "Testimonio del expediente sobre arbitrios para la subsistencia del Hospicio," AGI, México, vol. 2791, exp. 13.

6 The report also attributed the improvements to such measures as establishing the Monte de Piedad and Royal Cigar Factory, dividing the city into eight cuarteles with thirty-two *alcaldes de barrio*, reorganizing the judicial system, and stationing the *tropa veterana* in Mexico City. "Informe" (1947), 201.

7 Viera (1952), 70. The only other eyewitness account from the first few years is Martín Josef Verdugo's petition to the Poor House administrator of November 7, 1777, in which he claimed to have observed "the beautiful order that prevails and the dedication with which the unfortunates are treated." Enclosed in "Recivos, 1774–75," AHSSA, BP-EA-HP, bk. 1.

8 See lengthy file in AGI, México, vol. 2791, exp. 13. Royal approval, in the Real Cédula of November 26, 1782, actually came nearly a year after the funds began reaching the Poor House in December 1781. 1804 report, f.8.

9 This petition accompanied "La Junta remite testimonio de las constituciones al Consejo" (March 21, 1785), AGI, México, vol. 2791, exp. 16.

10 See 1804 report, ff. 8–9. According to the *Suplemento*, 513, the textile workshops were established in 1780.

11 *Instrucciones* (1873), 2:131.

12 Decree of March 27, 1786, AHCM, Actas de Cabildo, vol. 106, ff. 24v–25.

13 See esp. the decrees of March 27, April 10, May 9, September 15, and December 5, 1786, in AHCM, Actas de Cabildo, vol. 106, ff. 24–94; and AGN, Bandos, vol. 14, exp. 24.

14 Chase (1975), 13.

15 See notation in 1804 report, f. 8. This document does not specify whether the fourteen hundred people were "maintained" all at once. They probably were because, given the high turnover rates, the asylum often took in that many people over the course of a normal year.

16 Although Humboldt lists 58 percent of the adult inmates as women in 1790,

this figure is unreliable. An error must have occurred in copying from the totals of the Revillagigedo census. The figure of 19 percent children is plausible (1966), 4:292.

17 Among the fifty-seven children admitted in 1774 were three sets of siblings who came on their own; in 1776 there were only five among fifty-five children. Only two, Agustín and Antonio Fonseca, were clearly identified as niños. Some of those identified as siblings could even have been adults. "Recivos," 1774–75 and 1776, AHSSA, BP-EA-HP, bk. 1.

18 *Constituciones . . . de la Real Casa del Señor S. Joseph de Niños Expósitos de esta ciudad de México. . .* , AGN, Bandos, vol. 9, exp. 5, 27. Avila Espinosa shows, however, that the majority of the foundlings died or left in infancy and only a few stayed on into their teens (1994).

19 "Razón de los Pobres de ambos Sexsos, que se confirmaron en este Rl. Hospicio de Mexico. . . ," August 2, 1779, APSV, Confirmaciones 1766–85, vol. 5.

20 "Recivos," 1774–75 and 1776, and "Salidas," 1774 and 1776–78, in AHSSA, BP-EA-HP, bks. 1, 2.

21 The petitions were on behalf of two married couples, four women, and two men; all but one were elderly and infirm. Two women and one couple were released. AGN, Templos y Conventos, vol. 47, exp. 9, ff. 1037–59v.

22 In addition to the 1785 petitions I used, Martínez Barbosa cites several others from 1787 and 1788 (1994), 63. I found only two such petitions in the 1790s, one from 1799 cited by Martínez Barbosa and one from 1792, in AGN, Policía, vol. 30, ff. 10–11 (July 31, 1792).

23 For example, Eusebio Díaz de Garcidiez obligated himself "to provide the daily maintenance of Estevan García Pineda (alias Campana), take care that he not beg any alms, and . . . should he do so, return him to the Hospicio de Nuestra Señora de Guadalupe y el Señor San Josef, which cares for the poor." Slip dated April 11, 1774, in "Salidas" 1774, AHSSA, BP-EA-HP, bk. 2.

24 This estimate assumes that there were six hundred inmates at the end of the year and that some unnumbered children left the Poor House with their parents, as was sometimes noted on the exit slips.

25 The total exit permits issued by December 23, 1774 (nine months after the asylum opened), was 273, with the numbers running separately for women (126) and men (147). These figures suggest that men and women were equally likely to be released since men held a slight edge in both the releases and the makeup of the inmate population. For 1776–78 only 88 slips survive, with totals given only sporadically. Four cumulative totals for female releases allow the calculation of female turnover rates. A total of 581 women had left by October 5, 1777; 699 by February 12, 1778; and 887 by November 2, 1778. Thus, 306 women (and perhaps additional unnumbered children) had been released in thirteen months. Assuming the average releases of 5.5 women per week held steady for the entire year, some 286 female inmates would have left the Poor House in a twelve-month period. If the same male/female ratios were maintained as in 1774 (when 1.17 men left for every woman), some 334 men, or a total of approximately 620 paupers, would have left in 1778.

26 These estimates are supported by summary statistics of December 31, 1803, which

claim that 24,819 paupers came through the asylum in thirty years. See 1804 report, f. 11v. The number in the early years must have been much higher than the 827 annual average, for far fewer entered in the later years.

27 Zavala (1968), 287–88, 300–309; Archer (1973).

28 Archer (1973), 383. Martínez Barbosa notes that seven mecas were transferred to the asylum from the barracks of the militia regiment in 1780 (1994), 68.

29 Muriel (1974), esp. 143–46, 169.

30 The priest's explanation at the end of the 1782 list referred to "an Otomita who does not understand" in addition to the "mecas who are not able." Since the Otomís had for centuries been in contact with the Spanish colonizers, it is possible that the Otomí inmate was retarded or disabled in some other way that prevented him or her from understanding Spanish and/or Christian doctrine. "Padrón para el cumplimiento anual de Nta. Madre Iglecia de los Pobres de ambos Sexos que contiene este R. Hospicio oy 23 de Marzo de 1782," GDCLDS, Mexico D.F., microfilm roll no. 35978.

31 Because this note is inserted in the exit records, it appears that the youth was sent home. "Salidas" 1774–75, AHSSA, BP-EA-HP, bk. 2. The other examples are taken from notations on the "Recivos" 1774–75, bk. 1.

32 Because a quarter of them are for a family group, the 131 entrance slips for 1774–75 and 136 for 1776 include approximately two hundred people for each year. The other boletos may have been lost, although it is also possible that they were only issued for a restricted category of paupers. Since the proportion of women and children is higher in the slips than in the summary statistics (women make up 50 and 59 percent of the adults in the *boletos*, compared with 38 and 44 percent in the summary statistics, while children make up 30 percent compared with 11 and 16 percent), Llanos y Valdés may have issued permission slips mainly to those wishing to enter voluntarily, among whom women and children as well as *vergonzantes* were disproportionately represented. Some slips do, however, note that the inmate was being forcibly confined.

33 Pescador (1992), 145–49; McCaa (1994), 24–25. Note that in the 1779 Confirmation list, the illegitimacy rate was highest among the castes (29 percent "natural"); 11 percent among the Spanish, and none among the Indian inmates receiving Confirmation. "Razón," APSV, Confirmaciones 1766–1785, vol. 5.

34 In Spain *pobres de solemnidad* were often issued formal *declaraciones de pobreza*. I have found no evidence, however, that the Mexican paupers had received an official declaration of pobre de solemnidad status. On Europe, see Martz (1983), 206; Perry (1980), 170; Geremek (1994), 24; and McCants (1997), 28, 200–201. On colonial Ecuador, see Milton (1999).

35 "Padrón de los Pobres de ambos sexos, que existen en este Real Hospicio de Pobres, para el Cumplimiento de N.a Santa M.e Yglesia," April 12, 1795; "Padrón de los Yndividuos de Plana mayor Empleados con sus correspondientes familias cada uno por separado, Pobres de Solemnidad que havitan en las viviendas de arriva, y Pobres de ambos sexos en las de abaxo que han cumplido con el precepto anual de Nuestra Santa Madre Yglesia en el presente año de 1808," GDCLDS, Mexico D.F., microfilm roll no. 35978.

36 The royal order was repeated on March 3 and 13 as well as on May 16, 1778. *Nov. rec.*, bk. 7, title 39, law 19.

37 1804 report, f. 9.

38 AGI, México, vol. 2791, exp. 12; Abadiano (1878), 26. I have found no evidence that the Poor House performed this function prior to the opening of the Departamento de Partos Ocultos in 1806. The 1804 report refers to Bucareli's addition merely as the "three patios de mugeres," f. 8.

39 These petitions are respectively enclosed among the "Recivos" for 1776 and the "Salidas" for 1776-78, AHSSA, BP-EA-HP, bks. 1, 2.

40 According to a notation on one of the 1776 entrance slips, Don Joseph Antonio Burillo was even granted the privilege of eating his meals in the Poor House refectory whenever he wanted, without having to live in the institution. I have found no other example of this practice.

41 The single 15-year-old mulatta María Gertrudis Islas, whose listing follows that of the vergonzante couple Doña Manuela Valencia and Don Manuel Aristorena, is labeled "esclava." The two Spanish sisters from Tianguistengo, 16-year-old Maria Gertudis and 12-year-old Cayetana Diaz, are not similarly labeled "servant." I have assumed they were serving Doña Maria Joaquina Yglesias and her three children, whose listing they follow, because they did not merit the honorific title of don and doña used by the others enumerated in the vergonzante section. See 1795 "Padrón," GDCLDS, microfilm roll no. 35978, ff. 38-40. The 1808 and 1811 censuses likewise include a few maids who served their vergonzante mistresses.

42 Listing for Doña Olmedo (1824), AGN, Archivo Histórico de Hacienda, vol. 117, f. 183; petition from Doña María Josefa Urías, AGN, Gobernación, Tramo 1, leg. 130 (February 21, 1833), exp. 7.

43 Cited in Seed (1988), 288-89.

44 1777 bylaws, art. 5.

45 Villarroel (1931), 95-96. Villarroel dated the first two volumes 1785 and the fourth 1787. The description of the Poor House is in the undated third volume (see Estrada [1979], ix-xii). Since Villarroel does not refer to the famine and epidemics of 1786, the earlier date is the most likely. Villarroel served in various bureaucratic posts, including positions in the financial office of the Tobacco Monopoly, and at the provincial treasuries of Puebla and Acapulco. He was also the commissioner overseeing the expulsion of the Jesuits from the Colegio de Tepozotlán. See Sacristán (1994b), 187.

46 *Instrucciones* (1873), 2:132-33.

47 "Comprobantes de la cuenta que dio Don Joseph Elizalde y Leon de 11 meses y el ultimo de D. Matías Gervete" (1778), AHSSA, HYH-HP, bk. 7.

48 1804 report, f. 10, cf. 1777 bylaws, art. 99.

49 "Testimonio de las constituciones," 1785, AGI, México, vol. 1791, exp. 16a.

50 It is impossible to quantify how many of the claimants were future employers since numerous artisans and shopkeepers who signed for an inmate, or occasionally an entire family, may have been relatives who merely declared their employment to show they were trustworthy. Note that I have found no evidence that the Poor House ever

charged a fee for consigning inmates as workers, as did the Puerto Rican Casa de Beneficencia with liberated slaves. Martínez-Vergne (1989).

51 The returns of "useless" youths are also noted in the 1807–8 entrance register, "Quaderno en que se apuntan las Entradas de los Pobres," AHSSA, BP-EA-HP, bk. 8.

52 These averages exclude the carpenters, masons, and peons who were paid by the day. The 1804 report states that two inmates had worked at each of these jobs for 250 days each year since 1774, but this precision and consistency is suspicious, f. 10.

53 None of the original board members remained, as is shown in appendix 4. Petition of January 1785, AGN, Templos y Conventos, vol. 47, exp. 9, ff. 1056–56v.

54 Only the 1790 figure lists women in the majority. I question the reliability of this statistic, however, since it comes from summary totals of the Revillagigedo census reprinted by Humboldt. It is possible that a transcription error occurred somewhere along the way. See appendix 1.

55 See the letter of the founding junta proposing the Poor House opening, January 12, 1774, BNM, Lafragua Collection, no. 118.

56 See 1779 Confirmation list, "Razón," APSV, Confirmaciones 1766–85, vol. 5; and 1782 Communion list, "Padrón," GDCLDS, Mexico D.F., microfilm roll no. 35978.

57 "Recivos," 1776, AHSSA, BP-EA-HP, bk. 1.

58 1795 "Padrón," GDCLDS, Mexico D.F., microfilm roll no. 35978.

59 Although children who had not yet been confirmed could not participate in the annual Communion, they are listed in both the 1782 and 1795 Communion lists. Indeed, the 1795 list specifies that it includes gentiles and children even though they could not participate in the annual obligation of the Church. Only an 1808 Communion list specifies that it excluded *los inhaviles*. The three documents are in GDCLDS, Mexico D.F., microfilm roll no. 35978.

60 The 1795 list did not give the race and place of origin of the baptized mecas, perhaps because it was considered obvious; the 1811 census specified that the mecas were Indians from "Apache" or "del Pitie." 1811 census, AGN, Padrones, vol. 72, f. 50. Only two of the nine baptized mecas in 1795 had last names; the others used Meca instead of a last name. 1795 "Padrón," GDCLDS, Mexico D.F., microfilm roll no. 35978.

61 It does suggest some irregularities in military recruitment. One Romualdo Rodríguez was only 15, legally too young to serve. Six men declared themselves to be Indian, another group legally excluded from the armed services. Seven more were mestizo. Only seven were born in Mexico City.

62 I am indebted to Christon Archer for suggesting this point to me in a letter of February 13, 1991.

63 Indeed, since the upper and middle classes in Mexico City only represented some 22 percent of the population (Arrom [1985], 7–8) and whites constituted 49 percent of the population, the majority of them could not be in the middle or upper classes.

64 See ibid., 105–11, 270–73.

65 See ibid., 313, n. 17; Pérez Toledo (1996), 150–58; and Moreno Toscano and Aguirre Anaya (1975).

66 See Gerhard (1972).

67 Not including the mecas, the 199 Mexican inmates came from the states of Mexico

(70), Puebla (34), Hidalgo (32), Querétaro (15), Guanajuato (13), Michoacán (7), Tlaxcala (5), Jalisco (5), Veracruz (4), Morelos (3), Guerrero (3), Oaxaca (2), Zacatecas (2), and 1 each from Nuevo León, Chihuahua, Coahuila, and Chiapas.

68 These documents are not entirely comparable because Poor House records only classified as "married" those who were legally wed, while census records included those in consensual unions among the married. See the discussion in Arrom (1985), 112–13.

69 For a discussion of family as a resource, see Arrom (1996a).

70 In most cases I have considered adults with children immediately following (rather than listed separately with the other children) as their parents, though they might just as easily have been aunts, uncles, or grandparents. This procedure undoubtedly misses the relationship between parents and older children, who were listed separately. It also misses the more distant family relationships, such as those between adult siblings or cousins, especially because the census, like all those of the period, is alphabetized by first rather than last names — except when the census taker interrupted the alphabetical order to include certain children after their presumed parents.

71 These were the 40-year-old Doña Ana Medina and the 27-year-old Doña Josefa Viduarri, identified in a city guide as Vidaurri y Medina. An 1807 notation refers to them as "las Medina." See Galván Rivera (1832), 108–9; and "Quaderno en que se apuntan las Entradas de los Pobres. . . ," AHSSA, BP-EA-HP, bk. 8, October 1, 1807.

72 See Arrom (1985), esp. chap. 4.

73 See Muriel (1974), esp. 143–46, 169, 223–27.

74 These are rough estimates based on the information in table 9C. The statistics for December 31, 1803, do not give the ages of disabled individuals, although the total number of adults and children are separately provided, with the unusual age break of 20. In calculating the proportion of disabled adults, I have assumed that none of the inmates under the age of 21 were disabled, which probably inflates the prevalence of disabilities in the adult population. The resulting estimate is that 52 percent of the men and 37 percent of the women suffered from a handicap or chronic illness.

75 Shaw (1975), esp. xviii.

76 See "Introduction," n. 14.

77 See Instrucciones (1873), 2:131–33, 566–67, 674–79; and Instrucción reservada (1960), 66–67.

78 Humboldt (1966), 2:50.

79 The 1804 report lists debts of 3,631.3 pesos to Simón de la Torre, 8,340.6 to the Casa de Yermo for lamb, and 1,818.5 to Domingo Castañiza, f. 8.

80 Florescano (1969); Garner (1985); Van Young (1992), chap. 2.

81 One small salary had, in fact, risen: the salary of 120 pesos, plus room and rations, for the rectora in the 1777 bylaws had been raised to 160 pesos, plus room and rations, by 1803. The scribe's salary had decreased, probably because many of his duties were taken over by the well-paid assistant administrator who was added sometime between 1777 and 1795. See table 7. The sum of 1,500 pesos allocated for a director in the 1769 and 1777 bylaws appears never to have been paid because neither Llanos y Valdés nor Torre drew a salary.

82 Humboldt's reproduction of 1790 census totals lists twenty-eight Poor House employees: two chaplains, two overseers, and twenty-four domestics (1966), 4:295.

83 Araujo stated that the sale of cloth manufactured by the inmates had produced 78,171.5 pesos over 29 years or an annual average of 2,696 pesos if the sales had held steady over the entire time period. There must have been earlier years when inmate earnings were much larger, for the 1803 earnings were only 951 pesos (344.8 from sales of cotton goods and 606.2 from wool and other fibers such as *pita*, from agave plants. 1804 report, ff. 7–8.

84 Abadiano (1878), 31.

85 Even a highly skilled cigarette roller, in a good year, earned only 70 pesos. Deans-Smith (1992), 191. See also Scardaville (1977), 66, 76, n. 59, 89.

86 Araujo claimed to have spent 58 pesos per inmate, a figure that is inconsistent with the other data he provides. Another suspect calculation came from Revillagigedo in 1794, who claimed that the asylum spent 50,000 pesos on 750 inmates, or 66 pesos a year. These figures are too round, and too high, to be believable. *Instrucciones* (1873), 2:131.

87 On salary trends, see Deans-Smith (1992), 195; and Scardaville (1977), 66, 89, 78, n. 83.

88 The police logs date from 1795 to 1807. Only 3.6 percent of those accused of vagrancy were sent to the Poor House—about the same number as were let go (3.6 percent) or sentenced to the armed services (3.7 percent). See Scardaville (1977), 301, 327–42.

89 Circular of February 6, 1798, AGN, Bandos, vol. 19, exp. 91, f. 162. A decree issued in Spain on January 11, 1784, similarly affirmed the charitable purposes of the realm's poorhouses. Although it discouraged the confinement of delinquents alongside the "worthy" poor, it did not explicitly prohibit it. The 1784 decree only stipulated that delinquents should be isolated from the other inmates in separate rooms or sections and that vagrants placed in asylums would have open-ended terms of confinement, as did beggars. *Nov. rec.*, bk. 12, title 31, law 12.

90 It still had six members in addition to its president, but the archbishop substituted for the second member of the cathedral chapter, the Poor House director had been added and the city attorney moved to an ex officio position, and the viceroy had been replaced by the oidor decano or *regente* of the Audiencia. In addition, there were two city councilmen and the prior of the Merchant's Guild, as before. Although it might seem as though the viceroy had lost control of the board to the archbishop, the Audiencia representative had always been the designated stand-in for the viceroy.

91 See *Suplemento*, 516, 525–27; and appendix 4.

92 The new Poor House board was approved by the crown on March 20, 1801. See *Suplemento*, 516, 520. The regent of the Audiencia was the president of the Poor House board in May of 1802. *Instrucciones* (1873), 2:677. It therefore appears that the viceroy "reassumed" the presidency sometime after that date.

93 *Instrucciones* (1873), 2:677–78.

94 See letter from Balthasar Ladrón de Guevara to Viceroy Iturrigaray, April 18, 1803, AGN, Historia, vol. 441, exp. 1. Torre still appears as Poor House director in subsequent pages of the same volume. According to a letter from González Carbajal to

the viceroy of January 5, 1810, he served with distinction as director without remuneration until 1806, when he became a member of the Junta de Caridad. In 1809 (but not 1806) he is listed as the Diputado del Hospicio, who had responsibility for the Hospicio section. *Suplemento*, 527; AGN, Historia, vol. 441, f. 62 (January 28, 1809) and f. 91 (January 5, 1810).

95 See Rivera Cambas (1880–83), 1:244; García Icazbalceta (1907), 7; and Zúñiga's will, dictated on October 8, 1797, shortly before his death, to the notary Domingo Becerra, AN, vol. 569, ff. 266–69. The disposition of his estate is outlined in detail in chart 2, which accompanies the *Suplemento*, following 528. Although he did bequeath a substantial 26,000 pesos to his niece, nephews, and cousin, far larger sums went to the capital's four prisons (54,000 pesos) to the founding of missions to convert the infidels (300,000 pesos), and to the Poor House (680,000 pesos plus a third of the product of his mines in perpetuity).

96 Alfaro gives the figure of 37,000 pesos, but this includes 10,000 pesos that Zúñiga bequeathed to rebuild the Poor House infirmaries (1906), 18. See chart 2 in *Suplemento*, following p. 528. The renovation took place in 1802–3 and included moving the infirmaries for men and women upstairs so that their occupants could (separately) hear the Mass taking place in the chapel below. 1804 report, ff. 8–9.

97 See chart 2 in *Suplemento*, following p. 528. Note that Alfaro puts the cost at 480,000 pesos (1906, 18), but I consider the earlier figure more reliable. On the construction of the addition, see various documents in AGN, Policía, vol. 30.

98 See comments in notes 1 and 2 to the chart in *Suplemento*, following p. 528.

99 See Marquina's "Instrucción" of January 1, 1803, in *Instrucciones* (1873), esp. 2:676–77.

100 Humboldt (1966), 2:50.

101 These mortality rates compare favorably with the 7 percent who died in 1794, the only other year for which such figures are available (see table 3).

102 The 1804 report says that 2,192.5 pesos had been paid to the "comisionados para recoger mendigos" over the past twenty-nine years, but it does not list any payments to a sentinel in 1803, f. 9.

103 Sedaño (1880), 286.

104 The rate of 15 pesos a month stipulated by the 1806 bylaws for pensioners in the Patriotic School and Department of Correction was evidently not paid for inmates in the Department of Worthy Paupers. See "Quaderno," AHSSA, BP-EA-HP, bk. 8, exit notation for December 1, 1807, and entrance notation for March 3, 1808.

105 Art. 17 of the royal decree of December 31, 1797, AGN, Bandos, vol. 19, f. 115.

106 The 1795 census lists the Poor House administrator as Juan Antonio de Araujo, a 46-year-old Spanish man with a wife and two children, who were served by a 30-year-old meca maid, María Antonia Meca. According to this information, Araujo would only have been 25 when the Poor House opened in 1774. By 1804 he would have been 55 years old.

107 AGN, Historia, vol. 441, exp. 1, f. 5.

108 Decree of January 25, 1800, AGN, Bandos, vol. 20, exp. 62, f. 162.

109 See Megged (1997), 12.

110 *Instrucciones* (1873), 2:675.

4 Reform of the Poor House, 1806–1811

1 Sedaño (1880), 286.
2 *Suplemento* no. 523-28.
3 This description is based on the one in *Suplemento*, 516-25.
4 Ibid., 524. The *Suplemento* published the membership of the Junta de Caridad, and the *Diario de México* 3, no. 277 (July 4, 1806), published its new bylaws, 261-68.
5 Decree of June 25, 1806, AGN, Bandos, vol. 22, f. 140.
6 *Suplemento*, 519, 521, 524.
7 See Caro López (1989), 185; and Tanck Estrada (1977), 16, 168-73.
8 Torre was one of three executors Zúñiga named in his will. See *Suplemento*, 515.
9 The drafting committee consisted of Azcárate, who eventually signed the "Prospecto," plus González Carbajal, Torre, Francisco Xavier Borbón, Ambrosio Sagarzurieta, Dr. Juan Antonio Bruno, Antonio Méndez Prieto, and Francisco Primo Verdad. *Suplemento*, 515-21.
10 An 1817 report confirms that the king "quiso que se arreglasen sus estatutos, como se ha hecho, a los del Hospicio de Cádiz." "Opinión del Síndico," December 29, 1817, AGN, Policía, vol. 30, f. 268.
11 See ibid.; and *Suplemento*, 516-17.
12 Ibid., 517.
13 An 1824 report states that the colonial board was supposed to have twenty-six members, including the viceroy and five Poor House employees (the chaplain, two *tenientes de policía*, and two of their assistants). "Estado general de la Casa del Hospicio de Pobres de Mejico, AGN, Archivo Histórico de Hacienda, vol. 117, f. 192 (hereafter cited as 1824 report).
14 The *Gazeta*'s list of forty-seven members omitted Francisco Xavier Borbón, fiscal de la Real Hacienda, who nonetheless appears in its listing of board assignments as a solicitor of funds for the fourth week of every month. *Suplemento*," 525-27. He also appeared as a member of the 1805 board, to which members were assigned for life terms.
15 1777 bylaws, arts. 21, 24.
16 The 1797 decree mandating the transfer of children came after the Patriotic School project was already under way (AGN, Bandos, vol. 9, exp. 5, 27). The transfers of young children may not have occurred, though. In the seven months covered by the 1807-8 entrance register, the only orphan sent from the Cuna (on January 27, 1808) was the 14-year-old María Ignacia Santelices Lorenzana. Three other Lorenzanas who entered the Poor House were adult paupers from the street.
17 Ann Blum points out that the Spanish term *adopción* (sometimes *proahijar*) could mean fostering or indenture, as well as what we consider adoption, and did not always make children automatic heirs (1998), 71-93.
18 *Suplemento*, 515.
19 Muriel (1956-60), 2:173.
20 For the 1807-8 registers, see "Quaderno en que se apuntan las Entradas de los Pobres (en borrador) y comienza el 3 de Agosto de 1807," AHSSA, BP-EA-HP, bk. 8. For the

1808 census, see "Padrón del Hospicio de Pobres," May 31, 1808, GDCLDS, Mexico D.F., microfilm roll no. 35978. For the 1811 census, see AGN, Padrones, vol. 72, ff. 39–58. For the correspondence, see AGN, Historia, vol. 441, exp. 1.

21 The 1808 Communion list does not appear to have been a one-day enumeration, either. Although signed on May 31, 1808, it contains a corrigendo who (according to the exit registers) had left on March 3. The sixty-seven children counted in the 1808 census appear to have been in the Department of Worthy Paupers rather than the school because they were listed among the inmates "living in the rooms below"—when we know that the school building was separate and the students, if counted, would be separately listed. Moreover, the proportion of children and their racial profiles match those of the inmate children rather than those of the students in 1811. Finally, a comparison of the girls age five to fourteen listed in 1808 with those in the 1811 census (boys' names are not available for 1808) shows that none of the 1808 girls were students three years later, although a few were still listed among the inmates of the Department of Worthy Paupers.

22 The 1808 total may be too high because the list appears to include inmates who were there at different times.

23 See the notation on chart 2, *Suplemento*, following p. 528.

24 *Suplemento*, footnotes on pp. 524–25.

25 The request was made on June 6, 1806. See correspondence between the Junta de Caridad and the viceroy, March-April 1818, in AGN, Policía, vol. 30, ff. 268–69v, 272–74v.

26 The *recaudador* (alms collector), José María Araujo, may have been related to the administrator Juan Antonio Araujo. After the alms collector died, the Poor House tried to recover the money from his father. AGN, Historia, vol. 441, ff. 150–51v (April 5, 1811). If the irregularities were already known in 1803, they might explain the scathing remark made by Viceroy Marquina about replacing "a particular penniless administrator who seeks the job to support himself, and his family." *Instrucciones* (1873), 2:677–78.

27 "Corrección de costumbres," *Diario de México*, July 13, 1807, 194.

28 The two 20-year-old José Arces may not be the same person. The 1808 census identifies José María Arce as an Indian from Santa Fe; the entrance register for December 15, 1807, identifies Don Juan José Aperechea y Arce as an español from the Real de Huautla. Although inconsistencies are common in the records, it is unlikely that a person would be identified as a Spanish don and an Indian at different times.

29 AGN, Historia, vol. 441, exp. 1, ff. 48–50.

30 1824 report, ff. 177–93. A board member was still assigned to supervise the Department of Correction in 1809, but not by the time of the next board listing in 1822. AGN, Historia, vol. 441, exp. 1, f. 63; Valdés (1822), 111. In his 1832 proposal to establish a reformatory for juvenile delinquents in Mexico City, Tadeo Ortiz flatly stated that no such facility existed in the Mexican capital (1952), 180.

31 Muriel (1974), esp. 110–43; "Informe" (1826), AHCM, Beneficencia, vol. 423, exp. 2, f. 3v ff.

32 AGN, Historia, vol. 441, f. 20.

33 The daily registers do not state whether or not these women were placed in the

asylum for correction, and other explanations are possible. For example, the slave may have been placed in the Poor House because she was useless as a worker. Two more examples may similarly bear no relation to punishment: one woman's record is followed by the notation "gives four pesos," and the 26-year-old mestiza Anacleta Aguilar's entry notes "brought by her father and mother." See entries for October 15, 1807, January 14, 1808, November 13, 1807, December 17, 1807, and February 15, 1808, in "Quaderno," AHSSA, BP-EA-HP, bk. 8.

34 Muriel (1974), 2:171–73.

35 Merely listed without identification in 1808, Doña Ana Medina is identified as the director in the 1824 report, ff. 182v–83. Vidaurri is identified as her relative in a city guide, which lists her full name as Vidaurri y Medina. Galván Rivera (1832), 108–9.

36 Valdés (1822), 110; 1824 report, f. 183; Galván Rivera (1832), 108–9; "Informe" (1835), AGN, Gobernación, Tramo 1, leg. 130, exp. 3.

37 Ortiz did not, however, propose that the new maternity home be exclusively for women of Spanish descent (1952), 178–79.

38 García Icazbalceta (1907), 17–18.

39 The salary is listed in the 1824 report, f. 182v. Vidaurri is listed as director in Galván Rivera (1832), 108–9.

40 *Suplemento*, 523.

41 The proportion of Spanish children in the Cuna is calculated from figures for 1805–12. Avila Espinosa (1994), 279, 299.

42 *Suplemento*, 523.

43 Tanck Estrada found that boys were 46 percent of the students enrolled in Mexico City's elementary schools in 1802 and 52 percent in 1838 (1977), 197.

44 See Arrom (1985), chap. 4.

45 I have found only one reference to a girl being "married off" with a dowry: María Matilde Ruiz left with a dowry on June 4, 1808. "Quaderno," AHSSA, BP-EA-HP, bk. 8, f. 55.

46 This figure excludes the mecas, whose ages are not stated in the 1795 or 1808 lists.

47 Chase (1975), 167.

48 In 1806 these items were paid for out of Zúñiga's estate, although in later years replacements would have to come out of the school's budget. *Suplemento*, chart 2, following p. 528.

49 Salary information from 1823 suggests that the Patriotic School spent at least 2,500 pesos on wages in 1811. If the school spent approximately 56 pesos per inmate, as in 1803, it would have spent 10,300 on its 184 students. These are only ballpark estimates, however, not corrected for inflation. They fail to take into account additional expenses for the school such as books, paper, and pencils; they do not take into account the presumably better quality of the clothing, and perhaps also the food, offered the students; and they omit the food and medicine undoubtedly consumed by the new employees and their many family members and dependents. On the other hand, the Patriotic School may have spent less on building maintenance than the Poor House did in 1803 because its physical plant was only 5 years old.

50 Even if, for the purposes of comparability, we include 25 students age 15 or older

from the Patriotic School, the Poor House only served 326 of the capital's adult paupers in 1811.

51 AGN, Historia, vol. 441, f. 52 (August 21, 1807).

52 The eighteen mecas were "delivered" to the asylum as an anonymous group, the sole people for whom no names, ages, or other details were given in the entrance register. We only know that one gave birth three days later to a baby, who was immediately baptized Petra and died the same night. Their entrance was authorized by the Exmo. Sr. Diputado. See 1807–8 entrance register, "Quaderno," AHSSA, BP-EA-HP, bk. 8, f. 23. The 1808 Communion list tells us little about the mecas, simply noting that there were "fifty-one gentiles," plus six more (three youths and three adult women) who were baptized and therefore listed among the inmates taking Communion.

53 The 56 percent of the entries containing the notation "por la tropa" may overstate the degree of compulsion because some paupers accompanied by a policeman or other law enforcement officer may have requested shelter in the asylum.

54 Another 1.6 percent were expelled for gross misbehavior, 5 percent were sent to a hospital, and 8 percent died.

55 AGN, Bandos, vol. 25, ff. 139–40.

56 Cases from May and June 1809, in AGN, Historia, vol. 441, exp. 1, ff. 65–67.

57 See, for example, the case of Cristobal de Santiago, "of a very advanced age, deaf, and blind," AGN, Historia, vol. 441 (1812), ff. 187–87v.

58 More than half the women aged 15 to 29 who sought temporary shelter in 1807–8 (ten of nineteen) were single mothers, all claiming to be married or widowed. Despite the numerous young mothers seeking refuge, the average age for women in the 1807–8 entrance register was 45.9, almost identical to the average age of 45.8 for women in the 1811 census. The younger women were balanced by the many elderly who came for short stays or to die in the asylum.

59 Reliable statistics on life expectancies are not yet available. Gayón Córdoba estimated that in 1851 the life expectancy for Mexico City dwellers reaching the age of 3 was approximately 37 years (1988), 11–14. McCaa estimated life expectancies at age 5 for Guadalajara in 1880 to be 37 years, apparently higher than the rural life expectancies of 29 and 34 in Oaxaca and Jalisco. He also calculated that at the beginning of the nineteenth century in Parral life expectancies at birth were barely 20 years (1993), 617.

60 He was one of forty inmates who died during the ten months from August 3, 1807, to June 3, 1808. Sixteen of them died in the space of six weeks in November and December 1807, as if the Poor House were swept by an epidemic. Unfortunately, the exit registers, where deaths were recorded, do not give the cause of death or the age and race of the deceased.

61 For the purpose of comparability, these figures are based on the entire population, including mecas and children (but excluding students), because the 1803 data do not provide information on mecas or permit a separate analysis of those age 15 or older.

62 Sagardo's petition of May 26, 1809, AGN, Historia, vol. 441, ff. 70–71.

63 Frexomil was listed in the 1795 Communion count as a 10 year old. The daily registers for 1807 show that she reentered the asylum on February 23, 1807, six months

before she was expelled. Another expelled woman, María Manuela Bravo, was sent to serve the administrator of the Poor House, Juan Antonio Araujo, on October 10, 1807. The asylum thus appears to have been reluctant to send loose women directly into the streets.

64 Correspondence from March 26, 1804, and June 25, 1807, AGN, Historia, vol. 441, ff. 4, 20.

65 Osores was presumably deposited in the asylum during her divorce proceedings. She was still in the Poor House three months after Viceroy Iturrigaray left Mexico on December 29, 1808. AGN, Historia, vol. 441, f. 51.

66 Although it was not part of the asylum's mission, the law listed the Hospicio de Pobres as an alternative *depósito* for women involved in suits against their husbands. See Haslip-Viera (1980), 194. In my study of eighty-one ecclesiastical divorce suits (Arrom [1985], chapter 6), I encountered no case where a woman was placed in the Poor House during divorce proceedings between 1800–57. In 1857 one woman was placed in the new Casa de Asilo (AGN, Bienes Nacionales, leg. 76, exp. 39).

67 The decline of Indian paupers was even more marked, from 33 to 27 percent if the mecas are included for both years.

68 The 1811 figures have an especially large margin of error because they are based on the sample described in Arrom (1985), 271, 311–12, n. 2. Herbert Klein analyzed a different sample of the 1811 census based on incomplete surviving totals rather than any sample design. He found Indians to comprise 27 percent of the city residents, castas 17 percent, and Spanish 57 percent (1996), 71, 91.

69 Unlike the entrance register, the exit register does not consistently give the race of people leaving the asylum, although race is listed for the women "returned" to the Poor House after working for a time as servants.

70 The matching of names also highlights the degree of inaccuracy in these censuses. Even though the titled inmates should have been among the best educated, a few gave the same age in both 1808 and 1811, or one that was more than three years' different. One Doña Catarina Hernández even changed her marital status from widowed to single. We have no way of knowing whether the married or widowed had ever been legally married or were only living in consensual unions. The 1777 bylaws only required the Poor House to check marriage certificates for those wishing to live with a spouse or to receive spousal visits within the institution.

71 1824 report, ff. 183, 190.

72 In 1811 Spanish women were much less likely to have migrated to Mexico City (as did only 38 percent of those in my census sample of all city residents) than Indian women (48 percent). See Arrom (1985), 108.

73 Sonia Pérez Toledo found that textile workers (among whom she included tailors and hatmakers) represented only 31 to 36 percent of all artisans in Mexico City in 1794 and 1842. I have followed her definition of *artisan*, a category that included carpenters and bakers, for example, because they were organized into guilds (1996), 138, 269–74.

74 Hernández Sáenz (1997), esp. 76.

75 The crisis in the textile sector escalated rapidly after 1804. See Bazant (1964); Chávez Orozco (1965); and Potash (1983), 10–11.

76 In Spain, for example, King Charles IV in 1794 decreed that all *expósitos* (foundlings) should be considered legitimate and therefore innocent of their parents' sins. See Sherwood (1988); and the decree of July 30, 1794, in Dublán and Lozano, no. 21, 1:34–36.

77 *Suplemento*, 515.

78 García Icazbalceta (1907), 7.

79 *Suplemento*, 525.

80 "Sobre arbitrios para auxiliar al Hospicio de Pobres de esta Capital," November 11, 1817, AHCM, Hospicio de Pobres, vol. 2295, exp. 18, ff. 1–2.

81 The board also requested that the ecclesiastical communities stop providing food at their doors and donate it as home relief to the pobres vergonzantes instead. These requests were made to the viceroy in the hope that he would convince the archbishop to issue the appropriate orders. *Suplemento*, 521.

82 Article signed S.C., *Diario de México*, Nov. 19, 1805, 210–11. See the sequel on page 238 of the November 25 issue, in which he proposes a reformatory for juvenile delinquents of both sexes.

83 See Ruiz Castañeda (1985), 262; Manrique de Lara and Monroy (1954), 47; and Di Tella (1996), 45, 60.

84 Villaurrutia was fifteen years old when he shared Lorenzana's return voyage to Spain in 1772. López de Escalera (1964), 1165.

85 Indeed one María Catalina Bermúdez, an "orphan and libertine woman," was turned away on March 26, 1804, despite the asylum's mission to care for orphans. AGN, vol. 441, Historia, exp. 1, f. 3.

5 Independence and Decline, 1811–1823

1 The Spanish constitutions of 1812 and 1820 assigned all hospitals and welfare institutions to the *ayuntamientos*, but it is unclear whether this provision ever applied in Mexico. Alvarez Amezquita (1960), 3:453; Muriel (1956–60), 2:283.

2 See Valdés (1822), 109.

3 This arrangement preceded the January 31, 1824, Constitutive Act of the Mexican Republic, cited in Velasco Ceballos (1943), 51. A decree of June 18, 1823, only four months after Iturbide resigned, mandated the creation of a new Poor House board, this time presided over by the governor of what would soon become the Federal District. Bocanegra (1892), 1:472.

4 AGN, Historia, vol. 441, ff. 62–63 (January 28, 1809), and f. 91 (January 5, 1810).

5 The committee began working after it was appointed by the Minister of Relaciones in May 1823. It is unclear whether the population figures are from January 1824 or from 1823, as were the fiscal data. The report is signed by aldermen Miguel Nájera, Vicente Valdéz, José Bernardo Baz, and Vicente Garviso. 1824 report, ff. 151–151 verso; 177–93.

6 Rivera Cambas (1880–83), 1:244; Velasco Ceballos (1935), 74. An 1806 report on the Poor House in the *Suplemento* does not mention any financial problems related to the Consolidation. Only one capital fund is accompanied by the notation "*consolidación*," the Obrapía of Don Juan Ruiz Aragón (Arangoite, according to an 1826 re-

port). It nonetheless continued producing income until 1812. See 1824 report, f. 184; and "Informe" (1826), AHCM, Beneficencia, vol. 423, exp. 2, f. 2v. Macedo says that only the ecclesiastical institutions were affected by the Consolidación (1900–1904), 712.

7 Muriel (1956–60), 2:283–85.

8 Humboldt (1966), 2:50; 1824 report, ff. 184, 186; "Informe" (1826), AHCM, Beneficencia, vol. 423, exp. 2, ff. 2. Cossío confirms that in 1824 the republican government recognized 279,394 pesos that the Poor House had invested in funds of the Consulado, the Tribunal de Minería, the Temporalidades, and the Renta de Tabaco (1917), 28.

9 Printed fundraising letter of September 30, 1817, AGN, Policía, vol. 30, f. 1.

10 See correspondence between the viceroy and the city council (1817–18), in AGN, Policía, vol. 30, ff. 1-2, 258, 268–69; and AHCM, Hospicio de Pobres, vol. 2295, exp. 18.

11 "Informe" (1826), AHCM, Beneficencia, vol. 423, exp. 2, ff. 2–3. The lottery was still producing 1,000 pesos per month in the early months of 1817. "Opinion del Síndico," December 29, 1817, AGN, Policía, vol. 30, f. 268.

12 Correspondence from city council to viceroy, October 24 and November 11, 1817, AGN, Policía, vol. 30, f. 258.

13 1824 report, f. 184; "Informe" (1826), AHCM, Beneficencia, vol. 423, exp. 2, f. 2v.

14 On the tablas, see the letter of November 27, 1833, in AGN, Gobernación, Tramo 1, leg. 130, exp. 2; and TePaske (1989), 73.

15 Correspondence between Poor House board and viceroy, November 11, 1817, AHCM, Hospicio de Pobres, vol. 2295, exp. 18, f. 2.

16 Abadiano (1878), 31. Fernández de Lizardi also emphasized the scarcity of private almsgiving during this period. Quoted in Sacristán (1994b), 236.

17 AGN, Historia, vol. 441, ff. 150–51v (April 5, 1811).

18 1804 report, ff. 8 and 11 verso.

19 AGN, Policía, vol. 30, esp. ff. 258–80v. The Poor House board's requests are summarized in AHCM, Hospicio de Pobres, vol. 2295, exp. 18.

20 Letter of September 30, 1817, in AGN, Policía, vol. 30, ff. 1-2.

21 "Opinión del Síndico," December 29, 1817, AGN, Policía, vol. 30, f. 268.

22 See, for example, complaints in AGN, Gobernación, Tramo 1, leg. 130, exp. 5 (1844).

23 Deans-Smith says that the Tobacco Factory was temporarily relocated in the Poor House in 1815 (1992), 250. Abadiano says that it took over the Patriotic School in 1819 but did not pay rent (1878), 31–32. See also Rivera Cambas (1880–83), 1:245.

24 Abadiano says that employees went fourteen months without receiving a salary (1878), 32, but the 1824 report lists a debt to employees worth slightly more than two years of their salaries by June of 1823 (f. 186). Of course, this debt may not have been distributed evenly. It is possible that some employees were paid after fourteen months while others—perhaps those receiving free room and board—forfeited their wages.

25 The 1824 report explained that properties on the Calle del Relox, San Pedro y San Pablo, and Callejón de Dolores brought in very little due to their "deplorable condition," f. 184.

26 The Constituent Congress of 1822 approved funds for the Poor House, perhaps recognizing the government's obligation to continue payments on Zúñiga's endowment. AGN, Governación, Tramo 1, leg. 130 (1833), exp. 2.

27 Ladd (1976), esp. 196–97.

28 Valdés (1822), 109–11; 1824 report, f. 192.

29 1824 report, f. 186.

30 Unless otherwise noted all information in this section comes from the 1824 report, ff. 177–93.

31 These were Pedro Prito, owed 1,133.7 pesos for bread; Eusevio Estavillo, owed 752.1 for lamb and beef; Juan José de Arizpe, owed 460 for chocolate; the House of Yermo, owed 46 for sugar; and 1,382.1 owed to various individuals. 1824 report, f. 186.

32 Four had been board members since at least 1806: Domingo de Lardizával was owed 900 pesos; Estevan Vélez de Escalante, 7,000; the Mariscal de Castilla, 4,918; and José María Fagoaga, 11,000. A new board member, Antonio Velasco de la Torre, was owed 1,100. 1824 report, f. 186.

33 AHCM, Actas de Cabildo, vol. 131-A, February 3, 1812, f. 19v.

34 Decree of August 9, 1830, in Dublán and Lozano, no. 858, 2:278–79.

35 Cases from February through August 1812, AGN, Historia, vol. 441, ff. 185, 180–80v, 193.

36 The 1806 "Prospecto" set the fee at 15 pesos a month, but Alfaro claimed (1906, 30) that the pension was only 10 pesos and rarely paid. The total paid by the seven pensioners in 1823 was 504 pesos (table 16). If all seven were there for the full twelve months, they paid 6 pesos a month.

37 The statistics for both dates may not be entirely comparable because of different age breakdowns. Unfortunately, the data do not allow accurate correlations of age with infirmity. The 1823 statistics do not give ages, only the categories of women, men, and students. The 1803 statistics use unusual age groups (breaking at age 20 rather than the more usual 15) for the total population, and do not provide age breakdowns for the health data. My figures are based on two questionable assumptions, that men and women in 1823 were 21 or older and that in both years the disabled were adults.

38 Although medicine and surgery were formally merged into one profession in 1831 (Hernández Sáenz, 1997, 265), the telescoping of three positions into one is more likely to reflect financial problems, especially because the new expanded term would have been *médico* not *cirujano*. The new definition of *doctor* did not include pharmacists, either.

39 1804 report, f. 10.

40 AHSSA, BP-EA-HP, leg. 3, exp. 24 (October 28, 1861).

41 By 1803 the rectora's salary had actually risen from 120 to 160 pesos; by 1823 it was back down to its 1777 level. Two other salaries listed in 1777 and 1803, but not in 1823, also remained stable: the 300 pesos a year paid to the mayordomo, and the 200 paid to the secretary. The inmate portero's salary also declined, from 96 to 84 pesos. Compare the 1824 report, ff. 182–83; the 1804 report, f. 11; and the 1777 bylaws.

42 The employees in 1829 were the administrator, José María Gómez; his assistant, Manuel Toledo; the chaplain, Joaquín Yáñez; the surgeon, José María Martínez; the *maestro de primeras letras*, José María Abarca; two wardens, Bartolomé Ayala

and Manuel Borjes; the *rectora de mujeres*, Josefa Merino; the *rectora de niñas*, Luz Figueroa; her assistant, Teresa Oropesa; and the portero, José María Priego. Listed in Galván Rivera (1829), 105.

43 The 1824 report distinguished between the professional employees, who earned from 240 to 1,000 pesos per year and were listed by name, and the others, who earned a mere 9 to 36 pesos a year and did not merit such recognition. The listing does indicate their gender, however (f. 182). The "professional" employees were the administrator, José María Pelaez; the chaplain Francisco de la Cuesta; the surgeon Juan Ca— de Oro; the schoolteacher, José María Abarca, his helper Manuel Toledo; two wardens, Bartolomé Ayala and Rafael Núñez; the rectora of the Hospicio (unnamed); and the rectora of the Patriotic School, Josefa Monares, who doubled as *portera* and maestra de amiga. The "nonprofessionals" were three male porteros and a sacristan, a female portera, another maestra de amiga, a cook and her helper, two *galopinas* (scullions), and an atolera.

44 The widows were "la viuda del difunto administrador" and the "viuda de Varela." The 1811 census had identified José María Varela as a 29-year-old Spanish *mandón del patio* (patio superviser) living in a household with his wife, his wife's sister, and a maid.

45 García Icazbalceta (1907), 12.

46 AGN, Gobernación, Tramo 1, leg. 130 (1833), exp. 1; (1841), exp. 3.

47 Report of Governor Baz, March 1, 1869, AHCM, Hospicio de Pobres, vol. 2295, exp. 65.

48 Manuel Payno (1966), 114–20. Although he wrote the novel in 1888–91, it was set in the mid-nineteenth-century capital, which Payno knew firsthand. The retired military officer Don Epifanio may have been modeled on Lt. Col. Francisco Barroeta, who administered the Poor House from 1833 until he was fired in 1841.

49 1824 report, ff. 180–81.

6 Republican Difficulties, 1824–1855

1 It is unlikely that the José María Gómez, who administered the institution in 1829, was the same Gómez Eguiarte of later years, who would only have been seventeen years old in 1829. They may have been related, perhaps father and son (see appendix 3).

2 The committee was appointed in May, and the formation of a new board was mandated in a June 18, 1823, decree, cited in Bocanegra (1892), 1:472.

3 See Acta Constitutiva de la República Mexicana, cited in Velasco Ceballos (1943), 51.

4 1824 report, f. 184. The largest single sum was the 250,000 peso Patriotic School endowment, which was invested in funds of the Consulado, ramo de Avería. Other funds were invested in the Consulado, Renta del Tabaco, Tribunal de Minería, and Temporalidades (table 16). Cossío puts the sum recognized by the government at 279,394 pesos (1917), 28. The Constituent Congress recognized its responsibility for these payments on June 20, 1822. AGN, Gobernación, Tramo 1, leg. 130, Tramo 1 (1833), exp. 2.

5 "Informe de la Comision [de Beneficencia] respectiva al Estado en que se hallan

el Hospicio de Pobres, la de Recogidas, y la de Expósitos," April 28, 1826, AHCM, Beneficencia, vol. 423, exp. 2.

6 Tayloe (1959), 62.

7 Velasco Ceballos (1935), 100.

8 See "Quaderno de borradores de sueldos" (1822–27), AHSSA, BP-EA-HP, bk. 9.

9 AHCM, Hospicio de Pobres, vol. 2295, exp. 21 (1827).

10 Ibid., exp. 20 (July 19, 1827), f. 13; and AHCM, Beneficencia, vol. 423, exp. 4 (1827), ff. 1–1 verso. See also the 1826 statement that the Poor House "no ha corrido a cargo de este Ex.o Ayuntamiento," in "Informe" (1826), AHCM, Beneficencia, vol. 423, exp. 2, f. 2; and Gamboa Ramírez (1994), 22. The city council again denied its responsibility for the Poor House in 1859. AHCM, Beneficencia y Asilos, vol. 416, exp. 3.

11 The timing of this takeover is unclear. By 1829 the Poor House was definitely under the control of the city council, since Galván Rivera included the Poor House as one of the commissions assigned to the aldermen (1829), 74. Only the Casa de Cuna and Hospital de San Andrés were still outside of city council jurisdiction by that time. Rivera Cambas (1880–83), 2:170; Orozco y Berra (1867), 197; Peza (1881), 16. The city council's jurisdiction was reiterated in the constitution of 1836 and in article 2 of the reform project of December 29, 1840. The Bases Orgánicas of 1843 gave the responsibility for welfare institutions to the Asambleas de los Departamentos. Muriel (1956–60), 2:286–87; Alvarez Amezquita et al. (1960), 1:236. The Minister of Relaciones also appears to have had some authority over the Poor House, at least in 1833–34 and 1847. AGN, Gobernación, Tramo 1, leg. 130 (1934) exp. 6; (1847), exp. 9. The Minister of Hacienda also exerted considerable power through his ability to release revenues collected from customs.

12 The adoption of the centralist constitution of 1836, with the accompanying change in status of the Federal District, led to considerable controversy over the governor's role in the Poor House. This controversy surfaced in AGN, Gobernación, Tramo 1, leg. 130 (1841), exp. 4. It was resolved by the new bylaws of 1843. On the conflict between the governor and city council, see also Rodríguez Kuri (1994); Gortari Rabiela (1994); and Warren (1996b), 128.

13 Galván Rivera (1828), 99–102.

14 The 1829 decree is cited in Rivera Cambas (1880), 1:244.

15 December 16, 1828, AHCM, Actas Secretas de Cabildo, vol. 290–A (microfiche 7/8). At the same time its funding was hampered by the dramatic drop in customs revenues from some eight million pesos in 1826–27 to some five million in 1829–30. See Di Tella (1996), 212.

16 A ladies' board supervised the Foundling Home from at least 1836 to 1846, and another oversaw the Hospital for Demented Women in 1844. See Arrom (1985), 43–45.

17 Bocanegra (1892), 1:472.

18 Malo (1948), 1:219.

19 Zerecero (1869).

20 Although members were appointed for life, the board did not always outlast changing administrations. A decree of July 18, 1823, called for the appointment of a totally new republican board (Bocanegra, 1892, 1:472). The colonial members were indeed

replaced when Tornel finally constituted the new republican board in 1828. In addition, board members frequently resigned, leading to many notations about the need to fill vacancies. See AGN, Gobernación, Tramo 1, leg. 130.

21 Abadiano (1878), 32. These donations may have come from José Francisco's estate, of which Francisco was named the executor. The former marqués (José Francisco) had already contributed some 11,000 pesos to the asylum during its independence crisis (1824 report, f. 186) and left instructions in his will that his executor should support institutions of public welfare. *Diccionario Porrúa* (1964), 534.

22 The recurrence of family connections among those involved with the Poor House is striking. For example, upon his father's death in 1809 Francisco Sánchez de Tagle replaced him on the Poor House board (AGN, Historia, vol. 441, f. 62). A Miguel Cervantes (possibly a son of the Miguel Cervantes who served on the 1822 board) served on the board in 1865. Governor Baz may have been related to José Bernardo Baz, the *síndico* of the city council who signed reports about the Poor House in both 1817 and 1824, or to Ignacio Baz, who served as regidor in charge of the Poor House in 1867. Other relatives who served on the board were Joseph Mariano Fagoaga (1806-22), Joseph María Fagoaga (1806-22 and 1833), José Juan Fagoaga (1822), and Francisco Fagoaga (1833-51); Juan Francisco de Azcárate (1806-22 and a signatory of the 1806 bylaws) and Miguel María Azcárate (1859); and Vicente Gómez de la Cortina (1806) and José Gómez de la Cortina (1836). One Antonio Terán, who served in 1806, may have been related to Gregorio Mier y Terán (1844) and Antonio de Mier (1865). Vicente Carbajal (1856) may have been related to Ciriaco González Carbajal (1806). See appendix 4.

23 AHCM, Hospicio de Pobres, vol. 2295, (1827), exp. 21.

24 See the decrees of March 3 and 7, 1828, in Dublán and Lozano, nos. 552-53, 2:61-63.

25 See Arrom (1988b); and Warren (1994), chaps. 4-5.

26 Although Bustamante's government is often portrayed as a conservative regime contrasting sharply with its liberal predecessor, both were similar in their policies toward the urban poor. See Costeloe (1975); and Bazant (1985), 3:434.

27 Decree of August 9, 1830, in Dublán and Lozano, no. 858, 2:278-79.

28 None of the five board members who signed had served on the 1828 and 1829 boards. See appendix 4.

29 Bustamante, "Pobres Mendigos," *Voz de la Patria* (September 4, 1830), 5-7.

30 Quoted in Shaw (1975), 198, from records of the Vagrants Tribunal, AHCM, Vagos, vol. 4152, exp. 73. Some workshops must still have existed, for the unemployed Luis Hunda, brought before the Vagrants Tribunal in 1831, requested work in the Poor House. See Pérez Toledo (1993), 40.

31 AGN, Gobernación, Tramo 1, leg. 130 (1833), exp. 6.

32 Ibid., exp. 2.

33 Abadiano gave the interest rate as 3 percent, perhaps because the government reduced it further at some later date (1878), 30.

34 Financial shortages were compounded by a scheme whereby government officials allegedly forced the asylum to buy spoiled corn. AGN, Gobernación, Tramo 1, leg. 130 (1833), exp. 1.

35 Ibid., exp. 16.

36 Ibid., exps. 2 and 6.

37 Decrees of December 8 and 9, 1833, in Dublán and Lozano, no. 1315-16, 2:643-44.

38 AGN, Gobernación, Tramo 1, leg. 130 (1834), exp. 26. The Ministers of Hacienda and Relaciones were also involved in facilitating the renewal of the Poor House. Ibid. (1833), exps. 17 and 20.

39 Richard Packenham's July 26, 1834 report, quoted in Gilmore (1957), 218-19.

40 See AGN, Gobernación, Tramo 1, leg. 130 (1833), exps. 6, 8, 9, 10, 17, 23, 24; (1835), exp. 36. See also Packenham, quoted in Gilmore (1957), 218-19, 223.

41 AGN, Gobernación, Tramo 1, leg. 130 (1833), exp. 11.

42 Tanck Estrada (1977), 193; *Diccionario Porrúa* (1964), 885.

43 AHCM, Actas de Cabildo, vol. 149-A (February 3, 1829); decree of January 18, 1834, AGN, Gobernación, Tramo 1, leg. 130 (1834), exp. 34.

44 Ibid. (1841), exp. 3.

45 A city guide of 1832 listed the Departament of Secret Births as having two employees, and Packenham in 1834 referred to a "department in the poor house of Mexico set apart for lying-in women," Galván Rivera (1932), 108-9; Gilmore (1957), 220. A report of May 25, 1835, did not mention it at all, probably because it had no residents on the day the inmate count was taken, "Hospicio de Pobres, Estado que manifiesta . . . ," AGN, Gobernación, Tramo 1, leg. 130, exp. 36.

46 Decrees of October 24, 1834, in Dublán and Lozano, nos. 1471-72, 2:752.

47 AGN, Gobernación, Tramo 1, leg. 130.

48 The use of the term *Junta de Beneficencia* for the Poor House board first appears in 1824, although it alternated with the term *Junta de Caridad* until the 1840s, when the term *Junta Directiva del Hospicio de Pobres* became increasingly common. See Dublán and Lozano, no. 858, 2:278; and AGN, Gobernación, Tramo 1, leg. 130, exps. 1-6, 36, 38. At this time *beneficencia* also meant "private philanthropy," as used by José María Luis Mora in his 1834 proposal for a Junta de Beneficencia Pública General in Mexico City to systematically encourage the philanthropy of the wealthy. See Velasco Ceballos (1938), 12.

49 See Bazant (1985), 436; and Costeloe (1993), 31.

50 *Diccionario Porrúa* (1964), 1478.

51 A few scholars have begun to move in this direction by emphasizing the populist overtones and educational programs of Santa Anna's early administrations. See Di-Tella (1996), esp. 238; and Fowler (1998), esp. chap. 6. However, since the last Santa Anna regime during which the Poor House benefited was in 1844, the year when he and his loyal adviser Tornel became estranged, it may be that much of the credit belongs to Tornel.

52 Decree of October 22, 1835, in Dublán and Lozano, no. 1634, 3:88.

53 Costeloe (1993), 131.

54 See references to this dispute in AGN, Gobernación, Tramo 1, leg. 130 (1841), exp. 4.

55 Agustín Reyes, "Memoria sobre la creación del Concejo Superior de Salubridad," in Abadiano (1878), 49-51.

56 Mayer (1844), 55. He was posted to Mexico City from 1841 to 1844.

57 AGN, Gobernación, Tramo 1, leg. 130 (1844), exp. 5.

58 "Libro 7° de Papeletas diarias" (1841–42), AHSSA, HYH-HP, bk. 10.

59 May 1, 1844, report, AGN, Gobernación, Tramo 1, leg. 130 (1844), exp. 5.

60 The date of Prieto's visit is unclear. He visited with Ignacio Trigueros, who was Santa Anna's Minister of Hacienda from October 1841 to October 1842 and then again from March 1843 to October 1844. Prieto (1906), 2:141–42. Perhaps this was the inspection mandated by the new Board of Health in January 1841. Prieto was also commissioned to inspect the Poor House with Manuel Gómez Pedraza in 1846. AGN, Gobernación, Tramo 1, leg. 130 (1846), exp. 2.

61 Prieto (1906), 2:141–42. I follow Shaw's translation (1975), 199.

62 AGN, Gobernación, Tramo 1, leg. 130 (1841), exp. 2. No employee was fired in the wake of the investigation, and one (Pedro Ibáñez), who was reported to have regularly beaten the students at meals, was still there in 1848 (1848 census, AHCM, Padrones, vol. 3409, cuartel menor 30, manzana 230).

63 Velasco Ceballos (1943), 51.

64 "Libro 7° de Papeletas diarias" (1841–42), AHSSA, HYH-HP, bk. 10. See also AGN, Gobernación, Tramo 1, leg. 130 (1833), exps. 1, 3, and (1844), exp. 1; and the description of abuses that the proposed regulations of 1861 attempted to correct in AHSSA, BP-EA-HP, leg. 2, exp. 5.

65 AGN, Gobernación, Tramo 1, leg. 130 (1833), exp. 14.

66 The records do not include the ruling on her petition. Ibid. (February 21, 1833), exp. 7.

67 A separate document stated that the Poor House "at most" received 1,600 pesos per month. See AGN, Gobernación, Tramo 1, leg. 130 (November 2, 1841), exp. 1.

68 Ibid. (1841), exp. 3.

69 See Ibid., exp. 2.

70 Ibid., exp. 2.

71 Ibid. (November 30, 1841), exp. 4.

72 Ibid. (1844), exp. 5.

73 "Papeletas diarias," AHSSA, HYH-HP, bk. 10. Many years later the Poor House doctor, Wenceslau Reyes, referred to the recurrent cholera epidemics that struck the asylum along with scarlet fever, measles, and mange (*sarna*). AHCM, vol. 2295, exp. 52, ff. 7v–8 (May 1868). See also Rivera Cambas (1880), 1:246.

74 See Pérez Toledo (1996), chap. 6.

75 Meyer links this decree to Santa Anna's attempt to improve social welfare services (1975), 61.

76 Prieto (1906), 2:142 (emphasis in the original).

77 A report of May 1, 1844, indicates that Trigueros used funds from the Ministry of Hacienda to renovate the Poor House. AGN, Gobernación, Tramo 1, leg. 130 (1844), exp. 5.

78 The bylaws were signed by the vice president of the Poor House board, Ignacio de Inclán. *Ordenanza* (1844).

79 Correspondence between the board vice president, Félix Osores, and the governor of the Department of Mexico, AGN, Gobernación, Tramo 1, leg. 130 (November 30, 1841), exp. 4. This draft was already mentioned in 1833. AGN, Gobernación, Tramo 1, leg. 130 (1833), exp. 4.

80 Di Tella (1996), 210.

81 See the reference to the colonial bylaws in 1824 report, f. 192.

82 The secondary sources contradict each other on whether the Casa de Corrección was founded in 1841 or 1842, whether it moved to the Recogidas or the Tecpam, and the name of its founder. See Abadiano (1878), 34; Alfaro (1906), 29; Rivera Cambas (1880–83) 2:82; Peza (1881), 38; and Galindo y Villa (1901), 85. Two government decrees suggest that it in fact opened in 1842. Dublán and Lozano, no. 2274 (February 5, 1842); no. 2297 (March 2, 1842), 4:108–10, 122–23. Correspondence from Manuel Gorostiza to city officials shows that it was not yet open on November 12, 1841 (AGN, Gobernación, Tramo 1, leg. 130, exp. 1). It appears that the Casa de Corrección was in the Poor House, and then the Recogidas, until it was united with the Colegio de San Antonio in the Tecpam in 1863. García Icazbalceta (1907), 213.

83 García Icazbalceta (1907), 29–32; Rivera Cambas (1880–83), 2:82. See also decree of October 21, 1853, in Dublán and Lozano, no. 4072, 6:720; and AGN, Gobernación, Tramo 1, leg. 130 (1842), exp. 4.

84 Desés is named in the "Presupuesto gral. pormenorizado de los gastos que se deben erogar en el mes de junio de 1861," AHSSA, BP-EA-HP, leg. 1, exp. 21, f.1. Although no employee is listed for the Department of Secret Births in 1848, its ama was likely to have been an inmate, as had been the case since its inception.

85 See 1824 report, f. 192; 1843 bylaws, chap. 2, art. 7; and García Icazbalceta (1907), 17–18.

86 Like the new bylaws, the renewed persecution of beggars was apparently the culmination of an earlier (but unsuccessful) initiative from Santa Anna's previous administration in 1841. See AHCM, Beneficencia y Asilos, vol. 416 (1843), exp. 1, ff. 10–10v; and AGN, Gobernación, Tramo 1, leg. 130 (November 12, 1841), exp. 1.

87 Decree of December 30, 1843, referred to in Velasco Ceballos (1943), 52; and Rivera Cambas (1880–83), 1:244.

88 Attempts to restore a lottery for the Poor House began in 1838. In 1843 the government decreed that the rifa del Hospicio be held on Sundays instead of Tuesdays (apparently a more profitable day of the week) because the proceeds were so small. Santa Anna also exempted the lottery from paying taxes for three years. AGN, Gobernación, Tramo 1, leg. 130 (March 20, 1843), exp. 2; (1844), exp. 5.

89 Report of May 1, 1844, ibid. (1844), exp. 5.

90 Peza (1881), 67–68; Alfaro (1906), 17.

91 Mayer (1844), 55.

92 W. Thompson (1846), 149.

93 Velasco Ceballos (1943), 52.

94 Abadiano (1878), 32; Alfaro (1906), 17, 29; Rivera Cambas (1880–83), 1:245. Alfaro's account contains some confusion over the cost of repairing the Poor House. On one page he says that it cost 30,000 pesos, while on another he says that it cost 120,000.

95 AGN, Gobernación, Tramo 1, leg. 130 (1846), exp. 2. A decree of February 19, 1845, stipulated that 2 percent of all customs revenues would be shared among the country's welfare establishments (Dublán and Lozano, no. 2801, 5:5–6). This was far less, however, than the 4 percent the Santa Anna government had assigned to the Poor House alone in 1843.

96 Other board members who contributed during this period included Dr. Felix Osores, Gregorio Mier y Terán, Juan Portillo, the canónigo Agustín Carpena, the presbítero Pedro Fernández, and Diego Somera. Roberto Manning promised a donation of 8,000 pesos, which was still unpaid in 1844. See AGN, Gobernación, Tramo 1, leg. 130 (1844), exps. 4–5.

97 Ibid. (1847), exp. 4.

98 Valle (1864), 7. The capital was governed by two city councils during this period—one allied with the occupation forces and another "in exile," based in Querétaro. Rodríguez Kuri (1994), 88–89. See also Gamboa Ramírez (1994), 41.

99 See Shaw (1975), 199.

100 During the brief periods when the city council ceased functioning in 1850 and 1852 the governor of the D.F. apparently controlled the institution. See Malo (1948), 1:349, 361, 370; and Abadiano (1878), 34.

101 There is some guesswork involved in determining which of the listed people worked for the Poor House and how they were related. The 1848 census does not note family relations. They must be deduced from the last names and the order of the listings.

102 Her nephew (or perhaps younger brother), the bachelor Manuel Arauz, may have run errands for the Poor House and collected a salary, since he was listed as a *correo* (courier). It is also possible that he, like the *agente de negocios* (business agent) and two young carpenters listed as other employees' relatives, merely lived in the building and worked elsewhere.

103 "Presupuesto General" (June 1861), AHSSA, BP-EA-HP, leg. 1, exp. 21, ff. 1–1 verso. See also Gardida's "Memoria" (December 31, 1863), AHCM, Hospicio de Pobres, vol. 2295, exp. 23.

104 AGN, Gobernación, Tramo 1, leg. 130 (1841), exp. 1. See also statistics in BNM, Collección Lafragua, no. 118 (1842) that cite 292 pobres and 34 additional employees, their families, and dependents.

105 Flores (1886–88), 2:297–98.

106 It spent 125 pesos in May of 1861, 54 for medicine, eyeglasses, and supplies and the rest as salaries for the four employees: the director (50), barber-surgeon (12), nurse (8), and inmate helper (1). "Presupuesto" (June 1861) AHSSA, BP-EA-HP, leg 1, exp. 21, f. 1 verso. The department still functioned in 1871. AHCM, Hospicio de Pobres, vol. 2296, exp. 160 (October 5, 1871). See also García Icazbalceta (1907), 17.

107 In 1863 Prieto was 314.75 pesos behind on his rent. García Izcabalceta (1907), 230.

108 "Casa del Hospicio de Pobres," AHCM, Padrones, vol. 3409, cuartel menor 30, manzana 230; García Icazbalceta (1907), 8–9, 19–20.

109 Morales (1994), 208.

110 Alfaro (1906), 19.

111 Ibid., 18–19.

112 Cited in Velasco Ceballos (1943), 53. Bazant confirms that budget deficits became unwieldy in 1851 (1985), 449.

113 Macedo (1900), 716.

114 According to an 1861 report, Doña Dolores Arauz did not draw a salary. In exchange for teaching the girls embroidery, she received free room and rations for her large family. "Presupuesto" (June 1861), AHSSA, BP-EA-HP, leg. 1, exp. 21, f. 1 verso. Gar-

dida's "Memoria" refers to her as an employee on December 31, 1863. AHCM, Hospicio de Pobres, vol. 2295, exp. 23.

115 See García Icazbalceta (1907), 13–14, 21–22; and Peza (1881), 68.

116 This colonial arrangement was still in place in 1907, as described by García Icazbalceta (1907), 13.

117 Payno (1966), 120; García Cubas (1986), 382.

118 Alfaro (1906), 19.

119 Funerals outside the gates were rare. See AHSSA, BP-EA-HP, leg. 4, exp. 7, f. 4 (January 1862).

120 Funerals with fifty or a hundred hospicianos were extremely rare; the vast majority of funerals were attended by twelve and a few by as little as five or six youths. See "Entierros (1853–59)," AHSSA, BP-EA-HP, bk. 11. The information on Alamán's funeral is in García Cubas (1986), 382.

121 Abadiano (1878), 32. Carpena had served on the board since at least 1844 and had made generous donations throughout the 1840s and 1850s to sustain the asylum (see Prieto, Memorias, 2:141). Osores's contributions apparently came in the early 1840s. AGN, Gobernación, Tramo 1, leg. 130 (1844), exp. 4–5.

122 Of these, 2,160 pesos were its regular annual ecclesiastical funding. 1804 report. For 1856 figures, see Alfaro (1906), 19.

123 On the growth of the country versus the city, see Arrom (1985), 285, table D.1.

124 See, especially, AGN, Gobernación, Tramo 1, leg. 130 (1841), exp. 4; (1833), exps. 2–3.

125 "Mendigos," Eco del Comercio, July 1, 1848, 4.

126 Decree of August 9, 1830, in Dublán and Lozano, no. 858, 2:278.

127 The Recogimiento had served as a barracks in 1829 and had closed since at least 1835. The reply to the other requests was "We will pick them up when we are paid what we are owed." AGN, Gobernación, Tramo 1, leg. 130 (1841), exp. 1.

128 Decree of Gov. Miguel M. de Azcárate, December 18, 1851, in Castillo Velasco (1874), 247. See also the decree of May 6, 1850, in Dublán and Lozano, no. 3435, 5:704–5.

129 "Proyecto de reglamento para la Casa de Asilo de Pobres Mendigos" (1852): 82–88.

130 Only some 20 percent were convicted. Shaw (1975), 280–93; Perez Toledo (1993). See also Arrom (1989) and Serrano Ortega (1996).

131 Letter from Olvera, April 25, 1828, in AHCM, Vagos, vol. 4151, exp. 5.

132 Aside from convicted vagrants and domestic servants (who would presumably vote as directed by their masters), male paupers could vote until they were disenfranchised in the 1836 Bases Constitucionales. The city council members were buffered from reliance on the popular vote, however, by a system of indirect elections. See Legislación electoral (1973), 34, 44; Tena Ramírez (1973), 207–8; Shaw (1975), 319–22; and Warren (1996a), 41.

133 In addition, the ayuntamiento was asked to absorb the expenses of the tribunal, and staffing it added to the aldermen's work load. Still, the required police force and staff were already in place. See Arrom (1988a).

134 AHCM, Beneficencia y Asilos, vol. 416, exp. 2 (1855), f. 243.

135 In discussing the decree of December 1851, ordering the confinement of beggars,

Castillo Velasco explained that it could not be carried out because the Asilo had been closed by the city council (1874), 247. It apparently still existed in October 1857, when Doña Teresa Carrero was temporarily placed there during her ecclesiastical divorce proceedings. AGN, Bienes Nacionales, leg. 76, exp. 39. Marcos Arróniz also mentions a Casa de Asilo (1858), 117.

136 A Casa de Asilo de Mendigos, which appears in city council records from 1863 to 1868, may have been a new institution. See AHCM, Beneficencia y Asilos, vol. 416, exps. 4, 7 (1863); 6 (1868). By 1871 the governor of the D.F. was proposing the establishment of yet another asylum, the Casa de Corrección de Adolescentes y Asilo de Mendigos, because the city was "urgently in need of . . . a reformatory for adolescents and an asylum for the destitute elderly" (exp. 8, f. 1).

137 In 1852 this society ran twenty schools with four thousand students. See González Navarro (1985), 104. A similar organization was proposed by José María Luis Mora in 1834. Velasco Ceballos (1938), 12.

138 Peza (1881), 149–60.

139 "Proyecto de Reglamento" (1852), 83. An 1866 report from the Junta de Caridad of Guadalajara, which opened an asylum for beggars during the Second Empire, similarly laments that "very few of these truly needy wretches came" to the asylum. AHCM, Consejo General de Beneficencia, vol. 418 (1866), exp. 111, f. 5.

7 La Reforma, Reorganization, and Crisis, 1856–1863

1 See, for example, González Navarro (1985), chap. 1, esp. 40–54; and López Figueroa (1993), esp. 7–9, 50–65.

2 García Icazbalceta (1907), 82.

3 Salado Alvarez (1917), i–v.

4 Cuevas (1967), 755.

5 Velasco Ceballos (1935), 103–4.

6 Macedo (1900–1904), 715–16.

7 González (1974), 377–80; Muriel (1956–60), 2:292–306.

8 See the law of June 25, 1856, and the reglamento of July 30, 1856, in Labastida (1893), 3–13.

9 Alfaro says that the thirteen *fincas* were worth 811,418 pesos before the Laws of Disentailment went into effect (1906), 19. Bazant cites the same figures (1971), 102.

10 Preamble to the law of June 25, 1856, in Labastida (1893), 3.

11 Bazant (1971), 53–55, 99.

12 Ibid., 102; Cossío (1917), 29. Cossío (1917, 29–30) and Alvarez Amezquita et al. (1960, 3:412) refer to a petition of June 28, 1856, by some of the Poor House tenants, who refused to buy its property and ceded their rights to Dr. Agustín Carpena, the treasurer of the Poor House board, so that he could protect the asylum's assets. I have found no evidence, however, that Carpena bought these properties in his own name. Peza mentions only that Carpena did much to protect the Poor House during those difficult times (1881), 68.

13 García Icazbalceta (1907), 230–31; Cossío (1917), 29; Alvarez Amezquita et al. (1960),

3:411. Although Cossío and Alvarez Amezquita refer to the Frenchmen as Deschamps, I have followed García Icazbalceta's nomenclature since his account was closer in time to the events.

14 Blackmore's contract called for monthly payments of 107.7 pesos (to amortize a debt of 8,000 pesos), which he claimed to have made regularly. See AHSSA, BP-EA-HP, leg. 2, exp. 24 (October 29, 1861); leg. 3, exp. 19 (July 5, 1861); leg. 4, exp. 11 (May 8, 1862). Cossío claims, without providing further details, that "later" several mortgages were canceled by the Secretaría de Relaciones (1917), 29.

15 Bazant (1971), 136–38.

16 Velasco Ceballos (1943), 53.

17 Bazant (1971), 114.

18 García Icazbalceta (1907), 230–31. As late as June 1868 José María Gómez Eguiarte, the administrator of the Poor House from at least 1829 until 1861, still owed 1,500 pesos at 6 percent interest. AHCM, Beneficencia, vol. 415, exp. 11, f. 3.

19 Salado Alvarez (1917), iii.

20 "Extracto de papeletas diarias" AHSSA, BP-EA-HP, leg. 1, exp. 1. (1859).

21 Ibid.

22 Ibid., exps. 1 (1859) and 4 (1860).

23 "Extracto de papeletas diarias" (1859), AHSSA, BP-EA-HP, exps. 1 (1859) and 4 (1860).

24 AHCM, Beneficencia y Asilos, vol. 416, exp. 3 (November 15, 1859), f. 4.

25 Velasco Ceballos (1934), 108.

26 Bazant (1971), 167–81. The funds of ecclesiastical welfare institutions were also excluded according to clarifications of later laws. See the decrees of February 5 and April 15, 1861, in Dublán and Lozano, no. 5198, 9:55; no. 5312, 9:158.

27 Decree of February 28, 1861, in ibid., no. 5257, 9:101–3, published on March 2, 1861. See also the secularization decree of February 2, 1861 (no. 5188, 9:32–33), and attempts to protect welfare institutions on March 13, 1861 (no. 5270, 9:113), March 14, 1861 (no. 5272, 9:114–15), and January 30, 1862 (no. 5549, 9:376–77).

28 These were the Poor House, the Tecpam de Santiago, the Casa de Corrección, the Casa de Niños Expósitos, five hospitals (San Andrés, San Juan de Dios, San Pablo, San Hipólito, and Divino Salvador), and two prisons (Belén and Diputación), which were studied by García Icazbalceta sixteen months later (1907).

29 Art. 17 of the February 28, 1861, decree did, however, charge the city council with remaining "vigilant of the good order and policía of all the houses of charity." Dublán and Lozano, no. 5257, 9:103.

30 The duties of the General Office of Public Beneficence were spelled out in a reglamento published on May 5, 1861. Dublán and Lozano, no. 5343, 9:191–98.

31 García Icazbalceta (1907), 93–95.

32 The additional employees, who earned lower salaries, were a collector of funds, four scribes, and a portero. Decree of February 28, 1861, in Dublán and Lozano, no. 5257, 9:101, arts. 3–4.

33 The 1877 Dirección had only six staff members, compared to twelve in the 1861 office. The highest paid employees in 1877 were the secretary and treasurer, who each earned only 1,200 pesos. The 1877 budget was only 3,960 pesos, compared to 18,600 in 1861. See Abadiano (1878), iv.

34 García Icazbalceta (1907), 101. He favored a central office whose employees did not have tenure and who could be fired for incompetence.

35 Cited in Valadés (1976), 121.

36 Bazant (1971), 209.

37 Decree of July 7, 1862, in Dublán and Lozano, no. 5677, 9:486–87.

38 Decree of August 30, 1862, in ibid., no. 5726, 9:523; Bazant (1971), 209–11.

39 "Informe emitido por el Sr. Abogado Defensor de los fondos de Beneficencia Pública," June 12, 1861, AHSSA, BP-EA-HP, leg. 2, exp. 2.

40 García Icazbalceta lists unpaid interest of 65,786 pesos as of the end of 1858 and another 59,197 accrued at 3 percent from 1859 to 1863 (1907), 232.

41 For 1856 see table 23; for 1861, see "Estado que manifiesta . . . ," AHSSA, BP-EA-HP, leg. 1, exp. 16 (April 31, 1861).

42 Alvarez Amezquita et al. (1960), 3:434–35.

43 Velasco Ceballos (1934), 103–8.

44 AHSSA, BP-EA-HP, leg. 3, exp. 44 (1861), leg. 4, exp. 6 (1862); García Icazbalceta (1907), 83–84, 225. In June 1867, when he returned to power, President Juárez thus found it necessary to prohibit for a second time the many lotteries, "which daily take place in the capital." Decrees of June 28, 1867, and February 29, 1868, in Dublán and Lozano, no. 6280, 10:279.

45 AHSSA, BP-EA-HP, leg. 2, exps. 10, 15, 20 (September 1861); leg. 3, exps. 18, 20, and 27 (October–November 1861).

46 "Presupuesto" (1861) and "Papeletas diarias" (1862), AHSSA, BP-EA-HP, leg. 2, exp. 21, f. 2; leg. 4, exp. 2.

47 Ibid., leg. 3, exp. 17 (November 18, 1861); leg. 2, exp. 20 (September 1861); leg. 3, exp. 14, fourth pamphlet (December 26, 1861).

48 Bazant (1971), 463.

49 "Noticia de las cantidades que debe el Hospicio de Pobres de Mégico" (January 5, 1863), AHSSA, BP-EA-HP, leg. 4, exp. 18, f. 2.

50 A footnote to García Icazbalceta's report states that the Poor House had lost 63 percent of its original edifice: 38,075 of the original 60,565 square meters (1907), 8.

51 See the description in ibid., 117–20; and Tomás Gardida's "Memoria" (December 31, 1863), AHCM, Hospicio de Pobres, vol. 2295, exp. 23.

52 García Icazbalceta (1907), 227.

53 The expenditures for the month of August 1863, for example, were 2,083 pesos. García Icazbalceta (1907), 218. For December 1861 they were 1,843 pesos. "Cuenta de entrada y salida" (December 1861), AHSSA, BP-EA-HP, leg. 3, exp. 38.

54 *Diccionario Porrúa* (1964), 111.

55 For a full transcription of Arriaga's report, see the appendix to Arrom (1996b), 47–53.

56 Marginal note of June 18, 1861, on Arriaga's report, AHSSA, BP-EA-HP, leg. 2, exp. 2, ff. 1–2.

57 López Figueroa (1993), 9.

58 Juan N. del Valle also referred to the *juntas de caridad* that governed the capital's welfare establishments in 1861, even though they had occasionally been referred to as *juntas de beneficencia* in earlier decades, as in the document naming José Ramón

Malo to the Poor House board on April 27, 1847. AGN, Gobernación, Tramo 1, leg. 130, exp. 9.

59 Decrees of February 28, 1861, and August 20, 1862, in Dublán and Lozano, no. 5257, 9:101–3; no. 5726, 9:525.

60 Velasco Ceballos (1934), 108.

61 AHSSA, BP-EA-HP, leg. 2, exp. 5 (July 8, 1861).

62 Ibid., leg. 4, exp. 15 (October 21, 1861).

63 "Informe" (May 31, 1861) ibid., leg. 1, exp. 21, ff. 1, 5.

64 "Cuenta de entrada y salida" (December 1861), ibid., leg. 3, exp. 38, f. 3v.

65 This conclusion is in keeping with arguments made during the debates of the 1857 Constitutional Convention, where anticlerical liberals opposed freedom of religion because they saw the Catholic Church as an important force for inculcating morality and maintaining order. See Sinkin (1973), 7.

66 "Presupuesto" (June 1861), AHSSA, BP-EA-HP, leg. 1, exp. 21, f. 2.

67 Letter of November 18, 1861, in ibid., leg. 3, exp. 3.

68 Ibid., exp. 1 (November 22, 1861). See also leg. 3, exp. 35 (December 18, 1861).

69 Petition of October 21, 1861, ibid., leg. 2, exp. 23. See also petition from the blind soldier Bartolo Herrera and his 11-year-old stepson, in leg. 3, exp. 6 (October 31, 1861).

70 See also the admission of the children related to Colonel Novoa on November 22, 1861, in ibid., exp. 9.

71 Ibid., exp. 30 (December 4, 1861).

72 Letter of November 21, 1861, in ibid., exp. 7. See also exps. 11 and 30 (November 22 and December 4, 1861).

73 Ibid., exp. 13 (November 27, 1861).

74 Ibid., exp. 2 (November 21, 1861), f. 2.

75 Ibid., ff. 6–9.

76 Ibid., leg. 2, exp. 14 (August 19, 1861).

77 Correspondence of September 30, 1861, in ibid., exp. 18.

78 Ibid., leg. 3, exp. 40 (December 20, 1861).

79 The customary fees were waived in order to expedite the adoption. Note that there are some discrepancies between the girl's story and that of the Poor House staff. Ibid., exp. 15 (October 6 to November 28, 1861).

80 Caballero did consider his family eligible for free funeral services, however. See ibid., exp. 14 (December 5, 1861).

81 The Liberals apparently intended to add a shoemaking workshop as well, since the Defensor de los Fondos de Beneficencia authorized 6 pesos per month as salary for a *maestro de zapatería*. "Presupuesto" (June 1861), ibid., leg. 1, exp. 21, f. 1 verso. However, no such master appears in detailed financial records from September 1861 to January 1862 (leg. 3, exp. 37), in Gardida's "Memoria" of December 31, 1863 (AHCM, Hospicio de Pobres, vol. 2295, exp. 23), or in García Icazbalceta's 1864 report (1907), 97.

82 AHSSA, BP-EA-HP, leg. 3, exp. 37, ff. 4–4v.

83 Ibid., exp. 38, ff. 6–6v. See also leg. 4, exp. 7 (January–February 1862).

84 The *Diccionario Porrúa* considers Castañeda a Conservative (1964, 284), but he evidently cooperated with the Juárez regime.

85 Officers of the Junta Directiva (November 1861), AHSSA, BP-EA-HP, leg. 1, exp. 9.84.

86 See Galván Rivera (1829), 105; and 1848 census, AHCM, Padrones, vol. 3409, cuartel menor 30, manzana 230.

87 "Sobre destitución del administrador por la renta fraudulenta de las casas. . . ," AHSSA, BP-EA-HP, leg. 1, exp. 9; and AHCM, Hospicio de Pobres, vol. 2295, exp. 27 (1863).

88 Gómez Eguiarte's illness had begun by September 1861 and became acute later that fall. See numerous documents in AHSSA, BP-EA-HP, leg. 2, exp. 20 ff.; and leg. 3, signed by the assistant administrator, J. G. Aragón, because of the former's sickness.

89 See Peza's praise of Larrañaga's heroic efforts to save the asylum (1881), 70; and Larrañaga's report of August 29, 1863 in AHCM, Hospicio de Pobres, vol. 2295, exp. 26, f. 2.

90 García Icazbalceta (1907), 82.

91 A maternity hospital (authorized in a decree of November 9, 1861) apparently did open briefly, but the school (proposed in a decree of April 15, 1861) did not. See Peza (1881), 97–99; Rivera Cambas (1880–83), 2:280–82; and Velasco Ceballos (1943), 53.

8 Recovery during the Second Empire, 1863–1867

1 For a treatment of Maximilian's legislative accomplishments, see Barroso Díaz (1981a).

2 González (1974), 380.

3 Velasco Ceballos (1935), 97.

4 See, for example, Corti (1929). An exception is Barroso Díaz's unpublished law thesis (1981b), 59–77. Meyer also provides a brief, positive assessment of the imperial policies (1975), 62.

5 Erika Pani does note the Second Empire's attempts to incorporate women into public life (1995), esp. 431.

6 Alessio Robles (1944), 38. The *Diccionario Porrúa* (1964) and other liberal works downplay his conservatism and present him merely as a devoutly Catholic bibliophile.

7 García Icazbalceta (1907), 140. The preface (vii–3) explains that the order to begin the investigation, signed by the prefecto político, dates from July 9, 1863. The report was published posthumously.

8 Gardida's "Memoria" (December 31, 1863), AHCM, Hospicio de Pobres, vol. 2295, exp. 23.

9 See list of employees in "Presupuesto general" (June 1861), AHSSA, BP-EA-HP, leg. 1, exp. 21, f. 1. Borja was listed as a 28-year-old widowed employee in 1848 (AHCM, Padrones, vol. 3409, cuartel menor 30, manzana 230). She was still in the Poor House, among the ancianas stricken with typhoid, in 1867–68. AHCM, Hospicio de Pobres, vol. 2295, exp. 52, f. 13.

10 For more details, see "Presupuesto" (June 1861), AHSSA, leg. 1, exp. 21, f. 1 verso.

Arauz had been the embroidery teacher for at least fifteen years. See 1848 census, AHCM, Padrones, vol. 3409, cuartel menor 30, manzana 230.

11 He was probably the same D. Nicolás Triuleque whose mother received free funeral attendants in 1861. He earned a salary of 320 pesos that year. "Presupuesto" (June 1861), AHSSA, BP-EA-HP, leg. 1, exp. 21, f. 1.

12 Two 1861 documents corroborate this charge by describing an incident of a girl speaking to her lover from a balcony and by referring to other meetings between lovers. AHSSA, BP-EA-HP, leg. 3, exp. 37, f. 61 verso; leg. 3, exp. 24.

13 In addition to Gardida's description of the lack of discipline among the elderly, see also García Icazbalceta, who claimed that the elderly begged during their leaves from the asylum but were never punished (1907), 15–16. Republican documents also suggest that they drank alcoholic beverages since pulque appears regularly in lists of purchased supplies such as "Presupuesto" (June 1861), AHSSA, BP-EA-HP, leg. 1, exp. 21.

14 Blum similarly concluded that "the operative model for the Hospicio was that of a patron-client household" and also found this pattern in the Foundling Home (1998), 126.

15 García Icazbalceta (1907), 24, 127–30, 141.

16 Ibid., 120–44.

17 Ibid., 120, 130–31.

18 The military hospital was moved to the building that housed the Casa de Correción. This reformatory was combined with the Tecpam de Santiago on September 7, 1863. García Icazbalceta (1907), 213; AHCM, Hospicio de Pobres, vol. 2295, exp. 26, ff. 2–4.

19 Gardida's "Memoria" (December 31, 1863), AHCM, Hospicio de Pobres, vol. 2295, exp. 23, f. 25.

20 García Cubas (1904), 39–43; González (1974), 406–10.

21 García Icazbalceta (1907), 113–14. See also Martínez de la Torre (1875).

22 In addition, each nun was to receive a one-time sum of 25 pesos to cover moving expenses. See Article 9 of the contract between the city council and the Society of St. Vincent de Paul, September 21, 1863, in Gardida, "Memoria" (December 31, 1863), AHCM, Hospicio de Pobres, vol. 2295, exp. 23, ff. 27–30, appendix.

23 Compare García Icazbalceta (1907), 212, 222; "Presupuesto" (June 1861) AHSSA, BP-EA-HP, leg. 1, exp. 21; and ibid., leg. 3, exp. 37. It is unclear exactly which employees were let go. It appears that the administrator, rectora, vice rectora, and girls' teacher were dismissed. Although some of these employees (including the rectora, vice rectora, and girls' teacher) had been elderly inmates, they nonetheless drew salaries. It is possible that there was a male administrator above the sisters, as García Icazbalceta proposed as the model for all welfare institutions. If so, however, he does not appear in the surviving Poor House records of the imperial period, which are signed by the Superiora Melchora Yriarte. Moreover, if García Icazbalceta's wage information is correct, his monthly salary cannot have been as high as the 83.3 pesos earned by the previous administrator (1907), 112–13.

24 Appendix to Gardida's "Memoria" (December 31, 1863), AHCM, Hospicio de Pobres, vol. 2295, exp. 23, art. 3a.

25 Rivera Cambas incorrectly wrote that the sisters left in 1866 (1880–83), 1:245. Internal Poor House documents show that, on the contrary, they were firmly in command
until September 17, 1867, when the superiora, Melchora Yriarte, submitted a letter
of resignation. AHCM, Hospicio de Pobres, vol. 2295, exp. 42. The sisters had an old
connection to the Poor House since they had been temporarily lodged there in 1846,
soon after they arrived in Mexico from France. AGN, Gobernación, Tramo 1, leg. 130
(1846), exp. 1.

26 Peza (1881), 16. They were already in charge of the Hospital de San Pablo. Abadiano
(1878), 38.

27 Circular of May 28, 1861, in Labastida (1893), 366. See also the decree of February 19,
1861, on page 361.

28 Decree of February 26, 1863, cited in González (1974), 408.

29 García Icazbalceta (1907), 182.

30 They had also refurbished the Department for Curing Eyes, which had been totally
separate from the Poor House since its founding. See "Presupuesto" (June 1861)
AHSSA, BP-EA-HP, leg. 1, exp. 21. The nuns agreed to nurse its few patients. Gardida,
"Memoria" (December 31, 1863), AHCM, Hospicio de Pobres, vol. 2295, exp. 23.

31 "Informe" (March 1, 1869), AHCM, Hospicio de Pobres, vol. 2295, exp. 65, f. 26.

32 See ibid., exp. 30 (1865); and AHCM, Actas del Consejo General de Beneficencia,
vol. 422, exp. 11 (March 13, 1866). The Poor House never regained its entire former
building, not only because much of it had been sold but because the street of Providencia now intersected it.

33 García Icazbalceta (1907), 83–84, 225–27.

34 Ibid., 214, 231–32. Note that this figure is far lower than Alfaro's estimate of 811,418
pesos (1906, 19), which Bazant rightly questioned (1971, 102). García Icazbalceta
does not explain the terms on which the Regency agreed to repay its debt to the Poor
House, but interest rates listed in his appendix range from 3 to 6 percent (1907),
230–33.

35 García Icazbalceta (1907), 21; Valle (1864), 423.

36 García Icazbalceta (1907), 114.

37 Monthly expenses had leveled off to 3,625 pesos by August of 1865. AHCM, Actas del
Consejo General de Beneficencia, vol. 422, exp. 54.

38 See García Icazbalceta (1907), 214; and Valle (1864), 423, who gives a similarly positive assessment of the Poor House's financial situation in 1864.

39 García Icazbalceta (1907), 137–38.

40 Valle (1964), 379.

41 García Icazbalceta (1907), 137–38, 212–23.

42 Letter from the Prefecto del Valle to the Consejo General de Beneficencia, February 10, 1866, in AHCM, Consejo General de Beneficencia, vol. 420, exp. 113.

43 See correspondence of June 20, August 20–21, and August 28, 1866, in ibid., vol. 421,
exp. 174. The order referred to may have been that of February 24, 1866.

44 Gardida, "Memoria" (December 31, 1863), AHCM, Hospicio de Pobres, vol. 2295,
exp. 23, f. 22.

45 Ibid., vol. 2295, exp. 29. The child was sent to the Poor House by order of the municipal prefect.

46 Ibid., exp. 26, ff. 2–4.

47 Ibid., exp. 43.

48 See Tanck Estrada (1977), 197. Note that neither the opening of the Reformatory for Juvenile Delinquents in 1842 nor of a vocational school for boys in 1856–57 had reduced the proportion of boys in the Poor House.

49 On staff shaping the nature of U.S. asylums, see Porter (1993).

50 García Cubas (1986), 496, 498.

51 "Informe de la Comisión de Vigilancia del Hospicio de Pobres," October 1, 1865, AHCM, Consejo General de Beneficencia, vol. 418, exp. 47.

52 Preamble to decree of April 10, 1865, *Diario del Imperio*, April 10, 1865: 341; Barroso Díaz (1981a), 63–64.

53 In addition to the internal records of the Poor House and of the Consejo General de Beneficencia, see Barroso Díaz (1981a), 545; and Martin (1914), 183.

54 Bazant (1971), 271–72.

55 *Diario del Imperio*, April 10, 1865: 341–42.

56 Indeed, Justo Sierra labeled Maximilian's Indian policies socialist. Cited in Barroso Díaz (1981b), 97. The junta mostly catered to Indians, as can be seen in documents in the AGN, Ramo de la Junta Protectora de las Clases Menesterosas. On Maximilian's Indian policies, see, for example, González y González (1965), 102–10; and Pani (1998).

57 *Diario del Imperio*, 2d supplement to no. 83 (April 10, 1865), 342.

58 It also specified that the vice president of the council would be the Minister of Gobernación and that the emperor himself would appoint all members. "Reglamento Interior del Consejo General de Beneficencia," Orizaba, May 11, 1865, in *ibid.*

59 *Diario del Imperio*, June 20, 1866, 1. It was moving in this direction by June 7, 1865. Barroso Díaz (1981b), 73.

60 *Diario del Imperio*, April 10, 1865, 342–43.

61 These boards were already in place by the end of June 1865. The nine Mexico City institutions with such boards were the Poor House, Casa de Maternidad, Casa de Niños Expósitos, Tecpam, and the hospitals of San Andrés, San Juan de Dios, San Pablo, Hombres Dementes, and Mujeres Dementes. AHCM, Actas del Consejo General de Beneficencia (June 29, 1865), vol. 422, exp. 4.

62 Ibid., exp. 2 (May 11, 1865).

63 Decree of June 20, 1866, in *Diario del Imperio*, June 20, 1866, 1.

64 The Maternity Hospital was originally located next to the Poor House in a section of its former building, but it later moved to larger quarters. Orozco y Berra (1867), 201–2; Alvarez Amezquita et al. (1960), 3:450–51; Peza (1881), 22–23.

65 Abadiano noted that the empress gave the Maternity Hospital special protection, even sending it obstetrical equipment after she returned to Europe (1878), 20–21.

66 Rivera Cambas (1880–83), 2:280–82.

67 Richard Packenham noted the absence of a system of home relief in his report on the Mexican poor in 1834. See Gilmore (1957), 219. By mid century the Mexican Society of St. Vincent de Paul, which García Icazbalceta headed, may also have provided home relief as it did in Europe. See Lis (1986), esp. 129–30, 207.

68 Decree of April 1866, quoted in Gonzalez Navarro (1985), 103.

69 *Diario del Imperio*, April 10, 1865, 342.

70 *Memoria* (1867), 25.

71 Ibid. The Maundy Thursday ceremony is described in Archbishop Labastida's speech, included on p. 10.

72 This report suggests that the ladies' board may have met separately from the men's. "Informe que rinden las señoras de la Comisión de Vigilancia del hospital de San Pablo," Aug. 3, 1865, AHCM, Consejo General de Beneficencia, vol. 418, exp. 40. Unfortunately, there is no equivalent information on the ladies of the Poor House board.

73 See, for example, *Estracto* (1865); and *Obras* (1865).

74 In addition to the ladies' board established for the Poor House in 1828 there was one for the Casa de Cuna, one for the Hospital del Divino Salvador, and another to teach female prisoners of the Acordada how to read and write. See Arrom (1985), 14–26, 38–52, 166–71, 259–68.

75 Carlota, "Informe del Consejo General de Beneficencia," *Diario del Imperio*, April 10, 1866, 368, in AGN, Gobernación, vol. 1884. On the asylums of Querétaro and Guadalajara, see the July 1865 reports of those consejos, in AHCM, Consejo General de Beneficencia, vol. 418, exps. 38, 111.

76 Letter of April 15, 1866, to S.M. la Emperatriz, *Diario del Imperio*, April 16, 1866.

77 Maximilian's decree of June 20, 1866, also granted municipal hospitals revenues from prohibited games. *Diario del Imperio*, June 20, 1866.

78 The other beneficiaries were the Tecpam (3,000 pesos); the Hospital of Guanajuato (900); various welfare institutions of Guadalajara (5,343); the Hospital de San Roque in Puebla (564); and the hospitals of Zacatecas (2,400), Cuernavaca (140), Irapuato (120), Orizaba (500), and Toluca (300). See Carlota's "Informe," *Diario del Imperio*, April 10, 1866, 368.

79 See art. 17 of 1866 bylaws; and Barroso Díaz (1981b), 75. The city council assigned the Poor House 625 pesos per month from fines on prohibited games (minutes of September 26 and October 10, 1865, AHCM, Actas del Consejo General de Beneficencia, vol. 422, actas 6, 7. After May 1866 it also assigned the Poor House part of the proceeds from Maximilian's rifas de beneficencia.

80 P. F. Martin (1914), 179.

81 AHCM, Actas del Consejo General de Beneficencia, vol. 422, exp. 11; AHCM, Consejo General de Beneficencia, vol. 420, exp. 119.

82 A short early draft, dating from 1865, gave the direct supervisory role to the Prefecto Político. See "Reglamento interior del hospicio que designa las obligaciones de los Empleados y Profesores," AHSSA, BP-EA-HP, leg. 6, exp. 1.

83 See documents from May and November of 1861 in ibid., leg. 3, exp. 40; and leg. 1, exp. 21, f. 7. In a letter of October 7, 1865, José María Godoy referred to the Escuela de niños del Hospicio. *AHCM*, Consejo General de Beneficencia, vol. 418, exp. 47.

84 The report is in AHCM, Actas de Consejo General de Beneficencia, vol. 422, acta 2.

85 See Carlota's "Informe" *Diario del Imperio*, April 10, 1866, 368.

86 Despite the bylaws, the state's attempt to limit the authority of pauper parents in 1866 and 1871 was unsuccessful. See Blum (1998), 204–6, 222–23.

87 Conversations with Ann Blum helped me develop this idea. See also her discussion in (1998), 119-20.

88 AHSSA, BP-EA-HP, leg. 4, exp. 15 (October 21, 1861).

89 The plan proposed on January 16, 1865, to manufacture some of the army's uniforms in the Poor House (as well as the Tecpam and Carcel de la Ciudad), apparently never materialized. AHCM, Hospicio de Pobres, vol. 2295, exp. 33.

90 The sisters took half the profits for the Poor House and then deducted the cost of materials from the girls' portion. Ibid., exp. 43, f. 2.

91 AHCM, Actas del Consejo General de Beneficencia, vol. 422, exp. 2 (May 11, 1865).

92 AHCM, Hospicio de Pobres, vol. 2295, exp. 43 (Oct. 26, 1867).

93 See AHCM, Actas del Consejo General de Beneficencia, vol. 422, exps. 12-14; and AHCM, Consejo General de Beneficencia, vol. 421, exp. 174.

94 The twenty-one boys under 8 years of age were to be transferred from the Tecpam. Decree of June 22, 1866, in ibid., vol. 421, exp. 174.

95 Decree of July 3, 1866, in AHCM, Hospicio de Pobres, vol. 2295, exp. 36.

96 In August of 1865 the asylum must have housed at least 512 inmates since the mother superior requested shoes for 512 people at 6 reales per pair. AHCM, Consejo General de Beneficencia, vol. 418, exp. 47.

97 Memo of October 26, 1867, in AHCM, Hospicio de Pobres, vol. 2295, exp. 43, f. 2v.

98 Its expenses exceeded its revenues by 1,268 pesos in July 1866. Ibid., exp. 35, f. 6. Poor House expenditures apparently increased from January to July, for a report sent by the Prefecto del Valle to the Consejo on February 10, 1866, lists the January expenses as only 3,300 pesos. AHCM, Consejo General de Beneficencia, vol. 420, exp. 113.

99 AHCM, Hospicio de Pobres, vol. 2295, exp. 43, f. 2. This calculation is based on the profit of 34 and 39 pesos for August and September 1867 after deducting the cost of materials and setting aside a portion for the girls.

100 See art. 17 of 1866 bylaws. The estimate of earnings from funerals is based on García Icazbalceta (1907), 84.

101 These records are in the archive of the city council, which recovered jurisdiction over the asylum in 1867. AHCM, Consejo General de Beneficencia, vol. 420, exp. 137.

102 Carlota's "Informe," *Diario del Imperio,* April 10, 1866, 368.

103 Maximiliano (1865), 8; decree of February 28, 1861, in Dublán and Lozano, no. 5257, 9:101-3.

104 AHCM, Actas del Consejo General de Beneficencia, vol. 422, exp. 1 (April 19, 1865). On the emperor's plan to encourage private philanthropy by bestowing medals on major donors, see Barroso Díaz (1981b), 71-72.

105 Sor María Ville resigned because she did not receive permission from her superior. See Carlota's "Informe," *Diario del Imperio,* April 10, 1866, 368; and AGN, Gobernación, vol. 1884, exps. 2-1, 2-2, 2-4.

9 The Liberals Return, 1867–1871

1 See the decrees of March 30 and October 31, 1868, in Dublán and Lozano, no. 6306, 10:293–94, and no. 6441, 10:441–42; and Bazant (1971), 276–81.

2 Decree of February 29, 1868, in Dublán and Lozano, no. 6280, 10:279. A decree of June 28, 1867, referred to in the later decree, had already abolished the lotteries, but those whose profits were applied to establishments of beneficence and public education were allowed to continue from July until February while municipal funding was regularized.

3 Decrees of July 10 and July 14, 1871, in Dublán and Lozano, nos. 6912, 6914, 10:531–34.

4 The government also granted war widows and orphans pensions equivalent to half the soldier's salary. Decree of December 29, 1871, in ibid., no. 6982, 10:728.

5 The December 2, 1867, Law of Public Instruction was revised on May 15, 1869. Ibid., no. 6182, 10:193–205; Monroy (1974), 663–64, 667.

6 The new secondary schools included the Normal School for Teaching the Deaf-Mute (1867), the National Preparatory School (1868), the Secondary School for Girls (1869), and an Escuela de Artes y Oficios for Women (1871). With these initiatives President Juárez finally implemented the decrees of President Comonfort's first Liberal administration in 1856 and 1857. See Dublán and Lozano, nos. 4675, 4680, 4865, 4962, 4931, vol. 8. The School for the Blind opened in 1871. Peza (1881), 87.

7 Decree of December 30, 1871, in Dublán and Lozano, no. 6983, 10:731. See also the law of October 31, 1868, which exempted the funds of Instrucción Pública y Beneficencia from certain taxes. Velasco Ceballos (1943), 54.

8 The exact nature of the dispute is not spelled out in the Poor House documents, but several oblique references support this theory. I am indebted to Ann Blum for helping me unravel this puzzle. See also Blum (1998), 104; AHCM, Hospicio de Pobres, vol. 2295, exp. 42 (September 2–28, 1867); and AHCM, Empleados-Hospicio, vol. 918, exp. 1.

9 AHCM, Hospicio de Pobres, vol. 2295, exp. 42, ff. 1–2; AHCM, Empleados-Hospicio, vol. 918, exps. 1, 3.

10 The highest-paid woman in 1861 was the rectora, who earned 258 pesos a year. The assistant administrator earned 500. See table 25.

11 "Proposiciones de la Comisión del Hospicio sobre arreglo de este establecimiento" (January 7, 1868), AHCM, Hospicio de Pobres, vol. 2295, exp. 55.

12 "El C. Gobernador llama la atención . . ." (March 1, 1869), ibid., exp. 65, f. 26.

13 It is unclear who replaced Aguilar after he died in the typhoid epidemic. By May 1868 the city council had received two applications for his vacant position (AHCM, Empleados-Hospicio, vol. 918, exps. 4, 5). This second administrator was fired on January 9, 1869, and was immediately replaced by a Señor Márquez (AHCM, Hospicio de Pobres, vol. 2295, exp. 65). Soon thereafter Luciana Arrázola de Baz took the position. She resigned in December 1869 when Juana Rodríguez de Herrera took the position of director of the girls' department and the post of administrator simul-

taneously (see AHCM, Empleados-Hospicio, vol. 918, exp. 8; and AHCM, Hospicio de Pobres, vol. 2295, exp. 113, f. 4).

14 The Comisión del Hospicio was held in quick succession by the aldermen Ignacio Baz, Juan Abadiano, Aniceto Ortega, and Bustamante. The latter, who rarely visited the asylum because of his bad health, was replaced with yet another alderman in the summer of 1870. AHCM, Hospicio de Pobres, vol. 2295, exps. 65, 87, and 99.

15 The first director, Doña Rosa Espinosa, served during the five months from October 1867 to March 1868. She was replaced by Doña Juana Rodríguez de Herrera, who resigned three months later, on June 9, because she had to attend to "extremely grave family business" in Chihuahua. Both her successors were fired in quick succession: Doña Merced Lizarraga by November 24, 1868, and Doña María Lascuráin vda. de Ortiz Yzquierdo on January 9, 1869. The new director, Doña Dolores Estrada, must not have lasted long, either, for when Rodríguez returned in the fall of 1869 she took over from Doña Luciana Arrázola de Baz. See ibid., exps. 42, 65; AHCM, Empleados-Hospicio, vol. 918, exps. 7, 8, 9.

16 Reports from the Board of Health (May 11, 1868, ff. 1–6v) and the Poor House doctor (May 22, 1868, ff. 7–11), AHCM, Hospicio de Pobres, vol. 2295, exp. 52. The Board of Health put the inmate population at between seven and eight hundred (f. 2); the doctor put it at eight hundred (f. 8v).

17 Ibid. (May 11–28, 1868).

18 Report of the Comisión del Hospicio, Jan. 7, 1868, ibid., exp. 55, f. 1. The committee had been studying the problems in the Poor House since at least October 12, 1867. Ibid., exp. 43, ff. 1–2.

19 Among the twenty-six girls aged 20 to 24, 57 percent had lost both parents and the rest had lost one; all ten girls over age 25 had lost both parents. Report of Poor House administrator, November 6, 1867, ibid., exp. 43.

20 Reports from Abadiano and the Poor House doctor, May 22 and May 28, 1868, ibid., exp. 52.

21 In its meeting on January 7, 1868, the city council decided to postpone action on the committee's recommendations until it received a report from a Comisión de Beneficencia y Hospicios, which was studying all the welfare institutions in the capital. I have been unable to locate this report. Ibid., exp. 55, f. 3.

22 In early 1869 Señora Juárez, as president of the Junta de Protección del Hospicio, invited Doña Juana Rodríguez to take charge of the asylum. AHCM, Hospicio-Empleos, vol. 918, exp. 8.

23 "Reglamento para el Hospicio de Pobres," *La Gaceta de Policía*, October 11, 1868, 1–3.

24 A chaplain was on the payroll as late as 1869, when he was fired as part of Governor Baz's reforms. AHCM, Hospicio de Pobres, vol. 2295, exp. 65, f. 27v.

25 Decree of December 2, 1867, in Dublán and Lozano, no. 6182, 10:193–205. The curriculum was otherwise remarkably similar.

26 Rather than opposing adoption, the 1866 bylaws probably forgot to mention it. Adoption appears to have been possible under the clause that allowed the girls to go live with families who wished to take them. In any case, the 1868 bylaws discouraged adoption "because past experience has shown that we should be very frugal with this type of concession" (bylaws, chap. 8, art. 9).

27 "Representacion de dho. Establecimiento para que no se admita la renuncia de su comision al C. Abadiano," August 7, 1868, AHCM, Hospicio de Pobres, vol. 2295, exp. 57.

28 "El Hospicio: Espantos," *La Orquesta*, January 7, 1869, inserted in ibid., exp. 65.

29 There is a discrepancy in the records concerning her age. Although the January 1869 report said that Paz Estrada was 28, a report of November 1867 had listed her age as only 17 years. Ibid., exps. 43 and 65.

30 City council report, January 9, 1869, ibid., exp. 65, ff. 6–13.

31 Abadiano attempted to sue the article's author for slander, but took no further action upon discovering that the author was protected by the *fuero constitucional* (perhaps it was Baz who as governor enjoyed constitutional immunity?) See memo of January 8, 1869, ibid., f. 5.

32 According to Martínez de la Torre's *Discurso* (1875, 15), Baz published his report in *Siglo XIX* (vol. 7, no. 66). I am indebted to Ann Blum for this reference. The manuscript report is in AHCM, Hospicio de Pobres, vol. 2295, exp. 65, ff. 23–28.

33 In 1867 only 48 percent had been too old, but the figure is not entirely comparable because it was based on the proportion aged 13 or older, not 12 or older as in 1869.

34 Report of June 19, 1871, AHCM, Hospicio de Pobres, vol. 2296, 127, f. 3v.

35 The director and administrator were immediately suspended on January 9 "for the duration of the trial." The director, Doña María Lascuráin de Ortiz, unsuccessfully appealed her suspension on January 11. See ibid., vol. 2295, exp. 65 (1869).

36 The uniforms cost 6,575 pesos. See reference in report of February 1, 1870, in ibid., exp. 113.

37 Baz's report of March 1, 1869, ibid., exp. 65, f. 27.

38 Letter of December 5, 1871, AHCM, Empleados-Hospicio, vol. 918, exp. 8; report of June 19, 1871, AHCM, Hospicio de Pobres, vol. 2296, exp. 127, f. 4.

39 She was a longtime member of the Lancasterian Company, which in an obituary praised her for putting "her talent, money, prestige and influence" at their disposal. Mendieta Alatorre (1972), 209.

40 Ibid., 179–211.

41 Ibid., 175.

42 AHCM, Hospicio de Pobres, vol. 2295, exp. 113, f. 4.

43 On Señora Baz in the Poor House, see AHCM, Empleados-Hospicio, vol. 918, exp. 8; Hospicio de Pobres, vol. 2295, exps. 61, 69. On the Maternity Hospital, Tecpam, and Foundling Home, see Abadiano (1871), 20, 35; and Blum (1998), esp. 134–37.

44 Decision of the city council, May 13, 1870, AHCM, Hospicio de Pobres, vol. 2295, exp. 94, f. 3.

45 See files of January 31 and February 13, 1872, ibid., vol. 2296, exps. 163–64; and her petition for a raise on November 27, 1871, AHCM, Empleados-Hospicio, exp. 8.

46 No precise statistics are available for 1867 or 1868, but in their reports of May 1868 the Poor House doctor and the Board of Health placed the number of inmates at "around seven hundred" and "between seven and eight hundred." AHCM, Hospicio de Pobres, vol. 2295, exp. 52, ff. 2 and 8v. The month of January alone had brought the influx of "forty plus" new inmates. Ibid., exp. 113 (February 2, 1870).

47 "Ynforme que rinde la encargada del establecimiento," July 6, 1870, ibid., exp. 119.

48 It is hard to believe the children rose at 4:30, earlier than was required in any of the Poor House bylaws. A cryptic reference to extra bread rations for "the women who are nursing their babies" also makes one wonder whether the only paupers in residence were the students and the elderly listed in the statistics. Ibid., f. 2.

49 See report of July 31, 1871, ibid., vol. 2296, exp. 155, f. 3.

50 On the problems with the printing press, see also ibid., vol. 2295, exp. 87 (March 8, 1870).

51 Da. Josefa Rodríguez' report of December 4, 1871, ibid., vol. 2296, exp. 145, ff. 3-3v.

52 Ibid., vol. 2295, exp. 111 (November 30, 1870); vol. 2296, exp. 155 (December 4, 1871), ff. 7-8.

53 AHCM, Empleados-Hospicio, vol. 918, exp. 15 (October 28, 1870).

54 AHCM, Hospicio de Pobres, vol. 2296, exp. 134.

55 Correspondence of June 19 to July 18, 1871, ibid., exp. 127.

56 Ibid., vol. 2295, exp. 94 (May 7, 1870). See also vol. 2296, exps. 131 (July 1871); and 139 (September 5, 1871). The Poor House was also able to fend off pressure to rehabilitate young prostitutes, as seen in documents proposing the establishment of a separate asylum for them (vol. 2295, exp. 61 [Oct. 10, 1868]).

57 Ibid., vol. 2295, exp. 89 (March 26, 1870).

58 Ibid., vol. 2296, exp. 127 (June 19, 1871), f. 3.

59 Ibid., exp. 139 (September 5, 1871).

60 See, for example, Gaceta de Policía, October 11, 1868, 1; and AHCM, Hospicio de Pobres, vol. 2296, exps. 130-31 (1871).

61 See Gelt's accusations and Señorita María Herrera's resignation on March 6, 1871, AHCM, Empleados-Hospicio, vol. 918, exp. 8.

62 Because she had allegedly deposited the girls' earnings with a relative instead of with the Treasury or the Monte de Piedad, as required by the 1868 bylaws, she was dismissed in December 1876. See Blum (1998), 144.

63 October 30 to November 17, 1871, AHCM, Hospicio de Pobres, vol. 2296, exp. 143. The inmates also became clients of the state, as evidenced by the boys' attendance at the "Bando Nacional que declara el Presidente Juárez" in 1871 (exp. 155).

64 See Alfaro (1906), 12.

65 See memos in AHCM, Hospicio de Pobres, vol. 2295, exps. 74 (April 1869), 113 (March 25, 1870), 118 (October 17, 1870); and vol. 2296, exps. 113, 136-37 (February 2, September 4, and September 9, 1871).

66 AHCM, Hospicio de Pobres, vol. 2296, exp. 158 (October 23, 1871).

67 Ibid., exps. 138, 145 (September 29 and December 4, 1871).

68 Ibid., vol. 2295, exp. 113 (February 2, 1870), f. 5.

69 See, for example, ibid., vol. 2296, exps. 147 (November 7, 1871), 155 (October 25, 1871).

70 Ibid., vol. 2295, exps. 106, 113 (March 21 and October 25, 1870).

71 See ibid., exps. 97, 102, and 119.

72 In December 1871 the Poor House also looked into ordering a billiard table (mesa de boliche) for the students' entertainment. See ibid., vol. 2296, exps. 151, 154, 155.

73 Memo of May 7, 1870, ibid., vol. 2295, exp. 94.

74 "Ynventario general de los objetos en el Hospicio de Pobres," ibid., exp. 113, (January 28, 1870), ff. 12–12v.

75 Ibid., exps. 107 (October 25, 1870), 112 (December 23, 1870); vol. 2296, exps. 146 (Oct. 27, 1871), 149 (December 21, 1871). A reference to Abadiano's visits during the "time of the posadas" also suggests that this part of the Christmas celebration was still enacted in the asylum in 1868. Report of January 9, 1869, vol. 2295, exp. 65, f. 8.

76 See López Figueroa (1993), 103–5; Alfaro (1906), 41–42; and the denunciation in *El Monitor Republicano*, on April 16, 1878, that the "Reform laws were not being imposed in this Establishment" (AHSSA, BP-EA-HP, leg. 6, exp. 1). The religious paraphernalia in the chapel was not sold until 1924. Blum (1995), 20.

77 See Reis (1995); and Voekel (1997).

78 *Código Penal* (1871), arts. 857–58, 860–62, 620.

79 See AHCM, Beneficencia y Asilos, vol. 416, exps. 6, 7 (1868 and 1869).

80 The city council's reluctance to intern any but children in the Poor House is also evident in the pension it granted a family with serious birth defects that prevented them from working. The sole example I have found of municipal home relief, it suggests that the aldermen no longer considered confinement of an entire family appropriate, as they had in the late eighteenth century. AHCM, Beneficencia, vol. 415, exp. 21 (August 29, 1871).

81 The first and third petition were approved, but the second was denied because Portillo's daughters were over the age of twelve. See AHCM, Hospicio de Pobres, vol. 2296, exp. 126 (June 15, 1871); vol. 2295, exps. 90 (March 29, 1870), 95 (May 13, 1870).

82 See, for example, the director's memos of May 7, 1870, and November 16 and December 4, 1871. Ibid., vol. 2295, exp. 94; and vol. 2296, exps. 144–45.

83 Ibid., vol. 2296, exp. 145 (December 4, 1871), ff. 1, 5.

84 Abadiano (1878), iv–v; also see the introduction by Eduardo Liceaga, xvi.

85 See Liceaga's introduction to Abadiano (1878), xvii.

86 Alfaro (1906), 58.

87 Hamnett (1994), 198.

Conclusion

1 After 1884 the Hospicio served a younger clientele than in the past. The 1884 bylaws mandated that it only take girls from the ages of 2 to 14 and boys from 2 to 10. After that, they were supposed to be transferred to the Escuela Industrial de Huérfanos. Those between the ages of 2 and 6 were to be placed in a separate "preschool" section, an 1884 innovation. "Reglamento del Hospicio," approved June 4, 1884, AHSSA, BP-EA-HP, leg. 12, exp. 11.

2 See notation of June 4, 1808, in "Quaderno," AHSSA, BP-EA-HP, bk. 8.

3 Anne McCants (1997) found a similar pattern in Amsterdam's municipal orphanage during the seventeenth and eighteenth centuries. Rather than taking in all orphans, it favored the offspring of "middling" families, thus functioning "to keep people from the middle rungs of the city from sliding down" (19, 200–201). In Mexico, a

racially mixed colonial society, the traditional impulse to aid those from one's own social class took on an additional twist. On the discriminating nature of traditional charity, see Geremek (1994), 24–27, 40.

4 For the charge of despotism, see the minutes of March 6, 1827, in AHCM, Vagos, vol. 4151, exp. 4.

5 On the persistence of the moral economy of begging, see especially Beneficencia Pública (1931), 40–91, 97; Fernández de Lizardi (1942), 205; Mayer (1844), 55; Ortiz (1952), 177–78; García Cubas (1986), 224–25; Palavicini (1945), 4:78; Sacristán (1994b); and González Navarro (1985), 71–79, 99. On the conventions of begging, see also Geremek (1994), 48–50.

6 Van Young (1988), 153.

7 On the existence of a tacit social contract, see Arrom, "Rethinking Urban Politics in Latin America before the Populist Era," in Arrom and Ortoll (1996), 5–7.

8 Beneficencia Pública (1931), 48; Tanck Estrada (1977), 226.

9 Van Young (1994), 344.

10 See decree of August 19, 1879 in Castillo Velasco (1874), 246–47; and descriptions of roundups in the 1920s and 1930s in Beneficencia Pública (1931); and Ochoa (1998).

11 Rivera-Garza (1995), chap. 3.

12 By 1872 there were also three casas de asilo for the children of poor workers, which had likewise closed by 1874. AHCM, Beneficencia y Asilos, vol. 416, exps. 8–10, 19, 71, 96.

13 According to Peza, the asylum housed 206 paupers in 1880. *Beneficencia*, 73. See also Velasco Ceballos (1943), 22; Galindo y Villa (1901), 93–96; AHCM, Beneficencia y Asilos, vol. 419, exp. 105 (1899).

14 See Blum (1998), 153–54, 184–85, 269–74, 412, 418–21, 529.

15 On the colonial "safety net," see Van Young (1988), esp. 141, 150–53.

16 Much more research is needed on the situation of nineteenth-century *cofradías*. See Brading (1983), 11–16; and Bazarte Martínez (1989). Artisans' mutual aid societies only partially filled the gap they left and then only late in the nineteenth century. See Pérez Toledo (1996) and Illades (1996).

17 Löwenstern (1843), 117.

18 See Schwartz (1988), esp. 129–30, 241; and Geremek (1994), 214–18. Repressive policies also appear to have failed in Salvador, Brazil, where a beggars' asylum was established in the late nineteenth century. See Fraga Filho (1996), esp. 151–56.

19 Norberg (1985), 215. See also Ransel (1988), who documents the degeneration of an institutional ideal; and Altschuler and Saltzgaber (1988), who argue that local officials in charge of implementing New York state poorhouse policies did not share the state government's desire for social control (1988).

20 Katz (1983), 25. See also the critique of workhouses in James Taylor, "The Unreformed Workhouse, 1776–1834," in E. W. Martin (1972), 57–83.

{ GLOSSARY }

English cognates and foreign words used only once and defined in the text do not appear here.

aduana: customs house or agency; also customs tax

alcalde: ward magistrate

alcancía: money box, used to collect alms for an institution

ama de confianza: trusted housekeeper; here, female supervisor

anciano/anciana: elderly person

arroba: unit of weight equal to twenty-five pounds

atolera: woman who makes atole, a corn beverage

audiencia: high court under direct royal jurisdiction

ayuntamiento: city council, municipal government; also known as the cabildo

caballería: a land measure of approximately 105 acres

casa: house

casta: caste; a person of mixed racial heritage

castizo/castiza: person of mestizo and white parents, in theory of three-quarters European and one-quarter Indian heritage

celador/celadora: supervisor or watchman; also a kind of policeman

Consolidación de Vales Reales: a measure decreed in 1804 to consolidate government treasury debts by calling in Church-held mortgages

consulado: merchant guild, commercial tribunal

corregidor: royal district governor

corrigendo/corrigenda: young person placed in custody for reform and punishment; juvenile delinquent

cuartel: ward, one of the administrative units into which Mexico City was divided in 1782

desnudos: literally, naked ones; here, ragged paupers whose torn clothes barely cover their flesh

doctrinero: a type of priest; here, a layperson who teaches Catholic doctrine

don/doña: honorific title denoting high status

egido (today *ejido*): common land, usually belonging to indigenous communities

español/española: Spanish; here a person who passes as white; refers to those born in America as well as Spain

fiador: person who guarantees by bond

fianza: the guarantee provided by a fiador

fiscal: government attorney

gente de bien: literally, good people; loosely, the well-to-do

juez de letras: judge trained in the law

junta: committee or governing board

lépero: literally, a leper; in Mexico a pejorative term for a lower-class ruffian; also a vagrant

limosnas: alms

limosnero/limosnera: beggar

lobo/loba: person of mixed Indian and black descent

maestro/maestra: master artisan; a primary school teacher if qualified by *de primeras letras* or *de amiga*

matrimonio: marriage; a married couple

mayordomo: male steward; here, the man in charge of the departments for men and boys

meca: shortened form of Chichimeca, an indigenous person from the "barbarous" north of Mexico

mendigo: beggar; a vagrant, or "false beggar" if qualified by *fingido*

milpas: fields, usually for growing corn

montepíos: pensions paid by a royally sponsored agency

morisco/morisca: literally, Moslems converted to Christianity; in Mexico, a light-skinned mulatto

niño/niña: child; usually refers to those under 15 years of age

oidor: "hearer" of cases; audiencia judge

ordenanzas: ordinances; statutes governing an institution

pardo/parda: literally, dark; a person of partly black descent

patronato real: royal patronage over the Church, including the right of the Spanish crown to nominate candidates for ecclesiastical office and supervise Church administration

peso: monetary unit worth eight reales until the decimal system was established during the Second Empire

petate: sleeping mat woven from palm thatch or grass

pobres de solemnidad: the "solemn poor," paupers from respectable families fallen on hard times who were traditionally eligible for special public assistance

populacho: pejorative term for the masses

portero/portera: gatekeeper

primeras letras: primary education, specifically the first subjects taught in elementary school

pulque: alcoholic beverage made from the fermented sap of the maguey (a type of agave)

real: a monetary unit worth one-eighth of a peso or 12 granos; also, royal

real acuerdo: council of royal advisers

recogida: women secluded in a recogimiento or anyone secluded in an institution

recogimiento: retirement home, or house of refuge for women

rectora: female warden; here, a woman in charge of departments for women (mujeres) and girls (niñas)

refectolera: person who serves meals in institutions

Reforma: the reform movement led by the Liberals in Mexico from 1854 to 1867 *regidor:* alderman, city councillor

reglamento: set of rules governing an institution; statutes

tablas de carnicería: taxes on the butchering of cattle

Temporalidades: assets of the suppressed Jesuit order, also the royal bureau administering these

tinterillos: unlicensed attorneys who often represented poor people in court

verdaderos pobres: the "true" poor, who deserve assistance because they are elderly, sick, or disabled

vergonzantes: the "shamefaced poor," who are too proud to beg; in Mexico, used interchangeably with pobres de solemnidad

vinaterías: establishments that sell wine

vocal/vocales: members of a governing board

volo: coins customarily thrown by godparents at a baptism to the beggars gathered in the churchyard

{ BIBLIOGRAPHY }

Archives

AGI: Archivo General de Indias, Seville
  México
AGN: Archivo General de la Nación, Mexico City
  Archivo Histórico de Hacienda
  Ayuntamiento
  Bandos
  Bienes Nacionales
  Cédulas Reales
  Gobernación
  Historia
  Padrones
  Policía
  Templos y Conventos
AHCM: Archivo Histórico de la Ciudad de México, Mexico City
  Actas de Cabildo
  Actas del Consejo General de Beneficencia (422)
  Actas Secretas de Cabildo
  Beneficencia (415 and 423)
  Beneficencia y Asilos (416)
  Consejo General de Beneficencia (418–21)
  Empleados-Hospicio (918)
  Hospicio de Pobres (2295–96)
  Padrones
  Vagos
AHSSA: Archivo Histórico de la Secretaría de Salud, Mexico City
  BP-EA-HP: Fondo Beneficencia Pública, Sección Establecimientos Asistenciales,
    Serie Hospicio de Pobres
  HyH-HP: Fondo Hospitales y Hospicios, Sección Hospicio de Pobres
AN: Archivo Notarial, Mexico City
APSV: Archivo de la Parroquia de la Santa Veracruz, Mexico City
  Confirmaciones 1766–85

BNM: Biblioteca Nacional de México, Mexico City
    Lafragua Collection
GDCLDS: Geneological Department of the Church of the Latter Day Saints, Salt Lake
    City, Utah
        Mexico D.F.

Newspapers

Diario del Imperio, 1865–66.
Diario de México, 1805–07.
Eco del Comercio, 1848.
Gaceta de Policía, 1868.
Gazetas de México, 1795–1806.
El Monitor Republicano, 1878.
La Orquesta, 1869.
El Redactor Municipal, 1842.
Revista Mensual de la Sociedad Promovedora de Mejoras Materiales, 1852.
Siglo Diez y Nueve, 1841.
Voz de la Patria, 1830.

Printed Works

Abadiano, Juan. *Establecimientos de beneficencia: apuntes sobre su orígen y relación de los actos de su junta directiva*. Mexico City: Imp. de la Escuela de Artes y Oficios, 1878.
Aguilar, Gilberto F., and Roberto Ezquerro Peraza. *Los hospitales de México*. Mexico City: Casa Bayer, 1936.
Ajofrín, Francisco de. *Diario del viaje que por orden de la sagrada Congregación de Propaganda Fide hizo a la América Septentrional en el siglo XVIII el P. Fray Francisco de Ajofrín*. Ed. Vicente Castañeda y Alcover. 2 vols. Madrid: Real Academia de la Historia, 1958.
Alessio Robles, Miguel. *La filantropía en México*. Mexico City: Ediciones Botas, 1944.
Alexander, John K. *Render Them Submissive: Responses to Poverty in Philadelphia, 1760–1800*. Amherst: University of Massachusetts Press, 1980.
Alfaro, Martiniano T. *Reseña histórico-descriptiva del antiguo Hospicio de México*. Mexico City: Imprenta del Gobierno Federal, 1906.
Almonte, Juan Nepomuceno. *Guía de forasteros, y repertorio de conocimientos útiles*. Mexico City: Imprenta de Ignacio Cumplido, 1852.
Altschuler, Glenn, and Jan Saltzgaber. "The Limits of Responsibility: Social Welfare and Local Government in Seneca County, New York, 1860–1875." *Journal of Social History* 21, no. 3 (1988): 515–37.
Alvarez Amezquita, José, Miguel E. Bustamante, Antonio López Picazos, and Francisco Fernández del Castillo. *Historia de la salubridad y de la asistencia en México*. 4 vols. Mexico City: Secretaría de la Salubridad y Asistencia, 1960.
Archer, Christon I. "The Deportation of Barbarian Indians from the Internal Provinces of New Spain: 1789–1810." *The Americas* 29, no. 3 (1973): 376–85.

Arrillaga, José Basilio. *Recopilación de leyes, decretos, bandos . . . de la República Mexicana.* 4 vols. Mexico City: Imprenta de J. Fernández de Lara, 1828–65.

Arrom, Silvia Marina. *The Women of Mexico City, 1790–1857.* Stanford: Stanford University Press, 1985.

———. "Beggars and Vagrants in Mexico City, 1774-1845." Paper presented at the meetings of the American Historical Association, December 1988. (1988a)

———. "Popular Politics in Mexico City: The Parián Riot, 1828." *Hispanic American Historical Review* 68, no. 2 (1988): 245–68. (1988b)

———. "Vagos y mendigos en la legislación mexicana, 1745-1845." In *Memoria del IV Congreso de Historia del Derecho mexicano.* ed. Beatriz Bernal, 2 vols. Mexico City: UNAM, 1988, 1:71–87. (1988c)

———. "Documentos para el estudio del Tribunal de Vagos, 1828-1848: respuesta a una problemática sin solución." *Anuario Mexicano de Historia del Derecho* 1 (1989): 215–35.

———. "Desintegración familiar y pauperización: los indigentes del Hospicio de Pobres en la ciudad de México, 1795." In *Familia y vida privada en la historia de Iberoamérica,* ed. Pilar Gonzalbo Aizpuru and Cecilia Rabell Romero. Mexico City: UNAM and El Colegio de México, 1996, 119-31. (1996a)

———. "¿De la caridad a la beneficencia? Las reformas de la asistencia pública desde la perspectiva del Hospicio de Pobres de la ciudad de México, 1856-1871." In *Ciudad de México,* ed. Illades and Rodríguez, 21–53, 1996. (1996b)

———, and Servando Ortoll, eds. *Riots in the Cities: Popular Politics and the Urban Poor in Latin America, 1765–1910.* Wilmington, DE: Scholarly Resources, 1996.

Arróniz, Marcos. *Manual del viajero en Méjico, ó compendio de la historia de la ciudad de Méjico . . .* Paris: Librería de Rosa y Bouret, 1858.

Avila Espinosa, Felipe A. "Los niños abandonados de la Casa de Niños Expósitos de la ciudad de México, 1767-1821." In *La familia en el mundo iberoamericano,* ed. Pilar Gonzalbo Aizpuru and Cecilia Rabell. Mexico City: UNAM, 1994, 265–310.

Barroso Díaz, Angel. "Maximiliano: legislador liberal (reflexiones sobre el Segundo Imperio)." In *Memorias del II Congreso de Historia del Derecho Mexicano,* ed. José Luis Soberanes Fernández. Mexico City: UNAM, 1981, 539–55. (1981a)

———. "Política legislativa indigenista y eclesiástica del segundo imperio mexicano." Licenciatura in law thesis, Universidad Iberoamericana, 1981. (1981b)

Bazant, Jan. "The Evolution of the Textile Industry in Puebla: 1544-1845." *Comparative Studies in Society and History* 7, no. 1 (1964): 56–69.

———. *Alienation of Church Wealth in Mexico: Social and Economic Aspects of the Liberal Revolution, 1856–1875,* ed. and trans. Michael Costeloe. Cambridge: Cambridge University Press, 1971.

———. "Mexico from Independence to 1867." In *The Cambridge History of Latin America,* ed. Leslie Bethell. Cambridge: Cambridge University Press, 1985, 3:423-70.

Bazarte Martínez, Alicia. *Las cofradías de españoles en la ciudad de México (1526–1869).* Mexico City: UAM-Azcapotzalco, 1989.

Beezley, William H., Cheryl E. Martin, and William E. French, eds. *Rituals of Rule, Rituals of Resistance: Public Celebrations and Popular Culture in Mexico.* Wilmington, DE: Scholarly Resources, 1994.

Bellows, Barbara L. *Benevolence among Slaveholders: Assisting the Poor in Charleston, 1670–1860.* Baton Rouge: Louisiana State University Press, 1993.

Beneficencia Pública del D.F. *La mendicidad en México.* Mexico City: A. Mijares y Hno., 1931.

Blum, Ann Shelby. "Captive Client or Fluid Boundaries? Child Circulation in the Welfare System, Mexico City, 1870–1940." Paper presented at the meetings of the American Historical Association, January 1995.

————. "Children without Parents: Law, Charity, and Social Practice, Mexico City, 1867–1940." Ph.D. diss., University of California, Berkeley, 1998.

Bocanegra, José María. *Memorias para la historia de México independiente, 1822–1846.* 2 vols. Mexico City: Imp. del Gobierno Federal en el ex-Arzobispado, 1892.

Borah, Woodrow. "Social Welfare and Social Obligation in New Spain: A Tentative Assessment." *Congreso Internacional de Americanistas, España 1964: Actas y Memorias 36,* no. 4 (1966): 45–57.

————. *Justice by Insurance: The General Indian Court of Colonial Mexico and the Legal Aides of the Half-Real.* Berkeley: University of California Press, 1983.

Brading, David A. "Tridentine Catholicism and Enlightened Despotism in Bourbon Mexico." *Journal of Latin American Studies* 15, no. 1 (1983): 1–22.

————. *Church and State in Bourbon Mexico: The Diocese of Michoacán, 1749–1810.* Cambridge: Cambridge University Press, 1994.

Bremner, R. H. "Modern Attitudes towards Charity and Relief." *Comparative Studies in Society and History* 1, no. 2 (1958–59): 377–82.

Brown, Julie V. "Peasant Survival Strategies in Late Imperial Russia: The Social Uses of the Mental Hospital." *Social Problems* 34, no. 3 (October 1987): 311–29.

Calderón de la Barca, Frances. *Life in Mexico: The Letters of Fanny Calderón de la Barca with New Material from the Author's Private Journals,* ed. Howard T. Fisher and Marion Hall Fisher. 1843; rpt. New York: Doubleday, 1966.

Callahan, William J. "The Problem of Confinement: An Aspect of Poor Relief in Eighteenth-Century Spain," *Hispanic American Historical Review* 51, no. 1 (February 1971): 1–24.

Carasa Soto, P. *Pauperismo y revolución burguesa: Burgos, 1750–1900.* Valladolid: Universidad de Valladolid, 1987.

Caro López, Ceferino. "Beneficencia, asistencia social y represión en Murcia durante el siglo XVIII." *Estudios de Historia Social* 2 (1989): 165–200.

Carr, Raymond. *Spain, 1808–1975.* Oxford: Oxford University Press, 1982.

Carreño, Alberto María. *Los españoles en el México independiente (un siglo de beneficencia).* Mexico City: Imp. de Manuel León Sánchez, 1942.

Castillo Velasco, José María del. *Colección de leyes . . . del Distrito Federal . . .* Mexico City: Imp. de Castillo Velasco, 1874.

Centro Mexicano para la Filantropía. "Understanding Mexican Philanthropy." In *Changing Structure of Mexico: Political, Social, and Economic Prospects,* ed. Laura Randall. London: M. E. Sharpe, 1996, 182–99.

Chambers, Clarke A. "'Uphill All the Way': Reflections on the Course and Study of Welfare History." *Social Welfare History* (December 1992): 492–504.

Chandler, D. S. *Social Assistance and Bureaucratic Politics: The Montepíos of Colonial Mexico, 1767–1821*. Albuquerque: University of New Mexico Press, 1991.

Chase, Bradley Lewis. "Medical Care for the Poor in Mexico City, 1770–1810: One Aspect of the Spanish Colonial Beneficencia." Ph.D. diss., University of Maryland, 1975.

Chavez Orozco, Luis. *El comercio exterior y el artesanado mexicano (1825–1830)*. Mexico City: Banco Nacional de Comercio Exterior, 1965.

———. "Orígenes de la política de seguridad social." *Historia Mexicana* 16, no. 2 (1966): 155–83.

———. *La agonía del artesanado*. Mexico City: Centro de Estudios Históricos del Movimiento Obrero Mexicano, 1977.

Clement, Patricia Ferguson. *Welfare and the Poor in the Nineteenth-Century City: Philadelphia, 1800–1854*. Rutherford, NJ: Fairleigh Dickinson University Press, 1985.

Código penal para el Distrito Federal y Territorio de la Baja-California sobre delitos del fuero común, y para toda la República sobre delitos contra la Federación. Mexico City: Imp. del Gobierno, 1871.

Cohen, Stanley, and Andrew Scull, eds. *Social Control and the State*. New York: St. Martin's Press, 1983.

Constitución federal de los Estados Unidos Mexicanos sancionada por el Congreso General Constituyente el 4 de octubre de 1824 . . . Guadalajara: Poderes de Jalisco, 1973.

Cook, S. F. "The Hunger Hospital in Guadalajara: An Experiment in Medical Relief." *Bulletin of the History of Medicine* 8, no. 4 (1940): 533–45.

Cooper, Donald B. *Epidemic Disease in Mexico City, 1761–1813: An Administrative, Social, and Medical Study*. Austin: University of Texas Press, 1965.

Cope, R. Douglas. *The Limits of Racial Domination: Plebeian Society in Colonial Mexico City, 1660–1720*. Madison, University of Wisconsin Press, 1994.

Corti, Egon Caesar. *Maximilian and Charlotte of Mexico*. Trans. Catherine Phillips. New York: Alfred A. Knopf, 1929.

Cosío Villegas, Daniel, ed. *Historia moderna de México: la República Restaurada, la vida social*. 2d ed., vol. 3. Mexico City: Editorial Hermes, 1974.

Cossío, José Lorenzo. *Datos históricos sobre las propiedades urbanas de la instrucción pública y de la beneficencia privada*. Mexico City: n.p., 1917.

———. *Guía retrospectiva de la ciudad de México*. Mexico City: n.p., 1941.

Costeloe, Michael P. *La primera república federal en México (1824–1835): un estudio de los partidos políticos en el México independiente*. Trans. Manuel Fernández Gasalla. Mexico City: Fondo de Cultura Económica, 1975.

———. *The Central Republic in Mexico, 1835–1846: Hombres de bien in the Age of Santa Anna*. Cambridge: Cambridge University Press, 1993.

Couturier, Edith. "The Philanthropic Activities of Pedro Romero de Terreros: First Count of Regla." *The Americas* 32 (July 1975): 13–30.

———. " 'For the Greater Service of God': Opulent Foundations and Women's Philanthropy in Colonial Mexico." In *Lady Bountiful*, ed. McCarthy, 119–41, 1990.

Cray, Robert E., Jr. *Paupers and Poor Relief in New York City and Its Rural Environs, 1700–1830*. Philadelphia: Temple University Press, 1988.

Crowther, Margaret A. *The Workhouse System, 1834–1929: The History of an English Social Institution.* Athens, GA: University of Georgia Press, 1982.

Cruz, Francisco Santiago. *Los hospitales de México y la caridad de Don Benito.* Mexico City: Editorial Jus, 1959.

Cuevas, Mariano. *Historia de la nación mexicana.* 1940; rpt. Mexico City: Editorial Porrúa, 1967.

Darío, Rubio. *El Nacional Monte de Piedad, fundado en el año de 1775.* Mexico City: n.p., 1947.

Davies, Keith A. "Tendencias demográficas urbanas durante el siglo XIX en México." *Historia Mexicana* 21, no. 3 (1972): 481–524.

Davis, Natalie Zemon. "Poor Relief, Humanism, and Heresy: The Case of Lyon." In *Society and Culture in Early Modern France,* Stanford: Stanford University Press, 1975, 17–64.

De Swaan, Abram. *In Care of the State: Health Care, Education, and Welfare in Europe and the USA in the Modern Era.* New York: Oxford University Press, 1988.

Deans-Smith, Susan. *Bureaucrats, Planters, and Workers: The Making of the Tobacco Monopoly in Bourbon Mexico.* Austin: University of Texas Press, 1992.

———. "The Working Poor and the Eighteenth-Century Colonial State: Gender, Public Order, and Work Discipline." In *Rituals of Rule,* ed. Beezley, 45–75, 1994.

Di Tella, Torcuato. "The Dangerous Classes in Early Nineteenth-Century Mexico." *Journal of Latin American Studies* 5, no. 1 (May 1973): 79–105.

———. *National Popular Politics in Early Independent Mexico, 1820–1847.* Albuquerque: University of New Mexico Press, 1996.

Diccionario Porrúa de historia, biografía y geografía de México. Mexico City: Editorial Porrúa, 1964.

Dublán, Manuel, and José María Lozano, eds. *Legislación mexicana o colección completa de las disposiciones legislativas expedidas desde la independencia de la República.* 34 vols. Mexico City: Imp. del Comercio 1876–1904.

Durkheim, Emile. *Moral Education: A Study in the Theory and Application of the Sociology of Education.* Ed. and trans. Everett Wilson. New York: Free Press of Glencoe, 1961.

Dwyer, Ellen. *Homes for the Mad: Life inside Two Nineteenth-Century Asylums.* New Brunswick: Rutgers University Press, 1987.

Elias, Norbert. *The Civilizing Process: The History of Manners.* Trans. Edmund Jephcott. 1939; rpt. New York: Urizen Books, 1978.

Estracto de los reglamentos generales de la asistencia pública . . . de la junta de beneficencia del primer cuartel de Paris. Mexico City: J. M. Andrade y Escalante, 1865. Copy in AGN, Gobernación, vol. 1884.

Estrada, Genaro. "Introducción" to *Enfermedades políticas que padece la capital de esta Nueva España,* by Hipólito Villarroel. Mexico City: Miguel Angel Porrúa, 1979.

Evans, Albert S. *Our Sister Republic: A Gala Trip through Tropical Mexico in 1869 . . .* Hartford, CT: Columbian Book Company, 1870.

Fairchilds, Cissie C. *Poverty and Charity in Aix-en-Provence, 1640–1789.* Baltimore: Johns Hopkins University Press, 1976.

Farris, Nancy M. *Crown and Clergy in Colonial Mexico, 1759–1821.* London: Cambridge University Press, 1968.

Fernández de Lizardi, José Joaquín. *The Itching Parrot*. Trans. Katherine Anne Porter. 1816; Garden City, NY: Doubleday, Doran, 1942.

———. *El Periquillo sarniento*. 1816; rpt. Mexico City: Editorial Porrúa, 1974.

Finzsch, Norbert, and Robert Jütte, eds. *Institutions of Confinement: Hospitals and Prisons in Western Europe and North America, 1500–1950*. Cambridge: Cambridge University Press, 1996.

Flores, Francisco A. *Historia de la medicina en México desde la época de los indios hasta la presente*. 2 vols. Mexico City: Oficina Tip. de la Secretaría de Fomento, 1886–88.

Florescano, Enrique. *Precios del maíz y crisis agrícolas en México (1708–1810)*. Mexico City: El Colegio de México, 1969.

———, and Isabel Gil Sánchez. "La época de las reformas borbónicas y el crecimiento económico, 1750–1808." In *Historia general de México*, ed. Centro de Estudios Históricos. 4 vols. Mexico City: El Colegio de México, 1976, 2:183–301.

———, et al., eds. *La clase obrera en la historia de México*. Mexico City: Siglo Veintiuno Editores, 1980.

Flynn, Maureen. *Sacred Charity: Confraternities and Social Welfare in Spain, 1400–1700*. Ithaca: Cornell University Press, 1989.

Foucault, Michel. *Madness and Civilization: A History of Insanity in the Age of Reason*. Trans. Richard Howard. 1961; New York: Random House, 1965.

———. *Discipline and Punish: The Birth of the Prison*. Trans. Alan Sheridan. 1975; New York: Random House, 1979.

Fowler, Will. *Mexico in the Age of Proposals, 1821–1853*. Westport, CT: Greenwood Press, 1998.

Fraga Filho, Walter. *Mendigos, Moleques e Vadios na Bahia do século XIX*. São Paulo and Salvador: Editora HUCITEC and EDUFBA, 1996.

Francois, Marie Eileen. "When Pawnshops Talk: Popular Credit and Material Culture in Mexico City, 1775–1916." Ph.D. diss., University of Arizona, 1998.

French, William E. *A Peaceful and Working People: Manner, Morals, and Class Formation in Northern Mexico*. Albuquerque: University of New Mexico Press, 1996.

Galindo y Villa, Jesús. *Reseña histórico-descriptiva de la ciudad de México*. Mexico City: Imp. de F. Díaz de León, 1901.

Galván Rivera, Mariano. *Guía de forasteros de Méjico para el año de 1828*. Mexico City: Galván Rivera, 1828.

———. *Calendario manual y guía de forasteros de Méjico para el año de 1832*. Mexico City: Galván Rivera, 1832.

———. *Calendario manual y guía de forasteros de Méjico para el año de 1829*. Mexico City: Galván Rivera, 1829.

Gamboa Ramírez, Ricardo. "Las finanzas municipales de la ciudad de México, 1800–1850." In *La ciudad*, ed. Hernández Franyuti, 1:11–63, 1994.

García Cubas, Antonio. *El libro de mis recuerdos: narraciones históricas, anecdóticas y de costumbres mexicanas anteriores al actual orden social*. 1905; rpt. Mexico City: Editorial Porrúa, 1986.

García Icazbalceta, Joaquín. *Informe sobre los establecimientos de beneficencia y corrección de esta capital* . . . Mexico City: Moderna Librería Religiosa, 1907.

Garland, David. *Punishment and Modern Society: A Study in Social Theory*. Oxford: Clarendon Press, 1990.

Garner, Richard. "Price Trends in Eighteenth-Century Mexico." *Hispanic American Historical Review* 65, no. 2 (May 1985): 279–325.

Gayón Córdoba, María. *Condiciones de vida y de trabajo en la ciudad de México en el siglo XIX*. Mexico City: INAH, 1988.

Geremek, Bronislaw. *Poverty: A History*. Trans. Agnieszka Kolakowska. 1988; Oxford: Blackwell, 1994.

Gerhard, Peter. *A Guide to the Historical Geography of New Spain*. Cambridge: Cambridge University Press, 1972.

Gilmore, N. Ray. "The Condition of the Poor in Mexico, 1834." *Hispanic American Historical Review* 37, no. 2 (May 1957): 213–26.

Ginzberg, Lori. *Women and the Work of Benevolence: Morality, Politics, and Class in the Nineteenth-Century United States*. New Haven: Yale University Press, 1990.

Góngora, Mario. "Estudios sobre el Galicanismo y la 'Ilustración Católica' en América española." *Revista Chilena de Historia y Geografía* 125 (1957): 96–148.

Gonzalbo Aizpuru, Pilar. "La casa de los niños expósitos de la ciudad de México: una fundación del siglo XVIII." *Historia Mexicana* 31, no. 3 (1982): 409–30.

———. "Hacia una historia de la vida privada en la Nueva España." *Historia Mexicana* 42, no. 2 (1992): 353–77.

González, Armida de. "Los ceros sociales." In *Historia Moderna de México*, ed. Cosío Villegas, 3:369–450, 1974.

González Angulo Aguirre, Jorge. *Artesanado y ciudad a finales del siglo XVIII*. Mexico City: SEP/80, 1983.

González y González, Luis. "El indigenismo de Maximiliano." In *La Intervención Francesa y el imperio de Maximiliano: cien años después, 1862–1962*, ed. Arturo Arnaiz y Freg and Claude Bataillon. Mexico City: Instituto Francés de América Latina, 1965, 103–11.

González Navarro, Moisés. *La pobreza en México*. Mexico City: El Colegio de México, 1985.

Gordon, Linda. *Heroes of Their Own Lives: The Politics and History of Family Violence: Boston, 1880–1960*. New York: Viking, 1988.

Gortari Rabiela, Hira de. "Política y administración en la ciudad de México: relaciones entre el ayuntamiento y el gobierno del Distrito Federal y el Departamental, 1824–1843." In *La ciudad*, ed. Hernández Franyuti, 2:166–83, 1994.

Greenleaf, Richard E. "The Obraje in the Late Mexican Colony." *The Americas* 23 (January 1967): 227–50.

Grob, Gerald N. *Mental Institutions in America: Social Policy to 1875*. New York: Free Press, 1973.

Guedea, Virginia. "El pueblo de México y las elecciones de 1812." In *La ciudad*, ed. Hernández Franyuti, 2:125–65, 1994.

Gutton, Jean-Pierre. *La Société et les pauvres en Europe (XVIe–XVIIIe siècles)*. Paris: Presses Universitaires de France, 1974.

Hamnett, Brian. *Juárez*. London: Longman, 1994.

Haskell, Thomas L. "Capitalism and the Origins of the Humanitarian Sensibility." 2 parts. *American Historical Review* 90, no. 2 (1985): 339–61; 90, no. 3 (1985): 547–66.

Haslip-Viera, Gabriel. "Crime and the Administration of Justice in Colonial Mexico City, 1696–1810." Ph.D. diss., Columbia University, 1980.

———. "The Underclass." In *Cities and Society in Colonial Latin America*, ed. Louisa Schell Hoberman and Susan Migden Socolow. Albuquerque: University of New Mexico Press, 1986, 285–312.

Hernández, Shannon McGhee. "Charity, the State, and the Social Order in Nineteenth-Century Guatemala: 1778–1871." M.A. thesis, University of Texas, 1992.

Hernández Franyuti, Regina, ed. *La ciudad de México en la primera mitad del siglo XIX*. 2 vols. Mexico City: Instituto Mora, 1994. (1994a)

———. "Ideología, proyectos y urbanización en la ciudad de México." In *La Ciudad*, ed. Hernández Franyuti, 1:116–60, 1994. (1994b)

Hernández Sáenz, Luz María. *Learning to Heal: The Medical Profession in Colonial Mexico, 1767–1831*. New York: Peter Lang, 1997.

Herráez, Julia. *Beneficencia de España en Indias (avance para su estudio)*. Seville: Escuela de Estudios Hispanoamericanos, 1949.

Himmelfarb, Gertrude. *The Idea of Poverty: England in the Early Industrial Age*. New York: Knopf, 1984.

Holloway, Thomas H. *Policing Rio de Janeiro: Repression and Resistance in a 19th-Century City*. Stanford: Stanford University Press, 1993.

———. "Doing Favors for Street People: Beggars and Vagrants in 19th-Century Rio de Janeiro." Paper presented at the meetings of the Latin American Studies Association, April 1997.

Howard, David A. *The Royal Indian Hospital of Mexico City*. Center for Latin American Studies Special Studies, no. 20. Tempe: Arizona State University, Center for Latin American Studies, 1980.

Humboldt, Alexander von. *Political Essay on the Kingdom of New Spain*. Trans. John Black. 4 vols. 1811; rpt. New York: AMS Press, 1966.

Ibar, Francisco. *Muerte política de la República mexicana . . .* Mexico City: Imprenta á cargo del Sr. Tomás Uribe y Alcalde, 1829.

Illades, Carlos. *Hacia la república del trabajo: la organización artesanal en la ciudad de México, 1853–1876*. Mexico City: El Colegio de México and UAM-Iztapalapa, 1996.

———, and Ariel Rodríguez. *Ciudad de México: instituciones, actores sociales y conflicto político, 1774–1931*. Zamora: El Colegio de Michoacán and UAM, 1996.

"Informe sobre pulquerías y tabernas el año de 1784." *Boletín del Archivo General de la Nación* 18 (April 1947): 187–236.

Instrucción reservada que dio el virrey don Miguel José de Azanza a su sucesor . . . Mexico City: Editorial Jus, 1960.

Instrucción del Virrey Marqués de Croix que deja a su sucesor Antonio María Bucareli. Ed. Norman Martin. Mexico City: Editorial Jus, 1960.

Instrucciones que los vireyes de Nueva España dejaron a sus sucesores. 2 vols. Mexico City: Imp. de Ignacio Escalante, 1873.

Israel, J. I. *Race, Class, and Politics in Colonial Mexico*. Oxford: Oxford University Press, 1975.

Jiménez Salas, María. *Historia de la asistencia social en España en la edad moderna*. Madrid: Consejo Superior de Investigaciones Científicas, 1958.

Jones, Colin. *Charity and Bienfaisance: The Treatment of the Poor in the Montpellier Region, 1740–1815*. Cambridge: Cambridge University Press, 1982.

Katz, Michael B. *Poverty and Policy in American History*. New York: Academic Press, 1983.

———. *In the Shadow of the Poor House: A Social History of Welfare in America*. New York: Basic Books, 1986.

Kingman Garcés, Eduardo. "De la antigua caridad a la verdadera beneficencia: formas históricas de representación de la pobreza." In *Antigua modernidad y memoria del presente: culturas urbanas e identidad*, ed. Ton Salman and Eduardo Kingman Garcés. Quito: FLACSO, 1999, 281–309.

Kittleson, Roger. "Beggars False and True: The Asilo de Mendicidade and the Construction of a Povo in Porto Alegre." Paper presented at the meetings of the Latin American Studies Association, April 1997.

Klein, Herbert. "The Demographic Structure of Mexico City in 1811." *Journal of Urban History* 23, no. 1 (1996): 66–93.

Labastida, Luis G. *Colección de leyes . . . relativos a la desamortización de los bienes de corporaciones civiles y religiosas . . .* Mexico City: Tip. de la Oficina Impresora de Estampillas, 1893.

Ladd, Doris. *The Mexican Nobility at Independence, 1780–1826*. Austin: University of Texas Press, 1976.

Laguarta, Pablo Lorenzo. *Historia de la beneficencia Española en México (síntesis)*. Mexico City: Editorial España en América, 1955.

Lamas, Adolfo. *Seguridad social en la Nueva España*. Mexico City: UNAM, 1964.

Lavrin, Asunción. "Diversity and Disparity: Rural and Urban Confraternities in Eighteenth-Century Mexico." In *Manipulating the Saints: Religious Brotherhoods and Social Integration in Postconquest Latin America*, ed. Albert Meyers and Diane E. Hopkins. Hamburg: Wayasbah, 1988, 67–100.

Leacock, Eleanor Burke, ed. *The Culture of Poverty: A Critique*. New York: Simon and Schuster, 1971.

Lebsock, Suzanne. *The Free Women of Petersburg: Status and Culture in a Southern Town, 1784–1860*. New York: Norton, 1984.

Legislación electoral mexicana, 1812–1973. Mexico City: Diario Oficial, Secretaría de Gobernación, 1973.

Lewis, Oscar. "The Culture of Poverty." *Scientific American* 215, no. 4 (1966): 19–25.

Linati, Claudio. *Costumes civils, militaires et religieux du Mexique*. Ed. Justino Fernández. 1828; Mexico City: Imprenta Universitaria, 1956.

Little, Cynthia J. "The Society of Beneficence in Buenos Aires, 1823–1900." Ph.D. diss., Temple University, 1980.

Lis, Catarina. *Social Change and the Laboring Poor: Antwerp, 1770–1860*. New Haven: Yale University Press, 1986.

Lis, Catarina, and Hugo Soly. "'Total Institutions' and the Survival Strategies of the Laboring Poor in Antwerp, 1770–1860." In *The Uses of Charity*, ed. Mandler, 38–67, 1990.

López Cámara, Francisco. *La estructura económica y social de México en la época de la Reforma*. 2d. ed. Mexico City: Siglo Veintiuno, 1973.

López de Escalera, Juan. *Diccionario biográfico y de historia de México.* Mexico City: Editorial del Magisterio, 1964.

López Figueroa, Felipe Valentín. "Pobreza, caridad y beneficencia, un ejemplo: el Hospicio de Pobres de la ciudad de México, 1857-1876." Licenciatura thesis, Escuela Nacional de Antropología e Historia, INAH, 1993.

López Monjardin, Adriana. *Hacia la ciudad del capital: México, 1790-1870.* Departamento de Investigaciones Históricas Cuaderno de Trabajo, no. 46. Mexico City: INAH, 1985.

López-Portillo y Weber, José, Justino Fernández, and Ignacio Díaz-Morales. *El Hospicio Cabañas.* Mexico City: Editorial Jus, 1971.

Lorenzana, Francisco de. *Memorial que presentan a todas las comunidades, y gremios los pobres mendigos de México, por mano de su Arzobispo.* [1770]. Copy in AGI, México, vol. 2791, exp. 10b.

Löwenstern, Isidore. *Le Mexique: Souvenirs d'un voyageur.* Paris: Arthus Bertrand, 1843.

Lyon, G. F. *Journal of a Residence and Tour in the Republic of Mexico in the Year 1826.* 2 vols. London: John Murray, 1828.

Macedo, Miguel. "La asistencia pública en México, hasta 1900." In *México: su evolución social,* ed. Justo Sierra et al. Mexico City: J. Ballescá y Cía, 1900, 2:706-24.

———— "Charity." In *Mexico: Its Social Evolution,* ed. Justo Sierra et al., trans. G. Sentiñón. Mexico City, J. Ballescá, 1900-1904, 2:706-23.

MacLachlan, Colin M. *Criminal Justice in Eighteenth Century Mexico: A Study of the Tribunal of the Acordada.* Berkeley: University of California Press, 1974.

Malo, Ramón. *Diario de sucesos notables de Don José Ramón Malo.* Ed. Mariano Cuevas. 2 vols. Mexico City: Editorial Patria, 1948.

Mandler, Peter, ed. *The Uses of Charity: The Poor on Relief in the Nineteenth-Century Metropolis.* Philadelphia: University of Pennsylvania Press, 1990.

Manrique de Lara, Juana, and Guadalupe Monroy. *Seudónimos, anagramas e iniciales de escritores mexicanos . . .* Mexico City: SEP, 1954.

Márquez Morfín, Lourdes. *La desigualdad ante la muerte en la ciudad de México: el tifo y el cólera (1813 y 1833).* Mexico City: Siglo Veintiuno, 1994.

Marroquí, José María. *La ciudad de México.* 3 vols. Mexico City: J. Aguilar Vera y Cía, 1901-3.

Martin, E. W., ed. *Comparative Development in Social Welfare.* London: George Allen and Unwin, 1972.

Martin, Norman. *Los vagabundos en la Nueva España: siglo XVI.* Mexico City: Editorial Jus, 1957.

————. "La desnudez en la Nueva España del siglo XVIII." *Anuario de Estudios Americanos* 29 (1972): 261-94.

———— "Pobres, mendigos y vagabundos en la Nueva España, 1702-1766: antecedentes y soluciones presentadas." *Estudios de Historia Novohispana* 5, no. 8 (1985): 99-126.

Martin, Percy F. *Maximilian in Mexico: The Story of the French Intervention (1861-1867).* New York: Charles Scribner's Sons, 1914.

Martínez Barbosa, María Xóchitl. "El Hospicio de Pobres de la ciudad de México: origen y desarrollo (1774-1806)." Licenciatura thesis, Universidad Iberoamericana, 1994.

Martínez de la Torre, Rafael. *Discurso que pronunció el Dip. Rafael Martínez de la Torre en la sesión del día 3 de diciembre de 1874 sosteniendo la existencia legal de las Hermanas de la Caridad conforme á las instituciones de la República y leyes de Reforma.* Mexico City: Imp. de Díaz de León y White, 1875.

Martínez-Vergne, Teresita. "The Liberal Concept of Charity: *Beneficencia* Applied to Puerto Rico, 1821–1868." In *The Middle Period in Latin America: Values and Attitudes in the 17th–19th Centuries,* ed. Mark D. Szuchman. Boulder: Lynne Rienner, 1989, 167–84.

————. "The Allocation of Liberated African Labour through the Casa de Beneficencia: San Juan, Puerto Rico, 1859–1864." *Slavery and Abolition* 12, no. 3 (1991): 200–16.

Martz, Linda. *Poverty and Welfare in Habsburg Spain: The Example of Toledo.* Cambridge, Cambridge University Press, 1983.

Matos Rodríguez, Félix. *Women and Urban Change in Nineteenth Century San Juan, Puerto Rico (1820–1868).* Gainesville: University Press of Florida, 1999.

Maximiliano. *Reglamento interior del Consejo General de Beneficencia.* Mexico City: Imp. de Andrade y Escalante, 1865. Copy in AGN, Gobernación, vol. 1884.

Mayer, Brantz. *Mexico as It Was and as It Is.* New York: J. Winchester, New World Press, 1844.

McCaa, Robert. "The Peopling of Nineteenth-Century Mexico: Critical Scrutiny of a Censured Century." In *Statistical Abstract of Latin America,* ed. James Wilkie et al. Los Angeles: University of California Press, 1993, 603–33.

————. "Marriageways in Mexico and Spain, 1500–1900." *Continuity and Change* 9, no. 1 (1994): 11–43.

McCants, Anne E. C. *Civic Charity in a Golden Age: Orphan Care in Early Modern Amsterdam.* Urbana: University of Illinois Press, 1997.

McCarthy, Kathleen, ed. *Lady Bountiful Revisited: Women, Philanthropy, and Power.* New Brunswick: Rutgers University Press, 1990.

McLeod, James A. "Public Health, Social Assistance, and the Consolidation of the Mexican State, 1888–1940." Ph.D. diss., Tulane University, 1990.

McWatters, David L. "The Royal Tobacco Monopoly in Bourbon Mexico, 1764–1810." Ph.D. diss., University of Florida, 1979.

Megged, Amos. "Poverty and Welfare in Mesoamerica during the Sixteenth and Seventeenth Centuries: European Archetypes and Colonial Translations." *Colonial Latin American Historical Review* 6, no. 1 (1997): 1–29.

Memoria que el Consejo Superior de las Asociaciones de Señoras de la Caridad de México dirige al General de Paris, de las obras que ha practicado . . . desde el 1 de julio de 1865 a 30 de junio de 1866. Mexico City: Marian Villanueva, 1867. Copy in BNM, Lafragua Collection, no. 33.

Mendieta Alatorre, Angeles. *Margarita Maza de Juárez: epistolario, antología, iconografía y efemérides.* Mexico City: Comisión Nacional para la Commemoración del Centenario del Fallecimiento de Don Benito Juárez, 1972.

Mesgravis, Laima. *A Santa Casa de Misericordia de São Paulo (1599?–1884): Contribução ao Estudo da Assistência Social no Brasil.* São Paulo: Conselho Estadual de Cultura, 1976.

Meyer, Rosa María. *Instituciones de seguridad social (proceso historiográfico).* Departamento de Investigaciones Históricas, Cuadernos de Trabajo, no. 10. Mexico City: INAH, 1975.

Michielse, H. C. M. "Policing the Poor: J. L. Vives and the Sixteenth-Century Origins of Modern Social Administration." Trans. Robert van Krieken. *Social Service Review* (March 1990): 1–21.

Milton, Cynthia E. "Defining the 'Solemn Poor': Perceptions of Poverty in Colonial Urban Quito (1678–1780)." Manuscript, University of Wisconsin-Madison, 1999.

Monroy, Guadalupe. "Instrucción Pública." In *Historia Moderna de México*, ed. Cosío Villegas, 3:633–743, 1974.

Morales, María Dolores. "Cambios en la traza de la estructura vial de la ciudad de México, 1770–1855." In *La ciudad*, ed. Hernández Franyuti, 1:161–224, 1994.

Moreno Toscano, Alejandra, ed. *Ensayos sobre el desarrollo urbano de México*. Mexico City: UNAM, 1974.

———, ed. *Ciudad de México: ensayo de construcción de una historia*. Mexico City: INAH, 1978.

———. "Los trabajadores y el proyecto de industrialización, 1810–1867." In *La clase obrera*, ed. Florescano et al., pp. 302–50, 1980.

———, and Carlos Aguirre Anaya. "Migrations to Mexico City in the Nineteenth Century." *Journal of Interamerican Studies and World Affairs* 17, no. 1 (1975): 27–42.

Muriel, Josefina. *Conventos de monjas en la Nueva España*. Mexico City: Editorial Santiago, 1946.

———. *Hospitales de la Nueva España*. 2 vols. Mexico City: Editorial Jus, 1956–60.

———. *Los recogimientos de mujeres: respuesta a una problemática social novohispana*. Mexico City: UNAM, 1974.

Nacif Mina, Jorge. "Policía y seguridad pública en la ciudad de México, 1770–1848." In *La ciudad*, ed. Hernández Franyuti, 2:9–11, 1994.

Norberg, Kathryn. *Rich and Poor in Grenoble, 1600–1814*. Berkeley: University of California Press, 1985.

Novísima recopilación de las leyes de España . . . 6 vols. Madrid: J. Viana, 1805–7.

Nuevo Febrero mexicano: obra completa de jurisprudencia teórico-práctica . . . 4 vols. Mexico City: S. Pérez, 1850–52.

Obras de caridad que se practican en varios establecimientos de beneficencia: apuntes escritos para el Consejo de Beneficencia. Mexico City: J. M. Andrade y Escalante, 1865. Copy in AGN, Gobernación, vol. 1884.

Ochoa, Enrique C. "Public Welfare and the Campaign against 'Beggars' in Mexico City during the 1930s." Paper presented at the meetings of the Latin American Studies Association, September 1998.

Olejniczak, William. "Working the Body of the Poor: The Ateliers de Charité in Late Eighteenth-Century France. *Journal of Social History* 24, no. 1 (1990): 87–107.

"Ordenanza de la división de la nobilísima ciudad de México en cuarteles . . ." Ed. Eduardo Baez Macías. *Boletín del Archivo General de la Nación* 10, nos. 1–2 (1969): 51–125.

Ordenanza para el régimen y gobierno del Hospicio de Pobres de esta capital. Mexico City: Imp. de la Casa de Corrección, 1844. Copy in AHSSA, BP-EA-HP, leg. 2, exp. 5.

Orozco y Berra, Manuel. *Memoria para el plano de la ciudad de México formada de órden del Ministerio de Fomento*. Mexico City: Imp. de Santiago White, 1867.

———. *Historia de la ciudad de México desde su fundación hasta 1854*. Ed. Seminario de Historia Urbana del DIH-INAH. Mexico City: SepSetentas, 1973.

Ortiz, Tadeo. *México considerado como nación independiente y libre.* 2 vols. 1832; rpt. Guadalajara: Ediciones I.T.G., 1952.

Ortiz Escamilla, Juan. "Insurgencia y seguridad pública en la ciudad de México, 1810–1815." In *La ciudad*, ed. Hernández Franyuti, 2:95–124, 1994.

Ouweneel, Arij. *Shadows over Anahuac: An Ecological Interpretation of Crisis and Development in Central Mexico, 1730–1800.* Albuquerque: University of New Mexico Press, 1996.

Padilla, Antonio. "Pobres y criminales: beneficencia y reforma penitenciaria en el siglo XIX en México." *Secuencia* 27 (September–December 1993): 43–69.

Palavicini, Félix F. "Asistencia Pública." In *México: historia de su evolución constructiva.* Mexico City: Editorial "Libro, S. de R. L.," 1945, 4:62–98.

Palomares Ibáñez, Jesús María. *La asistencia social en Valladolid: el Hospicio de Pobres y la Real Casa de Misericordia (1724–1847).* Valladolid: Servicio de Publicaciones de la Diputación Provincial de Valladolid, 1975.

Pani, Erika. "El proyecto de estado de Maximiliano a través de la vida cortesana y del ceremonial público." *Historia Mexicana* 45, no. 2 (1995): 423–60.

———. "¿'Verdaderas figuras de Cooper' o 'pobres inditos infelices'? La política indigenista de Maximiliano." *Historia Mexicana* 47, no. 3 (1998): 571–604.

Park, Deborah Carter, and J. David Wood. "Poor Relief and the County House of Refuge System in Ontario, 1880–1911." *Journal of Historical Geography* 18, no. 4 (1992): 439–55.

Pascoe, Peggy. *Relations of Rescue: The Search for Female Moral Authority in the American West, 1874–1939.* New York: Oxford University Press, 1990.

Pascua, Anastasio de la. *Febrero mejicano, o sea la librería de jueces, abogados y escribanos . . . nuevamente adicionado . . .* 9 vols. Mexico City: Imp. de Galván a cargo de M. Arévalo, 1834–35.

Payno, Manuel. *El fistol del diablo: novela de costumbres mexicanas.* 1845–46. 2d ed. Mexico City: Editorial Porrúa, 1973.

———. *Los bandidos de Río Frío.* 1889–91. 3d ed. Mexico City: Editorial Porrúa, 1966.

Pérez Estevez, Rosa María. *El problema de los vagos en la España del siglo XVIII.* Madrid: Confederación Española de Cajas de Ahorros, 1976.

Pérez y López, Antonio. *Teatro de la legislación universal de España e Indias . . .* 28 vols. Madrid: Imp. de M. González, 1791–98.

Pérez Toledo, Sonia. "Los vagos de la ciudad de México y el Tribunal de Vagos en la primera mitad del siglo XIX." *Secuencia* 27 (September–December 1993): 27–42.

———. *Los hijos del trabajo: los artesanos de la ciudad de México, 1780–1853.* Mexico City: El Colegio de México and UAM-Iztapalapa, 1996.

Perry, Mary Elizabeth. *Crime and Society in Early Modern Seville.* Hanover, NH: University Press of New England, 1980.

Pescador, Juan Javier. "Devoción y crisis demográfica: la cofradía de San Ygnacio de Loyola, 1761–1821." *Historia Mexicana* 39, no. 3 (1990): 767–801.

———. *De bautizados a fieles difuntos.* Mexico City: El Colegio de México, 1992.

Peza, Juan de Dios. *La beneficencia en México.* Mexico City: Imp. de Francisco Díaz de León, 1881.

Pike, Ruth. "Penal Servitude in the Spanish Empire: Presidio Labor in the Eighteenth Century." *Hispanic American Historical Review* 1, 58 (1978): 21–40.

Piven, Frances Fox, and Richard A. Cloward. *Regulating the Poor: The Functions of Public Welfare.* New York: Vintage, 1971.

Platt, Anthony M. *The Child Savers: The Invention of Delinquency.* Chicago: University of Chicago Press, 1969.

Pogolotti, Marcelo, ed. *Los pobres en la prosa mexicana.* Mexico City: Editorial Diógenes, 1978.

Poinsett, Joel Roberts. *Notes on Mexico Made in the Autumn of 1822 . . . 1824;* rpt. New York: Praeger, 1969.

Porter, Susan L. "Gendered Visions of Poverty: Admissions Policies in American Orphanages, 1800–1850." Paper presented at Ninth Berkshire Conference on the History of Women, June 1993.

Potash, Robert A. *Mexican Government and Industrial Development in the Early Republic: The Banco de Avío.* Amherst: University of Massachusetts Press, 1983.

Prieto, Guillermo. *Memorias de mis tiempos, 1828–1853.* 2 vols. Mexico City: Vda. de Ch. Bouret, 1906.

"Prospecto de la nueva forma de gobierno político y económico del Hospicio de Pobres de esta Capital." *Diario de México,* July 4, 1806, 261–68.

"Proyecto de reglamento para la Casa de Asilo de Pobres Mendigos." *Revista Mensual de la Sociedad Promovedora de Mejoras Materiales* 1 (1852): 82–88.

Pullan, Brian. *Rich and Poor in Renaissance Venice: The Social Institutions of a Catholic State to 1620.* Cambridge: Harvard University Press, 1971.

Ransel, David. *Mothers of Misery: Child Abandonment in Russia.* Princeton: Princeton University Press, 1988.

Real ordenanza para el establecimiento e instrucción de intendentes de ejército y provincia en el reino de la Nueva España, 1786. Ed. Ricardo Rees Jones. Mexico City: UNAM, 1984.

Reher, David S. "¿Malthus de nuevo? Población y economía en México durante el siglo XVIII." *Historia Mexicana* 41, no. 4 (1992): 615–64.

Reis, João José. *A Morte é uma Fêsta: Ritos Fúnebres e Revolta Popular no Brasil do Século XIX.* São Paulo: Companhia das Letras, 1995.

Rivera Cambas, Manuel. *Mexico pintoresco, artístico y monumental.* 3 vols. Mexico City: Imp. de la Reforma, 1880–83.

Rivera-Garza, Cristina. "The Masters of the Streets: Bodies, Power, and Modernity in Mexico, 1867–1930." Ph.D. diss., University of Houston, 1995.

Rodríguez Kuri, Ariel. "Política e institucionalidad: el Ayuntamiento de México y la evolución del conflicto jurisdiccional, 1808–1850." In *La ciudad,* ed. Hernández Franyuti, 2:51–94, 1994.

Ross, Edward. *Social Control: A Survey of the Foundations of Order.* New York: Macmillan, 1901.

Rothman, David J. *The Discovery of the Asylum: Social Order and Disorder in the New Republic.* Boston: Little, Brown, 1971.

———. "Social Control: The Uses and Abuses of the Concept in the History of Incarceration." In *Social Control,* ed. Cohen and Scull, 106–17. 1983.

Ruiz Castañeda, María del Carmen. *Catálogo de seudónimos, anagramas, iniciales y otros alias usados por escritores mexicanos y extranjeros.* Mexico City: UNAM, 1985.

Rumeau de Armas, Antonio. *Historia de la previsión social en España: cofradías, gremios, hermandades, montepíos.* Madrid: Editorial Revista de Derecho Privado, 1944.

Russell Wood, A. J. R., *Fidalgos and Philanthropists: The Santa Casa de Misericordia of Bahia, 1550–1755.* Berkeley: University of California Press, 1968.

Ryan, Mary P. *Cradle of the Middle Class: The Family in Oneida County, New York, 1790–1865.* New York: Cambridge University Press, 1981.

Sacristán, María Cristina. "Filantropismo, improductividad y delincuencia en algunos textos novohispanos sobre pobres, vagos y mendigos (1782–1794)." *Relaciones* 36 (fall 1988): 21–32.

———. *Locura e Inquisición en Nueva España, 1571–1760.* Mexico City: Fondo de Cultura Económica, 1992.

———. *Locura y disidencia en el México ilustrado, 1760–1810.* Zamora: El Colegio de Michoacán and Instituto Mora, 1994. (1994a)

———. "El Pensamiento ilustrado ante los grupos marginados de la ciudad de México, 1767–1824." In *La ciudad*, ed. Hernández Franyuti, 2:187–249, 1994. (1994b)

Salado Alvarez, Victoriano. "Prologue." In Cossío, *Datos históricos*, i–v (1917).

Salazar, Flora. "Los sirvientes domésticos." In *Ciudad de México*, ed. Moreno Toscano, 124–32, 1978.

Salvatore, Ricardo D., and Carlos Aguirre, eds. *The Birth of the Penitentiary in Latin America: Essays on Criminology, Prison Reform, and Social Control, 1830–1940.* Austin: University of Texas Press, 1966.

Santamaría, Francisco J. *Diccionario general de americanismos.* 3 vols. Mexico City: Editorial Pedro Robredo, 1942.

Sarrailh, Jean. "Note sur la réforme de la bienfaisance en Espagne à la fin du XVIIIe siècle." In *Eventail de l'histoire vivante: hommage à Lucien Febvre.* Paris: A. Colin, 1953, 2:371–89.

Scardaville, Michael C. "Crime and the Urban Poor: Mexico City in the Late Colonial Period." Ph.D. diss., University of Florida, 1977.

———. "Alcohol Abuse and Tavern Reform in Late Colonial Mexico City." *Hispanic American Historical Review* 60, no. 4 (November 1980): 643–71.

———. "(Hapsburg) Law and (Bourbon) Order: State Authority, Popular Unrest, and the Criminal Justice System in Bourbon Mexico City." *The Americas* 50, no. 4 (1994): 501–25.

Schwartz, Robert M. *Policing the Poor in Eighteenth-Century France.* Chapel Hill: University of North Carolina Press, 1988.

Scott, James C. *Weapons of the Weak: Everyday Forms of Peasant Resistance.* New Haven: Yale University Press, 1985.

Scull, Andrew T. *Museums of Madness: The Social Organization of Insanity in Nineteenth-Century England.* New York: St. Martin's, 1979.

Secretaría de la Asistencia Pública. *La asistencia social en México.* Mexico City: Talleres Gráficos de la Nación, 1940.

Sedaño, Francisco. *Noticias de México, recogidas por D.F.S., vecino de esta ciudad desde el año de 1756, coordinadas, escritas de nuevo y puestas por órden alfabético en 1800.* Ed. Joaquín García Icazbalceta. Mexico City: Imp. de J. R. Barbedillo y Cía., 1880.

Seed, Patricia. *To Love, Honor, and Obey in Colonial Mexico: Conflicts over Marriage Choice, 1574–1821.* Stanford: Stanford University Press, 1988.

Seminario de Historia Urbana del Departamento de Historia, INAH. *Ciudad de México: ensayo de construcción de una historia.* Mexico City: INAH, 1978.

Serrano Ortega, José Antonio. "Levas, Tribunal de Vagos y Ayuntamiento: la ciudad de México, 1825–1836." In *Ciudad de México,* ed. Illades and Rodríguez, 131–54, 1996.

Shaw, Frederick. "Poverty and Politics in Mexico City, 1824–1854." Ph.D. diss., University of Florida, 1975.

Sherwood, Joan. *Poverty in Eighteenth-Century Spain: The Women and Children of the Inclusa.* Toronto: University of Toronto Press, 1988.

Shubert, Adrian. " 'Charity Properly Understood': Changing Ideas about Poor Relief in Liberal Spain." *Comparative Studies in Society and History* 33, no. 1 (1991): 36–55.

Sinkin, Richard. "The Mexican Constitutional Congress, 1856–57: A Statistical Analysis." *Hispanic American Historical Review* 53, no. 1 (1973): 1–26.

Smith, Bonnie G. *Ladies of the Leisure Class: The Bourgeoise of Northern France in the Nineteenth Century.* Princeton: Princeton University Press, 1981.

Sosa, Francisco. *El episcopado mexicano: biografía de los Ilmos. Sres. arzobispos de México . . .* 2 vols. 1877. Rev. 3d ed. by Alberto María Carreño. Mexico City: Editorial Jus, 1962.

Soubeyroux, J. "El encuentro del pobre y la sociedad: asistencia y represión en el Madrid del Siglo XVIII." *Estudios de Historia Social* 21, no. 2 (1982): 147–58.

Suárez, Marcela. *Hospitales y sociedad en la ciudad de México en el siglo XVI.* Mexico City: UAM-Azcapotzalco, 1988.

Tanck Estrada, Dorothy. *La educación ilustrada (1786–1836).* Mexico City: El Colegio de México, 1977.

Tayloe, Edward Thornton. *Mexico, 1825–1828: The Journal and Correspondence of Edward Thornton Tayloe.* Ed. C. Harvey Gardiner. Chapel Hill: University of North Carolina Press, 1959.

Taylor, William B. *Magistrates of the Sacred: Priests and Parishioners in Eighteenth-Century Mexico.* Stanford: Stanford University Press, 1996.

Tena Ramírez, Felipe. *Leyes fundamentales de México.* 5th ed., rev. Mexico City: Editorial Porrúa, 1973.

TePaske, John Jay. "The Financial Disintegration of the Royal Government of Mexico during the Epoch of Independence." In *The Independence of Mexico and the Creation of the New Nation,* ed. Jaime Rodríguez O. Los Angeles: University of California Press, 1989.

Thompson, E. P. "Time, Work Discipline, and Industrial Capitalism." *Past and Present* 38 (December 1967): 56–97.

———. "The Moral Economy of the English Crowd in the Eighteenth Century." *Past and Present* 50 (February 1971): 76–136.

Thompson, Waddy. *Recollections of Mexico.* New York: Wiley and Putnam, 1846.

Tikoff, Valentina. "Orphans as Agents of Empire: The Naval Orphanage of San Telmo in Seville, 1681–1847." Paper presented at the meetings of the American Historical Association, January 2000.

Trattner, Walter I., ed. *Social Welfare or Social Control? Some Historical Reflections on Regulating the Poor.* Knoxville: University of Tennessee Press, 1983.

Turner, John Kenneth. *Barbarous Mexico.* 1910; rpt. Austin: University of Texas Press, 1969.

Tyor, Peter L., and Jamil S. Zainaldin. "Asylum and Society: An Approach to Institutional Change." *Journal of Social History* 13, no. 1 (1979): 23–48.

Valadés, José C. *Maximiliano y Carlota en México: historia del Segundo Imperio.* Mexico City: Editorial Diana, 1976.

Valdés, Alejandro. *Guía de forasteros de este imperio mexicano, y calendario para el año de 1822.* Mexico City: Valdés, 1822.

Valdés, Dennis Nodin. "The Decline of the Sociedad de Castas in Mexico City." Ph.D. diss., University of Michigan, 1978.

Valle, Juan N. del. *El viajero en México: completa guía de forasteros para 1864* . . . Mexico City: Andrade y Escalante, 1864.

Valle Arizpe, Artemio de. *La lotería en México.* Mexico City: Talleres Gráficos de la Lotería Nacional, 1943.

Van Young, Eric. "Islands in the Storm: Quiet Cities and Violent Countrysides in the Mexican Independence Era." *Past and Present* 118 (February 1988): 130–55.

————. *La crisis del orden colonial: estructura agraria y rebeliones populares de la Nueva España, 1750–1821.* Mexico City: Alianza Editorial, 1992.

————. "Conclusion: The State as Vampire—Hegemonic Projects, Public Ritual, and Popular Culture in Mexico, 1600–1990." In *Rituals of Rule,* ed. Beezley, 343–74. 1994.

Vázquez de Warman, "El pósito y la alhóndiga en la Nueva España." *Historia Mexicana* 17, no. 3 (1968): 395–426.

Velasco Ceballos, Rómulo. *Caridad y asistencia pública en México: las loterías.* Mexico City: Talleres Gráficos de la Nación, 1934. (1934a).

————. *Las loterías: historia de estas instituciones, desde la Real fundada en 1771, hasta la Nacional para beneficencia pública.* Mexico City: Talleres Gráficos de la Nación, 1934. (1934b)

————. *El niño mexicano ante la caridad y el estado.* Mexico City: Editorial Cultura, 1935.

————. *Asistencia pública: un año bajo la administración del Presidente Cárdenas.* Mexico City: DAPP, 1938.

————. *Fichas bibliográficas sobre asistencia en México.* Mexico City: Secretaría de Salubridad y Asistencia, 1943.

Venegas Ramírez, Carmen. *Régimen hospitalario para indios en Nueva España.* Mexico City: SEP-INAH, 1973.

Viera, Juan de. *Compendiosa narración de la ciudad de México.* Ed. Gonzalo Obregón. 1777; Mexico City: Editorial Guarania, 1952.

Vigneaux, Ernest. *Souvenirs d'un prisonnier de guerre au Mexique, 1854–1855.* Paris: Librairie de L. Hachette et Cie., 1863.

Villamil, Antonio. *Memoria histórica del Nacional Monte de Piedad.* Mexico City: I. Escalante, 1877.

Villarroel, Hipólito. *México por dentro y fuera bajo el gobierno de los vireyes, ó sea enfermedades politicas que padece la capital de la N. España.* Ed. Carlos María de Bustamante. Mexico City: Imp. del C. Alejandro Valdés, 1831.

Villaseñor y Sánchez, Joseph Antonio. *Theatro americano, descripción general de los reynos, y provincias de la Nueva-España* . . . 2 vols. Mexico City: Imp. de la vda. de D. Joseph Bernardo de Hogal, 1746.

Viqueira Albán, J. P. *¿Relajados o reprimidos? Diversiones públicas y vida social en la ciudad de México durante el Siglo de las Luces.* Mexico City: Fondo de Cultura Económica, 1987.

Voekel, Pamela. "Peeing on the Palace: Bodily Resistance to Bourbon Reforms in Mexico City." *Journal of Historical Sociology* 5, no. 2 (1992): 183–208.

———. "The Religious Roots of Mexican Liberalism." Paper presented at the meetings of the Latin American Studies Association, April 1997.

Warren, Richard. "Vagrants and Citizens: Politics and the Poor in Mexico City, 1808–1836." Ph.D. diss., University of Chicago, 1994.

———. "Entre la participación política y el control social: la vagancia, las clases pobres de la ciudad de México y la transición desde la Colonia hacia el Estado nacional." *Historia y Grafía* 6 (1996): 37–54. (1996a)

———. "Desafío y trastorno en el gobierno municipal entre la Independencia y la Reforma: el ayuntamiento de México y la dinámica política nacional, 1821–1855." In *Ciudad de México*, ed. Illades and Rodríguez, 117–30, 1996. (1996b)

———. "The Discourse of Masses and the Masses of Discourse: Crowds and Popular Political Culture in Mexico City from Independence to the Reform." Paper presented at the Conference on Mexican Popular Political Culture, 1800–2000, Center for U.S.-Mexican Studies, University of California-San Diego, April 1998.

Weber, Max. *The Protestant Ethic and the Spirit of Capitalism.* Trans. Talcott Parsons. 1905; London: Allen and Unwin, 1930.

Woolf, Stuart J. *The Poor in Western Europe in the Eighteenth and Nineteenth Centuries.* London: Methuen, 1986.

Zavala, Lorenzo de. *Ensayo histórico de las revoluciones de México, desde 1808 hasta 1830.* Mexico City: De la Vega, 1845.

Zavala, Silvio. *Los esclavos indios en la Nueva España.* Mexico City: Colegio Nacional, 1968.

Zedillo Castillo, Antonio. *Historia de un hospital: el Hospital Real de Naturales.* Mexico City: IMSS, 1984.

Zerecero, Anastasio. *Memorias para la historia de las revoluciones en México* . . . Mexico City: Imp. del Gobierno, en Palacio, 1869.

Zúñiga y Ontiveros, Mariano de. *Calendario manual y guía de forasteros en México, para el año de 1800.* Mexico City: Zúñiga y Ontiveros, 1800.

{ INDEX }

Page numbers followed by an "i" refer to illustrations and their captions, by a "t" to tables and their captions, and by an "f" to figures and their captions. Dates are italicized to distinguish them from page numbers.

200–201, 212, 225, 344 n.116. *See also* Patriotic School

Suffrage, 35, 204, 283, 344 n.132

Tablas de carnicería, 52t, 55, 109t, 130, 161, 163, 317 n.46

Taxes, 180, 184, 187, 196, 338 n.15, 342 n.95; income from, 52t, 55, 199, 209t, 211, 317 n.47, 317 n.49; proposals for, 53, 54, 163. *See also* Tablas de carnicería

Tayloe, Edward Thornton, 178

Tecpam, 195, 237, 260, 342 n.82, 350 n.18, 351 n.48, 354 n.89, 354 n.94

Temporalidades de los ex-Jesuitas, 51, 52t, 55, 57, 160–61, 161t, 197, 317 nn.49–50, 335 n.8, 337 n.4

Ternel de Velasco, Petra, 180

Thompson, E. P., 14, 301 n.5

Thompson, Waddy, 196

Tolsá, Manuel, 64i, 65

Tornel, José María, 180, 184, 186, 187, 194, 338–39 n.20, 340 n.51

Torre, Simón de la: 112, 123; contributions by, 52t, 318 n.56, 326 n.79, 329 nn.8–9; positions of, 159, 326 n.81, 327–28 n.94, 327 n.94

Tribunal de Minería, 160, 161t, 335 n.8, 337 n.4

Tribunal de Vagos. *See* Vagrants Tribunal

Trigueros, Ignacio, 188, 193–94, 341 n.60, 341 n.77

Triuleque, Nicolás, 349 n.11

Tyor, Peter, 9

Unemployment, 18, 26, 148, 204, 223, 308–9 nn.58–59

Upper class: ambivalence about Poor House experiment, 4, 156, 283; aversion to the poor, 7, 33–35, 38–40; duty to poor, traditional view of, 32; gap between popular culture and, 38–39, 313 n.140; proportion of population, 302 n.15, 325 n.63. *See also* Moral economy of begging

Urban crisis, 6–7, 17–18, 38, 202

Vagrants (mendigos findigos/false beggars), 23i; arrests of, few, 41, 204, 283–84, 344 n.130; definitions of, 2–3, 25–29, 35–36, 39–40, 308–9 nn.58–60, 309–10 nn.70–71, 309 n.67; depictions of, 13, 18–20, 23–24, 23i, 27–28, 183, 196; exclusion of from Poor House, 98, 111, 125, 319 n.82; forced employment of, 24, 111, 125; legislation on arrests of, 21, 306–7 nn.37–38, 307 n.43; legislation on confinement of, 21, 24, 25, 307 n.40, 308 nn.52–53, 309 n.60; legislation on employment of, 13, 21, 24, 25, 36, 307 n.45, 308 nn.52–53; sentence limits for, 22, 307 n.43; target of Poor House decree, 13, 19. *See also* Worthy vs. unworthy paupers

Vagrants Tribunal (Tribunal de Vagos), 29–30, 35–36, 182, 203–4, 308–9 n.58, 310 n.79, 312 n.119, 344 n.130, 344 n.133

Van Young, Eric, 284

Velasco Ceballos, Rómulo, 207, 228, 334 n.3

Velasco de la Torre, Antonio, 336 n.32

Vélez de Escalante, Estevan, 336 n.32

Verdaderos pobres, 1, 11–13, 22–24, 22i, 111, 125–26, 143, 149, 282. *See also* Disabled persons; Elderly persons; Ill persons; Worthy vs. unworthy paupers

Verdugo, Martín Josef, 321 n.7

Vergonzantes, 89–93, 102, 105–6, 118, 131t, 151–52, 168, 189–90, 282–83, 324 nn.40–41, 359 n.3; exclusion of from bylaws, 278

Vértiz, José María, 199

Veterans, 222

Vicario de Moreno, Luisa, 180

Vicario de Quintana Roo, Leona, 180

Viceroys, 49, 112, 124, 158, 327 n.90, 327 n.92. *See also specific viceroys*

Victoria, Guadalupe, 182

Vidaurri y Medina, Josefa, 134, 152, 168, 331 n.35

Viera, Juan de, 77, 97

Vigneaux, Ernest, 6

Silvia Marina Arrom holds the Jane's Chair in Latin American Studies at Brandeis University. She is the author of *The Women of Mexico City, 1790–1857* (1985) and editor (with Servando Ortoll) of *Riots in the Cities: Popular Politics and the Urban Poor in Latin America, 1765–1910* (1996).

*

Library of Congress Cataloging-in-Publication Data
Arrom, Silvia Marina, 1949-
Containing the poor : the Mexico City Poor House, 1774-1871 / Silvia Marina Arrom.
p. cm.
Includes bibliographical references and index.
ISBN 0-8223-2527-6 (cloth : alk. paper)
ISBN 0-8223-2561-6 (pbk. : alk. paper)
1. Almshouses—Mexico—Mexico City—History. 2. Mexico City (Mexico)—Social policy. 3. Mexico City (Mexico)—Economic conditions. I. Title.
HV63.M6 A77 2000
362.5'85'097253—dc21   00-029396